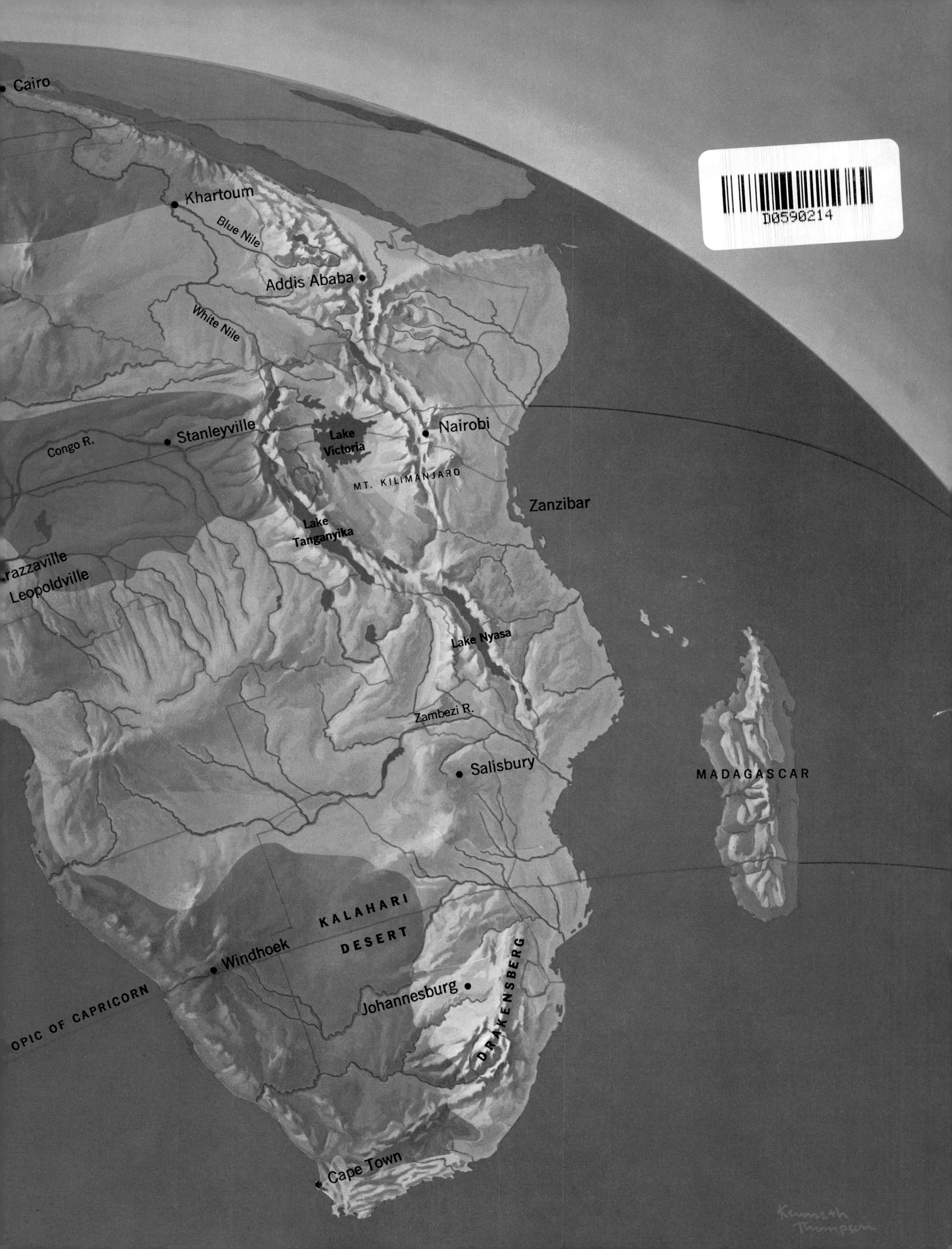

Cairo

Khartoum

Blue Nile

D0590214

Addis Ababa

White Nile

Nairobi

Stanleyville

Congo R.

Lake Victoria

MT. KILIMANJARO

Zanzibar

Lake Tanganyika

razzaville

Leopoldville

Lake Nyasa

Zambezi R.

Salisbury

MADAGASCAR

KALAHARI DESERT

Windhoek

OPIC OF CAPRICORN

Johannesburg

DRAKENSBERG

Cape Town

Kenneth Thompson

AFRICA

Photographs by

Alan Root

Clem Haagner

Emil Schulthess

W. T. Miller

D. C. H. Plowes

Bernhard Grzimek

C. A. W. Guggisberg

C. A. Spinage

Weldon King

Sven Gillsater

and others

Maps drawn by Kenneth Thompson

A F

A Chanticleer Press Edition

The Continents We Live On

RICA

A NATURAL HISTORY

Leslie Brown

Hamish Hamilton · London

Fourth Printing 1967

© 1965 by Random House, Inc.

All rights reserved under International and Pan American Copyright Conventions. *First published in Great Britain, 1965, by Hamish Hamilton Ltd., 90 Great Russell Street, London W.C. 1*

Planned and produced by Chanticleer Press, New York

Manufactured by Conzett & Huber in Zurich, Switzerland

This book must not be offered in or imported for sale into the United States of America or Canada.

Contents

Foreword

Any book of this length on so vast a continent as Africa can be little better than a vignette, and the accounts given here of several major regions are necessarily brief. It is almost impossible, for instance, to convey in one short chapter the vastness and diversity of such areas as the Sahara and the equatorial forest; whole books devoted entirely to these regions could only be summaries. Then again, the larger mammals that are of such surpassing interest in Africa have been made a major theme of this book; that has tended to leave little space for the almost equally interesting birds, reptiles, fish, plants, or rock formations. In general the presentation of the material takes the form of a discussion of the origin of a particular habitat, with reference to climate and geology, and rather more detailed descriptions of the habits of some of the more interesting inhabitants of the region.

The material for this book has been gathered in the course of twenty-five years of living in Africa, where I have served as an Agricultural Officer in Nigeria and Kenya. This has been augmented by travel to other countries. In the course of the past two years the need to learn more about other parts of Africa has taken me to Ethiopia, Morocco, and over most of the southern third of Africa. Although library facilities are not generally so good in Africa as they might be, I have read books and papers in many centers of research. But I have depended much more on firsthand knowledge and on discussion with others who have lived in Africa for a long time and know the conditions thoroughly.

For several reasons gathering material for this book has not been too easy. Africa is still a difficult continent to explore. Even now, if one wants to get off the beaten track at all, it is necessary to plan itineraries according to the weather and the available roads; for instance, if one goes to Ethiopia by road from Kenya in October one cannot return before December because of the rains in northern Kenya. There are many places that can still be reached only on foot, and one can still be bitten by a mamba, die of malaria, or be eaten by a maneating lion.

To the natural difficulties of terrain, poor communications and health hazards have in recent years been added the infinitely more tiresome problems brought about by political upheaval. Based in Kenya, I have sometimes been unable to visit or communicate with other parts of Africa. I had to abandon a possible trip to Somali because of the state of Anglo-Somali relations. The former Belgian Congo has been in chaos for most of the time, and a good deal of correspondence between Kenya and South Africa has gone astray. Despite these various difficulties I have visited various areas of the continent from the Mediterranean to the Cape, and my own knowledge of Africa and its problems has been greatly advanced thereby.

Much of this book has been written—as perhaps it should have been—on the tail board of my safari Landrover after a hard day's drive over bad tracks, while I have fortified myself with an indigenous brew—strong black coffee. As an introduction to this fascinating continent it may serve, but no traveler in Africa should forget that this is still a land of discovery. A vast amount of new information is being brought to light each year about even the commonest animals, which, until recently, no one thought to study in detail. An apparently commonplace occurrence beside the camp breakfast table may easily prove to be something unheard of. The visitor to Africa would do well to observe small and common animals and birds as well as the grand drama of the great mammals of the plains.

The scientific (Latin) name of a species has, in general, been given only the first time a plant or an animal is mentioned. For the convenience of the reader, however, such a name has sometimes been repeated in a later chapter.

For assistance and criticism in the preparation of this book I am indebted to the following: R. I. G. Attwill; B. H. Baker; Professor L. C. Beadle; Dr. E. Beals; Dr. R. C. Bigalke; Professor G. J. Broekhuysen; R. H. Carcasson; Kai Curry-Lindahl; Dick Estes; Dr. P. E. Glover; Dr. P. J. Greenway; Major I. R. Grimwood; C. A. W. Guggisberg; Dr. W. D. Haacke; Dr. H. Klingel; Dr. C. Koch; Dr. J. B. Panouse; Dr. O. P. Prozesky; Dr. Thane Riney; Dr. E. A. Schelpe; Dr. W. Steyn; Dr. Lee M. Talbott; Dr. A. Tjonneland; L. D. E. F. Vesey-Fitzgerald; Colonel Jack Vincent; Murray Watson; V. Wilson and Dr. J. M. Winterbottom. Thanks are due too to the editors of Chanticleer Press and Susan Grafman, who helped so much over photographs and dealt with voluminous correspondence. We have not always agreed, but at least points of difference have been hammered out, frequently at a white heat.

Karen, Kenya — LESLIE BROWN

Vast Africa

With an area of 11,699,000 square miles, Africa is the second largest continent in the world, exceeded only by Asia. Among other noteworthy features it contains the world's greatest desert, the Sahara, and the world's longest and probably most famous river, the Nile. And the marvelous basin of Ngorongoro is the largest volcanic crater in the world. In volume the Congo is the world's second greatest river, smaller only than the Amazon. Lake Victoria is the world's second largest lake. The Great Rift Valley, the most extraordinary feature of its kind visible on the earth's surface, runs right through a vast section of the eastern part of the continent. In its trough it holds Lake Tanganyika, the world's second deepest lake (only Lake Baikal in the U. S. S. R. is deeper) and, at Lake Magadi, the second largest deposit of natural soda in the world. The soda lakes of the Rift are rendered unique by the glorious spectacle of millions of flamingos, perhaps the greatest bird spectacle in the world. Africa is thus a continent with many matchless features.

Africa is ancient. The continent has been a stable landmass for a very long time. Over great areas the underlying rocks of the pre-Cambrian Basement Complex, the oldest known rocks in the world, are exposed to view. At times, seas have submerged parts of it, and deposited vast quantities of limestone and sandstone, while in the northern part of the Rift Valley and elsewhere are enormous masses of more recent volcanic rocks. Volcanic activity continues in one or two places, and is still capable of altering the face of these regions. What are called "young fold mountains," ranges formed by the folding of beds of old rocks in response to relatively recent movements of the earth's crust, are found in Africa only—in the north, in the Atlas Mountains, and in the south, near the Cape of Good Hope.

Africa is unique in spanning the whole climatic range from the subtropics in the north to the subtropics in the south. It contains all types of country from the starkest desert to lush rain forest three hundred feet tall, and from mangrove swamps and coral beaches to strange alpine plants on high equatorial peaks. The vegetation occurs in rather neat belts on either side of the equator, and the seasons in these belts are controlled chiefly by the oscillation of the earth on its horizontal axis, which means summer weather in the south during the northern winter.

The type of vegetation that occurs in different parts of Africa, or even closely adjacent parts of the same region, can usually be explained by the following basic formula. Take any soil, water it with a given amount of rain at stated intervals, and a certain type of vegetation will result. To take the uncomplicated case of a fertile, free-draining, loamy soil on flat terrain, the vegetation supported by such soil differs according to the rainfall. In five inches of rain per annum it is desert; in fifteen inches of rain it is grass steppe with acacia and other bushes; and in fifty inches of rain it may be either forest or savanna according to whether the rain falls in one season followed by a long drought, or whether it is well distributed throughout the year, as happens on the equator. The broad distribution of Africa's vegetation belts can thus be explained.

Smaller differences, which often appear to refute the analysis above, can be explained by the closer application of the same formula. The soil varies according to local topography. Within a mile or so one may pass from a hilltop of barren rock supporting only succulents, through a strip of grassland and savanna on steep stony ridges, where much of the rain runs off, and into luxuriant tropical forest at the base of the hill. Finally, along drainage lines, there will often be heavy clay soils, seasonally waterlogged or flooded, that will grow only tall grasses and scarcely any trees. Such local differences are not explained by change in total rainfall, but by the soil type and topography. To carry the argument a stage further, the vegetation on top of an individual termite mound is often quite different from that at the base. Again, differences in soil type and drainage can account for this.

The broad belts of vegetation occurring in this way divide the continent into a number of conveniently distinct regions, which have been used as a basis for describing different ecological provinces in this book. Some are immense, others relatively small. They differ a little from place to place within themselves, and trained scientists can split each of these major regions into various minor types. But to the ordinary traveler one stretch of savanna or forest looks much like another. The fine differences that can be pointed up on a large-scale map can only be indicated here. The reader must not be surprised if a mountain with a patch of forest on its summit is dealt with in the middle of what is shown as an area of desert. Such local variations are part of the charm and interest of Africa.

Africa is still relatively little known. Apart from the Mediterranean coasts, which have been known for thousands of years, it is only in the last century or so that much has been learned about the interior. The implacable barrier of the Sahara Desert has long prevented southward exploration on foot. Roman centurions penetrated up the Nile to the swamps of the Sudd and were beaten there; so were many later explorers. The tropical sea coasts were uniformly malarial and hot, and many explorers died in their attempts to penetrate to the interior. But some who came back told of wonders, and stimulated further probing till the continent gave up its major secrets.

High, cold Africa. A great glacier in the Ruwenzori range, or Mountains of the Moon, Congo, at an altitude of about 14,500 feet. (Kai Curry-Lindahl)

Since the early explorers, the time spent pacifying indigenous peoples and taming the land has permitted too few to observe and to ponder. And even in this brief time many a wonder of Africa has already vanished beyond recall. In the last twenty-five years a great deal of research has been done, much of it still unpublished. Political turmoil in parts of Africa has recently interfered with the research that was beginning to shed light on many problems. In many parts of Africa discoveries still lie upon the doorstep: one has only to step outside to observe some creature whose habits are relatively little known.

There is splendid, and in some places sublimely beautiful scenery in Africa. But there are fewer scenic and geological wonders here than on several other continents. Africa is a land of immense spaces, often of a monotonous sameness punctuated by isolated hills and ranges covered with vegetation in high rainfall areas. Yet even such spaces, if they abound in birds and beasts, have the charm of wilderness. One may still camp in unspoiled wild country without much likelihood of seeing other human beings.

Above all, Africa is famous for its animal life. Although it is the savannas and grasslands that support the greatest number and variety of animals, the forests too contain remarkable beasts, such as the okapi and the gorilla. The richness of the larger African fauna may be gauged by comparing it to a continent such as North America. The latter has about twenty species of land mammals larger than a dog. Africa has one large species of bovine, one of deer, four of pigs, three of sheep and goats; in addition it has five pachyderms (an elephant, two hippos and two rhinos), four species of wild horses and three of anthropoid apes not found in North America at all. And there are over sixty species of the hollow-horned ruminants known as antelopes, varying from the huge Derby eland weighing almost a ton to the pygmy antelope weighing less than ten pounds. Even if it seems unfair to compare tropical Africa with temperate North America, the difference would be nearly as great if the comparison were made with South America or India.

It is this richness and variety of large mammalian fauna that, from a naturalist's viewpoint, marks the continent as unique. Unfortunately, a great part of this fauna has already disappeared. Thoughtless destruction was the fashion of the times among early European settlers. Destruction of habitats by the indigenous people, much accelerated recently by population increases, is pushing other animals toward extinction at an alarming speed. And in the last fifty years the fate of this wonderful range of animals has too often been butchery or commercial exploitation. Only in the last decade or so have they been studied in any detail.

The remaining animals can perhaps be saved if action is taken in time; but for some the danger is acute. Although conservation and careful utilization of the natural resources are often discussed in Africa they are not yet an everyday approach to life. Politics in the past twenty years have increased the difficulties of conservationists, and far too many constructive measures have been senselessly rendered futile by political opposition. Fortunately some large areas have been saved, and for some of the finest aggregations of animals the future seems reasonably secure. But it remains to be seen how well the new governments will protect their resources from destruction. Some are doing well; others are not.

As the larger mammals of Africa are of surpassing interest they are the main zoological theme of this book. But that is not to say that birds, reptiles, fish or other wildlife, or botany or geology, are not equally interesting. Africa has some two thousand species of fish, compared with about fifty in Europe. There is an abundance of birds second only to South America, and the residents are increased each year by myriads of migrants from the Eurasian landmass. Birds include the largest living species, the ostrich, while the three million flamingos of the Rift Valley are an unparallelled spectacle. There is still an immense field left for the study of the detailed habits of birds, small mammals, reptiles and insects.

The flora of Africa is especially remarkable in two areas: first, in the alpine zones of the high mountains of East Africa, with their unique gigantic forms of groundsel and lobelia and all manner of other curious plants: and second in the Cape subtropical region, which has almost as many species (25,000) as the whole of the huge equatorial forest zone. This is plainly a remnant of what was once a widespread flora. But the vegetation is always of interest in its role as a habitat for animals and birds.

It would be pleasant to think of the continent of Africa as uninhabited and unspoiled by man. But for millennia Africa has been inhabited by man in large numbers, and the evidence is mounting that man first evolved in Africa. The effect of man upon habitats and wildlife has been intensified in the last half century by the rapid increase in population that has followed development by colonial powers.

Man's influence on environments cannot therefore be ignored; it is always necessary to ask the question, "Has man been here?", when assessing a particular situation. With very few exceptions man is the destroyer in Africa. Forests are cut down, savannas and grasslands burned, wild animals wastefully slaughtered, and steppes degraded to near-desert through overgrazing by the too-numerous domestic stock of pastoral peoples. There are exceptions to this general rule, where man, to serve his own ends, has attempted to conserve or prevent waste, as for instance in irrigation schemes or in building dams to hold water. Some creatures, like the plague finch *(Quelea quelea),* do thrive as a result of man's presence. But generally both the environment and its wildlife are degraded by man, and the continent as a whole is in slow decline. To replace exploitation by conservation, to save the remaining wonders for future generations, and to ensure the survival, under better and more stable conditions, for all forms of life, including man, is the major challenge of all who live in Africa and love it.

Low, arid Africa. The Kalahari sand dunes of South West Africa glow in the evening light. The tree is Boscia albitrunca, common in many dry parts of Africa. (C. J. Uys)

Link to Southern Europe

Mediterranean Africa

1

Most of the continent of Africa falls within the Ethiopian Region, which is one of the six great zoogeographical regions of the world. The northernmost territories of Africa, however, which border the Mediterranean Sea from Morocco to Egypt, belong to the Palearctic Region, and their flora and fauna are more akin to southern Europe than to Africa proper. This area we may call Mediterranean Africa.

Mediterranean Africa, now a rather narrow coastal strip, was at one time much wider. It may have extended as much as 1250 miles into what is now the Sahara Desert. Here Mediterranean and Sudanese fauna and flora would have mingled without the formidable desert barrier that now separates them. The southern limit of moist climate has retreated in face of the gradual desiccation of the African continent which followed the retreat of ice in northern Europe. In some areas the Sahara reaches the Mediterranean Sea, but in others, notably in Morocco and Algeria, the Mediterranean strip is still wide and varied in character. In fact, in Morocco eight distinct bioclimatic stages can be distinguished between the sea coast and the spine of the High Atlas Mountains, which is the present southern boundary of Mediterranean Africa.

Remnant Mediterranean influences can still be perceived along the Atlantic coast southward to Mauretania, and on mountain ranges far within the Sahara. But it is convenient to define this zoogeographical extension of Europe as that part of the African continent between the Atlantic and the spine of the Atlas Mountains, ranging east from there to the mountains of Tunisia, the Jebel Akhdar of Cyrenaica, and then disappearing towards Egypt. The Nile delta, a moist and fertile area, is not properly part of this region, but is the result of rainfall and erosion occurring two to four thousand miles away in the very heart of Africa.

MEDITERRANEAN CLIMATE

Climatic conditions throughout the world are broadly determined by such elemental factors as latitude and the oscillation of the earth on its horizontal axis. If, instead of oscillating, the earth were merely to spin on its vertical axis, temperate latitudes would have neither summer nor winter but roughly the same temperature all the year round. The primary factors are to some extent modified by the shape of a continent, topographical features, or by wind and ocean currents. Nevertheless, in any given latitude one may expect to find certain climatic features. In this way, immediately north and south of the tropics, there are climatic belts circling the earth that have what is described as a Mediterranean climate.

In this type of climate the winters are cool and moist; severe cold and deep snow occur only in high mountains. Winter is followed by a mild wet spring in which plants grow vigorously; there is often an abundance of flowers, both wild and cultivated. During the long, hot, dry summer most growth withers and dies, and the land looks parched and bare. Then comes autumn, snowfall on the heights, and again winter, the latter often very pleasant and sunny.

These climates are found not only in the Mediterranean region but in California, Chile, at the southern tip of Africa, and in Australia. The similarity in the climate of these areas can be demonstrated by a study of certain plants in northwest Africa. There the typical local vegetation is *maquis*—a dense shrubbery composed of tree heather *(Erica arborea),* palmetto, broom *(Cytisus),* furze *(Ulex)* and small evergreen oaks and pines. Among this one may find, growing wild and happily naturalized, the prickly pear cactus *(Opuntia),* from America (which can become a pest species if not watched); the Australian *Eucalyptus,* which, rather than any native tree, is commonly chosen for reafforestation projects; and, on Atlantic coastal sand dunes in Morocco the South African *Mesembryanthemum,* a succulent plant with beautiful flowers, has been pointed out to me as a native wildflower.

GATEWAY TO AFRICA

At the Strait of Gibraltar there is a point where Europe is separated from Africa by a narrow strip of sea only twenty miles wide. Here migrant birds have to face neither the wide Mediterranean nor the Sahara barrier but can fly straight from one continent to another without meeting much of an immediate climate change.

Cape Spartel, where the Mediterranean and Atlantic coasts of Africa meet, is the western tip of a long spine of limestone hills that climb eastward into the mountainous Rif. It is one of the best places to watch bird migration. The cape itself is rocky, covered with maquis of palmetto, heath, and sun rose *(Cistus),* all wind-blown and stunted, typical of the vegetation along the Mediterranean coast to the east.

Large soaring birds, such as buzzards, eagles, vultures, or storks, avoid flying over open water. When migrating they use thermal air bubbles to gain height, then glide till they approach the ground again. In this way they conserve energy. Thermal bubbles are formed over land which is unevenly heated because of its varying surface; they do not occur over the sea. Thus most of the large land birds of western Europe

The Mediterranean coast of Morocco. Overgrazed hillsides are covered with a shrubby growth called maquis and studded with flowers. (Leslie Brown)

Mediterranean Africa extends from the Atlantic coast of Morocco south to the Atlas, east to Tunisia, and along the Mediterranean coast to Cyrenaica; biologically it is part of Europe.

converge on the Strait of Gibraltar as they fly south in autumn and again as they fly north in spring. On the spring passage they gather at Cape Spartel and must then decide whether to cross the strait or stay in Africa. One might expect these birds to select a calm day, or a following breeze, for starting their flight northward. Nevertheless, large birds usually migrate when there is a stiff headwind. Then you may see hundreds of kestrels, harriers, honey buzzards, kites, and a few eagles setting out to cross the strait. In a following wind a bird's airspeed and height must be maintained by flapping, an exertion big birds seek to avoid. Against a headwind, however, they can maintain height without difficulty. By gliding against the wind they may cross the strait more slowly but are at least in no danger of falling into the sea. Most large birds, having gained enough height, can glide in a chosen direction at high speed, so that however strong the wind against them, they can eventually reach their destination with little effort.

Small birds often make the crossing here too. Most cross the open Mediterranean—to reach the south of France, Italy, or Spain—by night; in the darkness they are less exposed to predatory species. It is the large birds, however, that make Cape Spartel a spectacular migration station. Just as a driver of an automobile will take a main road even though it means traveling farther, large birds go hundreds of miles out of their way to avoid crossing a wide expanse of sea.

ATLANTIC DUNES AND MARSHES

A little way south of Cape Spartel there begins a line of sand dunes which stretches in a gentle curve for about a hundred miles. The dunes are characteristic of the Atlantic coast of this region, and they reappear again and again farther south, broken here and there by stretches of rocky coast. The dunes may reach a height of two hundred feet, and they are often lodged upon a substratum of sandstone. Their seaward side is shifting sand bound by marram grass, the same plant that binds dunes all along the coastline of Europe. Their landward side is covered with short turf thick with flowers. Here a small yellow vetch makes a golden carpet in spring, and there are abundant orchids, forget-me-nots, and other wild flowers. In early spring asphodel and wild onions bloom, and the dried stalks of these plants are later climbed by hordes of tiny dune snails. These snails then exude a mass of sticky mucus and spend the long hot summer dormant.

The dunes are really a narrow range of sandy mountains separating the coastal plain from the sea. Just inland the country is scarcely above sea level. Several large rivers, rising in the mountains of the interior, flow westward to the Atlantic. In times of winter rain or melting snow, and when wind and tide are against them, their swollen waters cannot escape through their narrow mouths. So they spread out behind the dunes to form huge flat brackish marshes. Many of these marshes have now been drained, but some still remain as winter haunts for thousands of migrant ducks and geese from Europe.

In spring, along the borders of these marshes, one seems to be unmistakably in southern Europe. The marshes themselves are bordered by the same marsh plants that are found in the Camargue (the great marshland in southernmost France) or Spain: *Salicornia,* wild yellow iris six feet tall, and the common reed *(Phragmites).* Lapwings *(Vanellus vanellus)* gyrate above the marsh grass in their spring flight, and from the open mudflats comes the courting call of the curlew *(Numenius arquata).* Marsh harriers *(Circus aeruginosus)* soar high above or plummet earthward in nuptial display. European storks *(Ciconia ciconia)* and buff-backed herons *(Bubulcus ibis)* walk among pastures and puddles left by the spring rains. If one shuts one's eyes to the human inhabitants, there is nothing obviously African about the scene.

On drier ground there are great areas of blowing sand or low undulating plains of gravel. Most of these are either cultivated, grazed short by innumerable sheep, or sometimes forested with introduced Eucalyptus. Again there is little apparently African about the scene; it could as well be in southern Spain. Soon, however, an African element does appear, for here breeds the Arabian bustard *(Choriotis arabs),* the common large bustard of the deserts and subdeserts of North Africa. In this sort of country in Spain we should have found the European great bustard *(Otis tarda).*

To the south the coastline becomes more rocky, but remains low-lying. Low rocky bluffs have been fretted into razor-edged convolutions by the constant pounding of the Atlantic surf. In the southern parts of this rocky coastline characteristic African plants appear, such as *Euphorbias*—giant members of the spurge family which in Africa take the place of, and come to resemble, the succulent New World cacti.

European and Mediterranean influences penetrate far down this coast into the tropics. On the remote islands of the Banc d'Arguin, off Mauretania, there are the largest known breeding colonies of the European spoonbill *(Platalea leucorodia)*. The birds mingle here with some tropical African species. Spoonbills ringed in the Netherlands have been found at the Banc d'Arguin, and greater flamingos ringed in the Camargue have been recovered in Mauretania. Indeed ringing records show that northwest Africa, between Tunisia and Mauretania, is a major winter haunt of waterfowl of all sorts from western Europe.

COASTAL PLAINS AND CORK OAKS

Inland of the immediate seaboard there is a broad, nearly flat plain rising gently, with a few small steps, to the foothills of the Atlas Mountains in the south and the Rif in the north. It is dissected by three large rivers and several smaller ones. These rivers run in rather narrow valleys cut through the limestone and sandstone of this plain, and along their meandering courses they form lagoons and swamps, thick with tamarisk and reeds. They are not like rivers in Africa proper; their banks are grown with willows, and they resemble rather parts of the Rhone in southern France or the Guadalquivir in southwestern Spain.

Most of the coastal plains are densely inhabited and cultivated. The climate is generally semi-arid, having less than twenty to twenty-five inches of rain a year. Most of this falls in the winter and spring, and in summer these plains become parched and bare. In spring, these cultivated plains are a sheet of flowers—orange and yellow *Compositae* predominating, with here and there masses of blue lupins, or yellow vetch. When occasionally one sees a camel feeding among these flowers, it looks incongruous. But in summer, when all is parched and brown, the camel looks in its element.

Because these plains have been continuously cultivated for centuries, it is scarcely possible to tell what they were once like. What wildlife they ever had has been reduced to the few species that can live with man—grain-eating birds, scavenging crows, small rodents, and a few predators such as weasels *(Mustela nivalis)* and kestrels *(Falco tinnunculus)*. But it is probable that at one time this coastal plain was a mixture of open grassy spaces and light woodlands of olive *(Olea europaea)* and cork oak. The olive survives only as a cultivated

The gorge of Ziz, southern Atlas Mountains. The river has cut its way through successive sedimentary strata forming broken cliffs almost bare of plants; date palms and tamarisk fringe the banks. (E. D. H. Johnson)

The cattle egret (Bubulcus ibis), common in most parts of Africa, mainly frequents wetlands in the Mediterranean region. (R. P. Bille) *Below: This bright yellow composite grows abundantly along the Mediterranean coast. (Leslie Brown)*

tree, but cork oak woodlands still exist practically in their natural state. They have been allowed to survive because they grow on sandy soils, which are useless to man for cultivation, and because they produce a valuable product.

The cork oak *(Quercus suber)* is a strange tree that is exploited for its bark. It grows in southwestern Europe as well as in Africa, but the largest forest of cork oak in the world is at Mamora in Morocco. Here one can see a remnant of the lowland forests that must once have covered a very much larger area of Mediterranean Africa. Although most luxuriant in the lowlands, the cork oak also grows in mountainous areas.

A mature cork oak forest consists of large, well-spaced trees, with grassy glades and little undergrowth. In spring the glades are bright with flowers, notably orchids and a huge yellow umbellifer. This should be ideal habitat for deer, and long ago it must surely have supported this animal. Nowadays, however, the glades are all grazed by domestic stock and few or no large wild animals remain.

To obtain cork, collectors strip off sheets of the outer bark at the base of the trunk of the cork oak. Curiously this does not seem to damage the tree, which quickly grows its bark again and can be restripped a few years later.

Various typically European and Asian birds breed in these cork oak forests. One noteworthy example is the imperial eagle *(Aquila heliaca)*, which in Africa breeds only in the cork oak forests of Morocco, and irregularly even there. This is an eagle of flat, low-lying country rather than mountains, and because of this it is more likely to be disturbed by man than is the golden eagle *(Aquila chrysaetos)*, which breeds in all mountainous areas of Mediterranean Africa as far south as the Spanish Sahara.

THE MEDITERRANEAN COAST

The Atlantic coast of this region is generally low-lying, but eastward from Cape Spartel, all the way to Tunisia, mountains descend straight into the sea and the coast is rocky and spectacular. Along the coast the climate is semi-arid, but a short distance inland rain is much more copious.

Typically, the lands bordering the coast here are covered with maquis. In spring the flaming yellow of the broom and furze breaks the dark green expanse of the oak and palmetto, and several species of white and purple sun rose flower among the growth. Wild lavender *(Lavendula pedunculata)* exudes its rich fragrance, and the rocks are grown over with spectacular yellow daisies. Against the deep blue of the Mediterranean, on a fine day, this galaxy of flowers is a glorious sight.

Although most of this maquis is browsed by goats and sheep it is not destroyed by them. Indeed, goats may even help to prevent invasion of the maquis by prickly pear cactus. This plant has been used to cover eroded ground; and in places inaccessible to goats, such as offshore islands or rock ledges, it has become dominant. Whenever goats can reach

Euphorbias on the Moroccan coast near Agadir. In Africa euphorbias often resemble the New World cactuses, but are actually giant members of the spurge family. (H. C. D. de Wit)

the prickly pear in summer droughts, they eat it down, and the maquis survives.

This Mediterranean coast used to be the haunt of the monk seal *(Monachus monachus)*. Seals are chiefly found in colder waters and they are scarcely represented in the tropics. Compared with temperate seas tropical waters are generally poor in fish life, and seals are common only where fish abound and can be caught easily. In the Mediterranean, fishing by human beings is intensive, and man may directly compete with the monk seal. There is a more direct threat: seals in water are relatively safe from their only enemy, man; but they must come ashore to breed and they are then within the reach of human interference. The seals used to drop their young in caves along this rocky coast. Though they have now virtually retreated from Mediterranean coasts, monk seals still survive and breed in caves along the Atlantic coast, where perhaps five thousand remain.

MAN THE DESTROYER

Most of Mediterranean Africa has been inhabited by man for thousands of years. So altered is the vegetation through man's cultivation and herding that we can scarcely imagine how this region once looked. With the vegetation has gone much of the wildlife, including almost all the large animals. Here and there remnants yield a clue; and man's own records help us to reconstruct a picture of the region when it was more thinly inhabited.

Where the Rif Hills stretch along the Mediterranean coast, one becomes painfully aware of man's major activity in Africa—destruction. Once these steep slopes were covered with maquis, merging into oak scrub higher up, and finally into forests of noble cedars, pines, and firs. The dense shrubbery and forests would have prevented erosion and preserved the indigenous wildlife were it not for man.

Instead, dense populations of human beings have exploited the conifers high up and have stripped most of the vegetation from the lower slopes of the Rif Hills to make way for crops. This has resulted in severe erosion, frequent landslips, and turbid floods in what ought to be clear streams. On one road down which I drove from the cedar-clad upper slopes of the Rif to the Mediterranean coast scarcely a hundred yards had been untouched by landslides within the last three or four years. A stream bed was plastered with clay and had, at the time of the snow melting, come down in a roaring flood, leaving a covering of silt over its boulder-strewn bed and spreading a whitish stain far out into the dark blue water of the Mediterranean.

Here, as elsewhere, such a condition can have only one end: in time the area will be deserted by man and will be reduced to a scanty cover of shrubs and grass on almost bare rock. This is happening rapidly in the Rif Hills; and most of Mediterranean Africa—unlike America and Australia—has been subjected to similar destructive processes for several thousand years. It is with some unease that one realizes that man is now the principal factor affecting the destinies of animals and plants, and it is no use pretending that he does not affect the land. Most of his use of the land in Africa is, as in the Rif, wasteful and destructive. In any discussion of the future of Africa the effects of this abuse must always be at the back of one's mind.

PINE-CLAD MOUNTAINS

The Rif Hills, which rise to over eight thousand feet, are a distinctive climatic and zoogeographic area of Mediterranean Africa. More than any other part of Morocco they are like the hills of southern Spain. For instance salamanders, which are typically northern in their distribution, are found in the Rif Hills, forming a clear link here between Africa and Europe. At high levels magnificent old Atlantic cedars *(Cedrus atlantica)* are interspersed with firs *(Abies pinsapo)*, and pines *(Pinus halapensis)*. Below the pines are found various types of oak: the evergreen oak *(Quercus ilex)*, some cork oak, and others. The undergrowth is inhabited by, among other creatures, foxes and wild boars.

The Rif is not the only conifer-clad massif in this part of Morocco. South and east lies the Moyen or Middle Atlas range, superficially not very different from the Rif. From cultivated lowlands one climbs into woods of evergreen oak, which give place to cedars and pines. In these beautiful forests it is very difficult to realize that one is in Africa at all. When snow lies deep it looks much more like some temperate ski resort in North America or Europe. These mountains have in fact the climate of a temperate resort, with a cold winter and heavy snowfall.

South and west of the Middle Atlas the country becomes drier; the effects of the Atlantic rain-laden winds are less clearly marked, and most of their moisture has already been shed. But both at the eastern and at the western extremity of the High Atlas range there is a humid climate with a cold winter. The beautiful conifer forests which characterize the Rif and Middle Atlas do not, however, persist this far to the west and south. Oak forests extend upward as far as pine trees, but the pines are of a different species, *Pinus pinaster*, and there are no cedars there.

In winter it is interesting to see how a broad-leaved tree like the evergreen oak supports heavy snow without breaking. In most temperate broad-leaved forests the trees shed their leaves with the approach of winter, and their bare branches cannot carry much snow. Conifers, of course, shed snow like the tiles of a house. The leaves of evergreen oak are stiff and harsh, and have evolved in such a way that they can withstand summer droughts. They do not fall off in winter, and the tree thus is heavily burdened with snow; it avoids breakage simply by being extremely flexible—almost rubbery. Under the weight of snow, young saplings are bent right down to the ground, and, as soon as the snow falls off or melts, the branches spring back into place again—sometimes with great force. Thus the oak forests survive the heavy snow of winter almost unscathed, whereas a rigid leafy tree would in the same conditions suffer severe, if not fatal, damage.

MONKEYS IN THE SNOW

The thickets of evergreen oaks that clothe the lower slopes of the Rif, Middle Atlas and the Atlantic side of the High Atlas

The Tessaout Valley drains a section of the High Atlas. The sparse bushes on the slopes show that even their 12,000-foot height does not save the mountains from desiccating Saharan winds. (Bleuler: Bavaria-Verlag)

ranges are inhabited by a basically European fauna. One of the commonest medium-sized birds to be found there is the European wood pigeon *(Columba palumbus)*; among small birds chaffinches and blackbirds are the most obvious. Booted eagles *(Hieraetus pennatus)* soar overhead and probably breed there, as they do in the mountains of southern Spain. Ravens scavenge in the pastures, and European storks wade at the edge of ponds and marshes. There is scarcely anything suggestive of Africa.

Yet in the larger mammals we see Africa asserting itself. While walking in the woods of the Middle Atlas one snowy evening I found the tracks of wild boar and foxes—typical European species—and of the Barbary ape *(Macaca sylvana)*. In Europe the Barbary ape is found only at Gibraltar, where it was probably introduced; it is not truly wild and depends largely upon human beings for subsistence. In the Middle Atlas, however, they are wild and relatively abundant.

This is one of the few places where monkeys' footprints may be seen in snow. Another place is the Himalayas, where the presence of the langur monkey is one possible explanation of reports of an "abominable snowman." But there are no wild monkeys at all in Europe, and nowhere else in Africa do monkeys regularly move about in the snow.

The Barbary ape is a large tailless member of the genus *Macaca,* widespread in Asia, where other species occur in tropical forests. Fairly closely related to baboons, Barbary apes go about in small troops, each with a social organization and hierarchy. Despite their long association with human beings little has been recorded in detail of their behavior, perhaps because they are generally shy and difficult to approach, but also because of general neglect of this region by observant naturalists.

Barbary apes are not strictly arboreal. They often descend to the ground, as their footprints in the snow testify. They are largely vegetarian, but they also eat insects. In these ways, too, they display a similarity to baboons in tropical Africa. However, it may be that they were once wholly aboreal but have since been forced, by steadily increasing desiccation and reduction of tree growth to take to life on the ground. Monkeys are especially helpless in the face of a powerful predator, and can only escape great danger by taking to trees; hence they come to ground with some reluctance.

THE LAST REMAINING PREDATORS

The African character of the fauna of this area is even more clearly demonstrated by its predators than by its herbivores. Within a few miles of each other, and in exactly the same sort of upland country of oak interspersed with open spaces, I saw a European red fox *(Vulpes vulpes)* and a jackal *(Canis aureus)*. The jackal is the ancestor of most breeds of domestic dog, and it has a very wide distribution over Asia and Africa; in Europe it occurs as a remnant population. These two animals, the fox and the jackal, might be expected to compete with one another, for both are scavengers and also catch small rodents, birds, frogs, insects, or anything else they can find. The fox is perhaps more active as a predator and less of a scavenger than the jackal, so that their somewhat different eating habits probably allow them to inhabit the same area without coming into conflict.

The many wild pigs and Barbary apes of this region used to be the main prey of leopards *(Panthera pardus)*. But there are now estimated to be less than fifty leopards left in the whole of the Middle and High Atlas regions, and this remnant is being steadily reduced. Human populations with their domestic stock push farther and farther into mountain regions, and the leopards, unfortunately, kill some domestic stock. In turn, men kill the leopards; it is probable that their fate in this part of Africa is sealed.

Today all sorts of rumors are current about the leopards of the Atlas; they are said to be unusually large and ferocious, and many are said to be black. But the fact is that they are ordinary spotted leopards of no greater size than elsewhere, and their range, which is extensive, includes much of Asia as well as most of Africa. The final extermination of the leopard in northwest Africa will mean that the pig and the monkey will have thereafter no other enemies but man, and they may well multiply until they become more of a nuisance than leopards ever were.

Lions, the most magnificent of African predators, existed in northwest Africa until very recent times, but must now be regarded as extinct. In Roman times they were common, and they certainly existed in Mediterranean Africa until late in the last century. They even persisted in parts of Morocco, in the High Atlas, into the 1920's. Their disappearance must have been hastened by the decline in the numbers of their natural prey, large ungulate animals of the plains. This decline must have made them increasingly dependent upon domestic stock, and thus brought them more and more into conflict with human beings. Their last main stronghold was in the interior of Algeria, where they were hunted to extinction late in the nineteenth century. In Morocco their final disappearance may have been as much due to some unknown disease as to hunters, and reduced the population to a remnant incapable of reproducing itself.

The smaller predators again demonstrate that this area links Africa to Europe. The European weasel *(Mustela nivalis)* is the commonest of its tribe in Morocco. The European otter *(Lutra lutra)* is found north and west of the Atlas, and in some streams on the southern side. The genet cat *(Genetta genetta)* and the mongoose *(Herpestes ichneumon)* are common both to southern Europe and North Africa. But the European badger does not occur, its place being taken by the African honey badger or ratel *(Mellivora capensis)*. This animal penetrates only into the southwesternmost part of Mediterránean Africa, in the Sous valley and adjacent mountains; its presence, nevertheless, is a link with Africa proper.

BARBARY STAGS AND HARTEBEEST

Many animals in Africa are wrongly referred to as deer. The only true wild deer of the African continent is the Barbary race of the European red deer *(Cervus elaphus barbarus)*. Whether any of them now survive is problematical, for their habitat is restricted to low-lying forests in a small area on the borders of Algeria and Tunisia. At one time they extended far into what is now the Sahara, when marshy forests covered

An intermontane basin of the High Atlas near Rich, Morocco. Approaching the Saharan fringe, the vegetation is that of an overgrazed subdesert steppe. (E. D. H. Johnson)

much of North Africa. Their range has been reduced, first by desiccation, secondly by cultivation and human occupation. About three hundred existed up to 1959, along the Algeria–Tunisia border, but by 1962 these were thought to have dwindled to a hundred.

Barbary red deer are a small and rather degenerate race of the European species. Since they live in thick forests, they are probably more akin in general to the lowland red deer of continental Europe than to the upland deer of Scotland. Like other deer, the males shed and then grow their antlers again every year. It is this that distinguishes them from the hollow-horned ruminants, which include wild cattle, buffalos, and all the African antelopes.

The bony antlers of deer are sexual characteristics peculiar (in all but the reindeer) to the males. When they are fully grown and hard, stripped of the covering of skin and blood vessels—called the velvet—inside which they grow, the stags are ready to breed. In deer the breeding season is short and clearly defined, and in the Barbary stag the rut, as it is called, occurs from September to October. This allows the females or hinds to bear their calves the following spring, in May and June when food is relatively abundant. The Barbary deer have an advantage denied to most red deer—the winters in their territory are fairly mild and moist, so that they can survive them in good condition.

Apart from pigs, the only other large herbivores which inhabited this region in historical times were bubal hartebeest, the northwestern representatives of the tribe of hartebeest found all over Africa from Morocco to the Cape. Formerly hartebeest were divided into a number of species, but today several are considered as races of one species. The bubal hartebeest, the nominate race—*Alcelaphus buselaphus buselaphus*—is, sad to say, now extinct.

The bubal hartebeest inhabited the lowland plains of Morocco, Algeria and Tunisia, as well as parts of Egypt. Its range may possibly have extended as far as what was formerly Palestine and also Arabia (which, although outside Africa, is counted as part of the Ethiopian Region), but there is no certainty of this. Living in the lowlands as it did, it was bound to come into conflict with and be eliminated by man's cultivation, unless preserved in sanctuaries. The bubal hartebeest became extinct late last century when it could have been saved if anyone had thought about it. Even in the first quarter of this century, when efforts were being made, in South Africa for instance, to save the last remnants of threatened species, no one seems to have thought of the poor bubal hartebeest. It has vanished leaving little trace of its habits.

The bubal hartebeest seems to have been a small animal by comparison with other hartebeest, and of a tawny red color. In response to the cold winter climate it grew a longish coat, which tended to curl, and it developed a whorl of hair on its forehead. It lived in small groups, but we cannot say whether this was normal, for this habit has been typical of the hartebeest whenever it has begun declining in numbers. Of course the bubal may have been a small and rather degenerate race of hartebeest, differing somewhat in its habits from its near relatives.

The bubal hartebeest, typically African, and the Barbary stag, typically European, underline the dual origin of the fauna of Mediterranean Africa. Here we have an Ethiopian animal, the hartebeest, in the Palearctic Region; and as we shall see, there are places where typically Palearctic animals, notably sheep and goats, penetrate into the Ethiopian Region.

The stag and the bubal hartebeest were probably the only common animals big enough to serve as prey for the lions of this region in the last few centuries. With their complete disappearance, or reduction to remnants, the fate of the lions was sealed. The leopard, that more versatile and solitary predator, can hang on where the larger, more gregarious lion must die out.

THE BARREN HEIGHTS OF THE ATLAS MOUNTAINS

The wettest parts of this region are the Rif Hills and the Middle Atlas. On the inland side of the Middle Atlas, in the mountains of interior Algeria and Tunisia, and in the High

Left: Rivers in the south Atlas often run in precipitous gorges. The clear waters of the Dadès are bordered with wild oleander. (Afrique Photo) Right: Gentler slopes of intermountain basins bear more vegetation but the eroded banks and wide bed of a small river testify to violent floods born of overgrazed hillsides. (Peter W. Haeberlin)

Atlas itself the climate is much drier. There is one small area of high rainfall where the High Atlas approaches the Atlantic; but elsewhere there is less rain and snow on these great mountains, despite their height, than in the much lower Middle Atlas and Rif. To the south the High Atlas rises abruptly to about fourteen thousand feet from the Atlantic coastal plain. In the north their bases are on plateaus between them and the Middle Atlas. Their lower slopes are barren and rocky, with only some juniper and oak scrub. From here one climbs through a belt of evergreen oaks until one reaches pines *(Pinus pinaster),* and above that onto arid stony slopes grown with spiny shrubs. The ultimate summits of the mountains always retain some snow even in summer. Thickets of wild oleander border the streams, and there is little flat land or grass. Every available inch of moist valleys is cultivated—like a sort of artificially irrigated savanna of fruit trees. In these gardens are bulbuls *(Pycnonotus),* typically African birds, alongside typically European species.

Almost flat intermontane basins occur at intervals inside the Atlas ranges. These are semi-arid and strongly reminiscent of similar basins in the American Rockies. Crossing the Atlas in the north the traveler becomes aware that each successive basin is drier until finally he reaches the true desert. The western slope of each mountain wall is wetter and better vegetated than the eastern slope, and long before the traveler has crossed the last ridge he is aware that he is approaching the Sahara.

Gazelles are typically desert or dry steppe animals, and these regions were once inhabited by the Atlas or Cuvier's gazelle *(Gazella gazella).* This creature differed from most gazelles in that it ranged over the mountain slopes up to eight thousand feet. It was formerly abundant but has been exterminated by the local inhabitants to such an extent that it now survives only in a few places and in small numbers. Perhaps gazelles are easier to exterminate in mountainous country than in flat open desert where it is very difficult to get close to them.

Mountain birds of this area include the lammergeier *(Gypaetus barbatus),* raven *(Corvus corax)* and alpine chough *(Coracia graculus)*—all typically Palearctic species. The lammergeier, or bearded vulture, has a habit of breaking large bones by dropping them on rocky slopes; it then eats the fragments or scoops out the marrow with its specialized tongue. Despite its magnificent appearance it is a scavenging vulture by nature. It is commonest where large numbers of domestic stock, existing under poor conditions, provide a more copious and reliable food supply than do wild animals. The lammergeier's bone-dropping provides only a minor source of food; its principal diet is carrion.

Ravens are normally the largest of the crow species in any habitat. Here they are found without any smaller crows, and they consequently perform all corvine functions, scavenging about villages and houses as well as hunting carrion over high pastures. The ravens of this region are smaller than those of the more northerly latitudes, and their call is higher pitched.

There is no more dramatic way to leave this region than to cross one of the passes of the High Atlas in a snowstorm. The traveler rises out of the oak woods by a road which follows a watercourse thick with oleanders. The vegetation at higher levels is reduced to spiny shrubs, foreshadowing what is to come. Next the snow covers all, as in any high pass, with ravens croaking and alpine choughs flying about in small flocks. Then one is over the top, the thick snow clouds born of Atlantic moisture grow thinner, and in a few minutes one emerges into a sunlit land of reddish rock and scree practically barren of vegetation. Beyond, the Sahara stretches unbroken for a thousand miles. Europe has been left behind, a few miles back, and vast stretches of greater Africa lie ahead.

Alpine meadow, snowfields, and slopes clad with cedar and pine near Mount Tidiquin, the highest point in the Rif Hills, betoken a much wetter climate in northern Morocco. (Leslie Brown)

Great Land of Thirst

The Sahara Desert

2

Sahara, or more properly *Sahra,* is an Arabic word signifying a dull-brown wilderness or emptiness. Indeed properly pronounced, it has the hot sound of a man gasping for breath. The word has become softer on European tongues, but the dread and fascination of the vast area it denotes remains.

The Sahara is the world's largest desert. In Africa it stretches from the Atlantic coast to the Red Sea but it should be considered together with the Arabian and Indian deserts in what has been called the Great Palearctic Desert. In Africa the desert is three thousand miles wide from coast to coast and more than one thousand miles from north to south. For centuries it formed an almost insuperable barrier to explorers; they could

Right: Dunes in the great eastern sand sea, or "erg," of Algeria. Such areas of constantly shifting sand contain very little life. (Pierre A. Pittet) Below: The addax, true desert antelope, is highly nomadic and able to go without water for long periods. Its large hoofs assist it in walking on loose sand. (François Edmond-Blanc)

pass it only by sailing around the coast of West Africa or by laboriously following certain caravan routes. The Nile, which might have afforded passage to ships, is blocked in Egypt by cataracts.

The Sahara includes great mountain ranges and apparently illimitable flat plains of stone and gravel. Huge expanses of unrelieved sand dunes daunt the traveler and form a refuge for strange animals. Oases of water, sometimes clear and sweet, sometimes bitter and poisonous, well up amid the emptiness. Appalling heat alternates with piercing cold. Born of the extremes of heating and cooling, violent winds, charged with sand or dust, scour the surface, shifting anything that is not fixed, cutting and withering plants and harassing all animals and birds. Winds alternate with long periods of utter calm, with stars brilliant in the night sky, and silence absolute, broken by no bird or mammal or even insect. In the softness of sunset light, the desert can be beautiful beyond words, but life in it is a struggle continually dominated by the need for water.

In the great desert are found the hottest places on earth. Surface temperatures of 170° F have been known, and the hottest place of all, El Azizia in Libya, has recorded 136.4° F in the shade. A furnace at midday in summer, the desert cools rapidly at night, so that there may be a diurnal variation of more than 60° F. The sky is almost always cloudless, but it is partly obscured by a haze of fine dust. The relative humidity is usually less than ten per cent and in places rain may fall only once in ten years. The winds, chiefly northeast trade winds, but also westerlies nearer the Atlantic, sometimes blow with such force that a man cannot walk against them.

Terrible yet fascinating, the Sahara has been the subject of entire books and it has been well documented from the time of the Egyptians and Romans. In covering an area of about 3,500,000 square miles, almost half of Africa, in one chapter, one can pick out only a few salient features.

THE ORIGINS OF DESERTS

The Sahara is a desert simply because insufficient rain falls to balance the evaporation caused by the sun's rays and the transpiration of plants drawing on stored water resources. In the Sahara, the rainfall is everywhere less than ten inches per year, and over immense areas less than five inches. At the same time evaporation from open water surfaces in a year is seven or eight feet. If there were any rain in summer, water would evaporate even faster. The Sahara is the exemplification of a desert, and will remain one except in the remote possibility of another pluvial period.

The fundamental reasons for deserts are climatic. An arid zone girdles the earth between the temperate zone and the tropical savannas and forests. The extent of this zone depends upon other features such as the shape of the continents, the proximity to oceans, and the existence and aspect of big mountain ranges. It so happens that in this part of Africa a naturally arid zone coincides with the largest continental landmass in these latitudes, a landmass unrelieved by high mountain chains athwart the prevailing trade winds. Since there is thus nothing to make rain, the desert prevails. Even far out in the Atlantic Ocean in these latitudes there is a center of high-pressure systems that means fine clear weather and little rain.

The geological evidence makes clear that the Sahara must have been a desert for a very long time. It is a plateau, a huge shield of old rocks covering a vast area of the earth's surface. The underlying rocks are the pre-Cambrian gneiss of the basement complex, the ancient skeleton of Africa, and are the oldest rocks in the world. Above them have been laid huge areas of sandstone and limestone deposited in Cretaceous seas. But other enormous areas of sand and sandstone are not marine, for the sea never covered the eastern Sahara. Their origin is in the desert itself.

The geological structure of the Sahara is, broadly, a series

The Sahara, a huge desert tract stretching from the Atlantic to the Red Sea and from the Mediterranean to a line from mid-Mauretania to Eritrea; it is an important barrier.

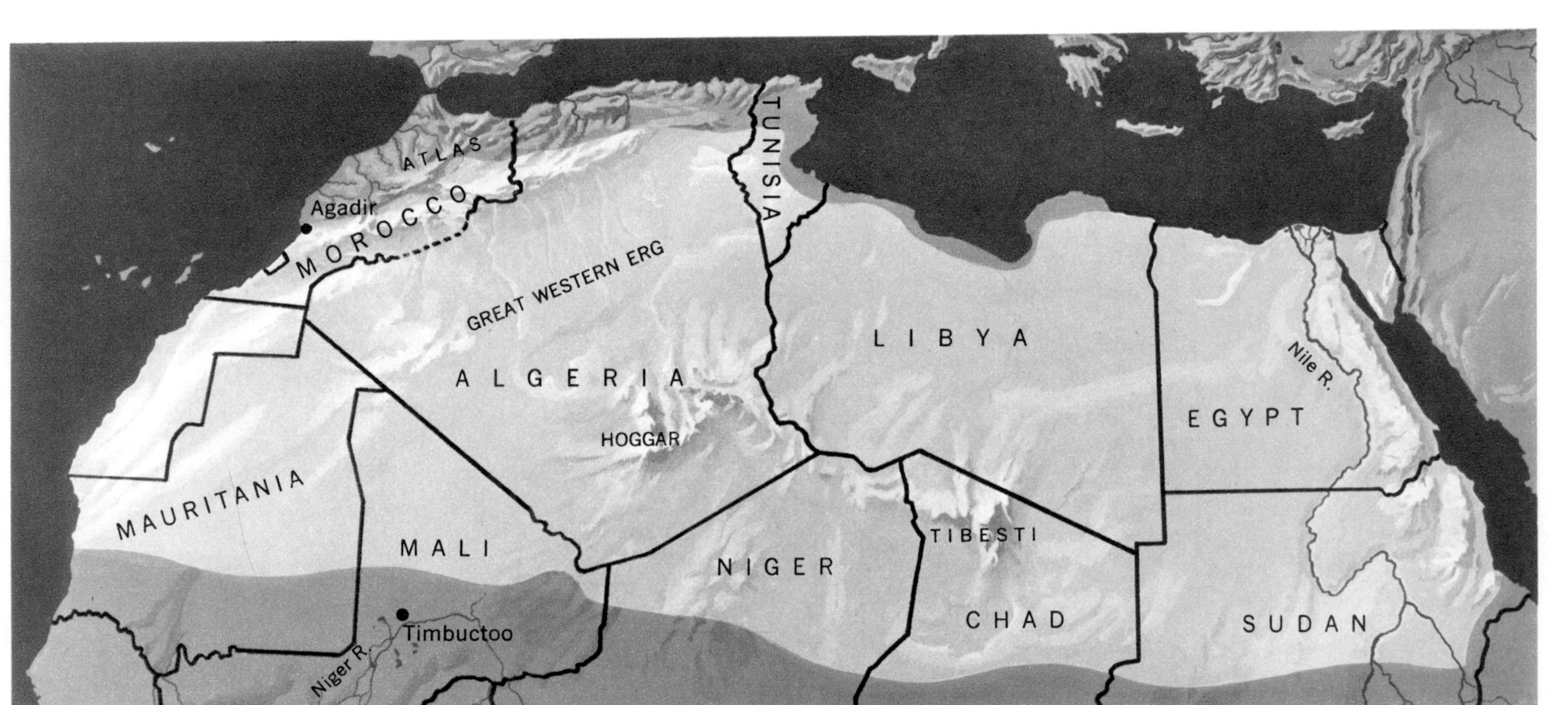

These mountainous dunes seem to threaten to engulf a traveler, but actually remain in much the same shape and position for many years. (Emil Schulthess)

of elevated areas enclosing hollows without an outlet; such hollows are called closed basins. In areas of high rainfall closed basins do not remain closed: rivers running into them eventually fill them with water, escape over a low point in the rim, and erode a deep valley running toward the sea. In a desert, however, rivers do not flow often enough to fill any large basins with water, much less escape from them. The great *chotts,* or depressions, in southern Tunisia, some of which are below the level of the Mediterranean, have never drained into that sea, though in periods when the sea level was higher than at present it may have overflowed into the Chott Djerid. In deserts such as the Sahara rivers running into closed basins deposit great masses of silt and sand, and the fact that the basins remain closed is proof that an arid climate has prevailed over very long periods.

Hence we may conclude that for untold millennia the interior of the Sahara has been too dry to produce any large perennial rivers. In relatively brief pluvial periods, probably corresponding with the temperate ice ages, there undoubtedly were large rivers in the Sahara. But they seldom flowed long enough to cut their way out of the basins to the sea, although they sometimes cut a channel from one basin to another.

THE BORDERS OF THE DESERT

Ecologists would scarcely agree as to where subdesert steppe ends and true desert begins. One will say that an area cannot be a desert if it has any vegetation whatever; another will place the limit at a point where a particular drought-resistant plant becomes the dominant constituent of the vegetation. In Algeria one can observe the transition from grass steppe covered with stiff-stemmed grass *(Stipa tenacissima)* and sage *(Artemisia)* to esparto grass *(Lygeum spartum)* and from that to the herbs *Haloxylon scoparium* and *Thymelaea macrophylla.* One ecologist will say that the boundary is where the *Stipa* ceases to thrive, others where even the plants better able to survive in lower rainfall die out.

There can also be a hydrographic boundary, the point at which rivers, if any, cease to flow. But such a boundary would embrace large areas between watercourses that could only be considered desert. The fact is that in many places there is no clear boundary between desert and steppe.

We have regarded the spine of the Atlas as the boundary between Mediterranean Africa and the Sahara, and certainly there is a very dramatic change there. But the southern slopes of the Atlas are normally called pre-Sahara by climatologists. This area contains a higher proportion of Mediterranean plants than Palearctic Desert or Sudanese subdesert species. But the main distinction is climatic; the pre-Sahara has a colder winter than the Sahara proper, with the temperature regularly below freezing point in the mountains. It is almost equally bare, but it is not quite so inhospitable as the Sahara proper.

The northern boundary of the Sahara proper is a series of depressions and low escarpments known as the Saharan Fault. This runs roughly from the mouth of the Wadi Dra on the Atlantic coast near Goulimine, then east to Erfoud, Figuig,

Biskra and the Gulf of Gabes, where it runs into the Mediterranean. There is often, but not always, a physical feature like an escarpment to mark this fault, and it is fairly clearly marked by average summer temperatures of 86° F and winter temperatures of 45° F.

Certain plants and animals do not pass this ecological barrier. The introduced date palm will not thrive beyond the fault. In the southwest the puff adder *(Bitis arietans)*, a snake of the Ethiopian region, does not occur north of the fault, nor strangely enough does the free-flying crow *(Corvus ruficollis)*. Though often not very obvious to the human eye, there are genuine differences between one bit of desert and another on the northern approaches.

The limits in the south are just as difficult to define exactly. In that region such rain as there is falls in summer, not in winter, and the desert climate is tropical rather than Mediterranean. The temperatures are much higher and never approach freezing point; consequently the evaporation rate is consistently higher. An average rainfall of fifteen inches per annum on the southern fringe of the desert would result in conditions as severe for plants as a rainfall of ten inches on the northern fringes. The most logical southern boundary is the area where the typical Sudanese subdesert vegetation begins to appear; as in the north this exhibits a gradual transition to moister conditions.

DEGREES OF DESERT

There are degrees of harshness within deserts. These variations may depend as much upon the topography and terrain, or the presence or absence of subterranean water, as on the actual rainfall itself. In mountainous areas where, in aeons of desert climate, all loose material has been blown or washed away, almost all rain either runs off at once or is evaporated from hot rocks. Even after a torrential storm the ground may be dry within a quarter of an hour. The water tears down a torrent bed in a column visible from the air in the form of a sort of chocolate-colored snake within the river.

In flat sandy areas a heavy rain sinks in; once water has sunk about one foot into sand it cannot be lost by evaporation or run-off. Moreover, in the Sahara, flat sandy areas are generally found at the bottoms of closed basins. They may be soaked at intervals with water from the run-off of a storm in mountains hundreds of miles away. The annual rainfall may be the same as that in rocky desert, but the conditions in the sand are less severe. The heat of the sun affects sand and rock differently. Since individual grains of sand are isolated from each other by air spaces, the surface of sand dunes becomes intolerably hot by day, but at night this surface heat is radiated rapidly. Rock deserts, on the other hand, absorb heat by day and retain it during much of the night; in summer they are never cool. For such reasons conditions of life are more severe in rock deserts than in sand dunes.

Actual rainfall in the Sahara varies from about ten inches per year to almost none. The accepted rainfall limit for true desert, as opposed to desert-steppe, is between four and five inches per year. But the amount of rainfall alone is not a good indication of conditions. It is better to use a formula in which rainfall, average temperature, and the evaporation rate are all taken into account. Such a figure will vary from the top of a rock to the sand on its shady side, or from the center to the outside of a bush. By taking advantage of such small local differences, animals and plants can often exist in areas where life is extremely difficult.

ERGS, REGS AND HAMADAS

There are three main types of desert terrain in the Sahara: ergs, regs and hamadas. Ergs are huge expanses of sand dunes such as the Libyan Desert or the Grand Erg Occidental. Regs are almost dead flat plains stretching into infinity on all sides, with a surface of coarse sand, gravel or stones, eternally scoured by the wind. And hamadas are upland plateaus that are cut by extinct watercourses and have a surface of stones, shale, or sheet rock.

We shall consider hamadas first since they are really the origin of the other two. In the western Sahara there are several big mountain massifs: the foothills of the Atlas, the great massif of Hoggar, the isolated eleven-thousand-foot mass of Tibesti, and lesser plateaus and mountain ranges such as Air, Tassili, and Adrar des Iforas. The summit peaks of these desert ranges have usually been denuded by ages of erosion so that the rocks stand forth like naked skeletons. The lower slopes form extensive hump-backed ridges or plateaus between radiating valleys. These plateaus are the hamadas, and they are often so extensive and flat that one hardly realizes they are elevated.

The rare rains of the desert are more likely to fall in mountain areas than in flat lowlands. When they fall on a rocky hamada they do not sink in; nor is there dense vegetation to

Left: Though vegetation is very sparse everywhere in the desert, sand can support more than stones and rock. (Afrique Photo) Right: A desert river in flood. Rare floods of this sort may do damage but they also rejuvenate vital subterranean water supplies far from the rain that caused them. (Pierre A. Pittet)

The small ripples of wind-blown sand repeat the motif of bigger dunes; the steep slope of dune or ripple is always away from the prevailing wind direction. (Emil Schulthess)

impede the flow. The water runs off as from the roof of a house, first into the gutters of the minor watercourses, then into bigger valleys. Here it charges along carrying masses of stones and silt. The storm water eventually reaches one of the closed depressions of the Sahara in the form of a devastating flood.

A one-inch storm with a one-hundred per cent run-off over a catchment of ten square miles would, theoretically, produce a flood flowing at fifteen miles per hour over three hundred feet deep in a confined rocky channel one hundred yards wide. Of course, a one-hundred per cent run-off is never achieved, but water does run off a hamada much of the time and the effect of a storm over one hundred square miles can be easily imagined.

Over aeons of time, the result of such storms are regs. The watercourses debouch into closed basins on almost flat ground and there they spread out. Their silt load is deposited in layers that build up to obstruct the flow. Then the river finds a new course and spreads its load of silt somewhere else. The stratified layers of silt deposited by these desert rivers over the ages form huge flat expanses, the regs.

The wind then gets to work. It scours the flat surface of the reg, impeded neither by vegetation nor by physical features. Any fine dust is removed first, then sand, which may accumulate somewhere else. But pebbles and larger stones remain

where the river left them. In time they form the unrelieved flat expanse of stones on the surface of a reg, often called a desert pavement. The stones protect underlying layers from further wind erosion, and are themselves protected from disintegration by a hard oxidized layer known as "desert varnish."

SEAS OF SAND

The ergs are the great expanses of sand dunes; they are the conception most people have of a desert. They are the result of the decay and wind erosion of regs. In the course of ages the smaller pebbles of the reg disintegrate into sand, which is then blown about by the wind. Since the reg itself is in a closed basin, as a rule the windblown sand cannot escape. It is deposited in certain areas according to the prevailing direction of the wind. In the Sahara most winds are from the northeast; consequently ergs will often be found at the western side of a closed basin.

The biggest of all ergs is the Libyan Desert, an expanse of sand as large as France. But there are many others of vast size, some more arid and inhospitable than others. It is an extraordinary feeling to stand on the edge of one of these great seas of sand. From atop a dune one gazes over apparently illimitable rolling hummocks of sand. If a traveler walks a little way into them he will be lost within minutes. He can backtrack his way out, of course, provided that sand has not meanwhile been blown into his footprints. On rock desert one can observe landmarks and undertake a day's exploration without fear. But woe betide anyone who goes far into an erg without a compass or a reliable guide.

Each erg is made up of dunes separated by bare ground. *Sifs,* or sabers, are long curved crests sloping gently toward the wind, with a steep, shifting, almost unclimbable slope on the lee side. Impressive and threatening, *ghourds* are masses of sand perhaps five hundred feet high. Simple dunes of several types may combine to form compound masses, sometimes called star dunes. Passes between these dunes, which are perennially free of sand, are called *gassi.* Sometimes these lead only a short way, but they may run through the whole erg.

One thinks of these dunes as continually shifting, and so, in a sense, they are. Yet individual dunes can be recognized from year to year over a long period. Sand continues to be blown off their tops, but other sand, blown off other dunes, or ultimately off regs, is deposited in its place. The shape of each dune is a near-permanent result of a combination of wind currents and possibly an underlying obstruction. A traveler may safely camp at the foot of a dune; it will not creep forward and bury him during the night.

Young dunes—young in the geological sense—are whitish; older dunes are golden. In the latter each grain of sand has had time to oxidize the iron compounds within it. The evening light glows from these golden dunes with a fantastically rich color. Sometimes, where river valleys flow into the ergs, the dunes may be partly stabilized by vegetation, but usually they are without plant growth of any sort. Some of the Saharan ergs are of comparatively recent origin. They are the result of the decay of regs which were formed by big rivers running off the uplands in the Quaternary pluvial periods coinciding with ice ages. Hamadas then had a wetter climate and supported steppe, with perennial grasses, giraffes, antelopes, elephants, and large herds of domestic stock—as the cave paintings of Tassili tell us. But there are some ergs that are much older.

Small rodents such as this rat of the genus Meriones are among the commonest mammals in the desert. They are most efficient in their ability to use sparse water. (Arthur Christiansen)

The Libyan Desert is an old erg in an advanced state of decay. In the young ergs that result from the Quaternary rivers the course of the river that formed them can sometimes be traced or guessed at. In any case the old river produces oases. But in the Libyan Desert there is no trace of old watercourses, and few oases. These facts indicate that the Libyan Desert is much older than other ergs in the Sahara.

There are even what might be called fossil ergs. The Nubian sandstone in which the famous temples of the Nile are carved consists simply of solidified ancient sand dunes, probably formed in Silurian times in much the same way as the ergs of Quaternary rivers. The fact that this sandstone exists at all is testimony to the enormous age of the Sahara as a desert.

FOSSIL RIVERS

The climate of the Sahara has been that of a desert for untold ages, with one marked period of change in recent geological time. In the Quaternary Ice Ages, the Sahara enjoyed a relatively wet climate, chiefly in the hills, but also, by reason of run-off, in the depressions.

Remnant vegetation of conifers and certain shrubs are evidence of the southward incursion of Mediterranean plants. In those days the much wetter climate on the heights of Hoggar, Tibesti and Tassili narrowed the great desert barrier to comparatively small areas. Mediterranean fauna and flora could move south, and Sudanese could move north. At some point about the Tropic of Cancer the two may even have met and intermingled. Some Sudanese fauna was able to colonize rivers which flowed north from this meeting point. The catfish *(Clarias lazera)* still found in some springs in the northern Sahara, and the Egyptian cobra *(Naia haie),* Cleopatra's asp, are two examples of Sudanese fauna that found their way north. Crocodiles have been found in lagoons at the foot of Tibesti and Hoggar.

There are many of these fossil rivers as, for example, the Wadi Saoura, which rises in the Atlas and is fed by the Wadi Guir, coming from Morocco. Confined between rocky walls, the Saoura penetrates far into the desert. It runs violently at least once a year and brings barbel as far as the irrigation canals of Touat. It is not quite dead, but it is dying, and one can trace the course of its struggle against the desert.

The Grand Erg Occidental, or Erg de Gourara, is a sea of dunes formed by the decomposition of the Saoura's Quaternary reg. Toward the end of its course the Saoura, marked by the date palms growing in its bed, flows almost straight between the edge of this erg and a line of cliffs. One may wonder how such a small river could stop the advance of such a vast sea of sand. But the behavior of the tributary Zousfana gives a clue to what is really happening.

Rising in the Algerian Atlas, the Zousfana is a much weaker stream than the Guir. The basin into which it once flowed strongly is, like others in the Sahara, filled by an erg, but here the erg has advanced so far westward in the course of time that it has blocked the Zousfana altogether. The river was forced to find an alternative route through a narrow rocky gorge, by which it joins the Saoura.

At present, the Saoura is strong enough to clean its bed

A "reg," a desert area covered with loose stones and gravel too large to be moved by the eternal winds of the area. (Pierre A. Pittet)

occasionally and run past its own erg. But a time will come, if desiccation continues, when the erg will advance still farther and choke the river altogether. Then it will be forced to spread out in a new place, or perhaps it will be "captured" by another river valley as it has captured the Zousfana.

This phenomenon of "capture" by one river of the waters of another is very significant in the Sahara. A strong-flowing river that eventually runs into the sea has greater power to erode the land surface than a "weak" river ending in a closed basin. Thus a strong river often eats back to the rim of such a basin and captures the waters of other rivers. This is why the Niger no longer flows into the basin of Taoudeni, north of Timbuctoo. Even the White Nile itself would probably not flow north through the Sahara without aid from a tributary of the Blue Nile, which has for ages been a strong river flowing into the Mediterranean. The White Nile is the only typical desert river that is not a fossil watercourse ending in a closed basin.

OASES AND TANEZROUFTS

From the viewpoint of living creatures, including man, the desert may be divided into small areas with water and vastly greater areas that lack it. The few surface rivers in the Sahara, other than the Nile, rise in the mountains of the Atlas and flow till they are absorbed in the desert sands. But there are important wet areas, both oases and *dayas,* upon which much of the life in the desert depends.

An oasis is a spot where permanent water is to be had either from springs or wells. In an oasis every drop of water is put to use by its human possessors. The use of water is closely regulated by law; but its use by man is of some value to wildlife. Oases are usually planted with forests of date palms *(Phoenix dactylifera),* but the more fertile ones also support fruit trees and crops. Their original vegetation may have been tamarisk *(Tamaryx aphylla* and *T. gallica),* oleander *(Nerium oleander)* and other shrubs, but this usually disappears.

A camel and her calf near the Red Sea Hills. Camels store fat, not water, in their humps. This one's shrunken hump indicates a period of privation. (Klaus Paysan)

Besides true oases, which are places of permanent habitation and cultivation, there are temporary desert pools. These occur in the bottoms of closed basins, chiefly among sand dunes or areas of rubble and rock. If the water in a basin is fresh, it indicates the subterranean flow of a fossil river and the basin is called a *daya*. If salt, it indicates that some fossil river has reached its final basin and it is known as a *sebkha,* a salt pan.

Both pools and oases are at times the haunts of migratory birds. Such ducks as pintail *(Anas acuta)* are often found on these pools. Doves and pigeons are common in oases, where they eat the cultivated grain and dates. Migrant passerine birds from Europe are found there in winter. But strangely enough they are not so vitally dependent upon these watering places as might appear.

It is important to remember that practically all drinkable water in the desert is used or controlled by man. There may have been a day when wild animals could come and go freely from oases, but that time has passed. The wild animals that can survive in the desert are either those that can do without drinking regularly or that man will tolerate in his midst. The jackal and the house fly are two animals that can exist only in the vicinity of water, and both are tolerated or endured by man.

In contrast to oases there are great areas with no water at all. The greatest of these, in the south central Sahara, is called the Great Tanezrouft—the land of thirst. Any man, mammal or bird that wishes to cross this area must do so in thirst or carry the needed water. The Great Tanezrouft is hundreds of miles across, but similar smaller areas occur all over the Sahara. Although the name "Tanezrouft" applies to a particular part of the south central Sahara it could equally well be applied to other completely dry areas.

LIFE IN THE DESERT

Animals and plants that live in the Sahara are divided into those that can live only near water, and those that can withstand open desert. There is no part of the Sahara absolutely without water, so there is no place without some life. Even in the most extreme forms of desert, where there is no rainfall for many years in succession, and where no ordinary vegetation is to be found, bacteria and fungi still manage to exist.

All animal life, either directly or indirectly, is dependent upon plants. Herbivores and insects eat plants, and carnivores, or lizards and frogs, eat the herbivores or the insects. Plants in the desert must not only contend with the difficulty of getting enough moisture to survive, but they must also defend themselves against animals desperately hungry and desperately in need of water. It is fascinating to see how these problems are overcome.

Desert rain falls in heavy storms at very long intervals. Some of it collects in hollows in watercourses and soaks deep beds of silt and sand. Here perennial plants and trees of considerable size can live. Early travelers often camped for the night under a good-sized terebinth tree *(Pistacia)* on the banks of a pool. Along all wadi beds that run down from the Atlas Mountains there are groves of tamarisk and of oleander. Away from the main wadi bed, but in situations where there is some subterranean moisture, there are often quite large acacia trees *(Acacia tortilis* and others). On the southern borders of the Sahara similar conditions result in lines of doum palms *(Hyphaene thebaica),* spiky desert date *(Balanites aegyptiaca),* and more acacias. Reeds and sedges often fringe the pools, or grow in backwaters and oxbows of the wadis.

But these are not the true plants of the desert. Out in the desert itself one is struck by the absence of plant life. The Sahara is unlike the deserts of North America, which have a relatively luxurious growth of cacti and other plants. One cactuslike plant, *Euphorbia echinus,* grows near the Atlantic but does not penetrate far into the true Sahara.

Perennial plants that survive from year to year and have green growth above ground must retain some water in their tissues. They achieve this either by storing water in an underground bulb or root, by reducing transpiration through the development of a waxy cuticle, or a hairy, spiky or folded surface, or they may grow flat along the surface to avoid high winds. Above all, the characteristic of many perennial desert plants is an immense root system in relation to the green top growth. There may be only one tiny little plant showing above the ground every thirty or forty yards, but its root system will spread far around it.

One plant which caught my attention on the hamadas of the South Atlas formed a gray-green cushion resembling moss. But I found it as hard as a rock. Its surface was made up of prickly little gray-green stars, performing the functions of leaves. Blown sand settled in the interstices of these stars and was in due course assimilated into the body of the plant so that it became a hard block of sandy material permeated with dry vegetable matter. Inedible, and not giving anything away, this plant, the Sahara cauliflower *(Anabasis arctioides),* had

Date palms in the bed of the Wadi Dra, southern Morocco. In the Sahara the date palm is, like the camel, introduced but vital. (Leslie Brown)

An ancient desert landscape of eroded towers cut from the solid rock by rivers and wind. (Emil Schulthess)

apparently solved supremely well the problems that faced it. The whole area where I found it was dotted with these hard little gray-green cushions as far as the eye could see.

PERENNIALS AND EPHEMERALS

The other major problem faced by desert plants is how to avoid being eaten. To protect themselves against animals, perennials are often spiny or repulsive, or both. In fact, any desert greenery is likely to have a repulsive smell, a bitter taste, or to be covered with spines.

Also, thorns may help to prevent water loss, though probably their main function is to ward off animals. One often sees sprigs of grass or other attractive fodder, which would certainly be eaten in the open, protected by some thorny shrub. It should not be assumed, moreover, that because some desert animals in America pay little attention to fearsome cactus spines, similar defenses are not successful in the Sahara. What one may certainly say of all desert plants is that if they lacked thorns, a vile taste, or a repulsive smell, they would be eaten as soon as they appeared above ground. Thorns are largely ineffective against the camel, but it should be added that the plants of the Sahara evolved before the introduction of camels about two thousand years ago.

To one kind of desert plant such protective devices are not essential. When a rare desert storm strikes, myriads of seeds that have been lying dormant for years germinate at once. They produce showy plants that are all leaves and flowers. In a very short time they have flowered, set their seed and with-

ered. Next time it rains there will be more seed to carry on the species in the same way. These are not annuals, for rain does not fall every year. They are ephemerals that flower briefly and are gone. The desert people call this type of growth *acheb,* and they eagerly seek it with their flocks. But the herds of animals that must subsist from year to year on the scanty growth of perennials cannot eat all this sudden flush of verdure. So enough of the ephemerals survive each storm to ensure the survival of the species.

ANIMALS OF THE DESERT

In the desert, animals have the same basic problems as plants: getting enough water in the first place, and secondly conserving it. For some this is easier than for others, but all desert animals are remarkably suited to their environment. Ergs are better habitats for animals than regs or hamadas. This is because they are soft and animals can burrow in them. Several animals, such as the fennec fox *(Fennecus zerda),* the fox *(Vulpes rueppellii),* the desert cat *(Felis margarita)* and jerboas *(Jaculus jaculus),* live mostly in ergs where they can dig a burrow or use one dug by another animal. Often such animals have hairy feet to assist them in running in sand.

Comparatively few desert animals actually have to drink water, though that is not to say that they will not drink when they can. Animals that had to drink regularly would fare badly in huge waterless areas; this applies more to small relatively immobile animals than to birds or to larger animals like gazelles that can travel long distances.

Of all vertebrate animals, amphibians are the least equipped to live in deserts. Newts have never managed to survive in the Sahara. But for frogs and toads, which need to spend only part of their lives in water, the desert is just habitable. Toads do better than frogs, perhaps because of their relatively dry skin: when a storm fills up temporary pools, the water often becomes alive with toads for a brief time. The growth stage of the tadpole is shorter here, the animal dropping its tail and becoming a toad before the ponds dry up.

For such animals the problem is how to survive till the next rains. Toads burrow into the earth or into crannies among stones, and so escape the extreme heat of the sun. In their burrows they become dormant; they breathe very slowly, and they may also lose an incredibly high proportion—up to sixty per cent—of their body water without dying. Put in water, an apparently desiccated toad will revive.

Reptiles are the best fitted of all vertebrates for life in deserts. For one thing, they live largely on other animals or insects, which are themselves of high water-content. Having taken in water through their prey, reptiles are better able than warm-blooded animals to conserve it: their skins are impermeable and they do not lose water by sweating. Their body temperature can vary with that of the air, and they can avoid the extreme heat of the sun, which is lethal above about 115° F to reptiles, by burrowing into the sand or getting into crevices. They can reduce water loss by breathing very slowly and, finally, their urinary system enables them to excrete the body's waste products in a solid mass from which almost all water has been reabsorbed.

Reptiles have one problem—to avoid being eaten by, for instance, predatory birds. Both the lanner falcon of the desert *(Falco biarmicus)* and the golden eagle live to a large extent upon spiny-tailed *Uromastix* lizards. These lizards, which are diurnal, are helpless against birds and are saved only by their cryptic coloration. Against other predators they have an effective defense in a spiny, armored tail with which they can inflict a damaging blow. Other reptiles avoid predators by cryptic coloration or by being nocturnal. Some lizards and snakes can bury themselves in sand in a very short time, and are then almost invisible.

THE IMPORTANCE OF MOBILITY

Birds and some of the larger mammals use mobility to overcome the problems facing them in the desert. Gazelles, for example, are the true animals of the desert, and two species—the dorcas gazelle *(Gazella dorcas)* and the rhim gazelle *(Gazella leptoceros)*—are common there. The latter is more like some of the Asian gazelles than most African species. It lives chiefly in upland areas while the dorcas gazelle can live equally well among dunes. The dama gazelle *(G. dama)* is a large animal that seasonally enters the southern desert fringes.

Gazelles cannot exist indefinitely in the open desert. They must have access to the kind of fodder that is to be found around wadi beds, temporary pools, or areas where the subterranean moisture is sufficient to maintain vegetation. Their long legs and slim bodies help them to move from one such locality to another at a good speed, and their water-economy, especially in the dorcas gazelle, is very efficient. They are extremely nomadic, and do not drink regularly.

Many birds fly long distances to water. Sandgrouse *(Pterocles)* in particular, inhabitants of deserts and semi-arid areas all over Africa, drink regularly. When sandgrouse drink they sometimes stand in the water and soak the feathers of their undersides. In aviaries male sandgrouse have been seen to offer the soaked breast feathers to their young so that these may drink the moisture from them. The range of sandgrouse is limited to convenient flight distance from water.

Birds have other advantages over mammals in the desert. Both must evaporate precious water to cool their bodies when the air temperature is higher than that of the blood, but the temperature of birds is relatively high—about 105–107° F—higher than that of most mammals. When sun temperatures are extreme, birds seek the shade of bushes and rocks, and they often nest in holes and crannies. Most of them thus avoid temperatures higher than that of their own blood. But some birds remain out in the open desert and make little effort to avoid the heat. In at least some of these the body temperature may rise in the heat of the day by as much as seven degrees; thus it can be 115° F before such a bird really feels the heat and seeks the shade. In addition, birds can extract more water from the body's waste products before excretion, since they do not urinate or produce any milk.

Even with these advantages not many birds are found in the desert away from water. Among the best known are two species of larks, *Alaemon alaudipes* and *Ammomanes deserti,* and the cream-colored courser *(Cursorius cursor).* Bustards *(Choriotis arabs),* occur in some areas, and predatory birds like falcons and eagle owls *(Bubo ascalaphus),* that get their water from their prey, are found in absolutely dry places.

THE ADDAX AND THE CAMEL

The worst problems are those faced by large animals that may be fairly mobile but are too big to burrow or to get into crannies, and whose body temperature is about 100° F, so

Left: Scorpions thrive in all desert areas; these are yellow Saharan scorpions. The hooked spine at tail tip is the sting. (Pierre A. Pittet) Right: The Aiguilles du Sisse, spiky remnants of an eroded old sedimentary formation. (Emil Schulthess)

that they are forced to evaporate water to keep cool by day and waste energy to keep warm at night. The most noteworthy of these large wild animals is the addax *(Addax nasomaculatus)*.

Addax live in the great sandy wastes, even in the very heart of an erg. They look fit and sleek despite their very scanty and scattered feeds. They are the size of a small donkey, and are related to the oryx but have spiral horns. These animals go in small herds or singly, gathering into larger groups on their seasonal migrations. Since they very rarely require water they can inhabit waterless areas, and they have large hoofs that help them to move among loose sand dunes. They have been exterminated in the northern parts of their former range, but still exist—although they are hard to locate—from Rio de Oro to the Sudan and north to the southern foothills of Hoggar.

No one knows quite how the addax manages to live in such conditions. Like other desert animals it avoids activity in the heat of the day and seeks shade when it can; but among dunes there is not much shade. As with the camel it has been wrongly supposed that it stores water in a special organ in its body. Perhaps a clue to its ability to survive in desert may be provided by the camel itself, though the two are not closely related.

Camels are nowadays entirely domesticated animals though they may appear semiwild and wander about unattended. Nor are they indigenous to the Sahara, having been introduced from Asia within the last two thousand years. These days it is impossible to think of the Sahara without camels; certainly many of the human inhabitants of the desert could not live without them.

Camels can go without water for long periods. The Arabs say that when camels are grazing on fodder from which they can obtain sufficient water without drinking that they are *jezzin*. Experiments have been carried out with camels to see just how long they can go without water, and how they manage to conserve it. A camel kept without water for seventeen days in early summer, and fed only dry fodder, lost a good deal of weight but it was still healthy at the end of the period. Camels kept without water in summer can lose up to twenty-seven per cent of body weight without dying. When allowed to drink they restore most of this loss in one great draught.

Moreover, the camel's body temperature can vary. Not only can it rise by as much as six degrees by day but it may also fall at night. Thus it is able to store heat at night and avoid excessive sweating by day. It is aided in this by a thick layer of hair or wool, which insulates its skin and helps its body to keep cool. When a camel is shorn its water loss is at once greater.

Even with these devices camels, like other mammals, inevitably lose some water in breathing, lactating and urinating. Although they can undoubtedly extract a large amount of water from their food, however dry it may seem, a time may come when even the camel will have to draw on the water in the tissues of its body to keep certain other processes working.

The circulation of the blood is vital to mammals. If the water in the blood were to fall below a certain level, the blood would become too viscous to pass through small blood vessels, the blood pressure would rise, and the animal would die. The camel has the extraordinary ability to draw upon the water in the other tissues of its body while keeping the water in its blood at the necessary level. It does not, of course, do these things consciously; but that it can do them at all is due to an extraordinary biological adaptation to conditions of the desert.

It is known that donkeys possess some of the capacities of camels; they too can go without water for very long periods, and they can lose up to thirty per cent of body weight without dying. The wild ass *(Equus asinus)*, the ancestor of the donkey, is a desert animal. Thus it is perhaps reasonable to assume that other wild creatures of extreme desert such as addax and gazelles also react to desert conditions in similar ways.

WILD SHEEP AND GOATS

On the south side of the Atlas Mountains, and in the isolated high massifs such as Hoggar, Tibesti and Air, lives the Barbary sheep *(Ammotragus lervia)*. It is strictly a mountain animal, shy and difficult to observe. It is a large creature, rufous-brown like the desert rocks; the male has a long beard and fine curved horns. It spends the day in mountain fastnesses, keeping to caves and gullies to avoid the sun, and descends to wadi beds to feed at night.

Barbary sheep have extraordinarily thick skulls. It is said that when pursued and in danger they can hurl themselves head downward over a cliff, land on their heads without injury, and so escape their pursuer. Although this seems most unlikely and the feat has never been observed by a naturalist, some scientists give credence to the tale. It seems more probable that the Barbary sheep has a thick skull to withstand the battering of head-on clashes between rutting rams—a practice indulged in by all male sheep at mating time.

The Nile Valley separates the mountain massifs of the interior Sahara from the Red Sea Hills of Nubia. In these desert mountains bordering the Red Sea lives the Nubian ibex *(Capra nubiana)*. Formerly ibex also lived in the dry beds of cliff-enclosed wadis running down through the desert toward the Nile, but in these more accessible places they have been exterminated in recent times. They do not live in the desert proper, but in the hills where the conditions are less extreme. They are magnificent stocky creatures, the males having splendid curved horns.

The Nubian ibex is also found across the Red Sea, in Arabia and Sinai. Both it and the Barbary sheep are relics of an age when the Mediterranean and Palearctic fauna were able to advance southward across the desert to about the point, near the Tropic of Cancer, where Palearctic and Ethiopian faunas may have met and mingled. With increasing desiccation of their habitats they have been obliged to retreat into the hills, where they have gradually evolved an ability to withstand desert conditions.

BIRD MIGRATION ACROSS THE SAHARA

The birds that live in the desert are very few in comparison to those that annually traverse it. One would think the huge desert barrier would effectively prevent the passage of small and relatively helpless creatures. Yet hundreds of millions of small birds pass across it every year.

Beleaguered date palms menaced by encroaching sand dunes. Dates will grow in deep sand provided their roots can reach subterranean water. (Lionel Fava)

A desert river that rarely flows is cutting its way back into this flat plateau. All that remains of an older, higher plateau is the hills in the background, preserved by caps of harder rock strata. (Guy Le Rumeur)

Nor is the desert the only obstacle. Birds migrating from Europe must first make the crossing of the Mediterranean, averaging a distance of about three hundred miles. We know they cross on a broad front and that on average the crossing takes them about twelve hours. When they arrive on the southern shore there is little rest for them. Apart from the Jebel Akhdar and the moist region of northwest Africa there is no large area where they can rest and feed. To reach the lush savannas and forests of tropical Africa, where most of them winter, they must press straight on without a rest.

Taking the average width of the desert barrier to be about one thousand miles, and the average rate of flight of a migrant bird about twenty-five miles an hour, a tiny insectivorous migrant like a willow warbler *(Phylloscopus trochilus)*, which never flies more than a few hundred yards at a time in its breeding grounds, must be able to fly for about sixty hours nonstop to pass the desert. Head or adverse winds could increase this time, and the birds may make a longer diagonal crossing for the sake of a favorable wind.

It used to be thought that all migrant birds crossing the Sahara would pause at oases, take on a little food, and struggle on again. But the oases in the desert cover an infinitesimally small fraction of the total area and have been likened by one authority to a dozen teacups scattered across a football field. Even with all other areas that might possibly shelter and provide food for small migrant birds, less than one per cent of the desert's surface will serve for this purpose.

The population of European breeding birds that regularly winter in tropical Africa is estimated at about 600,000,000. The autumn passage occurs during about two months, between

August and October. The birds enter Africa from across the Mediterranean at the rate of about four thousand per mile of longitude per day. Oases may be a hundred miles apart, and if all the birds traveling on a hundred-mile front were to collect in one oasis for a rest, 400,000 would arrive each day. No such numbers are ever seen in an oasis. We may therefore conclude that birds do not usually rest at oases when crossing the Sahara, but make the flight without stopping.

Such migrants usually make shorter passages by night when they are safer from predators that hunt chiefly by day. But when crossing the Sahara they must fly for several days and nights without stopping. Since they have not often been observed we may conclude that they make the passage at a height so great as to be invisible to human beings on the ground. Recent radar studies have shown that some migrant birds fly as high as ten thousand feet so it is not surprising if trans-Saharan migrants remain largely invisible.

Some, of course, do come down at oases, where they find some shelter and water but not much food. Any temporary break in the monotonous flatness of the desert, whether it is a cairn, a rock cliff or an abandoned motor vehicle, will also lure migrant birds to shelter in its shade. But the proportion that do this is very small. They nonetheless serve to provide prey for two species of falcons, the sooty falcon *(Falco concolor)* and the lanner. The sooty falcon breeds very late in the year, and feeds chiefly on the southward-bound autumn migrants. The lanner breeds in April and takes a toll of the reduced number of migrants going north in spring. Neither is numerous enough to have any real effect on the number of migratory birds.

THE NILE VALLEY

By following the Nile, migrant birds might be expected to make the desert passage without enduring much hardship. The banks of the Nile away from the immediate vicinity of the water are sand or rock, but there is a narrow strip of vegetation that provides some food, and plenty of water. However, most birds that cross the desert pay little heed to the Nile.

Partial exceptions to this rule are the soaring birds that enter Africa through Suez. Unlike small birds, most of the big soaring birds do not cross the Mediterranean. The majority of the big birds from western Europe enter Africa through Spain and Cape Spartel, and most of the central and eastern European population, as also the Asian birds, enter through Suez. The desire to travel over land rather than over water is undoubtedly very strong. When big soaring birds arrive at the Gulf of Suez too far south they will turn northward again to bypass it rather than fly the mere fifteen miles across.

Eagles, buzzards, and kites migrate without stopping to feed, and once in Africa they push straight on to their ultimate destination. But for large soaring water birds like storks and cranes, the Nile is a valuable line of advance. Here on the sandbanks they can be seen mingling with the resident egrets, ibis and others.

The sandbanks in the middle of the Nile are scarcely less hot than the dunes of the desert itself. Yet numbers of birds breed on them, usually during the dry season when the sun is scorching, for that is the only time when the sandbanks are exposed. Some of the birds meet the difficulty in ingenious fashion.

The Egyptian plover *(Pluvianus aegyptius)* half-buries its eggs in the sand and covers them completely when forced to leave the nest. It also wets the sand around the eggs with water which it regurgitates. Several other sandbank birds bury their eggs but do not wet the sand. When disturbed, all are anxious to return to their eggs quickly—before the sun bakes them.

The Egyptian plover—the Trochilus of Herodotus—was reputed in fable to pick the teeth of crocodiles. When a crocodile lies on a sandbank with its mouth wide open, a bird certainly could remove scraps from between its teeth. Birds do not fear crocodiles on sandbanks, for the reptiles are not dangerous except when in the water. Nevertheless, no naturalist is recorded as having seen an Egyptian plover pick the teeth of a crocodile. It and other birds perform a service, however, in that they make an outcry when people approach. The crocodile takes heed of these warnings and moves into the water.

The Nile is not only a thread of water and a migration route connecting the Mediterranean with Central Africa. Its influence on rivers and lakes in the continent have been profound. Nilotic types of fish are found as far south as Lake Tanganyika, and rivers and lakes now unconnected with the Nile share its fish. It is thus quite appropriate to regard the Nile, as early explorers did, as a key to Africa far to the south. On its waters one can go from the Mediterranean part of the Palearctic Region to the southern Sudan. There all traces of Europe have been left behind and one is in Africa proper.

A Volcanic Tableland

The Ethiopian Highlands

3 Africa lacks such great mountain ranges as the Himalayas, the Andes or the Rockies. But, as any relief map makes clear, a number of large areas are thrust up above the general level of the land. Some of these support mountain ranges or isolated peaks more than ten thousand feet in altitude. Such mountains as the widely separated volcanic peaks of East Africa are connected by extensive plateaus at a much lower altitude.

Isolation makes the mountain areas of Africa especially interesting, and has resulted in many peculiar species of plants, birds and animals. This is particularly true of the Ethiopian highlands, which is by far the largest of these isolated blocks of mountains. This hill mass forms a natural region of Africa and gives its name to the whole Ethiopian Region, which includes all of Africa south of the Sahara as well as much of Arabia.

AN ISLAND IN A DRY LAND SEA

The Ethiopian highlands are not a true range of mountains but a huge plateau supporting ranges of higher peaks and many isolated, extinct volcanos. The massif is roughly pear-shaped, with the narrow or stalk end in the north. From here it extends nine hundred miles south till it drops, rather suddenly, into the plains of Borana and the Omo. On the east it shelves away gently through the grasslands of the Ogaden into the subdeserts of Somali, and on the west it drops sharply into the lowlands of the Sudan. At its broadest point, somewhere south of the middle, it is about six hundred miles across.

This highland mass stands like an island amidst the broad belts of vegetation which run right across Africa from west to east. The Ethiopian lowlands are, as a whole, not distinctively Ethiopian, though there are areas where local populations

The edges of the Ethiopian plateau break away into steep valleys and gorges denuded by centuries of man's use and misuse. (Anna Riwkin)

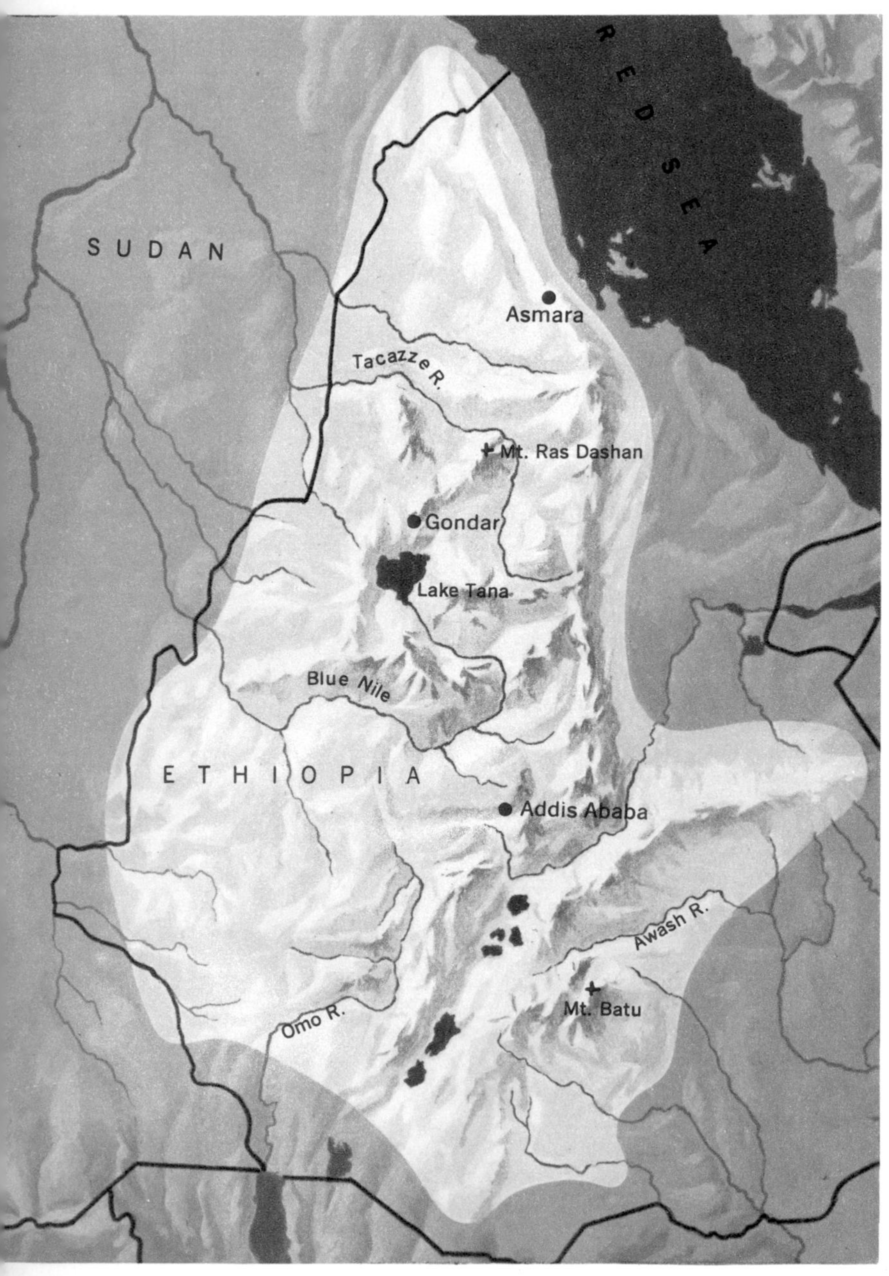

The Ethiopian highlands, the largest mountain block in Africa. It is wholly inland and surrounded chiefly by deserts, including the mountains of Ethiopia.

of unique wild animals or birds have been isolated. The vegetation of the lowlands, as well as the animals it supports, is more like that of the adjacent areas of the continent than like the highland mass. It is in the colder areas above about seven thousand feet that the special character of the Ethiopian highlands manifests itself.

Even these high plateaus are not all alike. To start with, the Great Rift Valley slices right through the highland mass, cutting off about a quarter of it in the southeast corner, including the high mountains of Arussi, Bale and Sidamo; there are great differences between these and the other mountains of Ethiopia. The floor of the Rift Valley itself constitutes a quite different kind of country, though the valley is enclosed by the highland block.

North and west of the Rift Valley many isolated peaks rise to subalpine levels from a great volcanic plateau. Vast mountain ranges are separated from one another by long stretches of rolling country, and the plateau is cut into smaller sections by the gorges of great rivers. Some mountain ranges, as in Semien, are so clearly separated from others that differences in fauna arise.

Such a highland mass, standing athwart the path of rain-laden winds from the Indian Ocean, is bound to make its own weather. Ethiopia is, and has been in the past, much wetter than the country around it, much of which is desert. Although there is no permanent snow, snow or hail lies on the highest peaks often enough to kill all but lowly forms of vegetation.

With its rainfall Ethiopia has an effect far beyond its borders. The rich silt of the Nile delta, on which the civilization of ancient Egypt arose and which is the lifeblood of modern Egypt, comes chiefly from the rapid erosion of volcanic heights in Ethiopia. Erosion caused by man is today proceeding so fast in Ethiopia that a millennium hence the plateau may be entirely different—largely bare rock incapable of supporting its present population and vegetation. This is a highland mass in the process of rapid change, chiefly caused by human misuse.

ETHIOPIA AND THE HORN OF AFRICA

Ethiopia shares the same history as the Horn of Africa, Somali and Arabia. Between the eras of reptiles and placental mammals this whole region repeatedly sank beneath the sea and then emerged again. This we know from the limestone, old coral reefs, shales and old coastal sandstone which today form plateaus and mountains thousands of feet above sea level. These rocks were laid down in relatively tranquil seas, but, in the Eocene period, which saw the disappearance of dinosaurs and the rise to dominance of mammals, there were tremendous volcanic eruptions and earth movements. Ethiopia was a great center of this volcanic activity. A great bulge or dome arose on the Horn of Africa, and many cracks and fissures developed in it. From these spouted vast quantities of fluid lava which spread gently over the land and solidified. The flattish tablelands so formed became the plateaus of Ethiopia as we know them today, a huge mass of lava sometimes as much as seven thousand feet thick laid on a foundation of older rocks like the icing on a cake.

Even then, violent activity in this part of Africa continued. A series of splits in the crust, in a general north-south direction, together with the sinking of blocks of land between the cracks, resulted in the Great Rift Valley. The faults or cracks marking the boundaries of this extraordinary geological formation completed the main features of the isolated block of the Ethiopian highlands as they are today.

THE ETHIOPIAN PLATEAU

The Ethiopian plateau is a horst—an isolated block of land left standing between lines of cracks or fissures in the earth's crust after the land all around it has sunk. If one stands on the edge of the great northeastern escarpment of Ethiopia,

The lower terraces of the Semien Mountains are clothed with savanna and scrub. The isolated rock blocks are the cores of old volcanic vents. (Toni Schneiders)

looking down from subalpine vegetation at ten thousand feet to deserts of burning lava at near sea level, it may seem that the earth movements that formed this huge crag must have been so violent that hardly any life could have survived them. But the movements took place over many millions of years. At the rate of half an inch a year, a land mass could move ten thousand feet up or down in a quarter of a million years. Such a rate of movement, if steady, would not seriously affect most inhabitants of the earth's surface. Scandinavia, for example, is thought to be rising at the rate of about a centimeter a year; this does not, needless to say, trouble the inhabitants. There is thus no reason to suppose the formation of the Ethiopian plateau was at any time catastrophically sudden.

Probably the plants and animals of the plateau were gently and imperceptibly left behind as the land on all sides dropped away from them. Many of them remain to give Ethiopia its present distinctive flora and fauna. Succeeding ages of climatic change, notably the pluvial periods, which in the tropics coincided with the ice ages of the temperate world, modified the distribution of forests, lakes, swamps and glaciers. But the country still bears the stamp of earth movements of a period more remote than that in which most of the great mountain ranges of the old and new worlds rose to their present heights. Ethiopia is ancient and it is isolated, and the combination of these two facts makes it especially interesting.

THE WORK OF RAINS AND RIVERS

Ethiopia makes its own weather conditions, and even today when Africa as a whole has a climate far drier than in the past, most of Ethiopia has a high rainfall. In past pluvial periods Ethiopia must have been very wet indeed, and the effects can be seen in the great gorges and ravines that dissect the plateau today. Chasms thousands of feet deep cut the plateau into peninsulas and isolated blocks inaccessible to each other. From the air these chasms have the form of a branching tree or of a frost crystal on a window pane. Dark green acacias and other forest trees at the bottom of the chasms indicate that the climate there is quite different from that of the plateau.

Small streams, obviously of no great volume even in rainy weather, may run into these chasms. These brooks could hardly have cut such huge gorges in hard rock. The explanation is of course that these little streams were once much larger. They joined to form enormous rivers draining the Ethiopian plateau. The Omo, for instance, raised Lake Rudolf some six hundred feet above its present level. The waters of the lake then escaped through a gorge in the northwest corner, now completely dry, and ran to join the Nile. Nile perch *(Lates niloticus)* thus entered Lake Rudolf, and are still there.

To cross one of these gorges may mean dropping five thousand feet, from a subalpine to a tropical climate, from bracing uplands to malarious acacia forests on the river bank. Barriers of this sort make crossing a gorge difficult for certain birds and animals, and some have become isolated. Others, like the bearded vulture or lammergeier *(Gypaetus barbatus)*, fly across such barriers with ease, but even some birds of strong flight, for instance the chough *(Coracia pyrrhocorax)*, are strangely isolated in Ethiopia.

Sometimes the waters have worn away the softer rock around whole sections of the plateau, leaving flat-topped hills, called *ambas*, surrounded by crags and scree. Some are completely inaccessible and have never been visited, and there will be much of interest to be found upon them when scientists eventually descend on them, probably by helicopter.

CHASM OF THE BLUE NILE

The greatest of the river gorges is that of the Abbai or Blue Nile. The river rises in a spring in the Damot Mountains and flows north into Lake Tana. Flowing east from the lake it soon reaches Tisisat and drops over one of the most spectacular waterfalls in Africa. Thereafter it plunges into the gorge and makes an almost complete circle until, about sixty miles south of its source at Gish Abbai, it has traveled about four hundred miles and fallen about six thousand feet.

The fish in Lake Tana prove that it was connected with the Nile system before the formation of the now impassable Tisisat Falls. At some stage a lava flow dammed the valley and formed the lake. Besides fish the lake once contained many hippos, but these have been virtually exterminated. Crocodiles are found in the river above Tisisat, but strangely enough they do not actually enter Lake Tana, though there is nothing to prevent them from doing so and they can walk quite well overland.

The Grand Canyon of Arizona would be lost in the Blue Nile Gorge. From the point where the river enters it to its outflow in the Sudan lowlands the gorge is over seven hundred miles long, and it is over seven thousand feet deep from the mountaintops bordering it to the acacias beside the river. On its sides the whole geological history of Ethiopia is displayed. As the gorge deepens it cuts first through the lava flows of the plateau top, then through limestone and sandstone, until the river finally flows over the hard rocks of the skeleton of Africa, rocks so old they cannot well be dated by fossil remains.

One would think that this great gorge, more than a mile deep and twenty miles across, would rival the Grand Canyon for spectacular effect. But it does not, because it runs through country with a high rainfall, so that its sides are clothed in vegetation. The rocks, too, are not the multicolored sandstones of the Grand Canyon, but chiefly dark lavas. Nor are they sculptured into the fantastic shapes characteristic of eroded sandstone. In the dry season the smoke of grass fires so thickens the atmosphere that one can scarcely see the far side of the gorge, but on a clear rain-washed morning the views across the gorge are magnificent.

The Blue Nile Gorge cuts off the highland plateau of Gojjam from the horseshoe-shaped plateaus of Shoa and Wollo. To the north the similar but less spectacular gorge of the Tacazze River cuts off the narrow plateau of Tigre from the high mountains of Semien. These great blocks are cut up by innumerable smaller gorges, resulting in an extraordinarily varied and contorted block of highland country. A typical view in Ethiopia is of a lip of crag, a vast gulf and, in the blue

Right above: A plant known as a red-hot poker (Kniphofia), growing at 11,500 feet on the edge of a five-thousand-foot abyss in the Semien Mountains. Right: Gelada baboons (Theropithecus gelada) perched on the edge of a four-thousand-foot crag. The big male, with a long cape of pale fur, grimaces at the intruder. (Both by Leslie Brown)

distance beyond, another plateau at about the same level with higher mountains rising from it. Rainwater, which is slightly acid, cuts fairly easily into lava or limestone, both of which are alkaline, and the great masses of rock which once filled the gorges have thus all been worn away.

There are three main divisions of the Ethiopian highland plateau. First the plateau of northern Tigre and Eritrea, composed of limestone and sandstone overlying still older rocks, but without the top layer of volcanic rock, and forming the neck of the pear-shaped mass. Then there are the volcanic plateaus of Shoa, Wollo, Semien, and, west and south of these, Jimma and Illubabor, all interconnected, but each slightly different. Finally, south and east of the Rift Valley, there are the volcanic plateaus and highlands of Bale, Arussi and Sidamo, rising to fourteen thousand feet, also cut by river gorges, but in many ways distinct from the rest of the Ethiopian highlands.

Each of these areas has its own character. In the north the rainfall is lower and the country harsher, and it does not seem surprising to see camels among fields of stunted grain. In the high cold central highlands the impression given is of a country which is a cross between greater Africa and some Middle Eastern land. And in the southeastern highlands one is unmistakably in a region with East and South African affinities, yet distinctively Ethiopian. Let us now take a closer look at these areas.

THE LIMESTONE PLAIN OF TIGRE

On the road from Addis Ababa to Asmara one emerges from high volcanic mountains onto a gently undulating plateau. This is at once reminiscent of Spain or North Africa; it is composed of limestone, here forming a plateau of its own. Still farther to the north even older rocks appear. The northern tip of the plateau drops sharply into a valley which separates the Red Sea Hills of the Sudan from the Ethiopian highlands. The western boundary of this limestone plateau is the Tacazze, beyond which rise the high mountains of Semien. The eastern boundary is the great Rift Valley scarp, dropping sharply to the Red Sea and the Afar depression. Relatively narrow—a hundred miles or so across—and of moderate height, the Tigre plateau attracts less rainfall than do the high volcanic hills to the south. This combination of geology and climate gives the plateau its special character.

Most of it is a gently undulating plain, cut into by gorges which become deeper and more precipitous where they run west to join the Tacazze. The plain is at a general level of six thousand feet and the climate is cool and dry. From the plateau rise isolated hills of bizarre shapes. They are sometimes as much as ten thousand feet high, but since individually they are not massive, they do not attract much rainfall.

A FAIR LAND RAVAGED

It is very difficult to visualize what this plain looked like before man made it his home. This is the oldest inhabited part of Ethiopia and the vegetation has been more drastically altered by man than elsewhere in the Ethiopian highlands. Here one can see the results of the feckless misuse, aggravated by a relatively dry climate, which surely helped to turn much of the Middle East into desert. One can actually relate the destruction of the countryside to the density of human population and the length of time man has been in the area.

The original vegetation of the Tigrean plateau is largely gone, and on all the steeper slopes centuries of abuse have stripped away the topsoil, leaving only stones and scrub. As erosion proceeds, more and more of each year's rainfall runs uselessly downhill into swift rivers. Once the topsoil cover has gone, a long interval must elapse before a very gradual soil-building process can restore something like the original conditions.

But it is possible to piece together what this land once was like. Relict plants give clues to the original vegetation. A tree still standing, its roots exposed, on a small hump of soil several feet above the stony plain, shows, for example, that the area was once covered with a blanket of soil as deep as the hummock. Small patches of forest survive in gorges too steep for man and his animals to reach and around churches and monasteries. These patches demonstrate that it is not lack of rainfall, but misuse by man that has changed the character of the country. A stroll round a church will probably reveal that the little wood enclosing it is of cedar *(Juniperus procera)* and brown olive *(Olea chrysophylla)*. Both are trees that grow in moderate rainfall; at one time they clothed most of the mountain slopes. If the church happens to be in a valley it will be surrounded by a small patch of broad-leaved trees, among which the white-flowered *Cordia abyssinica* is prominent, with perhaps a few big acacias. A wood of introduced *Eucalyptus* reveals that on the site of the church there were no trees, but only grassland, and that priests probably planted the trees. On the summits of high hills the cedar gives way to giant heath *(Erica arborea)*, once thirty feet high, but now only remnant scrub. A few red-hot pokers *(Kniphofia)* and giant lobelias may still persist in steep gullies. And on the plains a few larger acacias growing among the scrub remain as living proof that such trees once flourished there.

The picture that emerges is of hills once forested with successive zones of giant heath, cedar and olive, and, at the bottom, more luxuriant broad-leaved forest. The flatter, more open parts of the plateau must have been covered with waving fields of grass among which stood big table-topped acacias, much as in some of the more beautiful parts of East Africa today. But all this is gone. Where they are not cultivated the plains are covered with stunted acacia scrub, and perennial grasses have been replaced by annuals and weeds. Desert succulents such as aloes thrive in these conditions and there are acres of them with red or yellow flowers. Among the remaining larger trees are candelabra *Euphorbias*—not much use to man or beast, even for firewood. In places a hardy shrub, *Euclea,* with glossy bright green leaves manages to persist. Euclea is not much eaten even by goats and is notoriously difficult to destroy, even with modern chemicals.

Under the trees noble lions may once have rested and on the plains antelopes may once have grazed. But there are now no animals larger than a scavenging hyena or jackal and an occasional troop of vervet monkeys *(Cercopithecus aethiops)* living in remnant patches of woodland. In all of Africa no country has been more brutally ravaged by man.

The Blue Nile before it plunges into its deep gorge. The spray of the fall produces a patch of tropical forest. (Anna Riwkin)

The most successful species of wildlife in this area are those which have been able to benefit from the changes wrought by man. Pigeons, for instance, find the fields of grain to their liking and they can also find safe nesting holes in crags, bridges and buildings. Two species of large pigeons, the guinea pigeon *(Columba guinea)* and the white-collared pigeon *(C. albitorques)* are very common; the white-collared pigeon is found only in Ethiopia. Both birds glean the stubble in company with smaller turtledoves.

The destruction of woodland and its replacement by stones and scrub has favored the rock thrushes and chats. Every second bird one sees along a roadside is a chat or wheatear. Small finches and weavers are also noticeably thriving. Harriers and kestrels, winter migrants from Europe, hunt over open spaces; vultures and ravens abound, they too benefiting from dead domestic animals and refuse in villages. The lammergeier soars over the highest hilltops and the griffon vulture *(Gyps rueppellii)* frequents rock walls and gorges. What the vultures do not eat by day will be cleaned up by hyenas and jackals at night.

Hyenas are very common up to ten thousand feet. They come into the villages and towns to scavenge, and they are said to attack domestic animals or even sleeping men. For an animal like a hyena a large population of domestic animals living under conditions of overgrazing and semistarvation is a more reliable food supply than even the largest populations of healthy antelopes on fertile grass plains. Thus in northern Ethiopia hyenas and jackals have been able to thrive while other predators have virtually disappeared.

THE SEMIEN MOUNTAINS

West of Axum the land descends gradually toward the Tacazze River along a spur of the Tigre plateau. At the lip of the gorge, at about 4600 feet one can look across the chasm to a similar plateau beyond. On top of this plateau, adorned with steep turrets and bastions, and rising in three distinct steps is perched the north wall of Semien, containing some of the most spectacular scenery in the world.

The mountain mass is a broad plateau, cut off on the north and west in one enormous crag forty miles long and three to five thousand feet high. The low country at the base of the crag is savanna forest on old volcanic rocks, cut into by the deep gorges of clear streams. At the foot of the main cliff is a jumble of high ridges and deep ravines, very difficult to traverse. On top of these are perched huge cylinders, cones, and ridges of volcanic rock, a thousand or more feet high, with unscalable sides and untrodden summits, but dwarfed by the huge crag in the background. These are called *ambas* locally and are formed by erosion from the hard cores of old volcanic vents. Gullies thousands of feet deep are gradually cutting off sections of the mountain mass, and these in time will form other isolated and inaccessible peaks.

The main plateau south and east of the north wall is broad and grassy, draining southward through gorges that eventually join to form the Tacazze. The whole mountain mass is the remains of long extinct Hawaiian-type volcanos. Unlike conical or explosive volcanos these discharge their lava through large vents in relatively gentle streams. The lava flows over great areas, eventually solidifying in layers to form a huge, gently sloping dome of far greater bulk than in a conical volcano. In Semien the lava is as much as seven thousand feet thick on top of older rocks. The scenery looks violent but has been formed by essentially slow processes.

On the mountain plateau, at over nine thousand feet, there are great expanses of undulating cool grasslands, with remnant patches of *Hagenia* and occasional cedars *(Juniperus procera)* typical of the high Ethiopian plateaus. In the journey from two thousand feet at the Tacazze River to the Semien plateau one traverses many of the vegetation zones of lower Ethiopia, from savannas similar to those in West Africa to open downland. Almost anywhere else the great gorges that cut the plateau would command attention. But on the way to the higher peaks of Semien one has only to walk a little way to the north to come to the lip of the prodigious northwestern crag. There one looks down into depths which make the senses reel.

Remnant forests of *Hagenia* and cedar give place at about 10,500 feet to giant St.-John's-wort *(Hypericum)* and then to giant heath *(Erica)*. Despite much damage by men, there are still virgin stretches of giant heath here and there. Great red-hot pokers, each with a spike of orange flowers a foot long, flourish in rocky valleys. Wild roses and other northern plants mingle strangely with aloes and characteristic Ethiopian wildflowers, chiefly yellow *Compositae,* but including masses of blue labiates. It is a varied and beautiful flora made up of northern, Ethiopian, and lowland African elements.

At about eleven thousand feet the heath gives place to tussocky grassland dotted with the spikes of giant lobelias. Everlastings *(Helichrysum)* and sage *(Artemisia)* are also common. These open moorlands are strongly reminiscent of the grasslands on Mount Kenya or on other East African mountains.

The giant lobelias of Semien, with spikes up to twenty feet tall, are the largest I have ever seen. They flower every seven years or so, and the flowering spike then dies. Other high mountains in Ethiopia have their giant lobelias too, but one looks in vain for the giant groundsels which are common on the East African mountains. Nevertheless, the lobelias and some other plants proclaim the kinship between Ethiopian and East African heights.

BABOONS, RED WOLVES, AND RATS

On the plateau live huge herds of gelada baboons *(Theropithecus gelada)*. Found only in Ethiopia north and west of the Rift Valley, in Semien they occur in troops of as many as four hundred. They roost, and sometimes feed, on the enormous rock faces of the northwest escarpment, but most climb in the early morning to the alpine pastures of the plateau. Unlike most baboons they are so tame that they permit approach to within thirty yards before they shuffle away. The big males, with impressive capes of hair and tufted tails, look vaguely like lions as they lumber over the grasslands. Any of the full-grown ones could easily kill a man, but the relation between baboons and man is one of mutual indifference. It is a strange experience to wander among groups of these large terrestrial

The Omo River cuts into columnar basalt rock, a formation common in the volcanic Ethiopian massif. (Toni Schneiders)

Papyrus in a channel as well as meadows tight-grazed by cattle are characteristic of the shores of Ethiopian Rift Valley lakes. (Toni Schneiders)

monkeys and to listen to their high-pitched voices as they converse with one another or protest at the intrusion.

The turf of the moorlands is sometimes so honeycombed with rat burrows that it is impossible to walk without breaking into them. The rats provide an abundant food supply for various predators, avian and mammalian. The whole area reminds one rather of a temperate steppe or prairie, where great numbers of rodents are common. The little rats are preyed upon by everything from kestrels and lanner falcons to buzzards and big eagles. Yet they manage to abound.

The most interesting animal that eats the rats is the Semien fox, or Abyssinian wolf *(Simenia simensis)*. Little has been known about this animal in the past and the various names it has been given indicate the confusion as to its true relations. It looks vaguely like a small wolf, but is bright red, with a black, white-tipped brush. It does not howl like a wolf, but barks like a fox or screams like a vixen. Although it is much larger than an ordinary fox, I prefer to think of it as a fox rather than a wolf. It seems to live exclusively on rats, which it catches in the open.

Semien is a meeting ground of European, Ethiopian and distinctively African flora and fauna; this is its special interest. The birds of the plateau exemplify its character as a halfway house. Among the commonest are slender-billed chestnut-wing starlings *(Onychognathus tenuirostris)* and mountain chats *(Pinarochroa sordida)*, both common on East African mountains. The augur buzzard *(Buteo rufofuscus)*, another East African species, is the commonest predator. Then there are many characteristically Ethiopian birds, for instance the thick-billed raven *(Corvultur crassirostris)*, the spot-breasted plover *(Tylibyx melanocephalus)* and Erckel's francolin *(Francolinus erckelii)*. To complicate matters a common small bird is the ground-scraper thrush *(Psophocichla litsipsirupa)*, which is found in Ethiopia and southern Africa. Then there is the European chough *(Coracia pyrrhocorax)*, which is very common in Semien but found nowhere else in Ethiopia. Choughs are birds of strong soaring flight, and in Semien they descend to about nine thousand feet to feed on farmlands. Why they do not fly to other high plateaus, which they must surely be able to see, is a mystery.

THE WALIA IBEX

The plateau breaks off abruptly at the tremendous northwest cliff of Semien. Like many other cliffs of volcanic rock it consists of bays separated by knife-edge ridges or buttresses, the hard cores of old vents. The sun sets more or less along the line of this escarpment and to watch it go down, throwing the bays into deep shade and the castellated buttresses into relief, is to see rock scenery at its most magnificent.

On the cliff top, where the giant heath bushes are whipped about by strong winds, one has a feeling of a Mediterranean mountain-top. The turf is shot through with small flowers, and the scent of aromatic herbs is strong. A little way down, the cliff breaks into big ledges, hanging at a steep angle on the rock face. These ledges are forested with giant heath, each tree leaning out toward the abyss. Lichens festoon their ancient branches and beneath is a pasture of grass and herbs, blue with scabious—good feeding-grounds for any animal that can reach the ledges.

Here lives the southernmost species of ibex, the walia ibex *(Capra walie)*. Separated by four hundred miles of lower country from its nearest relative, the Nubian ibex of the Red Sea Hills, it has been isolated for so long that a distinct species has evolved. They are a major extension into the Ethiopian Region of a fauna with Palearctic affinities.

The ibex live at all heights on the escarpment from eight to at least eleven thousand feet. They seem to dislike the highest crags and prefer to spend their time on lower ledges or on buttresses jutting into the lowlands. Formerly they used to graze high up on the plateau, but continual persecution has forced them to abandon this practice. They also spend time in thick cover, browsing among the giant heath, where they are difficult to see. They are most easily observed when they move from one place to another across the cliff face. They spend the day out of sight in caves or under ledges.

The walia have no enemies but man, and probably they are now confined to the great northwest crag because it is the only safe refuge left to them. Possibly 150 to 200 of them remain, but this remnant seems to be breeding satisfactorily and could multiply and spread if unmolested.

ETHIOPIA'S HIGHEST MOUNTAIN

Ethiopia's highest mountain, Ras Dedjen (15,160 feet), is in Semien. Neither on it, nor on any other of the highest peaks in Ethiopia is there any permanent snow or glaciers. Moraines, those piles of rocks and debris which glaciers leave behind when they retreat, show that there were once two large glaciers in Semien. Snow then lay regularly down to twelve thousand feet, and even today it lies down to this level often enough to have a marked effect on the vegetation. Frost is regular above eleven thousand feet, and keen above twelve thousand. At such heights the daily variation in temperature is from warm sunlight to well below freezing, a range of about eighty degrees. This sort of variation is characteristic of East African mountains too, but height-for-height the climate of Semien is rather more severe than that, for instance, on Mount Kenya or Kilimanjaro.

The topmost screes are bare of plants. Grasses and giant lobelias persist to about 12,500 feet, but they are stunted and do not flourish as they do a thousand feet lower. Above the giant lobelias there is little but moss and lichens, though in sheltered spots a few lowly yellow composites survive. The only birds are big raptors such as the lammergeier, ravens and mountain chats. Gelada baboons, hardy creatures, traverse the very summit of Ras Dedjen itself.

These bare screes, where snow or drifts of hail often lie deep enough to stop plant growth, represent the alpine zones of temperate mountain ranges. But here the regular seasons of winter and summer are replaced by less clearly defined rainy and dry seasons and short periods of rain or drought. A plant growing here has scant chance to flower and seed but will be nipped by some unseasonable storm and subject to nightly frost. So it is not surprising to find bare screes despite the fact that the climate is, on the face of it, much less severe than that of the bare alpine zones of Europe or North America in winter.

THE LOWER PLATEAUS

The lower plateaus of Ethiopia run in a huge horseshoe around the bend of the Blue Nile, and are enclosed within that bend. South and west they extend to Jimma and to smaller isolated blocks near the Sudanese border. All these plateaus above a certain height were originally quite similar, but in areas of dense population human activity has largely stripped the ground of its cover of grass and trees.

From the plateau rise other large groups of mountains, as at Chokai, near Debre Medahan, or all along the great rift wall from Debra Sina to Dessie. All these highland blocks are much more densely inhabited than Semien, and the original zonation of vegetation has been largely destroyed or obscured by overgrazing and cultivation. It is difficult to say what they were once like, even on the lower plateaus. The natural vegetation has been reduced to remnants, and any large animals have long since been exterminated. But from the remnants and from a few less spoiled areas it is possible to reconstruct the scene.

Forty miles west of Addis Ababa at Menagasha, a remnant of cedar forest *(Juniperus procera)* has been almost miraculously preserved. The slopes of Mount Wuchacha are covered with a splendid stand of cedar with some *Podocarpus,* another characteristic highland tree in East Africa. Here the likeness to the slopes of Mount Kenya is strong, and a close look at plants and birds would be needed to place oneself exactly. For instance, the white-cheeked touraco *(Tauraco leucotis)* replaces Hartlaub's touraco *(T. hartlaubii)*. The larger fauna is strongly East African in its affinities. There are black and white colobus monkeys, leopards, and the black Menelik's race of the bushbuck. We have clearly come a step nearer East Africa from Semien.

Once, such cedar forests covered all the better drained slopes of Shoa, the ridges and the sides of volcanic peaks, while on the flatter lands there were grasslands and, along river valleys, stands of a noble table-topped acacia, *Acacia abyssinica.* These indicate a former landscape of cedar-clad hills and, at their bases, open rolling grasslands with long fingers of dark green acacias along drainage lines. Such areas are still be seen in the plateaus of southern Ethiopia almost in their virgin state, and the inhabited plateaus must once have looked like this too.

Any large animals that once lived here have long ago been

exterminated, though hyenas remain as scavengers. In such country—in the Mount Kenya foothills, for instance—the African buffalo *(Syncerus caffer)* would abound. But either this animal never existed in highland Ethiopia or it existed so long ago that no one remembers it. Nor are there any recent records of big herds of large antelopes, as would be found in similar areas in East Africa. If there ever were any lions, there are none now, though leopards manage to survive in the cedar forests of Menagasha.

THE THICK-BILLED RAVEN'S BEAK

If the larger animals have gone, birds and humbler forms of animal life remain. Many of these are distinctively Ethiopian. One very common species that will be seen by any traveler is the thick-billed raven *(Corvultur crassirostris)* previously mentioned in this chapter. It is found in every village from five to fifteen thousand feet up, and at any camp its wheezy croak wakes one in the morning. One of the largest and most imposing of ravens, it has an oval white patch behind the head and a great black curved blade of a beak, tipped with white. One may well wonder why it has this formidable appendage, and one raven in Semien demonstrated to me its purpose.

The bird was walking about in a pasture, and whenever it came to a lump of cowdung it scattered it with two or three scything sweeps of the beak, afterward searching for insects in the remains. It seemed clear that the beak was evolved for this purpose, to which it was perfectly fitted. But we know that cattle are comparatively recent introductions into Ethiopia: they are of the *Bos indicus* or zebu species, and accompanied man from the East. When these animals arrived, the thick-billed raven must already have been there and it must have been using its great bladelike beak to scatter the dung of animals similar to cattle. If these were buffalos no trace of them now remains. The raven, however, persisted and helps to complete our mental picture of the country as it once was before man's ravaging intrusion.

THE SOUTHEASTERN HIGHLANDS AND THE FORESTS OF BALE

The third major division of the Ethiopian highlands lies south and east of the Rift Valley. Although in many ways similar to the plateaus north and west of the rift, it is quite different from these. In the north, high ground along the rift wall south of Harar forms a narrow spine, rising to the south into a group of volcanic peaks—Cilalo, Badda, Encuolo and Cacca—which stand as cones or ridges on broad, forested bases.

Cacca and Encuolo drop away to the south onto a broad grass plain, at the headwaters of the Webi Scebeli River. South of this great plain rise the broad backs of the Mendebo Mountains of Bale province. Here there is more than a thousand square miles of mountain country more than 9500 feet high, culminating in the highest mountain in south Ethiopia, Mount Batu (14,131 feet).

Still further south this mountain mass descends into the forests of Sidamo, extraordinarily beautiful country where open glades alternate with blocks of dark green trees. Here colobus monkeys are common despite the fact that Ethiopians sell their skins for hearthrugs. There are also many birds familiar to East African slopes. We are in fact now entering country with many similarities to East Africa, and when the forests give way to savannas the likeness is almost complete. On this southward slope we are leaving Ethiopia behind.

The distinctive character of the Mendebos and other mountains farther north is immediately marked by the major fauna. Unique to this region, for it is found nowhere else in the world, is a splendid antelope, the mountain nyala *(Tragelaphus buxtoni)*. And here the Gelada baboon of the northwest is replaced by the still larger Hamadryas baboon *(Papio hamadryas)*. A bond too with the northern highlands is provided by the local race of the Semien fox, which is common. Colobus monkeys, bushbuck, and klipspringers are also found. Lions occur up to twelve thousand feet, and in the lower forests leopards were formerly common; they have become very rare.

As one climbs into the Mendebo Mountains from the north one passes first through a belt of cedar forest. This is extremely beautiful, for the aged trees have a weeping habit. Clear rushing streams descend through many little green glades, their level maintained by copious rains. There are no fish in these highland streams, since the lowland fish of the Webi Scebeli have been unable to pass the many waterfalls.

Above the cedars, and gradually becoming more dominant as one climbs, is a belt of Hagenia trees. Hagenia is found at high levels all over Ethiopia, but normally it has been destroyed or reduced to a remnant by human beings. Here, the Hagenia forests are pristine and the trees are huge. With increasing age and weight they incline down the slopes, and are often found lying on a patch of sunlit turf, their branches forming new and vigorous trunks. The trees bear masses of attractive reddish flowers, and a veritable garden of mosses, ferns and flowering plants often establishes itself on the broad, inclined trunks.

The Hagenia in turn gives way to forests of St.-John's-wort. In temperate climates St.-John's-wort is a lowly shrub, but here it grows to a height of fifty feet. This forest forms a unique habitat, clean underfoot, and rich in pasture of clover and fine herbs and grasses. Here for a certainty, and sometimes in the Hagenia forest lower down, will be found the mountain nyala.

THE ELUSIVE MOUNTAIN NYALA

The mountain nyala is a kudu-like animal belonging to the family *Tragelaphidae*—the spiral-horned antelopes. Like its relatives the kudu, bongo, eland and bushbuck, it is a cover- or bush-loving animal, and it epitomizes the shyness and secretive ways of most members of its family. It is found in all types of country from the higher cedar forests upward, but it is most common in the zone of giant heath *(Erica arborea)* which covers the top of the Mendebo Mountains. Nyala might spend more time in the forests of St.-John's-wort if these were not grazed continuously by domestic stock.

Right above: Ground-scraper thrush (Psophocichla litsipsirupa) on a stub of St.-John's-wort (Hypericum). This bird is distributed across Ethiopian and South Africa. Right: A glade in a St.-John's-wort forest in the Bale Mountains. Such country is the haunt of the mountain nyala. (Both by Leslie Brown)

Wattled cranes (Bugeranus carunculatus), the largest and most stately of African cranes, breed in Ethiopia and are a link with the South African bird fauna. (Clem Haagner)

It is very difficult to get more than a glimpse of mountain nyalas in dense cover, and they are best seen in the areas of giant heath which are regularly burned. Here the country is basically grassland with small bushes of giant heath. When these bushes are five to six feet high they grow together and are then burned by Galla drovers and graziers, leaving open ground spiked with the dead heath stems. Nyalas like to graze in this open ground but are very difficult to approach. They often lie down in a small hollow on top of a ridge or hummock, where they can disappear in a flash at the sight or sound of an enemy. When disturbed they can vanish almost as if by magic.

The nyala, more than any other animal, makes this a distinctive faunal region of Ethiopia, just as the walia ibex distinguishes Semien. The mountain nyala, is probably the nearest relative of the animal first called nyala, which inhabits Zululand, lives at low altitudes, and has a long shaggy coat of hair, but which possesses the same strongly lyrate spiral horns. The mountain nyala may thus be one of a series of important faunal links with South Africa. But much remains to be learned of its habits: the resemblance to the Zululand nyala may prove to be purely superficial.

Fortunately there are a good many nyalas left: the thousand-square-mile highland block of Mendebos may support between fifteen hundred to two thousand of them. These mountains are not yet so densely inhabited by human beings that their destruction is inevitable, and this may be one part of Ethiopia which it will still be possible to preserve.

HIGHLAND SWAMPS

Rain or hail falls almost every day in these mountains for eight months of the year; and for much of each day cloud or drizzle shrouds the landscape. The wet festoons the heath with dripping lichens, soaks the undergrowth of lady's mantle *(Alchemilla)* and tussock grass, and seeps in foglike tongues through the dark woods. The place has a haunted feeling about it and recalls a northern tundra rather than an African mountain.

Bogs form on the flat tops of the broad ridges, with little peaty pools in them. For me these bogs heightened the feeling of a northern land, for on the pools were migrant European wigeon *(Anas penelope)* whose clear whistling calls echo in spring from desolate northern waters. But on these same pools were yellow-billed ducks *(Anas undulata)* and Egyptian geese *(Alopochen aegyptiacus)*. European wigeon might be seen on other tropical waters, but the other two ducks would never be seen on a northern bog.

In these bogs there are also a few of Africa's most majestic crane, the wattled crane *(Bugeranus carunculatus)*, extraordinarily shy and wary though they seldom see human beings. The wattled crane breeds in Ethiopia and in Rhodesia and South Africa, but in none of the territory in between. They share this curious distribution with the ground-scraper thrush which also occurs farther north in Ethiopia. Some other birds, such as the mountain eagle owl *(Bubo capensis)*, are found all the way from the Cape to Ethiopia, but have intermediate forms in the East African mountains.

FROM IBEX TO WATTLED CRANES

At sometime in the far distant past the flora and fauna of Ethiopia must have been connected with that of South Africa. Hence the giant heaths, huge St.-John's-wort, everlastings and other plants characteristic of Ethiopia, the highlands of East Africa, and places farther south. With the occurrence of the wattled crane the links with the south become stronger. We are still in a halfway house between south and north, but in Bale we have come as it were to the south wall of the house.

A few hundred yards from the lonely swamp in the Bale Mountains where I came upon the cranes, I could walk to the edge of a crag and look over the forested headwaters of the Ganale Doria River, one of the big tributaries of the Juba. This was a true ecological frontier, for the forests below here become more and more East African in character and less Ethiopian. Scarcely touching the lower savanna forests in our journey so far from north to south, we have come, in effect, from a land with a strong Palearctic influence to one that is typically African. In the Semien Mountains choughs and ibex are Eurasian in their faunal affinities, but in Bale there are unmistakable similarities to the East African highlands and even to the flora and fauna of South Africa. Yet both areas, and the plateaus in between, would immediately strike a naturalist as being peculiarly Ethiopian—an impression which the Semien foxes, the mountain nyalas, or the thick-billed ravens would soon emphasize.

Ethiopia is unique but it spans, in its faunal affinities, almost the entire distance from the Mediterranean to the Cape of Good Hope, from wild roses to proteas, and from ibex to wattled cranes.

The Endless Steppe

The Sudanese Semi-arid Transition Zone

4

The southern border of the Sahara is not clearly defined: scientists still disagree over it. There is no physical feature to mark it, but a commonly accepted geographical boundary runs eastward from a point on the Atlantic coast about halfway between Cape Blanc and Cape Verde, swings a little northward near the Niger bend into the massif of Adrar des Iforas, then runs east through Agades and Kizimi in the Chad depression and into the Sudan. In the southern half of the

Right: A typical scene in Karamoja in the dry season: deep golden grass, distant mountains and an acacia tree. (F. G. H. Allen)   Below: This race of the Cape dikkop (Burhinus capensis) occurs in most of the acacia steppe and scrub in semi-arid areas. It lives on the ground, is largely nocturnal, and emits plaintive whistling cries. (Alan Root)

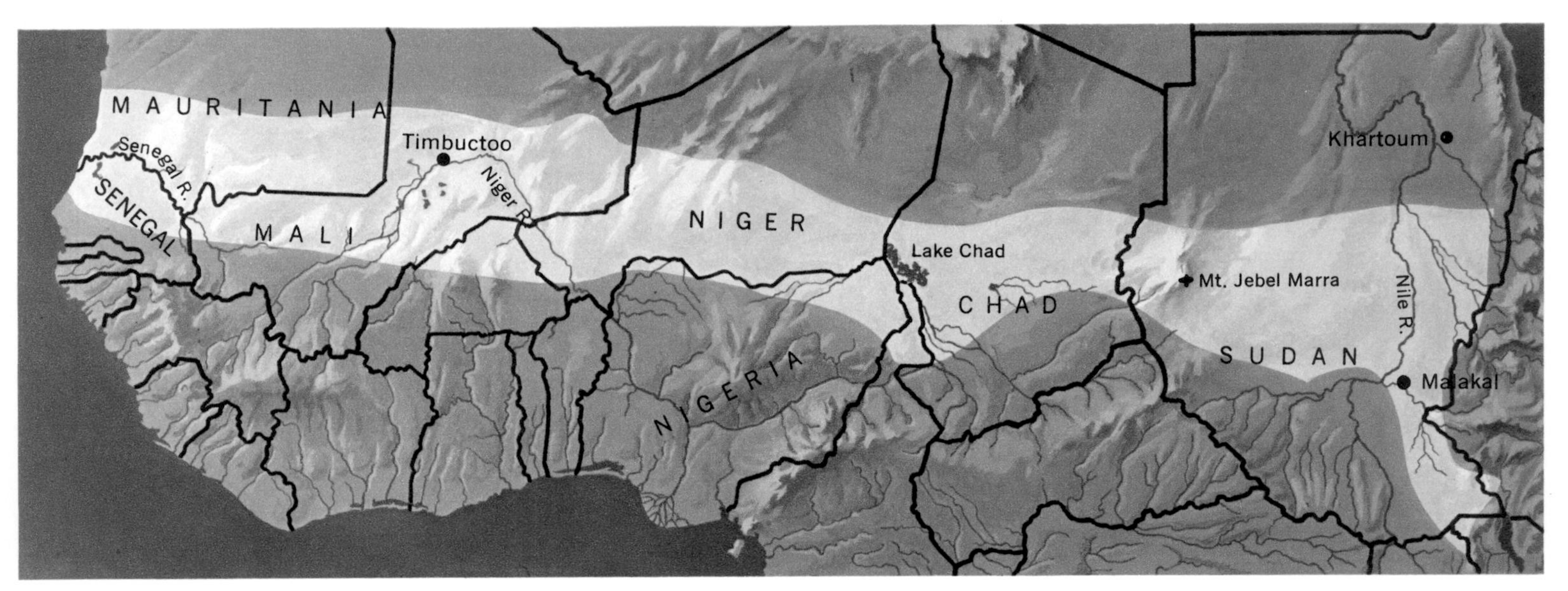

The Sudanese semi-arid zone, a broad strip of dry steppe and bush across Africa from Mauretania and Senegal to the Nile Valley in Sudan. It is a transition zone between desert and savanna.

Sahara the rainfall, such as it is, falls in summer rather than in winter (as in the north), and the vegetation changes from predominantly Saharan-Asiatic species to Sudanese desert plants.

In fact, there is no clear border of the Sahara in the south, but rather steady transition from desert to steppe. The arid open desert of sand or stones gives place to plains of grassland and scrub. Sand dunes become "fixed" with vegetation so that they can no longer move with the wind. Desert conditions disappear, and are replaced by semi-arid country in which the rainfall is still scanty and irregular, but is sufficient to maintain a much greater population of plants.

This zone is the first of several long belts of vegetation that run parallel across the continent from the Atlantic to the Nile Valley and sometimes beyond. There are no sharp boundaries between any of these zones, but no one standing in the heart of one of them would confuse it with another. As one moves south from the Sahara toward the coast of the Gulf of Guinea the amount of rainfall increases steadily. After a thousand miles of unbroken desert, with five inches of rain per year or less, the rainfall increases in the next eight hundred miles to well over one hundred inches per year at the coast. During this journey the country changes from barren rocks and sand to steaming mangrove swamps and raffia palms *(Raphia)*.

Ecologists who try to be as precise as possible divide this progressive change into five or six zones of vegetation. For our purposes we may divide it into three. The first of these zones is one of marked transition from barren desert through grass steppe to relatively lush savanna with good-sized trees and perennial grasses. The transition in this zone is greater than in either of the other two to the south of it. But at its center it consists of steppe grasslands stretching almost level as far as the eye can see, broken only by low trees and bush, or by an occasional hill. Much of this zone is heavily populated by men and their flocks of cattle, goats and sheep, and as a result the vegetation has been greatly modified, always for the worse. But some areas, for some such reason as a shortage of water for human needs, remain more or less in their natural state.

The change in climate is heralded by the appearance of quite large trees along watercourses. They include acacias, desert date *(Balanites aegyptiaca)* and the doum palm *(Hyphaene thebaica)*, a typically Sudanese tree. Such large trees indicate that fairly regular rain falls somewhere in the vicinity, runs off and collects in nearly flat watercourses as an underground store of moisture. Strips of perennial grasses also grow along the watercourses. As one moves south, and the rainfall becomes more copious and more regular, most of the landscape is covered with grass, especially *Aristida, Panicum turgidum,* and *Cenchrus biflorus,* with trees along watercourses and scrub here and there, especially where the country has been overgrazed by domestic stock. When all the country is covered with grass we can say that the desert has given way to semi-arid steppe.

It is characteristic of such regions that they vary greatly in appearance from year to year. All over the world, the lower the rainfall, the more erratic it is. An average rainfall of five inches per year may fluctuate from one to fifteen or even twenty inches in successive years. The maximum rainfall may be three or four times the annual average, and twenty times the lowest recorded rainfall. In high rainfall areas these fluctuations are not nearly so great. What this means, for many semidesert plants, is that they must be able to lie dormant as seeds through several years of drought, germinate quickly when there is adequate rain, then set seed again in the minimum possible time and await the next rainy period.

In areas on the desert fringe perennial grasses are scarce and most of the grass cover consists of annuals, such as *Aristida,* or ephemerals that grow vigorously in short periods of irregular rainfall. Some ecologists maintain that where any grass will grow perennials will grow, and that the dominance of annuals is due to interference by animals, chiefly the herds of domestic stock. Whether one agrees with this or not, the grasses in such semi-arid areas produce a flush of green grazing for perhaps two months in a good year; for the remaining time they are dry, and the whole steppe is whitish and sere. But the sharp onset of drought under a fierce sun often results in standing hay of surprisingly good feeding value. Semi-arid steppe, even in low rainfall, can support a remarkable number of animals.

To live for many years trees must survive droughts. When drought comes they shed their leaves; their bark, corky or protected by a waxy skin, helps to minimize water loss. Some trees are deep rooted and can tap water stored in the ground out of reach of shallow-rooted grasses. Others have long spreading root systems which draw water over a large area. In semi-arid climates, however, a tree cannot attain a great size, for as it grows its water requirement increases. There comes a time in a bad drought when it simply dies and stands like a skeleton, the perching post of birds of prey.

ACACIAS

Acacia trees are a feature of great areas of Africa. *Acacia* is a large genus of leguminous trees with feathery leaves, thorns, and sweet-scented flowers beloved of bees. It colonizes almost every area of Africa short of high wet forest, but is found in the greatest variety where there is rainfall of ten to thirty inches a year. Acacias vary from little bushes to majestic flat-topped trees sixty feet high with umbrella-like crowns 120 feet across. Acacias of one kind or other have become adapted to almost every variety of soil and climate. It would be easy for a trained ecologist to describe with reasonable accuracy the climate of a place if he knew the type of soil and the acacias growing in it.

The acacias of the desert fringe are mere bushes in the shape of an inverted cone. The trunk branches out a few inches above the ground and the limbs spread to form a flat-topped crown five to ten feet above the ground. This form of growth, common to many species, serves a dual purpose. The central growing points are always protected from smaller browsing animals by the outer ring of thorny branches, and the base of the tree is shaded from the rays of the sun, which may help to conserve water. The root system spreads out into open ground some distance from the tree.

Larger acacias of these semi-arid areas have a short thick trunk, and an umbrella-like crown of leaves. A common one in many parts of Africa is *Acacia tortilis*. It produces an abundance of spirally-twisted pods that fall to the ground and are greatly relished by wild and domestic animals alike. Even humans sometimes eat them.

Most African acacias are formidably armed with hooked thorns, or with long spikes, and many have both hooks and spikes. The thorns undoubtedly help to protect the older growth from browsing animals, but while they are growing they are soft and can be eaten. One species, the ant-gall acacia *(A. drepanolobium)*, has a most subtle form of self-protection. At the base of each pair of long spiky thorns a hollow, egg-shaped gall develops. As this dries it hardens, and it is then inhabited by colonies of small ants. When a browsing animal comes to feed on the young growing tips of the branches, the ants swarm out and soon make browsing uncomfortable. This acacia is almost thornless apart from its spiked galls, which are formidable enough.

AN ABUNDANCE OF WEAVERS

As has been explained, in the steppe country the grasses and herbs must seed copiously in order to ensure their survival. This results in an abundance of food for seed-eating birds and small mammals, and in this region game birds, various sorts of weaver birds, and doves are very common indeed. Bustards, larks and pipits that are not chiefly seed-eaters are also numerous in the open grassland.

Weaver birds are an almost exclusively African family, having only a few representatives in Asia. There are two main divisions of weavers, Ploceine weaver birds (named after the most numerous genus, *Ploceus)*, which weave their nests and hang them from trees, and Estrildine weaver birds (named after the genus *Estrilda)*, which build loose globular nests of grass heads and place them in a crotch or on a branch of a tree—or even on the ground. Between the two are certain intermediate types, including the very common sparrow weavers of the genus *Plocepasser*, which make woven nests that are looser and more clumsy than the neatest Ploceine weavers' nests, but stronger than those of Estrildine weavers.

Weaver birds are certainly the most numerous birds in this steppe country. The small Estrildines are largely associated with man and there is often a delightful little group of decorative species in a village or a camp. Such a group might include a blood-red fire-finch *(Lagonisticta)*, like an animated plum; a melba *(Pytilia)*, red, green and gray with barred underside; a few waxbills *(Estrilda)*, rather drab little brown birds; a pair or two of cordon-bleus *(Uraeginthus bengalus)*, blue and brown, the male brighter, with a distinctive purple throat-patch; a blue-black indigo finch *(Hypochera)* and a whydah or two *(Vidua)*. The whydahs and indigo finches are parasitic, laying their eggs in the nests of other Estrildine weaver birds. But unlike such true nest parasites as cuckoos, neither is harmful to its hosts. The incubation period is not abnormally short as in cuckoos and the young whydah or indigo finch is reared alongside the brood of the foster parent.

Ploceine weavers of this country are much larger than Estrildines and are generally yellow and black, with varying amounts of brown in their plumage. Some of them change

A red-fronted gazelle. Its tensed muscles and compressed tail attest its nervousness as it comes to drink. (Afrique Photo)

Scimitar-horned oryx on a steppe dotted with low thorny trees. This animal was domesticated by the ancient Egyptians. (Marcel Bonnotte)

their plumage seasonally, becoming drab brown or sparrow-like during the dry season and sporting brilliant livery during the brief rains, when they rear their broods. Unlike Estrildine weavers they normally breed in colonies, though some are solitary.

A Ploceine weaver's nest is a fascinating structure. The male alone makes it, selecting a pendent twig and weaving securely onto its tip a loop of grass or other fibrous material. Having made the loop, the bird stands inside it as he continues his work. On one side he fashions a domed nest chamber and on the other an entrance spout. He lines the nest chamber with soft grass heads and often places a nearly waterproof layer of grass or leaves on the roof. He then hangs upside down outside his residence, vibrating his wings and emitting continuous rasping calls till a female is attracted.

The Sudan dioch *(Quelea quelea)* is a Ploceine weaver of semi-arid areas throughout Africa that promises to rival the locust as a latter-day plague. In the dry season this species assembles in flocks of millions that migrate from place to place, destroying far more grain than they eat. They have done increasing damage in recent years, probably because the spread of agriculture has provided a more reliable dry season food supply. Curiously like locusts, these Ploceines have tight flocking habits and roost together in huge swarms in reed beds or clumps of bushes, which they often smash with their sheer weight. They breed in huge colonies of millions of pairs covering fifty to five hundred acres. The onset of wet weather stimulates them to breed, but they cannot build nests unless the rains are good enough to result in plentiful leafy grass. If this is not available, they cease breeding. In a good season they may produce two broods in six weeks, multiplying five or sixfold. Predators have little effect on their numbers, and man can control them only by blasting their roosting places, burning breeding colonies with flame-throwers, or by spraying poisons from the air.

THE WORLD'S LARGEST LIVING BIRD

The steppe is the home of the nominate race of the ostrich *(Struthio camelus),* the largest of all living birds, and formerly much more abundant than it is now. Ostriches also range into deserts, light thorn scrub, and the much more luxuriant grassland farther to the south.

A full-grown male ostrich stands about seven feet tall, is coal black with white wings and tail, while the bare skin of the neck and thighs is pinkish. In another race found in Somali the bare skin is bluish gray. Females are gray-brown,

Dama gazelles (Gazella dama), the largest of all gazelles, are long-legged, speedy animals adapted to life on the fringe of the Sahara. (Jean Dragesco: Atlas Photo)

and grown young resemble the female. Young birds have speckled and striped patterns which aid concealment in grass.

Ostriches travel about in pairs or troops and are very wary and difficult to approach. Capable of running at least forty-five miles an hour on their two-toed feet, they can outdistance most predators. Their long necks help them to detect the approach of an enemy long before most other wild animals would be aware of danger. If an ostrich bolts, gazelles or any other antelopes will usually take fright and follow, though they may not know what they are fleeing from.

Contrary to an old belief, ostriches do not bury their heads in the sand, but when nesting they do lay them flat along the ground at the approach of danger. Even an ostrich is remarkably inconspicuous in this position; a sitting female resembles a hump of earth or a pile of debris. But this concealing behavior is effective only by day; in the evening the coal black male takes over. He usually comes several hours before dark and he discloses the nest at once. Thus the best way to find an ostrich nest is to watch a lone male ostrich at dusk.

The ostrich is an exception to the rule that large birds lay few eggs and have long incubation and fledging periods. Several female ostriches lay in the same nest, which often holds twenty or thirty eggs, or even more. Only one bird, however, can incubate at a time, and so a sitting ostrich is often surrounded by conspicuous white eggs. Most of these eggs are wasted, but toward the end of the incubation period the ostrich actually removes some eggs from beneath its body and places them round the nest in small depressions; this helps to ensure simultaneous hatching. The eggs hatch in about twenty-eight days, and the young can run at once. They accompany both parents for some time and then form troops that may, in some parts of Africa, number as many as fifty but are usually smaller. The larger troops of young seem to be found in the more arid regions.

If ostriches were successful breeders they would soon become very numerous. But most eggs either fail to hatch because the parents do not cover them or because of attacks by predators. Hyenas eat a great many ostrich eggs and lions use the eggs as playthings—if they can first drive off the adult birds. However, the species has survived all these dangers and has only in recent years been much reduced by mounted human hunters.

THE ORIGINAL UNICORN

Several animals of these steppes are nomadic, traveling less than desert species but usually in larger herds. Most of the

animals from surrounding regions will concentrate in limited areas where adequate rain has resulted in good grazing. Seasonal migrations may also be made to avoid areas of waterlogged clay. The Sudanese steppe has fewer species of antelopes than the semi-arid bushlands of the horn of Africa, but shares some species with that region, while some are found only in the west. There are no zebras but there were formerly wild asses, and there are such species of gazelles as the dorcas, the red-fronted and the dama gazelles. The northern fringes, where steppe merges into the Sahara, is inhabited by the splendid scimitar-horned oryx *(Oryx algazel),* found only in the western half of Africa. The fauna is richer at the eastern end of this region, where Soemmerings's and Heuglin's gazelle augment it, and where kudus are found in hilly areas. A rather distinct race of greater kudu, a western representative of a typically East and South African beast, is found in northern Chad and Ubangi-Shari.

The scimitar-horned oryx, with its long gently curving horns, is the noblest oryx after the South African gemsbok. It inhabits the borders of the Sahara but does not go deep into true desert. It ranges through much of the northern fringe of the steppe from Rio de Oro to Sudan, but has been almost exterminated in Libya and Egypt. This creature, or the nearly extinct Arabian oryx, may be the origin of the fabled unicorn. A vaguely horselike animal, its long horns often appear from the side to be a single horn. The scimitar-horned oryx was once kept by the Egyptians as a domestic animal, and must have been well known to the ancients. Unicorns, on the other hand, were said to have straight horns, more like those of the Arabian oryx *(O. leucoryx)* or the beisa oryx *(O. gazella beisa).*

Very nomadic, the scimitar-horned oryx forms large herds on migration to favored grazing grounds where plentiful rain has fallen. A few large herds may contain a majority of the whole population of a part of the steppe, and by grouping together in this way they unfortunately make themselves vulnerable to attack by motorized hunting parties. In the dry season they are more widely scattered in waterless areas and are much safer. Old bulls are often solitary.

Oryx are found in the same area as the largest of all gazelles, the addra or dama gazelle *(Gazella dama).* This species is about the same weight as the East African Grant's gazelle *(G. granti),* but much more slender and with longer legs. Their slim bodies and long legs enable them to move fast over large distances. Almost white, addras lack the black side stripe that is found in most gazelles and is believed to break up the outline of the animal. Their whiteness sometimes helps to conceal them, but they can be very conspicuous against a dark ground. They range farther south in this zone than the oryx, and are both grazers and browsers of shrubs such as acacias, and even of a euphorbia, *Euphorbia balsamifera.*

Left above: Malachite kingfisher (Corythornis cristata), a tiny, brilliant bird of watersides, feeds both on insects and fish. Left: Egyptian geese (Alopochen aegyptiacus), common in such wet areas as the Niger inundation zone. Right: The bat-eared fox (Octocyon megalotis) is nocturnal, living in burrows by day, and feeding on insects and small mammals. The large ears are a feature of many desert and subdesert animals. (All by Clem Haagner)

THE CHEETAH—FASTEST OF ALL PREDATORS

To catch any of these steppe animals a predator must either be exceedingly cunning or so fast that it can run them down in the open. The cheetah *(Acinonyx jubatus)* adopts the latter method. It is found in this region, that is from Sudan west to Mauritania, but it is becoming scarce. It is more common in East Africa and it is one of several African predators also found, if rarely, in parts of Asia.

When hunting, a cheetah stalks to within a short distance of its prey, hiding behind tufts of vegetation. A slim and rangy animal, it is not conspicuous. Estimates of its speed in attack are variable, but trained cheetahs have been timed traveling at between sixty and seventy miles an hour—much faster than any antelope. If a gazelle, running all out, travels at nearly fifty miles an hour, then a cheetah could gain on it at the rate of about eight yards per second. But the cheetah can keep up this pace only for between a quarter and half a mile; once started on its sprint it has about fifteen to twenty seconds to catch its prey. To launch a successful attack it must therefore start from a distance of not more than two hundred yards from its prey.

At top speed the moving body of a cheetah bends almost into a circle, its hindfeet striking the ground well in front of its head. It covers the ground in great bounds and although the gazelle, swerving hither and thither, sometimes escapes, often the cheetah catches up with it, trips it with a paw, and instantly seizes it by the throat. The whole action is so fast that it must be seen on slow-motion film to be appreciated. If the chase does not soon seem promising the cheetah does not waste its energy but abandons the pursuit.

Cheetahs are less ferocious than lions or leopards, easily tamed, and Eastern potentates have trained them for the hunt. They purr and mew like cats, but they do not roar or growl like lions or leopards. Their claws are not completely sheathed and, like a dog's, are not sharp. All the cheetah's killing is done with the teeth. They are diurnal, hunting wholly by sight.

Scarcely less speedy and much more agile is another dryland predator, the caracal or desert lynx *(Felis caracal).* This medium-sized cat is exceedingly beautiful, golden brown in

color, with long black hairs on the tips of its ears, and a short tail. It preys upon hares, the larger rodents common in the steppe, and on birds. It can leap into the air to intercept a passing bird, catching it with its front paws. The largest animal it can kill is a young gazelle.

THE KORRIGUMS

In the south and east of this region the annual rainfall is higher. Here perennial grasses, chiefly *Cenchrus biflorus,* have largely replaced the *Aristida* characteristic of the northern desert fringe; and acacia bushlands or savanna are frequent. As on the northern fringe, the taller perennials first become luxuriant in the belts along watercourses, and with the increased rainfall to the south, they spread into the open country between drainage lines. Here there are no oryx, but giraffes *(Giraffa cameleopardis peralta)* occur in North Nigeria, North Cameroon and Chad, and there are still some red-fronted gazelles *(Gazella rufifrons).* Animals of the wetter savannas, such as hartebeest, roan antelopes, and even elephants, sometimes occur. But probably the most characteristic antelope of these grasslands is the bastard hartebeest or korrigum *(Damaliscus korrigum).* Not a true hartebeest, it vaguely resembles the hartebeest of the genus *Alcelaphus,* but its back slopes less and it has a shorter head. With its dark reddish brown body of a bluish satiny sheen it is a more handsome antelope than the true hartebeest; black patches decorate its head and legs.

This may once have been Africa's commonest large antelope, with a vast range, and occurring in large numbers. Three races of bastard hartebeest occur here, *D. k. korrigum* from Senegal to northern Nigeria, *D. k. purpurescens* in northern Nigeria, and *D. k. tiang,* called the tiang, in the Sudan and perhaps Chad. A fourth race, the topi, *D. k. jimela,* inhabits East Africa, reaching the coast and as far south as southern Tanzania. These races were formerly regarded as separate species, but all are probably one. With its wide range, the korrigum and its allied races was probably the only gregarious, plains-loving antelope that could rival the blue wildebeest *(Gorgon taurinus)* of South and East Africa in total numbers. At that it was more local than the hartebeest *(Alcelaphus buselaphus)* or the roan *(Hippotragus equinus).*

Bastard hartebeest are grazers and are partly nomadic. In places their seasonal migrations (especially among the tiang in the Sudan) still rival the spectacle of migrating wildebeest in the Serengeti Plains. In the west the korrigum tends to leave the dry northern parts of its range in March and congregate in the south when rain may have fallen on the fringe of the savannas. East of the Nile the tiang makes a seasonal migration in the opposite direction, from south to north, and abound in this area only part of the year. When traveling in strings across the flat plains of grass they often seem strangely indifferent to human beings and predators. The migrations of both the korrigum and the tiang tend to bring them to new grass following early rains, and the females then calve.

All races of this species have a curious discontinuous distribution; they are common in some areas but absent from some others apparently suited to their needs. Not enough is known of this antelope to explain fully either its distribution or its seasonal habits, but it may well be that its gregariousness is an important part of the explanation.

THE GREAT SWAMPS

Two vast areas of swamp and water, one permanent, the other seasonal, lend diversity to this region. Lake Chad is permanent, and receives the drainage of two large rivers, the Shari and the Kamadugu Yobe, that drain, respectively, the northern highlands of Cameroon and the northern third of Nigeria. The seasonal floods of these rivers expand Lake Chad into vast marginal swamps on black clay soil. The size and shape of the lake varies according to cycles of rainfall that occur at intervals of eleven and thirty-six years. In recent years it has been increasing in size, like some other African lakes.

Today Lake Chad has no outlet and is little more than a fraction of its former size. Once it was immense, occupying not only its present site but a huge basin four hundred miles to the north and three hundred feet lower. All this part of Africa was formerly much wetter and the rivers flowing into Lake Chad were much larger; their waters overflowed through the Bahr el Ghazal, a channel that is now dry. With increasing desiccation the rivers shrank and the alluvium brought down by the Shari became a barrier to the northward flow of their combined waters. The great lake to the north is now only a barren depression in the desert.

The Niger River rises in the highlands of Futa Jalon in Guinea, a forest area of very high rainfall. Running northeast it pushes out onto the plains and spreads over a huge area of almost completely flat country. The inundation zone covers about ten thousand square miles. The waters deposit their silt here and emerge at the northeastern end of this inundation zone, near Timbuctoo, quite clear. The flow of water from the April-September rains in the Futa Jalon highlands does not reach the Lower Niger till six months later.

Formerly the Niger ran on northward into the now dry Taoudeni depression, four hundred miles further north. This part of the southern Sahara contains abundant mollusk of species similar to those now found in the inundation zone. Nowadays the Niger drains away to the southeast, making a half-circle back toward the sea. This has been brought about by the phenomenon of river capture. In a past wetter period a more vigorous stream (now quite dry), draining the high massifs of Hoggar and Adrar des Iforas in the middle of the Sahara, captured the waters of the Niger and took them to the Gulf of Guinea. This process is being repeated today among the streams that run into Lake Chad. The Logone, a tributary of the Shari, comes very close to a headstream of the Benue, the Niger's main tributary, and sometimes overflows into it through an area of swamp. It is only a matter of time before the more vigorous, seaward-flowing Benue captures the Logone, and the waters of the Shari and Lake Chad will then be still further reduced in volume.

These great swamps provide a habitat for a multitude of birds and for water-loving antelopes such as the waterbuck

Right above: Mount Kadam, a peak in Karamoja, is in an escarpment of high mountains on the eastern edge of the Sudanese semi-arid zone. Right: Lilies such as this one spring up from parched soil after rain. (Both by Alan Root) Far right: Whistling thorn (Acacia drepanolobium). Colonies of ants live in the round galls, and the wind whistles eerily in the tiny entrance holes of their nests. The ants help to protect the tree from browsing animals. (Alan Root: Okapia)

Trapdoor spider dragging prey, a beetle, into its lair. The trapdoor serves as protection, concealment, and also to prevent the entry of very hot, dry air. (Alan Root: Okapia)

and the kob. Warthogs are common in the flood plains, and in the reedbeds of Lake Chad there is a race of the buffalo intermediate between the large black buffalo of the Sudan and the small, short-horned and often red buffalo of West Africa. Formerly very numerous, these and other animals have been pathetically reduced in number in the last fifty years. Near Lake Chad swamp-loving. animals come into close contact with semidesert species like the addra gazelle.

MULTITUDES OF MIGRANT DUCKS

Most of the ducks and other water birds that breed over the vast belts of taiga and tundra in northern Europe and Asia migrate to Africa in winter. Many of them reach the northern African tropics, but comparatively few pass the equator. Numbers of ducks and waders cross the Sahara, and others come down the west coast and travel inland to reach the Niger inundation zone. When the great flocks of migrant ducks and waders mingle with the abundant tropical species of herons, pelicans, and storks, the combination presents one of the great bird spectacles of the world.

The flood of the Niger takes several months to pass through the zone. Beginning in the south in May and June the waters rise and fill Lake Debo in the center; after that they move on to the north. The result is that the flood has begun to recede in the south before the northern end has its full allotment of water. When the northern waders and ducks begin to arrive in September the waders feed on exposed mudflats, while the ducks frequent the open water and rice fields. One wader, the black-tailed godwit *(Limosa limosa),* has so far departed from the usual habits of waders that it eats rice as well as worms and insect larvae in the mud.

The two most common migrant ducks here are the pintail *(Anas acuta)* and garganey *(Anas querquedula).* They are extraordinarily abundant between October and April, the flocks spreading across the sky on their evening flight from open water to feeding grounds. Probably one of the main reasons for their wintering in this zone is the rice fields; where they have become a serious pest. They mingle with resident African species of which the most common are the white-faced tree duck *(Dendrocygna viduata),* the knob-nosed goose and spurwing goose *(Sarkidiornis melanotis* and *Plectropterus gambensis).* The very beautiful little pigmy goose

(Nettapus auritus) and the Egyptian goose *(Alopochen aegyptiacus) are also found here.*

Ruffs *(Philomachus pugnax)* are the most common wintering waders; their numbers are legion. Possibly most of the European population of ruffs winter here. They are accompanied by at least fifteen other species of Palearctic waders and feed on the mudflats and shores together with about seven species of local resident plovers. Some ruffs remain all year round in the inundation zone, but they do not don full breeding livery, which includes a ruff of multicolored feathers in the male, essential to its remarkable communal displays on northern breeding grounds.

There is probably also a migration up the Niger from the savannas further south and east to take advantage of the temporarily favorable conditions here. Pink-backed pelicans *(Pelecanus rufescens)* appear in the floods, but they breed elsewhere. At the season of maximum flood in parts of the inundation zone, the lower Niger is bank-high with turbid water and provides no feeding grounds for the waders, pratincoles and terns that abound on its sandbanks in the dry season. The inundation zone of the Niger River is a magnet for all kinds of water birds from an immense area of the world's surface.

In traversing this region we began with the area where the great Sahara Desert gives way to small spiny shrubs along watercourses and concluded with a relatively lush land of perennial grasses and big trees, green for five or six months of the year. The rainfall in the former area was about five inches per year, in the latter about forty. Clearly this zone is very variable and could be divided into any number of subzones according to the degree of dominance of perennial grasses or certain trees. Yet broadly it covers the transition from desert to savanna. Trees in most of it are to some extent xerophytic, dropping their small leaves in the long, hard, dry seasons, and only in the south is the grass long enough to carry fierce grass fires. The southern boundary is not clearly marked any more than is the northern boundary with the Sahara. But when broad-leaved trees begin to dominate the arboreal vegetation we know we have left this vast transition zone and are in the savanna.

Land of Tooth and Claw

The Horn of Africa

5

Were it not for the highlands of Ethiopia, parallel belts of vegetation would stretch across the African continent from west to east. The Sahara does just this. But the semi-arid belt south of the Sahara, and the savannas still further south do not reach the east coast. East and south of the Ethiopian highlands, however, there is a large area of desert and semidesert. This region includes Somali and the deserts of Danakil, which fill the great northern funnel of the Rift Valley in northeast Ethiopia. South of Ethiopia the deserts swing inland, reaching across northern Kenya to the divide between Lake Rudolf and the Nile basin. In the south they are bordered by mountain ranges just north of the equator in Kenya and by the Tana River. Small as it is, the Tana is a barrier to the southward spread of certain species of animals.

Although large and varied, the entire region is either arid or semi-arid, and has similar faunal affinities throughout. The fauna is in many respects distinct from that of the great Sudanese semi-arid belt. It is much richer, and has links with the southern and eastern part of the continent rather than the west. Much of this region is bushland, but there are also areas of open lava desert hardly less cruel than the severest parts of the Sahara. Where there is bush there are also abundant succulents, euphorbias, *Cissus,* and sometimes acres of flowering aloes. Except in the west and in the southeast the region is generally enclosed between highlands and the sea.

SEABIRDS, OSPREYS AND BURROWING PLOVERS

If high average temperature is the criterion, the coasts of the Red Sea are among the hottest places on earth. It is not surprising that they are fearfully hot: the Red Sea lies in the Rift Valley, is enclosed by mountainous tracts, and has only a narrow outlet. Moreover, it is situated in the northern tropical belt.

This coast is one of the best areas of the world in which to observe life on coral reefs. Corals can grow only in warm seas, and are generally found along the eastern coasts of continents. The Red Sea reefs have been extensively studied by a team of French scientists who set up an underwater laboratory, in which they lived a month at a time and observed the fish and other creatures.

Offshore, the Red Sea is dotted with islands. Inaccessible, waterless, and devoid of vegetation, many of these are the haunts of multitudes of breeding seabirds. They are in the path of the northeast trade winds where landing is dangerous, so the seabirds are usually fairly safe from interference. Probably most of the seabirds from the northern Indian Ocean breed here—boobies, shearwaters, petrels, and tropic birds. Late in the season, when it can prey on small migrant birds from Asia, the sooty falcon *(Falco concolor)* also breeds on these islands. It winters in Madagascar.

Inshore there are smaller sandy islets and bars, and some sheltered lagoons and estuaries. Ospreys breed commonly on these, placing their huge stick nests on the ground, on low bushes, or on rocks. A strange characteristic of the osprey is that it does not breed in every area apparently suited to it. One would think that all it needed was a plentiful supply of fish and peace and quiet. But in Africa it breeds only on the Mediterranean coasts, and south to the Horn on the east and to Cape Verde on the west. It does not regularly nest in South Africa or anywhere in the southern hemisphere except Australia. This is one of those quirks of distribution that defy all reasonable analysis.

The crab plover *(Dromas ardeola),* an Asiatic and African species that breeds along the Somali coast in numbers, is the only species of this family that breeds in burrows. It is a migrant, moving south along the East African coast from August to May. Its nesting burrows are about five feet long, and it lays two chalky white eggs that are enormous in proportion to the bird itself. The burrowing habit is an adaptation that has permitted crab plovers to reduce the normal clutch size (three to four) of the plover family, while in the darkness of the hole the cryptic coloration that makes most plovers' nests so hard to find is unnecessary. Except for the fact that they eat crabs, little is known about these birds, despite their numbers.

COASTAL PLAINS AND HIGH PLATEAUS

Inland from the coasts there are flat plains of varying width. Scrub covered or subdesert steppes, they extend about as far south as the Juba River, where they merge with more luxuriant coastal savannas. Devoid of water for much of the year, they are exceedingly hot and arid. They are inhabited by certain hardy animals, notably Pelzeln's gazelle *(Gazella pelzelni)* which, like many gazelles, is able to live without water for long periods. This gazelle goes about in small herds, or sometimes singly; probably it is now rare.

The coastal plain varies in width, from two to two hundred miles, and is separated from the more elevated interior either by sharp escarpments or by gradual inclines. Much of this country is limestone, part of an ancient seabed that gradually

On Ol Donyo Mara, Samburu, Kenya, in the mountains between the subdeserts of the horn and the East African highlands. The gnarled old cedar (Juniperus procera) is a forest remnant. (Leslie Brown)

Desert steppe near the coast of the Red Sea. The scanty bushes and grass tufts prevent the sand from forming larger wind-blown dunes. (E. Aubert de La Rue)

emerged, perhaps 60,000,000 years ago. Although the rocks have a common origin, their topography is now very varied.

Parallel with the Red Sea coast is a range of mountains, the Golis range, that rises abruptly from the coastal plain or from foothills to seven thousand feet. It runs east to Cape Guardafui, and then pushes out into the Indian Ocean, reappearing as the Brothers Rocks and Socotra Island, which are simply mountain peaks with submerged bases. This range is the skeleton of the triangular jutting peninsula known as the Horn of Africa.

South of the horn the coastal plains rise more gently into the interior plateaus. The temperature drops and rainfall increases with the altitude. By the time the high plateaus of the Ogaden have been reached, at four thousand feet, the dry scorching climate of the coast has been left behind. One is in an area of cool grasslands and acacia scrub. Higher still, and on the tops of the Golis range, cedars, even if stunted, herald Ethiopian highland conditions.

VOLCANIC DESERTS

South of the Ethiopian highlands a belt of semi-arid country stretches five hundred miles inland, rarely rising above a thousand feet except on isolated mountains. Lake Rudolf, one of the largest alkaline lakes in the world, breaks the monotony of this great arid sweep, which continues westward beyond the lake through the deserts of Turkana. At the Uganda escarpment, the divide between the Nile basin and the Rift Valley, these northeastern deserts meet with the great Sudanese semi-arid belt; here there is a mingling of animals and plants characteristic of each of these regions.

Black lava boulders in the north Kenya deserts. Surprisingly, such country grows luxuriant grass in rare seasons of good rain. (Alan Root)

Great expanses of this flat country are covered with lava desert scarcely less pitiless than much of the Sahara. The ground is covered with loose boulders and stones, black or purplish, each often full of small holes, like a sponge. Between the boulders is fine red dust, which rises in clouds when dry and is as soft and slippery as butter when wet. During dry seasons the vegetation dies away, the black rocks of the desert absorb the heat, and ground temperatures of 150° F are common. Men and herds do not cover stretches of this desert in the middle of the day, but wait for the cool of evening and travel through the night.

In good seasons enough rain falls for grass to grow and seed. The desert is then covered briefly with a knee-high growth of annuals, chiefly three-awns grasses *(Aristida)*. As soon as the rain stops, this dries and then extends over the plain in an unbroken whitish sheet that hides the boulders. Most of the other vegetation is succulent, and much of it has the characteristic grayish-green look of plants which guard against loss of water by means of a waxy cuticle. Some, such as the desert rose *(Adenium somalense)*, produce a flush of extremely beautiful flowers, and a succulent, *Caralluma,* forms black stiff balls of small flowers that attract flies.

Similar, but still harsher deserts of volcanic rubble and lava occur in the northern funnel of the Rift Valley, on the plains of the Awash and the Danakil. Some of the temperatures recorded here are so extreme that it is difficult to believe that human or animal life could survive them. One explorer, L. M. Nesbitt, recorded 165° F in the shade at one gorge in the Afar depression, which is below sea level. In such temperatures anything a man touches, including his own clothes, is almost intolerably hot. Yet men and animals do live in these regions, and somehow survive the gruelling climate.

The Horn of Africa consists of rough deserts and semideserts encircling Ethiopia on the north and east.

Some of this lowland country is not volcanic, but is either limestone or sandy. Here trees and shrubs thrive better than on black lava, for whatever rain there is sinks into the soil and remains for a time available to plants. The country is then covered with a thin growth of low trees, acacias and *Commiphora* predominating. The rainfall increases toward the coast, and the bushland is more luxuriant. In Turkana, west of Lake Rudolf, there are broad belts of big acacias along the many sand rivers which drain eastward from the Uganda escarpment; but in the open, Turkana is much like the rest—sandy or lava subdesert.

ORYX, ZEBRAS AND GAZELLES

Harsh as this country is it supports numerous large animals. Grazing and browsing communities of these are rather strictly separated. Grazers are animals that habitually feed on grass. Browsers, on the other hand, feed chiefly on shrubs, trees, or creepers. Many animals both graze and browse, and so obtain a very varied diet.

The commonest grazers are Grant's gazelle *(Gazella granti)*, oryx *(Oryx gazella beisa)* and Grevy's zebra *(Equis grevyi)*. On the plateaus of Somali, and still farther to the north, Grant's gazelle is replaced by Soemmering's gazelle *(Gazella soemmeringii)*. Both are adaptable species, able to live not only in comparatively lush perennial grass steppe, but also in harsh desert where only a few blades of annual grass and scattered shrubs survive. On the high Somali plateaus another smaller species, Speke's gazelle *(G. spekei)*, is found. The males of this gazelle have a curious swollen pouch above the nostrils that becomes inflated in moments of excitement.

Grevy's zebra, which is much larger than the common zebra and has many narrow stripes, is very common in north Kenya and it reappears in northern Ethiopia in the deserts of Danakil. At close range these animals are unmistakably black and white, but at a distance they seem brownish and merge quite remarkably into the landscape of shimmering heat. They always seem to be in fine condition, even though grass may be very dry and scarce.

In the very harshest desert of this area a few remnant populations of the Somali wild ass *(Equus asinus somaliensis)* survive. One of these remnants lives in the scorching lava desert of north Danakil, and another farther south; no one knows just how many of these animals are left, but there are probably only a few hundred. The wild ass, a Saharan-Asiatic species found in various racial forms as far east as northwest India, is the ancestor of the domestic donkey; it seems less able to fend for itself than the almost untamable zebras. The wild asses that are quite common on the island of Socotra are probably domestic donkeys gone wild in comparatively recent years.

The beisa oryx is the commonest large grazing antelope. Handsome creatures with straight horns, they are distinct from the scimitar-horned oryx of the southern Sahara, but more closely related to the almost extinct Arabian oryx. The beisa is a northern representative of the splendid gemsbok of the Kalahari, and like several other animals of this region is a link with South African fauna. An active and powerful animal, it has been known, when attacked, to kill a lion with its horns.

In the southeastern corner of this region Hunter's hartebeest *(Damaliscus hunteri)* may be seen. In appearance halfway between a hartebeest and an impala, it is a grazer with the habits of a hartebeest. It often accompanies topi *(Damaliscus korrigum jimela)*, another grazer common in certain parts of this region, which is the eastern representative of the West African korrigum and the Sudanese tiang. How the unique Hunter's hartebeest has evolved in this one small area and nowhere else is a mystery. There are no more than a thousand or fifteen hundred of them and their range is contracting. About thirty have recently been transferred to the Tsavo National Park, south of the Tana—a natural barrier they could not cross unaided.

All the grazing animals of this area share the nomadic habit of the true desert animals of the Sahara to a greater or lesser

Right above: Thorn scrub of acacias and shrubs, typical vegetation of the semi-arid horn of Africa; here limestone crops out on the surface. (Carl Gans) Right: Vulturine guineafowl (Acryllium vulturinum) are abundant game birds of northeast Africa, traveling in large flocks, often far from permanent water. (Leslie Brown)

Goats browsing an acacia in the Danakil desert. The foliage thrives only where the animals cannot reach it by standing up or by climbing the center of the tree. On the right, one goat holds a branch with its forefeet while it nibbles. (E. Aubert de La Rue)

degree. Where grass is relatively plentiful, short local movements are all that is necessary. But where rainfall is really low, and where odd storms passing over one part of the country may leave neighboring areas completely dry, animals must be nomadic. They appear, as if clairvoyant, in areas where rain has just fallen, to take advantage of the often ephemeral growth of scanty green grass. There is, of course, no reason why they should not be able to see lightning many miles away and correctly interpret its significance. Perhaps, like vultures, they are guided by others of their kind to the whereabouts of food. A subdesert of this sort can never support, overall, the numbers of animals found in perennial grassland such as the highland plains of East Africa. And although a concentration of Grant's gazelle, Grevy's zebra and oryx may seem to indicate rich grazing potential, this is a misleading impression, for all these animals have undoubtedly gathered from far away and will start to move on in a short time.

ERRATIC RAINFALL

In areas where the rainfall is generally poor it is characteristically very variable and unreliable. When a rainstorm travels across this sort of country it follows a particular track; the next storm, however, may follow a slightly different track. Perphaps only in the belt where two rainstorms have overlapped, will the rain have been plentiful enough to stimulate vigorous plant growth. This incidence tends to attract birds, which may breed abundantly in an area watered by several storms, in preference to adjacent areas which received less rainfall.

In some parts of this region the rainfall comes in one season, from April to August; in others, in two seasons, from April to May and from November to December. A ten-inch annual rainfall in one season will produce strong growth for a short time, but the same rainfall over two seasons will result in desert. In neither season is it sufficient for grass to seed. And the lower the rainfall, the more erratic it becomes. Every animal or bird that lives in areas subject to these conditions must either be nomadic or be able to withstand prolonged periods of drought.

Where the rainfall is a little more plentiful, the onset of the rains is the signal for a tremendous outburst of breeding activity among the birds. Where the country a few weeks before was a desert of blowing dust with scarcely a green blade, with even succulent plants shriveled and curled, there is a sudden flush of greenery and flowers. Every thorn tree bursts into leaf, and the weaver birds—whose nests festoon the branches—work feverishly to rear their broods in the short period of abundance. The period is brief, but it suffices and the copious seeding of annual grasses provides food for the ensuing dry season, not only for weavers, but for a multitude of guineafowl, francolins, and other game birds. Bustards, which are characteristic birds of open dry steppes, are more numerous and varied in this area than anywhere else in the world.

GIRAFFES, GERENUKS AND DIKDIKS

In areas of scanty and irregular rainfall, but where the soil is deep enough, trees and bushes can benefit more from the water than can shallow-rooted grasses. Water lying deep in sand can be drawn upon by shrubs and small trees whose root systems are more vigorous and spreading than their growth above ground. The acacia trees and bushes that clothe much of this region have an umbrella shape and spreading root systems. They are able to stay green longer than the grass, and they usually break into flower and then into green leaf before any rain has fallen. They are perhaps stimulated by the great heat at the end of the dry season to leaf out before rain actually falls. Grasses can only flower at the end of the rains, and even then only if the rain has been sufficient; they sometimes shrivel and die before seeding.

It is therefore not surprising that browsing animals are just as common or commoner than grazing animals in this region. The varied assembly of browsing animals makes use of the tree growth at all levels. Elephants are fairly numerous in the southern parts of this region, and would occur in the north too had they not been exterminated by Ethiopians and Somalis. Rhinos also occur in the south, but are gone from the north. Both these animals are fairly dependent on water supply, and so are not found far away from rivers except in the rainy seasons. To make use of the tree and bush vegetation to the full, browsing animals largely independent of water or nomadic in habit are necessary.

Huge termite mounds are common in the bushlands of this region. The cylindrical ventilation shaft may be fifteen feet tall, and provides a perch for birds of prey, while barbets, swallows and bee eaters breed in the termite hill itself. (Henri Goldstein)

The three common animals which specialize in browsing

are: reticulated giraffes *(Giraffa giraffa reticulata);* the gerenuk *(Litocranius walleri),* a strange, long-necked gazelle-like creature able to stand bolt upright on its hindlegs; and the dikdik *(Rhynchotragus* and *Madoqua* spp.). These three use the vegetation from the tops of the acacias to ground level: the giraffe feeds on the acacias from their tops to about four feet above ground; the gerenuk browses up to eight feet, or bending down, feeds close to the ground; finally, the tangle of low branches and small shrubs is browsed by innumerable dikdiks. These three species can make almost perfect use of the acacias away from river basins. Dikdiks and gerenuks are not nomadic like giraffes, and hardly seem to need to drink at all.

Giraffes and gerenuks prefer flat country to steep hillsides and rough gullies. In such situations the bush is browsed by the greater and lesser kudu *(Strepsiceros strepsiceros,* and *S. imberbis).* These extremely beautiful antelopes, with long spiral horns in the male, are characteristic of southern and eastern Africa, and greater kudus extend west into the Sudanese semi-arid belt in northern Chad. Shy and difficult to see, they like to live in impenetrable thickets of bush on rocky hills; greater kudus are sometimes found in relatively open hilly country, and lesser kudus also inhabit the plains. Greater kudus tend to be found in small isolated pockets, but lesser kudus occur from Somali to the Tana River and beyond. Greater kudus are extremely susceptible to diseases like rinderpest, which has probably wiped them out in some localities that were apparently suited to them. Rinderpest entered Africa with domestic stock from the East in the 1890's, and some species of wild animals have not yet developed a resistance to the disease.

Two small browsing animals peculiar to this area are the dibatag *(Ammodorcas clarkei)* and the beira *(Dorcotragus megalotis).* Both have a predominantly local distribution, but in places it does frequent, the dibatag is quite common. It vaguely resembles a long-necked gazelle, but is more closely allied to the reedbuck. It trots, unlike the gerenuk, with its long neck raised, and browses on certain species of *Commiphora,* a spiny semisucculent tree which most animals find rather unpalatable. The beira, which is about twice the size of a dikdik and has very large ears, is found only on low stony hills in a small area of Somali.

Thus although this region has a low rainfall and vegetative growth is scanty and irregular, it contains a remarkable assortment of both browsing and grazing animals. They are preyed upon by lions and cheetahs, but nevertheless are scarcely kept in check by them. The lions kill the larger animals and they themselves generally stay in fairly thick bush near water. Cheetahs are found in light bushland or open plains, and are the main enemies of gazelles.

Left above: Gerenuk (Lithocranius walleri), a long-legged, long-necked antelope that lives by browsing trees up to eight feet above ground and is largely independent of water. (James R. Simon) Left: Ground squirrels are abundant small mammals in semi-arid parts of Africa. They live in burrows and rarely climb trees. (Alan Root: Okapia) Right: A reticulated giraffe, most beautiful of all giraffes, resting under an acacia tree festooned with weaver birds' nests. Giraffes browse thorn scrub up to eigtheen feet above ground. (Alan Root)

BIRDS OF PREY

Birds of prey are as common here as anywhere in Africa. They range from the tiny pygmy falcon *(Polohierax semitorquatus)* to the lappet-faced vulture *(Torgos tracheliotus)* with a nine-foot wingspan. In winter the resident hawks are augmented by thousands of migrants from Europe and Asia. Entering Africa through the Isthmus of Suez, they travel down the Nile or along the spine of the Red Sea Hills. They find relatively abundant food either in the Ethiopian highlands or on the plains of Somali in the November and December rains.

By day, hawks, eagles and vultures prey upon everything from insects to the dead bodies of large animals. By night, owls take up the task. Owls are neither so common nor so varied as daytime raptors, but they range from the very small insectivorous pearl-spotted owlet *(Glaucidium perlatum)* to one of the largest of all owls, Verreaux's eagle-owl *(Bubo lacteus).*

Diurnal birds of prey—even vultures—hunt exclusively by sight. Owls hunt both by sight at dusk, and by ear in pitch darkness. They have special hearing adaptations, including asymmetrical ears, facial discs that act like parabolic sound reflectors, and noiseless flight that enable them to pinpoint the rustle of an invisible animal. They do not feed on carrion at all; since carrion is static, they cannot locate it by ear, and like other birds owls have a negligible sense of smell. Carrion is cleaned up at night by hyenas and jackals, which are guided to their food by its smell.

Although many of the birds of prey of this area have individual preferences, they will also sometimes take unusual foods. Vultures normally eat carrion; Verreaux's eagles *(Aquila verreauxi)* eat rock hyrax; lanner falcons *(Falco biarmicus)* are swift bird-killers, and chanting goshawks *(Melierax* spp.) feed chiefly on lizards. But, when winged termites swarm, one may see large vultures and great eagles standing together on the ground around the outlet of the termite's nest seizing the insects before they can take wing, while smaller hawks and falcons join swallows, rollers and bee eaters to catch the flying termites aloft.

The termites swarm just after the first showers of rain, and myriads of winged males and females then emerge to make their brief nuptial flight and establish new colonies elsewhere. Although thousands are eaten by a wide variety of predators, enough survive, and termites are abundant throughout this region.

THE PLAGUE OF EGYPT

This region is a key breeding area for the desert locust *(Schistocerca gregaria),* much the most important of three species of migratory locusts found in Africa. Its invasion area stretches from the Atlantic to the Bay of Bengal and from the Caspian Sea to Tanzania, affecting sixty countries and the livelihood of 300,000,000 people. Modern research and efficient methods of control have enabled us almost to forget the locust, but many people still alive can remember the sudden descent of huge swarms that devastated crops and pasture alike. Only

Grevy's zebra, the handsomest of the world's wild equines, is fortunately still common in northern Kenya and parts of Ethiopia. (C. A. W. Guggisberg)

humans publicize the effects of the locust, but the plague must also have affected many wild creatures. Large nomadic animals or birds could move away from the devastation, but smaller sedentary creatures must often have perished.

This remarkable insect has a solitary as well as a gregarious phase in its life history. In the solitary phase it occurs as a relatively harmless grasshopper. The females lay their eggs in damp sand, each depositing fifty to a hundred eggs at a time. In ten to twenty days these hatch into nymphs, or hoppers, that emerge from the sand and move about freely. If the population of hoppers is dense they pass into the gregarious phase. Then they darken in color, and gather in bands which may number hundreds, thousands, or millions. Bands coalesce to form still larger bands, and the hoppers begin their devastating journey.

In five successive molts the hoppers travel perhaps two miles from their hatching area, eating every green blade they find. After the fifth molt they are adult winged locusts, but not yet sexually mature. Their first flights are short, but rapidly grow longer. Then they leave their hatching areas as migrant swarms which settle during the heat of the day or at night. During the five or six months of this migratory phase each of the millions of females lays several times in moist sand, each laying from three hundred to a thousand eggs in her lifetime. New generations of hoppers hatch and grow in vast numbers, and so the plague becomes ever more threatening.

A fair-sized swarm of flying locusts contains a thousand million insects; such a swarm would consume daily about three thousand tons of green food. Successive generations of the insects multiply into many such swarms, each darkening the sky over many square miles. When they settle the sheer weight of the mass of crawling insects breaks trees and crushes plants. For other living creatures the physical contact is intolerable.

The movement of swarms is probably controlled by the same air currents that result in rainfall. Thus an alighting swarm often finds the ground wet and is therefore able to breed at once. In northeast Africa three rainfall systems coalesce in a comparatively small area. Locusts can breed there in almost every month of the year, and hence this area is ideal for the production of a series of generations.

This appalling plague was not controlled until World War II; control has since intensified and become more efficient. Control is achieved by spraying insecticides from the air or ground on flying swarms and hoppers respectively—which is far more effective than the old method of baiting with arsenic, and much less harmful to wildlife. Outbreaks now occur chiefly in politically disturbed areas, where control operations are difficult or impossible. Through man's inability to live in accord with other men, this plague of Egypt may one day return.

Yet even locusts benefit certain other creatures. They are a valuable food supply for various birds and small animals; and some human beings and even gazelles eat them. The winter quarters of certain birds of prey and storks may in fact be related to the presence or absence of locusts. The European stork is well known as a follower of locusts in Africa, and concern has been felt in Europe that antilocust operations might deprive this bird of its winter food supply. Fortunately the storks can easily turn from locusts to other food and if they become extinct in Europe it will be due to a network of power cables in an industrialized countryside rather than to control of the locust plague in Africa.

A GREAT ALKALINE LAKE

On the western boundary of this region is a section of the Rift Valley. In the trough of this lies Lake Rudolf, 150 miles long and twenty to thirty broad. Fed by several large rivers, notably the Omo, which drains the southern highlands of Ethiopia, it has no outlet and is alkaline. Formerly six hundred feet deeper than it is now, and covering a much greater area, it used to escape into the Nile through a gorge near its northwestern end. This is now a totally dry defile, but the fish that

Left: Kori bustard (Choriotis kori), one of the world's largest flying birds; a big male weighs over twenty pounds. (Arthur Christiansen) Right: Female gerenuk, a long-necked supple beauty. (Julius Behnke)

Cheetahs are fairly common in the open plains and light thornbush of this region. They live on dikdiks and gazelles. (C. A. Spinage)

entered the lake through it are still there. Paradoxically, Lake Rudolf, no longer connected to the Nile, has a Nilotic fish fauna while Lake Victoria, now connected to the Nile system, does not. Chief among the Nilotic fish is the great Nile perch *(Lates niloticus),* which grows to well over two hundred pounds in weight.

Some of the world's biggest crocodiles abound in Lake Rudolf. They seem harmless to man and animals and feed on fish. In shallow water a group of these crocodiles may pen the fish against the shore, gradually working inward and gorging as they go. On a still night the snapping of their jaws can be plainly heard. Elsewhere crocodiles have been persecuted almost to extinction for their skins, but in Lake Rudolf they develop curious growths called buttons, probably because of the alkaline water; this makes their skins commercially useless and has saved them.

The shore is either rocky or, in shallow places, edged with reeds. Here are a multitude of ducks and geese, both indigenous species and winter migrants from Europe. In shallow lagoons along the shore, great white pelicans *(Pelecanus onocrotalus)* can be seen using the same technique as crocodiles to catch fish. They form in a line, and swim forward together. As if at a given signal, they plunge their bills into the water; underwater, the pouch spreads out like a landing net, and the fish are scooped up.

The shores of the lake are a paradise for water birds, and great numbers breed on islands in the lake. Shallow, and subject to windstorms, the lake is dangerous for small boats, and the islands have not been fully explored. This may be one place in tropical Africa where the osprey breeds; a crater lake on a small volcanic island is one of two known breeding places of the lesser flamingo *(Phoeniconaias minor).* Pelicans, spoonbills, herons, ibis and cormorants also breed on the islands in great colonies.

NATURE IN THE RAW

This region is often dry and harsh, either bare or covered with prickly trees or scanty grass, and apparently ill-suited to abundance of life. Yet all who know it agree on one point—it is wild, and creates a strong impression of nature in the raw, with its aridity, thorns, heat, scanty water, powerful predators and hunted prey, calamitous droughts or rare torrential rainstorms that turn deserts into swamps. Even the human inhabitants are chiefly nomadic stockmen who live in close association with wild beasts. Vultures and hyenas scavenge around camps and lions kill domestic stock—and sometimes men.

This wildness is nowhere more evident than on the El Barta and El Bonyuki plains in the southwestern corner of the area. Great expanses of sandy or stony soil, they are grown over with scarce grass and a gray-green shrub, *Disperma,* locally known as sage, but unrelated to true sage *(Artemisia)*. The high mountains of the Matthews range and the Ndotos, and the isolated mountain block of Nyiro border the plains on the north. To the south, escarpments rise into the foothills of Mount Kenya and the Leroghi plateau, and the highland grasslands of East Africa.

El Barta means "the horse," and it is not surprising that Grevy's zebra is very common in this area. Also found here are all those animals typical of the region—oryx, gerenuks, reticulated giraffes, and Grant's gazelles. Ostriches are very common, and elephants feed along the river courses. On the plains there are eland, impala, and some common zebras. These inhabit the East African grasslands, and their presence shows that this is a boundary or transition zone.

On the great mountains round about there are forests of unusual beauty. Composed of ancient podocarpus and cedar trees, they are often open below the canopy. The leaf-filtered sunlight falls upon fine grasses on the forest floor and there are many enchanting green glades in which buffalos and bushbuck graze at night. On the summit of Mount Nyiro, on a plateau several square miles in extent, frost sometimes whitens the grass of these glades in the morning. Here also are giant heath, giant St.-John's-wort, and other plants of Ethiopian and East African alpine zones.

Some animals, especially elephants, migrate up into these cool highland forests to escape the drought of the plains. Within a few miles they leave the true climate of this region and enter that of the greater East African heights. If we follow them we can survey the wild lands to the north from some rocky height. Thus, we too leave this harsh region for lands where life is easier, though not necessarily more interesting.

Bush Fires and Bishop Birds

The Guinea Savannas

6

We now enter another region that extends across Africa from the Atlantic coast at Senegal to the southern Sudan and the northern Congo. This is a huge block of nearly homogeneous wooded grassland or savanna that a man might traverse from end to end and still find himself looking at the same species of trees and grass. As one crosses it from north to south one sees a transition from smaller to bigger trees, ending in a wall of forest which makes a clear southern boundary. But the northern and southern parts of this region differ from each other much less than the northern and southern edges of the Sudanese transition zone to the north. The rainfall differs only about twenty inches from area to area, ranging from about forty to sixty inches, and the dry season in the south is about two months shorter than in the north.

The northern part of these savannas consists of a great belt of woodland dominated by two trees, *Isoberlinia doka* and *I. dalzielli.* So uniform is the association of these trees with tall stemmy *Andropogon* grass that Africans know this vegetation type by name. To the south of this belt there is a more varied belt of woodland, in which *Lophira, Daniellia oliveri, Bauhinia, Terminalia* and other trees are characteristic, again associated with *Andropogon* and other grasses. From north to south these belts are only about 250–350 miles wide, but each of them is about 3000–3300 miles long from west to east. They form a very distinct ecological zone across this part of Africa.

A savanna belt occurs here as a result of the interaction of soil and rainfall, as explained in the Introduction. Near the equator rain falls in two seasons, which in high rainfall areas merge into one another so that there is rain in every month. Beginning from about latitude 10°N. or S., however, the rain tends to fall in one clearly defined season. In the northern tropics the rain falls during the temperate summer, beginning about the vernal equinox, reaching a peak about midsummer, and tailing off in September and October. While the sun is high in the southern hemisphere it will be dry in the north, and vice versa. Thus, no matter how much rain falls in the rainy season in the northern tropics, there is a long dry season as well; it is this that gives rise to savanna.

During the rainy season in savannas there is always sufficient rain to produce exuberant growth. The controlling factor is not so much the total rainfall as the intervals at which the rain comes. Savannas are, after forests, the areas of greatest vegetative production in Africa. Consequently they support, as a rule, more animals and birds than any area except forest, and for some classes of animals their productivity greatly exceeds that of the forest.

RAIN AND FIRE IN THE SAVANNAS

In savanna the phrase "the rains broke" acquires dramatic force. The first tropical rainstorm after the long dry season is much more dramatic than the first day of spring weather in northern temperate zones, and its effect is immediate and greater. Just before the rains the atmosphere grows oppressive and the heat intense. Huge cumulus clouds build up daily, but they disperse. Then one day a larger cloud advances, heralded by a gale bringing with it the welcome smell of warm, wet earth. The sky darkens and thunder roars. Then the rain comes in a solid drumming sheet, and soon the ground is covered with water. When it passes, and the sun comes out, life springs anew from the land.

"Savanna" is a North American term used to describe an association of tall stemmy grasses and short or medium-sized, scattered, fire-resistant trees. There is comparatively little shrubbery, and bush thickets are confined to stream sides where there is more abundant water. Some so-called savannas are really grass plains which result from poor drainage or seasonal flooding during high rainfall. In such conditions large deep-rooted trees do not usually thrive, but grass can make luxuriant growth. Although there are some savannas of this type in Africa, most occur on fairly well-drained soils in undulating country.

During the rainy season a heavy storm falls every two or three days. The atmosphere is usually moist, and the ground hardly has time to dry out before the next storm. But the rains continue only for six months; for almost as long a period after that the southward shift of the sun brings drought, punctuated only by odd showers. In such conditions trees must shed their leaves just as certainly as when winter strikes in northern latitudes. The sudden onset of drought produces an effect of autumnal coloring in the leaves, and when they fall they carpet the ground with tinder-dry debris. Big evergreen trees cannot flourish except in river valleys. These conditions favor the growth of tall grass between the trees, and after the rains, dead dry grass forms a mass of inflammable material.

The balance between the trees and grass is delicate, and is maintained throughout the savanna belts of Africa by fire. In undulating country there are always some areas of shallow soil or heavy clay where grass will naturally predominate, alternating with areas of deeper, lighter soil suited to trees. Fire can start in these natural grassy areas and eat into the

The bushbuck (Tragelaphus scriptus) is one of the most widespread and adaptable of African antelopes. The western race, called the harnessed antelope, is the brightest in color. (Michèle Anna)

edges of woodland. The flames of a grass fire in savanna may be thirty feet tall. They scorch the mature trees, kill tree seedlings, and open up the growth; grass can then colonize these new bare spaces. Trees are forced to retreat, leaving only those that can survive the annual holocaust. Shrubs must regenerate from their rootstocks each year, just like raspberry canes each spring.

If fire is kept out of an area, the trees will thrive and shrubs grow taller. Gradually a closed canopy forms with thick bush underneath and, shaded from light, the inflammable grass withers away. The fire hazard is thus reduced. But the woodland so formed cannot approximate to true tropical evergreen forests. The rainfall regime still dictates that the trees must be deciduous, and as long as there are any areas of shallow soil where grass will naturally predominate there will always be a likelihood of fire eating into the edges of the woodland and recreating the open savanna.

In this northern savanna region the yearly cycle starts with the first rains in March or April. These fall on ground scorched by fire and parched by the sun, or covered with long dry grass. Almost overnight a green flush of grass appears and a canopy of variegated leaves springs forth on the trees. In a week a miraculous transformation takes place. The bare, black and dusty land is now a beautiful emerald-green parkland shaded by leafy trees. The air that was thick with haze and smoke is clear and sparkling, and exuberant plant and animal life begins anew.

As the rains continue, the ground gradually becomes more and more saturated, trees and grass grow rapidly; the growing grass impedes the violent run-off of heavy storms, and where the soil is deep and sandy the water sinks in to great depths. In hollows and valleys where there is clay, the ground becomes water-logged. This alternation of soggy and well-drained ground results in open treeless expanses in shallow valleys and in woodland on the ridges. The open spaces are characteristic of African savannas and are called *vleis, dambos, fadammas* and so on, depending on the language of the area.

Vervet monkeys (Cercopithecus aethiops) are common in forest strips along rivers and at the forest edge. (Afrique Photo)

Toward the end of the rains the grass shoots to a height of five or six feet, and sometimes more. Growth continues, but is no longer so rapid; the plants are storing in their roots the starch they need to produce the next year's foliage. The *dambos* begin to dry out, and flooded streams shrink. The grass seeds, and pods appear on the trees. The season of profusion is ending.

In these northern savannas blasts of a dry wind from the desert, the *harmattan,* follow the last storms in October and hasten the drying process. Some moisture still remains in the ground and most of this is pumped out by the vegetation in the last stages of its growth. By December the trees are bare of leaves, and the tall grass is dry and yellow. The crack of bursting seed pods punctuates a heavy silence in the heat of midday. The savanna is ready for the fire.

Fires may start naturally, but are far more often started by men. In fact many believe that savannas in their present form owe their existence entirely to man's use of fire, though this is open to question. It is sometimes difficult to ignite the grass, but once well ablaze the fire is a frightening spectacle. Suddenly the flames take hold with an angry roar, and in a few minutes there is a blackened expanse of ash in place of a four-foot tall mat of dead grass stems. The last green leaves that found shelter within the mat soon wilt and die, and thousands of small creatures are scorched to death. After the fire has passed it is difficult to believe that the parched and blackened expanse, tufted with burned clumps of grass and carpeted with crackling dead leaves, can ever again become a green and pleasant parkland. In the midday heat all life seems dulled, and the shrilling of cicadas is an omnipresent sound.

Just before the rains, some of the trees, drawing upon the last reserves of water in the soil and the starch in their own roots, miraculously produce a flush of new leaves. This fresh foliage, pale apple green, russet, or sometimes bright red, is a promise that life will again rejuvenate in the savanna.

"THE KING PUTS ON HIS ROBE"

The first rains start an immediate cycle of breeding among savanna birds. In the northern savannas the Africans have a charming phrase to mark the appearance in breeding dress of bishop birds. They—the Hausa of northern Nigeria—remark, *"Ga sarki ya sa alkyabba,"*—"See, the king puts on his robe!"

Bishop birds, which are Ploceine weaver birds, are very abundant in all savannas. In the dry season they resemble small dull sparrows and travel in flocks. But as soon as the rains begin they scatter and the males take on their brilliant breeding plumage. With their brilliant red and black, or yellow and black plumage, the most common bishops—of the genus *Euplectes*—are resplendent.

The flames of a bush fire in tall savanna grass frequently leap to twenty feet or more. A few minutes later the country is a blackened expanse of ash, and life is stilled. (Emil Schulthess)

The male of the orange bishop bird *(Euplectes orix)* is a brilliant orange-red with a black crown and belly, and brown wings. In display he resembles a miniature fireball perched upon a swaying stem of grass. By puffing up his bright red feathers he looks twice his size; and from time to time he rises into the air in a short whirring flight, singing a chirpy little song. Breeding usually in long grass in or near swampy places, he is visible at a range of half a mile. Each male bishop has a territory which he defends and into which come a few females that lay in small, oval nests low in the grass.

The yellow and black, or red and black long-tailed weavers of the genus *Coliuspasser,* often called widow birds or whydahs, tend to breed in drier savannas. They have similar habits in that the males display themselves from tall grass stems or low shrubs and attract females into their territory. But they also use their long tails in an aerial dancing display, most highly developed in some East African species.

There are fewer species of bishops and whydahs in West than in East Africa, but the tall grass savannas of West Africa seem alive with them in the rains. The displays of all these weavers somewhat resemble the displays of some American icterids, such as the red-winged blackbird. This is an example of a successful reproductive device which has evolved in quite unrelated groups of birds.

Other prominent birds of the savanna include glossy starlings *(Sturnidae),* which are dark iridescent blue and purple, rollers *(Coracias),* which are a pale and a dark blue and have harsh voices, hoopoes *(Upupa),* orange and black with fanned crests, and hornbills *(Tockus).* Doves and small pigeons are legion, and their pleasant calls salute the dawn and punctuate the midday heat. But game birds are fewer because of the intense fires.

DRY-SEASON MIGRANTS

Although most birds breed in the savannas during the rains there are some that avoid the wet weather and move northward soon after the rains begin. A number of these breed in slightly drier northern savannas, and others breed in semi-desert areas on the borders of the Sahara. But there are also birds that breed in the dry season in the southern savannas and move out during the rains to winter in the north. These movements are analogous to the migrations of palearctic birds in winter, but have been much less carefully studied, and are not fully understood.

The onset of the dry season is often heralded by a few days of the harmattan. The harmattan is really the north-eastern trade wind that blows across the Sahara Desert. In its passage it picks up a cargo of fine dust; at its thickest

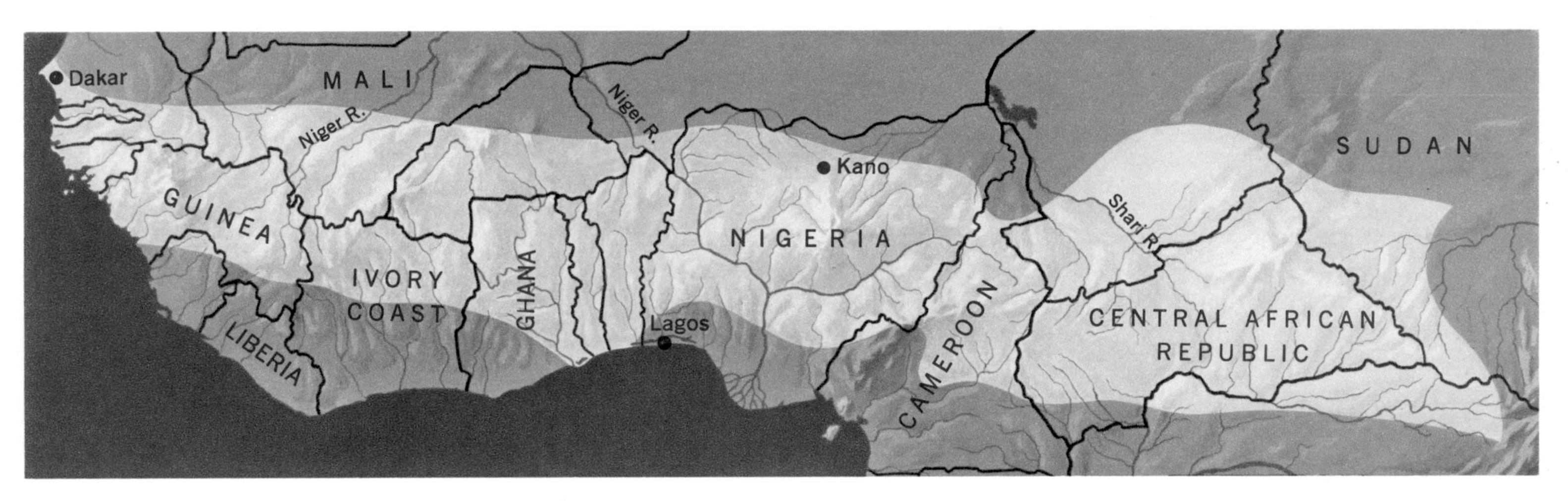

The Guinea savannas, a woodland belt from Senegal east to the upper Nile basin. It is bordered by steppes on the north and forests to the south.

this reduces visibility to two hundred yards or less. At the same time the humidity falls and the nights grow cold. In intense harmattan weather the temperature may vary fifty degrees between early morning and midday. The variation produces an illusion of very sharp cold at night, though freezing point is never approached.

The harmattan reaches these southern savannas in waves separated by periods of humid weather ending in a storm. With each wave of harmattan there seems to come a wave of fresh migrants, including such unlikely birds as white-headed kingfishers *(Halcyon leucocephalus)*, gray hornbills *(Tockus nasutus)* and white-throated bee eaters *(Aerops albicollis)*. Also among the migrants are various hawks, nightjars, rollers and others. There is no obvious reason why some of these birds should migrate at all; for instance, the insectivorous and fish-eating white-headed kingfisher can find food in the savanna at any time of the year, and in East Africa the same species is a permanent riverside resident. But in these savannas it breeds in the dry burned bush in holes or banks and moves out when the rains come.

The African black kite *(Milvus migrans parasitus)* and the red-tailed buzzard *(Buteo auguralis)* are two birds that move south into the savannas in the dry season, breed, and then move north again. Two other hawks, the grasshopper buzzard *(Butastur rufipennis)* and the diminutive, ternlike, swallow-tailed kite *(Chelictinia riocourii)*, reverse the sequence, breeding in the rains in semidesert bushlands to the north and migrating into the savannas in the dry season. The white-throated bee eater, which migrates through the savanna in great flocks to winter in the forest and in the south follows the same pattern. Thus these savannas may simultaneously harbor winter migrants from palearctic regions, dry-season breeding migrants, and dry-season non-breeding migrants.

Some of these West African migrations are no more than an ebb and flow between the northern subarid bushlands and the savannas, but some extend right across the equator. Abdim's stork *(Sphenorynchus abdimii)*, a bird that lives a life of continual abundance, breeds in the rains in the northern Guinea savannas and in the southern Sudanese transition zone; it is welcomed as a harbinger of rain by the people of the villages in which it breeds. Breeding completed, it moves south, passing through East African grasslands in October and November during rainy weather. It spends the northern dry season stalking about in wet grasslands from Tanzania south to the Transvaal in the southern rainy season. In former times it used to accompany swarms of locusts, but it can live equally well on grasshoppers and frogs. When the southern tropical rains tail off, it moves north again, once more following the onset of rains through East African grasslands in March and April. It arrives at its northern breeding grounds in April just before the main rains. It thus lives its whole life in savanna or grassland in wet weather, when there is an abundance of food.

A bird that migrates in the reverse direction is the pennant-winged nightjar *(Semeiophorus vexillarius)*. It breeds in the wet season in the southern tropics, between September and February. It then moves north and appears in the northern tropics during the rains. It too spends most of its life in moist savannas during the rains. Unlike most nightjars that nest on the ground, moreover, it breeds during the rains.

During the breeding season this nightjar grows a pair of extraordinary long white pennants on the ninth primary of each wing. In flight it looks as if it is trailing two long white tapes behind it. An even more remarkable breeding adornment is grown by the standard-wing nightjar *(Macrodipteryx longipennis)*. Its ninth primary is elongated into a flexible wirelike shaft with a raquet-shaped vane on the end. In display these "raquets" sail above the bird as if detached from its body. This nightjar too is a migrant, but is a dry-season breeder in the southern part of its range.

In any regular pattern of migration there must be an initiating factor that starts the movement, and an ultimate factor, or benefit to be gained by the migration. Various causes, including temperature, the abundance of food, the varying incidence of daylight from one season to another, and so on have been suggested to explain migration from northern lands. Intertropical migrations are often explained on the rather unsatisfactory grounds of local variations in food supply. But many intertropical and transequatorial migrations are too regular and too long to be so explained. An Abdim's stork in the Transvaal cannot know that when food supplies fail in its

Martial eagle (Polemaetus bellicosus), the largest eagle in Africa, is an inhabitant of savanna or steppes. It feeds chiefly on game birds, small antelopes and hyraxes. (Clem Haagner)

Hartebeest (Alcelaphus buselaphus) and warthogs (Phacochoerus aethiopicus) are two of the most widespread animals of savanna country. (Marc and Evelyne Bernheim: Rapho Guillumette)

"winter" quarters they will be abundant in the Sudan. Something must initiate such movements as are performed by Abdim's stork or the swallow-tailed kite. Since neither food supply nor photoperiodism (which is not likely to be marked in tropical latitudes) explains all cases it seems likely that the sudden and dramatic changes in the weather characteristic of savannas may be the real initiating cause of intertropical migrations.

TERRESTRIAL MONKEYS

Savanna is an environment in which the weight of edible grass which flourishes near ground level favors animals and birds that feed and breed near the ground. We can therefore expect large herbivores to be common. The fierce fires characteristic of savanna limit such sluggish creatures as tortoises and snakes, and kill millions of grasshoppers and small rodents each year, but birds and large animals can generally escape the fire.

Monkeys are normally arboreal but must adapt themselves to the savanna environment by becoming terrestrial. The two most common monkeys in the savanna are the very numerous olive baboon *(Papio anubis)* and the red hussar monkey *(Erythrocebus patas)*. Both of these get most of their food on the ground; they can climb well, but they chiefly use trees as roosts or observation points. Along river valleys strips of forest persist; here the vervet monkey *(Cercopithecus aethiops)* is common, but it makes only short excursions into grassland.

Baboons are generally disliked by farmers because they rob farmlands with great skill and intelligence. They are also reputed to be dangerous, capable of attacking *en masse*. It is doubtful if there is any real foundation for this belief. Baboons will certainly make threatening demonstrations with much loud barking, but supposed "attacks" upon human beings are usually inspired by curiosity that is misinterpreted as aggressiveness by the humans concerned.

Some people maintain that the baboon is a repulsive animal devoid of any virtue, but this is a prejudiced view. They are intelligent, well-organized monkeys, capable of showing great courage. They travel about in troops numbering from ten to over a hundred, and they often live near rocky hills where they can roost in remote caves or ledges at night. Early in the morning they come down and start foraging. They are basically vegetarian, but will eat insects and scorpions, and have been known to kill newborn antelope calves.

In each troop of baboons there is a small élite of large males that dominates all the others. The behavior of the

Patas monkeys (Erythrocebus patas) are large red terrestrial monkeys that run in large troops. These mothers are carrying well-grown babies slung under their bellies. (Jean Dragesco: Atlas Photo)

females, who also form a sort of dominance hierarchy, depends largely on the stage of their reproductive cycle. The dominant males of the central hierarchy mate with the females when they are most likely to conceive. Should the troop be attacked, say by a leopard or a dog, one or more dominant males will face the enemy, and sometimes give his life in the struggle that follows. With powerful jaws and three-inch canine teeth a male baboon is a redoubtable antagonist. Nevertheless he is no match for a leopard, and baboons make a tremendous outcry when they see a leopard or hear one grunting at night. Although leopards are supposed to be the natural enemies of baboons it is doubtful that they really kill many. Often a big troop of baboons will not give way to a leopard, though they will always do so to a lion.

ROAN AND HARTEBEEST

In these savannas several animals found over a wide range in Africa are common. One of them is the roan antelope *(Hippotragus equinus)*, the largest of the horselike antelopes, *Hippotraginae*. A relation of the oryx and the sable, it is found also in East and South Africa. So is the hartebeest *(Alcelaphus buselaphus)*, which we first met in North Africa as a recently extinct animal and which extends throughout savanna and grassland in various races to South Africa. There are also a fair number of African buffalos *(Syncerus caffer)*, intermediate in size and color between the large black buffalo of East Africa and the Sudan and the tiny red forest buffalo of the Congo; almost every variation from coal black to bright red can be seen in West African savannas. Near water there are the kob *(Kobus kob)*, the Defassa waterbuck *(Kobus defassa)* and the Bohor reedbuck *(Redunca redunca)*. The oribi *(Ourebia ourebi)* occurs in open savanna and the bushbuck *(Tragelaphus scriptus)* is common in thickets along watercourses. Several species of duikers (of the genera *Silvicapra* and *Cephalophus*) are also fairly common.

Elephants are not really at home in the Sudanese transition belt but are found in parts of this savanna. Of all the animals here they alone smash trees in their browsing, though they are not usually common enough for their browsing habits to affect tree growth over large areas. Rhinoceroses vanished a long time ago, except in the eastern end of this savanna zone.

The most striking and beautiful member of the savanna fauna inhabiting the northern fringe of this zone is the giant eland *(Taurotragus derbianus)*. The largest of the antelopes, a male of this magnificent species stands more than five and a half feet at the shoulder, weighs over fifteen hundred pounds, and may bear horns nearly four feet long. It must formerly have inhabited all the savannas from Senegal to the Sudan but the western race, *T. d. derbianus,* had been reduced to several dozen a few years ago and is separated by a wide gap in the range from other races that live in North Cameroon and the Sudan and are still quite numerous.

The savanna fauna of West Africa consists of fewer species than that of South or East Africa, but it is far more varied than, for instance, that of North America. Since they have comparable rainfall and food supply, the West African savannas should support just as many animals per square mile as do similar savannas in Rhodesia or Uganda. But throughout most of West Africa the human population is fairly dense and has hunted animals from time immemorial. Hunting pressure has greatly increased in the last fifty years or so, and with the spread of cultivation many hitherto remote areas have been colonized by man. Unless the fauna is soon preserved it may very well become extinct.

TSETSE FLIES AND OTHER INSECTS

Such wildlife as still survives in West African savannas is usually found only in areas rendered useless or unattractive to man by the presence of tsetse flies or *Simulium* flies. These, and several other insects, are the alternate hosts of disease-producing parasites of man or his domestic animals. The tsetse flies are the most widespread here and elsewhere in Africa, but *Simulium,* which causes blindness in human beings, is also important.

The tsetse fly has often been called the protector of natural Africa since it is the only force that in many areas has prevented man's misuse of soil and vegetation and the indiscriminate slaughter of animals. There are many species of tsetse, but all are dipterid bloodsucking flies of the genus *Glossina,* and all have a similar function. Some carry the parasite of sleeping sickness in man, and others carry parasites that are fatal to domestic stock. Thus they tend to exclude domestic stock, and sometimes man as well.

Tsetse flies ingest the fatal parasites when they feed on the blood of an infected animal. The trypanosomes, as they are called, pass through other stages of their life cycle in the salivary glands of the tsetse fly, and at the next feeding are injected into the blood of another animal. Thus a tsetse feeding on a warthog one day transmits the disease to a cow or a human being a few days later. Wild animals are immune or very resistant to the disease (trypanosomiasis) transmitted by tsetse, but man or domestic animals die. Some domestic animals have developed a degree of resistance, but none has been in Africa so long as the wild animals or the tsetse, and so a true immunity has not yet evolved.

West African tsetses carry very virulent forms of trypanosomiasis, and many local strains of the disease exist. A cow which may have shown resistance in one area will often die if transported two hundred miles to another. The menace of the tsetse can sometimes be removed by clearing pockets of vegetation, but often a wholesale clearing is necessary. This is generally uneconomic, and it often happens that small residual populations of tsetse remain when most of the vegetation has been cleared and the wild animals exterminated or driven away. Once a cow has the disease, the infection can be spread through a herd by other biting flies, such as stable flies *(Stomoxys).* I have lived in areas where scarcely a wild animal was left but where it was quite impossible to keep cattle uninfected by trypanosomiasis.

The wild animals, such as the buffalo, roan, and hartebeest, are not only beautiful or interesting, but in these savannas represent the most reliable source of meat protein for expanding human populations. It would therefore seem only wise to conserve the remaining stocks of wild animals and utilize their inherent capacity to resist the diseases that kill domestic stock.

An agama lizard on a tree trunk; they are abundant in West African savannas. (Arthur Christiansen)

GREAT RIVERS

The savannas of this whole region, from Senegal to the western Sudan, are drained by a few great rivers, the Senegal, the Niger, and its mighty tributary the Benue, the Volta, the Shari and the Kamadugu Yobe. Of these the Niger is much the largest, but the others have very much the same character. All fall within the same rainfall regime, rising in the period from April to May and shrinking in December to March.

In the dry season the flow is reduced to fast shallow ripples connecting huge still pools full of fish. Enormous banks of yellow sand are exposed, like miniature deserts and just as hot. In the rains the clear waters grow turbid and the rivers rise twenty or thirty feet and cover all the sandbanks. A river spreads out of its channel and over a vast area of flat alluvium known as a flood plain. This is often forested, or supports a

Female Buffon's kob and dog-faced baboons (Papio anubis). Baboons often warn other animals of the presence of danger. (Afrique Photo)

special kind of savanna with very tall stiff grass and small trees. These flood plains occur along the banks of all West African rivers.

The flood plain forests are a northward extension of the rain forest farther south. There species of trees and birds occur maybe three hundred miles north of the forest-savanna boundary. Little tongues of forest run far into the savannas up the valleys of any tributary, and small rivers running through savanna may suddenly meander in a flat place and form a little flood plain with a patch of forest. This mingling of savanna and forest along watercourses helps forest animals and birds to adapt to life in savanna.

The forests of flood plains hide buffalos, bushbucks and red duikers, while the grass swamps support waterbucks and kobs. The wet season, when the forests are intersected by innumerable water channels and the open areas are covered by ten-foot grass, gives the animals some respite from hunting. Then in the dry season, in the open plains, after the long grass has burned, they are difficult to approach unseen. On some flood plains wild animals have survived better than in the neighboring upland savannas.

In Nigeria, Africans told me that there were two kinds of waterbucks, one of the flood plain and one of the uplands. Certainly there seemed to be herds of waterbucks that never left the flood plain and others that stayed always in the uplands. Those of the uplands generally seemed redder and smaller than the flood plain animals. These two varieties were not even distinct races, but it seemed to me that I could see the beginning of the evolution of a new race or species of waterbuck, less dependent upon water than the typical species one sees. But it is unlikely that this process could ever be completed because of the imminent extinction of all waterbucks in savanna and flood plain alike.

PRATINCOLES AND BEE EATERS

Bird life along these rivers is splendid, especially in the dry season. At that time many birds breed on the huge sandbanks. The Egyptian plover of the Nile is found here, together with spurwing and Senegal wattled plovers *(Sarciophorus tectus* and *Afribyx senegallus)* and tiny white-fronted sand plovers *(Leucopolius marginatus)*. There are skimmers *(Rynchops flavirostris)*, strange ternlike birds with a lower mandible that

Male Buffon's kob (Kobus kob buffoni), a handsome red antelope found chiefly in good grazing lands near water. (Afrique Photo)

is much longer than the upper and is used to skim tiny fish from the surface of still pools. True terns—white-winged black *(Chlidonias leucoptera),* gull-billed *(Gelochelidon nilotica)* and little *(Sterna albifrons)*—sail over the water, and may be accompanied by black-backed gulls *(Larus fuscus).* Most of these are migrants, but the little tern breeds on sandbanks. In backwaters and in flood plain swamps there are storks, ibises, jacanas, ducks and geese.

The most attractive of all the sandbank birds are the gray pratincoles *(Galachrysia cinerea).* Distant relatives of coursers and terns they are delicate sprites, largely insectivorous and, in flight, buoyant as blown leaves. When one approaches their nests on sandbanks they strive to protect their young by attracting attention to themselves, dragging a pied wing in the prettiest act of deception imaginable. They lay their eggs in depressions in the sand, and the eggs themselves are exceedingly difficult to see since they have a faintly freckled sand color.

Another species of pratincole, the collared pratincole *(Galachrysia nuchalis),* is very dark and, though it would be conspicuous on sandbanks, it frequents the occasional rocky islands in the river's flow or stretches of rocky rapids where it is almost invisible; its eggs, too, match almost perfectly the dark rocks. Yet a third and larger pratincole, *Glareola pratincola boweni,* likes to rest and breed on mudbanks. It too is nearly invisible against this background.

Pratincoles are masters of concealment, but bee eaters are very conspicuous. On any of these rivers one is always aware of swarms of bee eaters. The three common species are the rosy bee eater *(Merops malimbicus),* the carmine bee eater

(Merops nubicus), and the red-throated bee eater *(Melittophagus bullocki)*. They may be joined by European bee eaters *(Merops apiaster)* on migration, and little bee eaters *(Melittophagus pusillus)* are widespread but found only in pairs.

Carmine and red-throated bee eaters breed in holes excavated in vertical banks. A colony of perhaps five thousand pairs of carmine bee eaters creates a brilliant red stain visible from miles away. Rosy bee eaters are unusual in that they nest in slanting burrows in flat sandbanks. The whole sandbank over a large area may be honeycombed with burrows; I have seen one colony that contained 18,500 holes.

Bee eaters are the common insectivorous birds seen hawking over the waters and sandbanks of these rivers. They are often accompanied by multitudes of European and other swallows. Six or seven species of swallows and martins occur here and one, the gray-rumped swallow *(Hirundo griseopyga)*, breeds in slanting burrows deep in flat sandbanks. Life can never be dull when there is this multitude of spritely birds to watch.

A young serval cat (Felis serval), a long-legged, big-eared predator of birds and smaller mammals. (E. S. Ross)

THE NIGER FLOOD

In the inundation zone of the Upper Niger the April-August rains in Sierra Leone and French Guinea produce a vast temporary lake and swamp. This drains out into the Lower Niger to the southeast; in Nigeria the river still runs high in December. By March the water falls, and in April the rains break in the savannas of Nigeria itself. The river then overtops its banks and spreads out over its flood plain. The sandy bed that was such an attractive breeding ground for so many birds is beneath twenty feet of turbid water. Most of the birds that graced the sandbanks must leave.

Some, like Egyptian and spurwing plovers, move only into local rice fields or canoe landings. Others, like herons and storks, find themselves forced to shift to fresh swamps and pools in the flood plain. Yet others, like the little terns, move downriver to the seashore. The movements of pratincoles are not understood, but it is probable that they move upstream into drier lands. What is certain is that the regular movements of birds follow the rise and fall of the Niger, which is part of the rainfall pattern in West Africa.

The Niger travels two thousand miles from its source before it receives the waters of its mighty tributary, the Benue, which drains almost the whole of the Cameroon highlands and is consequently a very large river. In the rains the flood of the combined rivers is over a mile wide and spreads over a flood plain seven or eight miles wide on either side of the river. The Niger then runs south, disappears into forests and loses itself among the many creeks and mouths of a huge delta before it meets the sea in the Bight of Benin.

The great Niger River drains and connects a huge area of land from the borders of the Sahara near Timbuctoo to the steaming swamps of its delta and from the heights of Guinea in the west to the Cameroon highlands in the east. Except for the Nile, it traverses and serves more varied country than any other African river. We can follow its flood waters out of this region and into the great forest to the south, where some of the flow was born.

The Great Swamplands

The Nile Basin

7

The great northern savanna belt that spans Africa from Senegal to the southern Sudan, western Kenya and Uganda changes little in all that vast distance. At its eastern end, however, it runs into an area of more complex geology, and abuts upon the ancient plateau of the eastern half of Africa. The Rift Valley and the Nile pass through parts of it, the Nile draining this area northward. Associated with the Nile are several of the great lakes of Africa: Lake Victoria, Lake Albert, and Lake Edward. The varying terrain, some unique animals and birds, and the multiplicity of rivers, lakes and swamps, all contribute to making the Upper Nile basin a distinct region of Africa.

Swamps border the Nile itself for hundreds of miles, extend over a huge area in the southern Sudan known as the Sudd, and cover great areas in Uganda. There are swamps elsewhere in Africa, but in this region they constantly claim attention with their vegetation of papyrus, reeds, aquatic grasses and water lilies.

Much of the Nile basin has a fairly high rainfall and gently undulating topography which, combined with high humidity and relatively short drought periods, result in a great expanse of swamp. Tropical swamps are formed by heavy rainfall that accumulates in hollows and cannot escape by rapid river flow. The excess moisture creates shallow, slow-moving sheets of water in low flat valleys. High temperature and strong sunlight assist plants to colonize this water and gradually these plants choke the flow. First, floating plants without root systems or with roots adapted to feeding in water form a loose mat on the surface. Such floating mats grow thicker with age, and in time other plants, with suitable root systems, are able to grow upon them. They in turn grow old, die, and form yet thicker mats on which still larger plants can flourish. The

Zebras, topis and impala form a large mixed herd in the Kagera Park. Each of these animals feeds on grass at a different stage of growth. (Emil Schulthess)

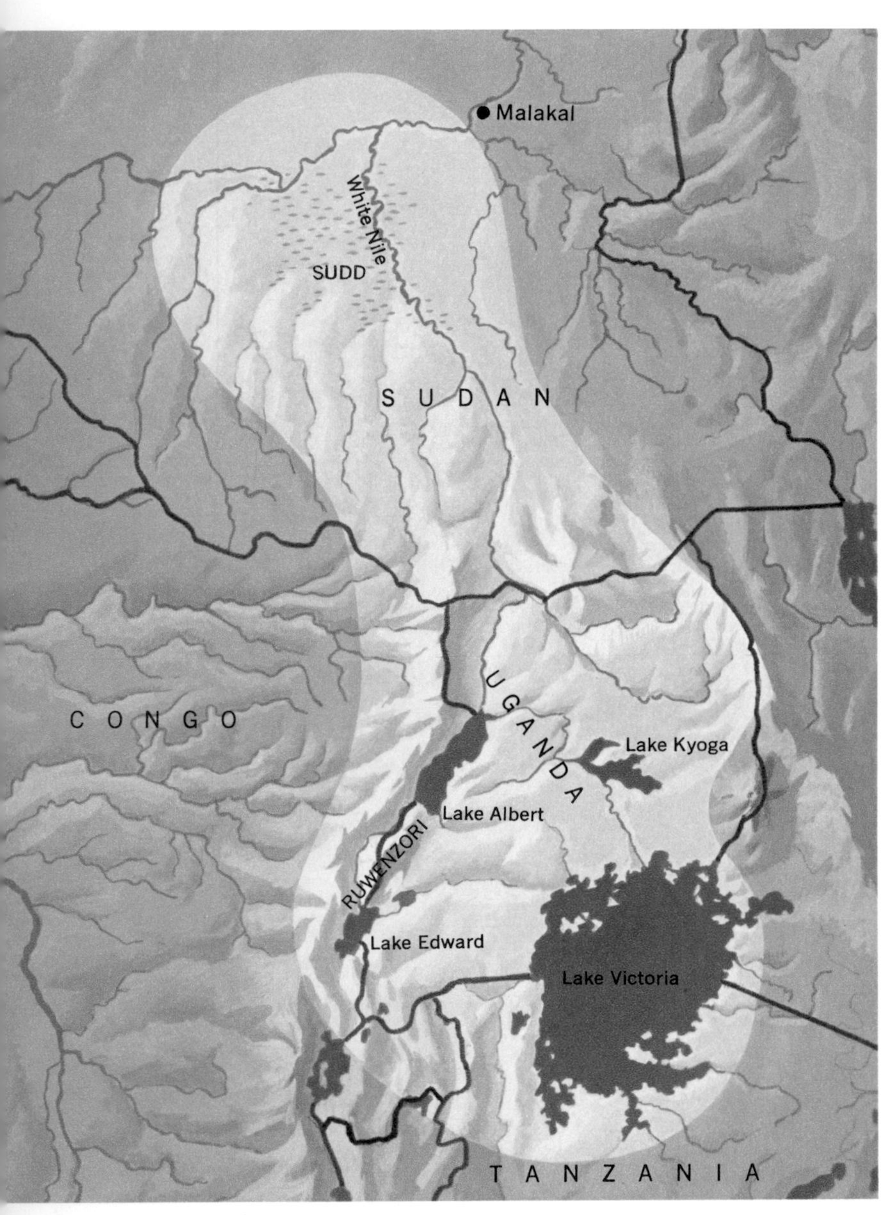

The Nile basin, an extensive flat swampy area in the Nile Valley in Sudan and Uganda. It is famous for its big game, great lakes and water birds.

end result is a soggy mass of dense vegetation, often strong enough to bear the weight of a large animal, but often separated from the solid ground underneath by several feet of water.

The topography of the Nile basin is peculiarly suited to the formation of these swamps. In the Miocene epoch (about 35,000,000 years ago) the present eastern shore of Lake Victoria was on a watershed whence rivers flowed westward. Earth movements and volcanic activity dammed the natural flow of the rivers and formed a series of lakes. The faulting of the Rift Valley intensified this process, and between the two branches of the Rift a shallow basin was formed by the sagging of the sedimentary rocks deposited on the lake beds. Lake Victoria now fills this basin, and the old watershed, from which rivers flowing westward originated, has almost been leveled. Some of the rivers now flow slowly east along practically flat valleys; others still flow west but very slowly. The valleys of all these rivers are filled with long tongues of gray-green swamp vegetation.

A GREAT SWAMP BARRIER

The greatest of all the swamps is the Sudd. It covers many thousand square miles of almost flat country in the southern Sudan, where the Nile takes an eastward turn and is joined by several other large rivers draining from higher ground to the west. So formidable a barrier is this great swamp that for centuries it prevented access to the Upper Nile by explorers coming up the river. Roman centurions actually reached the Sudd but could not pass it. The same fate befell several later explorers and it was not until Speke penetrated the continent from the east coast that the secret of the source of the Nile was revealed. In the past, steamboats have been trapped in the mass of choking, shifting vegetation, and their occupants have been known to die of starvation—since scarcely any food for humans can be found in the middle of the swamp. The only open channel is the Nile itself, which has been kept open by man.

The Sudd acts in a curious way to reduce the flow of the Nile. At high water, islands of vegetation break loose from the swamps fringing the river, float with the current, and jam up the channel. The blocked river then spreads out, covering a huge area with a sheet of shallow water. In the water swamp plants grow vigorously in the great heat, and several times as much water is transpired as could evaporate from the equivalent area of an open lake. The greater the flow of the river, the farther it spreads, and the greater the amount of water transpired by the swamp-loving plants. No matter how much water comes in from the south and west, there is comparatively little variation in the flow of the Nile at its northern outlet.

Outside the actual swamp of the Sudd there are more vast areas of flat ground which become water-logged or wet in rainy seasons. In the dry season this affords lush grazing, which attracts thousand of animals, wild and domestic, from the surrounding plains and savanna. Thus, as the water rises and falls, there is a related ebb and flow of animal life.

Although they avoid the dense swamp vegetation of the Sudd, some animals live in the wet grassland itself. The Nile lechwe *(Kobus megaceros)* is an isolated species whose nearest relatives dwell in great swamps in southern central Africa a thousand miles away. It has elongated hooves which spread out under the weight of its body, so as to prevent it from sinking into marshy ground. The undersurface of its pastern is bare, and when the lechwe runs, this naked pad adheres to slippery surfaces like the tire of an automobile. Lechwes spend much of their time grazing in large herds on water-logged ground where lions and cheetahs are at a disadvantage. To escape attack, they may plunge into water up to their necks.

With the lechwe lives a race of the common kob antelope of West Africa, the white-eared kob *(Kobus kob leucotis)*. For long regarded as distinct, this animal is probably developing through isolation into a clearly separate species. The color of the old males is strikingly different from other kobs, which are bright red. The white-eared kob is dark brown and, as its name suggests, it has white ears. These kobs are found on both banks of the Nile, whereas lechwes are confined to the Bahr el Ghazal area on the left bank.

The filamentous heads of papyrus form a tuft at the end of a long pithy triangular stem. (Emil Schulthess)

PAPYRUS AND NILE CABBAGE

The most obvious and distinctive plant of these swamps, papyrus *(Cyperus papyrus)*, is a huge sedge that forms a forest of stiff stalks fifteen feet tall. The stalks spring from a mat several feet thick, made up of the plants' own roots and dead vegetable matter. The triangular stalks are leafless, bearing at their tops a tuft of filamentous bracts, with flowers in their axils. The growth is so dense, and the stems so stiff and tangled, that a man must cut a path through a papyrus swamp. Little grows among papyrus but a few ferns and some climbers of the sweet potato family *(Ipomoea)*.

Papyrus is of course famous because the ancient Egyptians used it for making a form of writing paper. It is now too difficult to extract the stems from their watery environment in quantities sufficient for commercial purposes, and since animals seldom eat papyrus, and very few even penetrate the growth, the swamps remain almost undisturbed.

In the open water of these swamps there are sheets of a small, bright green, lettuce-like plant, the Nile cabbage *(Pistia stratioides)*. Each individual plant has a tuft of leaves and a shallow mat of roots which draws nourishment from the water. In shallow backwaters and ponds it can survive temporary drying out when the water level is low. When rivers flood, chunks of the mat or single plants are carried downstream, collect in the mouths of channels, and begin the process of choking streams. Found in all African river systems, it is nowhere more luxuriant than in the Nile basin. It looks edible, indeed succulent, but it has an acrid taste so that no animal relishes it.

These two plants, the papyrus and the Nile cabbage, dominate, respectively, the tall swamp growth and the open water of backwaters in this swampy region. In some swamps bulrushes *(Typha australis)*, sedges *(Cladium jamaicense)*, and reeds *(Phragmites mauritianus)* replace the papyrus. These are so closely allied to their European counterparts that some consider them identical species. They tend to grow in slightly drier conditions than papyrus, and each has its own local preferences. They form extensive swamps in eastern Uganda.

Crocodiles live on fish rather than flesh when the former is plentiful; this one seizes a tilapia. (Alan Root)

The swamps can be beautiful. Open water is often adorned by masses of blue and mauve water lilies, and still pools at evening reflect the color of the sky. But in general they are difficult places to explore, even with a boat, and have daunted many an investigator. Inside the growth, despite the huge quantity of accessible vegetable matter, there are few animals, perhaps because most of the leaves are harsh, sharp or unpalatable. Nevertheless, like any other unique habitat, such swamps have their own special inhabitants.

DEAD WATER

The swamp vegetation of papyrus, reeds, and other plants rests upon the solid bottom or floats on water which may be ten feet deep. Such water is dead, its oxygen having been exhausted by the upper layer of floating vegetation. Beneath, a layer of peat is formed from dead plant remains which have dropped from the floating mat. This peat differs from the peat of temperate bogs because it is not formed at the base of living plants. Devoid of oxygen, it does not decompose unless the swamp dries out, or is drained, and it is then exposed to the air.

The dead layer of water and of peat beneath the floating mat presents a problem to plants and animals that might colonize the mat. Even the roots of the swamp plants must be specially adapted or they would die for lack of air. Certain creatures have managed to overcome the difficulties and manage to live in great numbers in the dead mat of vegetable matter. The swamp worm *(Alma emini)* works in this mat like an earthworm, passing dead vegetation through its body and often completely covering the surface with its casts. It has a special organ on its hind end, an open blood-rich groove which enables it to absorb oxygen from the air while its head remains buried for feeding purposes. Even when the worm withdraws its hind end into the mud, this breathing organ still remains in contact with the air above. These worms can work down to a depth of two feet. They hasten the process of aeration and decomposition of the swamp mat, and by so doing make nutriments available to the plants that grow there.

One large species of animal lives in these swamps. It is the sitatunga *(Tragelaphus spekei)*, one of the spiral-horned antelopes, *Tragelaphidae*. It is closely related to the bushbuck, with which it will hybridize in captivity. Like the Nile lechwe it has greatly elongated hooves which spread out under pressure of its body, so that it does not break through the mat of plants and become bogged down in the water and mud. A very shy creature, it lives in the depths of the growth by day and emerges to feed on the verges by night. Although it is quite common, few people have seen a wild one. By living in the swamps the sitatunga escapes predators and makes use of a food supply inaccessible to antelopes that have normal hooves.

THE RIVER HORSE

The hippopotamus formerly abounded in these swamps and in the lakes and rivers of this region; indeed in some parts it is still very common. The second largest species of mammal in

The Rutshuru River drains the forested country on the Rift wall into Lake Edward. (Rune Hassner: Tio)

Africa, they are suited to an aquatic life: they can swim freely and can walk on the bottom. In clear water they can be seen moving about with a grace and ease that is almost unbelievable. On land they look ungainly, but can move with surprising speed.

Hippos live in small or large herds, though old bulls sometimes become solitary. They spend the day crammed together in water or in mud wallows, for the most part submerged, except for their backs, mostly to escape the heat of the sun. In deep water they surface periodically, simply in order to breathe. Their eyes and nostrils, as in some other aquatic mammals, are located on the top of their heads, and they have small ears which they shake vigorously when they surface. Where they are hunted, hippos hide in dense vegetation by day; from time to time their nostrils and eyes emerge as they surface to breathe. They emerge quietly, without snorting. In places where they are undisturbed, such as in the lakes and channels of western Uganda, they are tame, and herds of them lie about contentedly in the shallow water, scarcely moving when a human being approaches.

Hippos perform two vital functions, one engineering, the other chemical. By their great bulk and strength they help to keep open channels of water between masses of swamp vegetation. When they emerge at night to graze on the lush pastures at the water's edge they make wide paths through reeds or papyrus which help other creatures, including man, to reach the water more easily. By day their copious droppings fertilize the water itself: this enables quantities of minute blue-green algae to flourish, and these algae are in turn eaten by fish, notably the breamlike fish *Tilapia*. The hippo is thus vital to the health of populations of fish and also assists the uninterrupted flow of rivers.

Hippos are very large and powerful animals, and as a result they are usually beyond the strength of, and therefore are not threatened by, the predatory carnivores on shore. Even the lion is reluctant to tackle a full-grown hippo, though sometimes lions kill a few calves. In the absence of predation by large carnivores or man hippos can become too numerous for their habitat, and suffer from decimating outbreaks of disease. The banks of the Nile, for instance, and of the Kazinga

Overleaf: Great white pelicans and hippos at Lake Edward. The hippos rest in the water by day and emerge to graze at night. The pelicans fish by day and rest on shore at night. (Leslie Brown)

channel in the Queen Elizabeth National Park, have been so overgrazed by hippos that erosion is quite serious. Nowadays, while the main population remains healthy and unchecked by disease, hippos are regularly "cropped" by shooting in the Kazinga channel and Lake Albert, and the damage has thus been stayed.

CROCODILES AND NILE MONITORS

Crocodiles are still abundant in parts of this area. Before they were persecuted for their skins, they were found in far greater numbers. Crocodiles are perhaps the most dangerous predator to man in all Africa, but the degree of their danger to man seems to depend on the abundance of their immediate food supply. Where there are plenty of fish they prefer that diet, and rarely attack large mammals. But in some places, regardless of alternatives, they seize antelopes coming down to the water's edge to drink, and they do not always differentiate between man and other large animals. Even in areas where crocodiles are supposed to be harmless, it is foolhardy to go into the water; there can be exceptions to any local rule.

Among fish, crocodiles help to maintain the balance of species. If there are no crocodiles, carnivorous fish, such as catfish *(Clarias mossambicus)*, eat too many of the other fish and the value of fisheries is reduced. Even baby crocodiles are useful; they eat predatory insect larvae. Serious fishery problems have been aggravated by the virtual extermination of crocodiles in parts of Lake Victoria, and efforts are now being made to conserve these beasts.

Crocodiles come ashore to lay their eggs in sand, where the female often remains on guard near her nest. Many eggs are laid, which in due course hatch into little crocodiles fully able to fend for themselves. But they hatch only if the nests are not found by a big water lizard, the Nile monitor *(Varanus niloticus)*. Nile monitors are common all along the rivers of tropical Africa, and are especially numerous on some islands in Lake Victoria. They are carnivorous, but above all they like the eggs and young of birds and the eggs of crocodiles. They dig out the crocodiles' nests and any eggs they do not eat are often exposed and left to be eaten by such birds as marabou storks *(Leptoptilos crumeniferus)* and vultures.

Nile monitors may grow to over six feet in length, and can run swiftly and swim freely. If they cannot thus escape, they will sometimes retreat into a hole among rocks. From this kind of hideout it takes the full strength of several men to dislodge a monitor—by pulling on its tail—so strong is the grip of its long-clawed feet. Caught in the open the lizard blows itself up and hisses. Its tail, lashing from side to side, is an efficient weapon against smaller predators; it can bite fiercely, but if picked up by the tail it is helpless.

Pythons frequent all of tropical Africa but are commonest in swamps and along rivers. The African python *(Python sebae)* is a huge snake that may be twenty feet long. It kills its prey by constriction, and then swallows it whole. Contrary to general belief, the constriction does not smash the bones in the body of an antelope, but is merely used for killing it. The python's jaws are well able to accommodate large prey, since they are not hinged and can expand to an almost incredible extent. These reptiles are regarded as harmless to man, and they will normally try to flee when disturbed. But they can, by their sheer size and strength, inflict a very dangerous bite, and it is a mistake to tease a python apparently immobilized by a gargantuan meal.

WATER BIRDS

Lake Victoria and the other lakes of this region are dotted with many small islands where colonies of mixed fish-eating birds breed. These include three species of cormorants *(Phalacrocorax carbo, P. africanus* and *P. lugubris)*, the snake-bird or darter *(Anhinga rufa)*, and many kinds of herons. These latter vary from the giant goliath heron *(Ardea goliath)* to the very small green-backed heron *(Butorides striatus)*. In some colonies up to ten species of herons may be found. The commonest are probably the cattle egret *(Bubulcus ibis)* and the black-necked heron *(Ardea melanocephala)*. Both are herons which have given up a purely aquatic existence and have taken to foraging on land as well, which of course gives them a greatly increased range. Both feed on insects, and the black-necked heron also feeds on small grass mice.

Besides herons, sacred ibis *(Threskiornis aethiopicus)* and yellow-billed storks *(Ibis ibis)* may be found nesting here. The all-black open-billed stork *(Anastomus lamelligerus)* is another inhabitant of this area; its curious beak, like a pair of forceps, supposedly enables it to grip the snails and freshwater mussels on which it feeds. Pink-backed pelicans *(Pelecanus rufescens)* generally breed in colonies by themselves, but they sometimes have marabou storks with them. For some reason both these birds often choose to nest in a large tree far from any water, and the pelicans at least must then make a long journey to and fro each day to bring food to their young. Possibly such colonies mark the site of an old lake or freshwater lagoon where food was once abundant but which has since dried up.

These inland colonies of mixed fish-eating birds are just as impressive as bird colonies on seacoasts. There is the same feeling of great abundance and vigorous life. But in those I have watched, the survival rate has been very low. One colony was situated in spiky acacia trees, and at a stage when the young herons were becoming active they often fell and impaled themselves on the trees' long thorns. Few nests reared more than one young. In another island colony a group of Nile monitors and a fair-sized python climbed about in the trees and ate almost all the eggs and chicks, aided by a hippo that came ashore by night and knocked many young out of nests as it blundered among the bushes. If the young fell into the water they were eaten by small crocodiles or catfish. Despite these drawbacks the herons and storks survive, and are seen in numbers along all the waterways in this region. It seems that a high rate of breeding success is not essential to their survival.

WHALE-BILLED STORKS AND HAMMERKOPS

The most impressive of several unique birds in this region is the whale-billed stork *(Balaeniceps rex)*. It inhabits the papyrus swamps from the Sudd to Lake George and Lake Victoria, but is everywhere quite rare and seldom seen. It has a gigantic bloated bill shaped like an upturned boat, sober gray plumage, and wise-looking whitish eyes. The edges of its bill are sharp and presumably are an aid in holding and killing

The picture of contentment: basking hippos. They cannot stand long exposure to very hot sun. (Emil Schulthess)

the frogs and fish on which it feeds. It breeds deep in the swamps, and has never been studied closely.

Probably its nearest relative is a small brown stork, also with a boat-shaped bill, the hammerkop *(Scopus umbretta)*. Hammerkops inhabit rivers and ponds and are found near springs in dry country throughout tropical Africa. They are very remarkable birds indeed, and are particularly numerous in the Nile basin.

The hammerkop builds an enormous nest, quite unlike that of any other stork. The nest is a domed structure made with sticks mixed with mud; it has a small entrance hole overhanging the water, and a central chamber about four feet across and plastered inside with mud. Hammerkops take about a month to build their huge nests, and it is fascinating to watch them doing so. Starting with a bowl-shaped foundation of sticks and reeds, the birds build up from the back with strong sticks, by which is formed a sort of hood. At the same time they fashion a kind of spout, later to become the entrance tube. On top they pile about a foot's depth of reeds, sticks and grass. Achieving a depth of some six feet, the bird completes its nest by plastering the entrance tube and inner chamber with mud. The finished structure can support the weight of a man.

This great nest has only one chamber. It is well insulated from the sun and, when the hammerkop is brooding, a constant temperature—of about blood heat—is maintained within. The entrance is usually impregnable to snakes and small mammalian predators, but barn owls *(Tyto alba)* often get in and eject the hammerkop. Despite the elaborate nature of their home, hammerkops do not seem to breed very often or very successfully. I have seldom seen an occupied nest, and assume that they are long-lived birds.

YOUTHFUL FATHER NILE

The Nile, the longest river in Africa, drains all the watery areas discussed in the preceding pages. It is the southern branch, or White Nile that concerns us here. The Blue Nile drains the highlands of Ethiopia and joins the southern branch far to the north, at Khartoum. The White Nile is a more stable stretch of river than the Blue Nile, partly because it comes from a region of more regular, less distinctly seasonal rainfall, but even more because the flood waters of its major branches are collected and to some extent regulated by storage in two gigantic natural reservoirs, Lake Victoria, which is the second largest lake in the world, and Lake Albert.

The Nile runs out of Lake Victoria through a narrow gorge and then follows a turbulent course till it loses itself temporarily in the huge swamps of Lake Kyoga. A further turbulent reach, along which its roaring power must be seen to be appreciated, takes it to the Murchison Falls. Here it is compressed into a channel barely twenty feet wide, to plunge into a broad relatively calm channel connected to Lake Albert. Up to this point it is known as the Victoria Nile, but after it leaves Lake Albert it becomes the Albert Nile. Lake Albert lies in the western branch of the Rift Valley and is of very different character from Lake Victoria.

We are accustomed to think of the Nile as ancient, but the Victoria Nile is, by geological standards, quite young. On the site of Lake Victoria there was formerly another huge lake, known as Lake Karunga. This must have been connected with the Nile, for it contained Nilotic species of fish, including the Nile perch *(Lates)* and the lungfish *(Polypterus)*. In succeeding ages most of this old lake dried up, and only some of its original fish fauna survived, chiefly cichlids of the genus *Haplochromis* and the breamlike tilapia.

Later, after the extensive earth movements which formed the two branches of the Rift Valley, a shallow basin formed and filled with water. Still later, possibly within the last 200,000 years, further earth movements tilted the Lake Victoria basin so that it overflowed into what is now the Victoria Nile. The connection between the old Lake Karunga and the Nile was thus restored. But Nilotic fish have never been able to pass Murchison Falls, and the present fish fauna of Lake Victoria is composed chiefly of descendants of a few remnant species that survived when most of the old lake dried up.

Recently some species of Nilotic fish, the Nile perch and a tilapia, have been introduced above the falls. The Nile perch was put into Lake Kyoga only, but it has somehow found its way into Lake Victoria. The effects of these introductions will in time enable us to judge the impact of man's actions on the endemic fishes of Lake Victoria.

Still more dramatic events affected the waters of the other main branch of the White Nile, the Semliki River, which flows into Lake Albert. Lake Albert, Lake Edward, and Lake George all lie on the floor of the western branch of the Great Rift Valley at different altitudes. Once they were one continuous lake, or at least joined by a river that enabled Nilotic fish to reach Lake Edward. This we know from fossil remains. Later they were separated by high escarpments culminating in the great mountain range of Ruwenzori, the fabled "mountains of the moon," rising to almost seventeen thousand feet, with glaciers on the summits.

Then, probably only about seven thousand years ago, when primitive man was already living in the area, violent volcanic activity caused a series of tremendous explosions in the floor of the Rift close to Lake Edward. Huge clouds of ash and lumps of rock were blown into the air in a cataclysm that must have rivaled the greatest explosion in recorded history, the eruption of Krakatoa in the East Indies. The clouds of ash settled as a deep layer of dust at the north end of Lake Edward. The dust and poisonous volcanic substances destroyed most of the life of the area, including many of the Nilotic fish. But the Nile tilapia managed to survive, and thrives abundantly to this day.

Any mammals in the area, and such reptiles as crocodiles, were probably also destroyed by this cataclysm. Rapids in the Semliki have been sufficient to prevent the return of fish that could otherwise come upriver from Lake Albert. Crocodiles are held back by a much more tenuous barrier. They can walk well enough overland to bypass any of the waterfalls, but they greatly dislike dense forest. Both banks of the Semliki are clothed in such forest near the Beni Rapids, below which crocodiles abound. Were the forest cleared, the reptiles might well find their way past the rapids and return to Lake Edward—probably to the detriment of fish and other life in it.

BIG GAME ON THE SAVANNAS

On both sides of the Nile for many miles, in the Semliki Valley and in neighboring parts of the Rift Valley and eastern

Left: The African spoonbill (Platalea alba) has sharp serrations inside the flattened bill tip that help it to catch slippery prey in shallow water. (Julius Behnke)

Facing page, above left: Yellow-billed storks (Ibis ibis), black-winged stilts and a sacred ibis. Such groups of spectacular water birds are common around lakes in the Nile basin. (Julius Behnke) Right: A pair of crowned cranes (Balearica pavonina), a familiar bird in the Nile basin and East Africa. (Byron Crader) Below: Crocodiles formerly abounded but are now rarer. Despite the legend, birds do not pick the reptile's teeth when it is basking with its mouth open. (Byron Crader)

Congo, there is superb big-game country. Although fewer species occur here than in grassland to the east and south, these savannas probably support a greater biomass—the weight of living animals in a given area—than anywhere else in the world. Two facts account for this. First, this is a high rainfall area with lush growth. Second, a large proportion of the total population of wild animals is made up of very large species, such as elephants, buffalos, and hippos. The last, although aquatic, are land animals when it comes to feeding; they graze up to three or four miles away from river verges.

An average adult elephant may weigh four tons, a hippo two to three tons, and a buffalo one ton. Comparing these great beasts with small antelopes such as the hartebeest, which weighs about three to four hundred pounds, one elephant represents the biomass of twenty-five hartebeest—a fair-sized herd. Likewise a herd of fifteen kob antelopes equals only one bull buffalo, and a herd of a hundred buffalos would equal about twelve hundred kobs. It is the predominance of big animals in the fauna that explains the extent of the biomass in these regions. Conversely one might say that, if the grassland were less lush, these great herds of huge creatures could not survive.

In certain parts of these savannas counts have shown that a square mile supports more than a hundred thousand pounds of living animals. This is over twice the biomass of the apparently multitudinous populations of wildebeest, zebras, hartebeest and gazelles in places like the Serengeti Plains. Again, in the Murchison and Queen Elizabeth National Park of western Uganda, one may see fewer individual animals in a day than in the Nairobi National Park. But if the big herds of elephants and buffalos that graze on the plains were added to the hippos in the Nile and together converted, in terms of, say, the number of medium-sized antelopes which reach an equivalent biomass, it would be found that the number of antelopes would far surpass the greatest wildlife spectacles farther east.

Nor is the number of medium-sized animals negligible. Jackson's hartebeest, the topi, waterbuck, and Uganda kob are all numerous in parts of these savannas, and they provide a splendid spectacle in their own right. Up to two thousand topis may be seen together. The waterbucks of the Queen Elizabeth National Park are the finest in Africa—huge reddish animals with very long horns. They are so different in size and color from some other waterbucks that one could be forgiven for regarding them as a separate species. But there are intermediate linking populations which show clearly that they are indeed the same animals as the comparatively small, short-horned gray waterbuck to be found farther to the west and to the north.

Left: A favored drinking place attracts a wonderful assembly of animals and birds: elephants, pelicans and open-bill storks (Anastomus lamelligerus). (Alan Root) Right: A bull elephant shows considerable agility as, accompanied by cattle egrets, he leaves an aquatic feeding ground. (Uganda Ministry of Information)

Overleaf: Elephants, more numerous in the Nile basin than anywhere else, have a profound effect on the whole ecology of the region; here they feed largely on grass. (F. G. H. Allen)

A RAPIDLY CHANGING LANDSCAPE

In Uganda, both the Murchison and Queen Elizabeth Park owe their existence to epidemics of human sleeping sickness that swept Uganda in the early years of this century. The areas were at one time inhabited, but so severe was the disease that the human population had to be moved to other areas. They became game reserves and then national parks, and the population of large animals in them steadily increased.

There are now about 9,000 elephants, 8,000 hippos, and 10,000 buffalos in the Murchison Falls Park. Corresponding figures for the smaller Queen Elizabeth Park are 2,500, 12,000, and 12,000. It would not surprise me in the least to learn that all these figures were underestimates. The great herds of animals, fostered by protection, and increasingly unable to migrate out of the park because of human occupation on the boundaries, are rapidly altering the savannas they live on.

Elephants have almost destroyed tree growth over vast areas, not only in the Murchison Park, but in adjacent areas along the right bank of the Albert Nile. As this is an area of high rainfall the grass grows tall and lush when the trees are destroyed. The single-season rainfall, with a long dry season, results inevitably in very fierce fires. When such fierce annual fires sweep the country, young trees cannot grow to replace those destroyed by elephants. The whole countryside is being changed from fairly dense woodland to open, tall grassland. Even quite large forest trees do not escape. They are ring-barked either when the bark is torn off for food, or simply by elephants that use them for scratching themselves. With the increasing absence of trees, elephants have now been reduced to scratching themselves on the tall termite hills that dot the plains, which they thus shape into regular cones.

Elephants can feed on grass, and in these areas they have become almost entirely grass eaters. The fact, however, that an elephant's skeleton is very heavy, and that the tusks alone

Old bull buffalos (Syncerus caffer) have a reputation for savagery but like nothing better than a peaceful wallow in mud. (C. A. Spinage)

of a mature bull from this area often weigh between two to three hundred pounds, suggests an enigma. For its formation a mass of bone and ivory requires great quantities of calcium. It is possible that elephants formerly obtained this essential element from the bark of trees—which they have now destroyed. It remains to be seen whether the elephants can satisfy their needs equally well from grass, or whether, for lack of calcium in their diet, they will in time degenerate.

Buffalos, and smaller grazing animals like waterbucks, hartebeest and kobs, should benefit from the elephants' work. On the shores of the Nile and the lakes the voraciously grazing hippo so reduces the overall growth of grass that some bush species can survive fires and grow. The tops of these shrubs are browsed by elephants, so that a thicket six or eight feet tall is produced. Elephants and the hippos between them produce an environment which shelters a fair number of black rhinos, but only on the right bank of the Nile. The rhinos cannot cross the rushing river.

The end result of all these interacting factors is not yet in sight. But it seems quite certain that when an equilibrium between the animal populations and the vegetation they eat has been achieved, both the landscape and the population of animals that inhabit it will be quite different from what they were fifty years ago. The pity is that no one earlier this century recorded the numbers of various species of animals in these savannas.

A HELPLESS RELIC—THE WHITE RHINOCEROS

Grazing animals predominate throughout this area. There are few browsers other than elephants, which have been forced by their own activities to become grazers. Giraffes and the black rhinoceros are scarce, and typical browsers like kudus or impala are absent. Roan antelopes inhabit the drier savannas farther north, and are also grazers, as are waterbucks, kobs, and two races of *Damaliscus korrigum,* the topi and tiang.

On the left bank of the Nile is an isolated population of square-lipped or white rhinoceroses. They are not in fact white, but dark gray; the name is a corruption of the Afrikaans word *weit,* meaning broad, referring to the beast's huge square muzzle. This race of the white rhinoceros *(Ceratotherium simum cottoni)* is isolated from its nearest relatives in South Africa by over two thousand miles. Its situation is similar to that of the lechwe of the Nile swamps; like the lechwe it is found only on the left bank of the Nile. It too is a grazer, not a browser like the black rhinoceros.

At one time there must have been white rhinoceroses all the way from Natal to the Sudan. Even then the Nile, or perhaps the great lakes, must have prevented any eastward spread by these rhinos. The northern population may perhaps have been isolated from the southern when the equatorial forest extended much farther east, as it did in the pluvial periods that corresponded here with northern ice ages. The two races can only be distinguished from one another by certain details in the skull and teeth; superficially they are scarcely distinguishable.

The white rhino is the third largest land mammal in Africa, slightly smaller than a hippo, and almost twice the weight of its cousin the black rhino. It is a much more massive animal and, unlike the black rhino, is quite inoffensive. Indeed, on close acquaintance it seems so helpless and confused that one feels inclined to comfort this huge pachyderm. It can scarcely see, and depends for protection on its size, horns, and sense of smell. One that I watched, a huge bull, meandered to within ten yards of me before he realized that there was some unusual object in the shade where he had intended to lie down. Then he withdrew, and I could plainly perceive the bewilderment and fear on his grotesque visage.

There are less than a thousand white rhinos now on the left bank of the Nile, which hitherto has proved an impassable barrier to them. Some, therefore, have been transferred to Murchison Park, an addition to the big grazing animals already there. They ought to thrive, but since they calve only once every 2½ to 3 years, building up a healthy population will be a long slow process, and in the meantime they may become extinct in their original range. Like other rhinos they are persecuted for the sake of their horns, which are believed by eastern peoples to have aphrodisiac powers. Despite their size, they are utterly helpless against a skilled poacher armed with a rifle or poisoned arrows.

THE TERRITORIAL KOB

The Uganda kob *(Kobus kob thomasi)* is one of the most numerous grazing animals in the southern part of this area. It is the local representative of the typical kob of West Africa, and is found as far east as western Kenya, though there it is now almost extinct. It is a beautiful stocky red antelope, with fine horns in the males, and can leap almost as well as an impala.

The kob exhibits most remarkable territorial behavior, and studies of it have stimulated much research into this aspect of the behavior of other antelopes. Male kobs gather at specific places in open short grassland where they stand or lie about in a loose circle. Females due to mate enter the circle and usually select the most active male, but not necessarily the largest, among those assembled.

These territorial display grounds are an extraordinary sight. There are many of them in the Semliki Valley, some quite near main roads. The kobs lie about on the short grass, apparently inactive, each male well apart from his neighbor. The scene bears some resemblance to the communal display grounds of such birds as the blackcock *(Tetrao tetrix)* and the ruff *(Philomachus pugnax)*. These birds, however, differ from the kob in that the males display vigorously to the females, which the antelopes do not.

This territorial behavior in the kob appears to be dependent on density; that is to say, it occurs only where the animals are very common. Where kobs are relatively rare, individual males hold territories of greater size. The communal display grounds are not therefore vital to the survival of the kob as a species. Kobs are dying out in parts of their former range for reasons that are not entirely clear, and despite efforts to protect them.

In one way or another, the wild animals of this area, though perhaps less spectacular than the great mixed herds of the eastern grasslands, make the Nile basin no whit inferior in interest. And the great sheets of water and swampland add a unique habitat that is not found to the same extent elsewhere in Africa.

Apes, Pygmies and Peacocks

The Equatorial Forest

8

Africa contains a greater area of tropical rain forest than any other continent except South America. The forest spans three thousand miles from west to east and spreads almost one thousand miles from north to south in the Congo and Gabon. The area of the forests is estimated to be rather more than three million square miles, but this is an exaggerated figure because it includes some savannas. By far the major part is broad-leaved tropical forest situated in this one region, with its heart in an enormous block in the Congo drainage basin.

The Bight of Benin carves a huge slice out of the western half of Africa. If there were land where the sea is now, it would be forested; to the east of the bight the forest extends well south. But to the north the forest is comparatively narrow, extending at most two hundred miles from the coast. In Ghana and Togoland a tongue of savanna divides the forest and actually reaches the sea. The part to the west is known as the Upper Guinea Forest, and that to the east, as far as the Cameroon highlands, the Lower Guinea Forest. These divisions have some effect on the distribution of species.

The Cameroon highlands are a volcanic mass rising to thirteen thousand feet and dividing the Lower Guinea Forest from the great eastern block, with only rather narrow connections. There are thus really three divisions of this forest, the Upper Guinea, the Lower Guinea, and the Congo–Gabon heartland. But since all of these are really very similar in character, such divisions are chiefly for convenience. The whole region is dense tropical evergreen forest.

At one time, in the pluvial periods that corresponded to temperate ice ages, the forest extended very much farther east, north, and south than at present. It ran across the Rift Valley to East Africa and may in places have joined with forests typical of the coastlands of East Africa. It must have extended through southern Sudan to the edges of the Ethiopian highland block and on mountain ranges occurred at greater altitudes than today. In shrinking it has left behind islands and pockets of typical flora and fauna, but the region is still extensive enough to make it very difficult to cover in a single chapter.

THE SAVANNA BORDER

The borders of the forest and the savanna to the north, south, and east are still clearly defined in many places. Grass and the fire-resistant trees of savanna are found only a hundred yards away from forest giants. Each year the fire burns right up to the edge of the forest, but there it stops. In some areas, however, the savanna-forest boundary is less clearly defined.

The natural boundary between forest and savanna is a screen of low trees and dense shrubs which will not itself carry the fire, though each year such growth dies back from the heat of the flames and regenerates later. This belt of shrubs may be only ten yards wide, but it protects the edge of the forest itself. Its outer edge, composed of small shrubs and rather lush green grasses slows the attacking fire. Behind these are taller shrubs and small trees that are seldom scorched, and grow large enough to shade out potentially inflammable grasses. Behind these are still taller trees, and beyond them one is in the forest itself.

If it were not disturbed, this natural boundary would ebb and flow very slowly according to gradual changes in climate. It is a sharp dividing line between two forms of life: the one forest, with tall evergreen vegetation shading undershrubs but to all intents and purposes no grass; the other savanna, with a lush growth of grass and only small trees not a tenth of the bulk of the forest giants. On one side is sunlit, open woodland and breast-high green grass; on the other is deep, dim shade and an overwhelming mass of moist vegetation overhead. The contrast is from bright light to a dim coolness where a photographer's exposure meter will not register.

On its border with savanna, forest survives in many small isolated blocks where the soil is deeper and more suitable for large trees or in strips along river valleys. These areas are known as forest-savanna mosaic and, since savanna and forest species can come and go with ease between the two types of vegetation, they are a favored habitat of wild animals. In general it is the forest animals that take advantage of the open country, but waterbucks, for instance, often venture into small patches of forest.

In the absence of man little could affect the equilibrium on the savanna-forest boundary. Elephants can smash the protective screen of shrubs and so help the fire to creep into the edge of the forest itself. There are places where this can be seen happening and they look like wounds on a sensitive skin. But in recent years such destruction has been greatly accelerated by man. Remnant forest patches, especially in the forest-savanna mosaic, are being cut into at an alarming rate. When the forest is cut down it may be replaced within ten years by tall grass in what is called "derived savanna."

If man were kept out of recently "derived" savannas and these savannas were protected from fire, the forest would soon recolonize them. The conditions for forest growth have not been lost—only damaged. But it seems much more difficult to induce forest to colonize an area of old savanna. Even when fire is kept away from the boundary, forest will advance into savanna only by very slow degrees; it has to extend its protective band of shrubs first and colonize that rather than the open

The overwhelming mass of moist steamy vegetation near a forest waterfall. Creepers festoon the larger trees and make a continuous wall of growth. (Carl Frank)

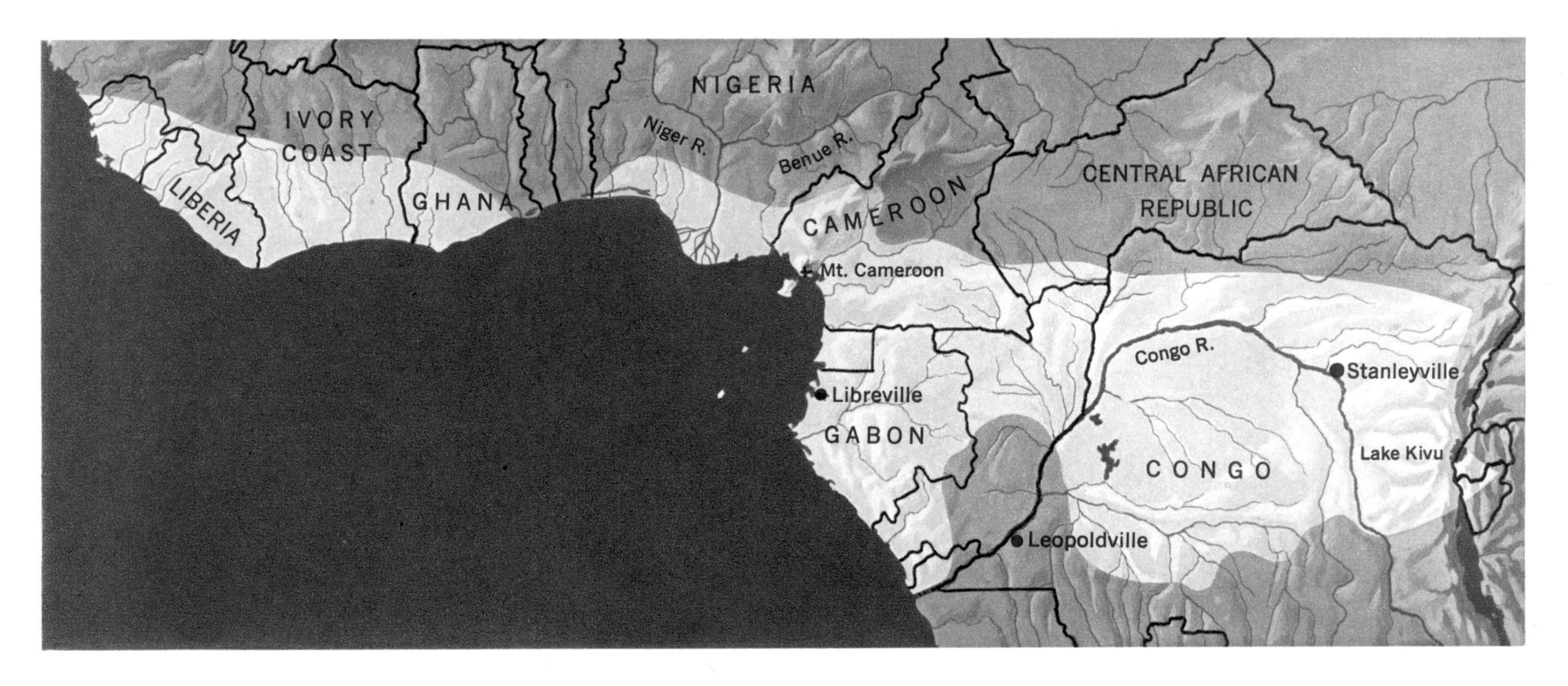

The equatorial forests, a huge block of tropical rain forest in the center of Africa, covers most of the Congo basin and the West African coastlands to Guinea.

grassland. Narrow though it is, the natural, fire-dominated boundary between forest and savanna evidently represents a very delicate balance. The savanna as the "aggressor" can more easily take advantage of any changes than can the forest, which is in slow retreat.

THE TROPICAL RAIN FOREST

The whole feel of a tropical forest is different from a temperate forest, however grand the trees of the latter may be. In temperate forests, broad-leaved or coniferous, the floor is shaded in summer by the leafage overhead. In coniferous forests the shade continues through winter, but a deciduous forest is open, the ground covered by dead leaves. Snow may cover the ground in both. In tropical forests deep shade is permanent, the temperature is always equable and the ground continuously moist. Conditions are ideal for rapid growth.

On the ground there is actually very little green vegetation. There is a layer of dead leaves, debris, and roots, with some moss and ferns, but this layer rots with surprising speed and is seldom as deep as the leaf mold of a temperate deciduous forest. The absorption of debris is accelerated by a great variety of living plants and animals, from rooting pigs and scratching squirrels and porcupines to termites, fungi and bacteria. One cannot see far in any direction between the stems of shrubs and the small trees, and the view is further obstructed by dead trunks bearing masses of ferns, moss, and creepers. At eye level there is a mass of shrubby foliage, and to see through it one must bend down. The bases of big creepers festooning the taller trees add further obstruction to passage. In some parts of the forest this shrubbery may be dense, in others relatively open, but it is seldom possible to see more than fifty yards in any direction.

Above the shrubs are small trees, forty to a hundred feet tall. These may be saplings of forest giants, but often they are species that never grow any bigger. They are known as the understory, and their chief value is as a nursery for the young of forest giants and as a feeding ground for animals and birds. Sometimes the understory is so thick that the true canopy can scarcely be seen above it.

Huge fluted trunks rear out of the understory. These are the bases of the crown or canopy trees, spaced at intervals of twenty to forty yards or more. The flutings of their boles spread into buttresses that writhe out over the forest floor some distance from the base of each trunk. These buttresses provide support for a massive tree that might otherwise stand insecure, with its permanently leafy crown always exposed to violent gusts of tropical winds. The lower limbs may be six feet thick, and each great trunk soars up a hundred feet or more before branching into a spreading crown. To view such a tree properly one must lie on one's back, and even then much of it may be invisible through the lower foliage.

Actually this description of three main layers of vegetation is too simplified. In each of the layers there are smaller and larger shrubs, saplings or canopy trees, so that in reality the forest consists of many layers of vegetation. The summit of one canopy tree may be a hundred feet above another, though both rear completely out of the understory. On the whole, however, any individual tree can be categorised under one of the three main types.

Tall rain forest of this type can be more than a little daunting to explore, and it is unwise to go far into it alone. Constant practice aids the development of the necessary bushcraft and sense of direction, but a beginner who strays more than fifty yards from a trail in flat forested country can quickly become lost. The equatorial forest is not to be trifled with.

Except for the oil palm (Eliaeis guineensis), tropical African jungles are generally poor in palm species. There are also wild date palms (Pheonix sp.) in such areas. (Carl Frank)

Above: Creeks and backwaters such as this afford the most convenient and silent way to approach the life of the forest. (Jean Macaigne)   Left: Duiker are the most numerous antelopes in such forests. Some, like this one, are gray and are no bigger than a hare. (Paul Popper)

Right above: Torrential tropical downpours run in streams from the foliage and form standing pools on the forest floor. (Paul Popper) Right: The caterpillar of a charaxes, one of the most typical of African butterflies. The markings on its body break its outline and assist in concealment. (E. S. Ross)

A full-grown male gorilla, rarely seen in the open, crosses a small patch of sedges, walking on the knuckles of the forelimbs and the soles of the hind limbs. Lowland gorillas have short hair. (Marcel Bonnotte)

Inside such a forest the light is dim and the atmosphere moist, windless and heavy. Far above, the soughing of wind can be heard in the crowns of great trees, but it is not felt among the bushes on the forest floor. The calls of invisible birds, the crash of a falling branch, the yell of a monkey or the shrilling of insects accentuate an impression of brooding silence. One feels inclined to tread carefully and quietly, testing each footstep. The general impression is one of awe. But knowledge will dispel this first feeling of vague apprehension, and to those who know it the rain forest is immensely fascinating and refreshing.

Tropical rain forests differ from temperate woodlands in their extraordinary variety. In tropical forests hardly two adjacent members of the crown species will be the same, though there are large areas where two or three species will be co-dominant. The understory is composed of different species from the crown and the shrubs of the floor are different again. Over all climb large creepers. Every high branch of a canopy tree bears masses of epiphytes, and huge rotting trunks obstruct passage on the floor and support a rich flora of moss and ferns. African mahoganies *(Khaya* and *Entandrophragma)* are common canopy trees, and oil palms *(Elaeis guineensis)* are very characteristic of lower levels.

The African tropical forest flora with perhaps twenty-five thousand species is not so rich as the South American with forty thousand. There are comparatively few species of palms, bamboos, aroids and orchids, while the masses of bromeliads (plants of the pineapple family) so characteristic of big tree branches in South America are altogether absent. Ecologists explain this by the supposition that in past times of great aridity the forest may have shrunk to very small areas in which only a limited number of plant species could survive. But there has always been some forest in Africa since the Mesozoic era, which ended about seventy million years ago.

Other forms of life are also abundant in these forests. There are perhaps fewer species of larger animals in the forest than outside it, but a few groups of antelopes are very well represented, while monkeys and apes are abundant. Some large animals never leave the forest, and rather few forest species are common to savanna as well. Smaller mammals include a good many species, such as the tree pangolin *(Uromanis longicaudata),* the potto *(Perodicticus potto),* or flying squirrels *(Anomalurus),* that occur nowhere else. Reptiles, amphibians, ants, butterflies and other insects and invertebrates are all richer in species inside than outside the forest.

Probably there are more birds in tropical forests than in any other ecological zone in Africa. But one cannot be certain of this because forest birds are often very difficult to see. Many skulking birds of the undergrowth are seldom noticed though they can be caught in mist nets, and the birds of the canopy can be heard but are usually seen only as dark blobs against the blue sky. I should not be surprised to learn that there were actually fewer birds per acre of forest than in some apparently unpromising environment such as semi-arid thornbush. Accurate estimates are difficult to make, for forest is not at all like, for instance, the East African grasslands, where everything is visible near ground level. The forest hides its secrets well.

AN INACCESSIBLE ABUNDANCE

Tropical forest is the highest expression of the basic formula describing soil, water, and plant relationships; it can only grow on deep free-draining soil in hot climates with at least fifty inches of rain a year, usually more. There must be some rain in any month of the year.

I do not suppose that anyone has ever weighed all the vegetation in an acre of tropical forest, but I am sure that it represents the greatest plant productivity anywhere on earth. One single small forest tree would weigh more than the ten to twenty tons of grass produced per acre by a tropical savanna. But unlike grassland the majority of this mass of vegetation is for two reasons inedible. First, most of it is hard wood; a healthy living tree protects itself even against the attacks of wood-boring insects. Secondly, it is nearly all more or less inaccessible to large, hoofed mammals, because it is out of reach standing twenty to two hundred feet above ground. For this reason no tropical forest supports anything like the number of hoofed mammals found in savanna.

I doubt if the entire annual growth of green vegetation in

The leopard is the largest forest predator, and one has even been known to kill an adult male gorilla. (Victor Borlandelli: Len Sirman Press)

an acre of forest would exceed the production of an acre of a tall grass such as elephant grass *(Pennisetum purpureum)*, which covers large areas near some African forest and can produce sixty to one hundred tons of edible green matter a year. Nevertheless, high above ground, trees and shrubs do produce a large amount of potential food, such as leaves, flowers and fruit, for herbivores. Naturally there are animals that can reach and make use of at least part of this elevated food supply; some of it, of course, falls to the ground and can be collected there.

In tropical forests, therefore, we must expect to find hardly any grazing animals unless they have access to savanna close by. Among the small and large browsers which feed on the leaves of shrubs and creepers close to the forest floor, are the elephant, buffalo, okapi, bongo, bushbuck and many kinds of duiker. There are numbers of expert climbers, such as gorillas, chimpanzees, monkeys and baboons, to make use of the leaves and fruits of the bigger trees. Finally there are giant forest hogs and bushpigs—grubbing or ground-feeding animals which consume fallen fruits and the tubers and roots of shrubs and creepers.

THE GREAT APES

Two great apes exist in African forests: the gorilla and the chimpanzee. The lowland gorilla *(Gorilla. g. gorilla)* occurs from southeastern Nigeria to the eastern Congo, and another race, *G. g. beringei*, inhabits certain montane forests. The chimpanzee *(Pan satyrus)* has a much wider range, from Sierra Leone in the west to Uganda in the east, and is able to survive in small forest pockets outside the main heartland. Some chimpanzees in Tanzania have even taken to a life in mixed savanna and forest. Neither gorillas nor chimpanzees are found in every area apparently suited to them. A pygmy chimpanzee sometimes regarded as a separate species, *Pan paniscus*, also occurs in a part of the Congo.

Great weight is a disadvantage in tree climbing; consequently gorillas live chiefly near the ground. A big male gorilla weighs four hundred pounds and seldom drags his bulk aloft despite his enormous strength and nine-foot reach. Female and young gorillas are more active, but cannot compare in agility with chimpanzees. The latter, which are much smaller and only a third of a gorilla's weight, climb into the tops of the highest trees and are marvellous to watch as they move about on great limbs more than a hundred feet up. On the ground both these apes progress on all fours, treading on the knuckles of their hands and the soles of their feet. Both can stand erect, but they do not walk about erect for long.

Gorillas have a quite unjustified reputation for savagery. Normally very shy and retiring, they will, if provoked, put on a fearsome demonstration, uttering frightful yells and beating their chests. But gorillas habitually beat their chests; the gesture is only used occasionally to threaten men. Tales of deliberate unprovoked attacks by gorillas are fables.

Apart from man, the only possible enemy of a gorilla is the leopard, yet it would be a bold leopard that tried conclusions with an irate male gorilla three times its weight—though this has been known to occur. Normally the two are mutually indifferent. But gorillas do fear snakes. And if gorillas were to restrict themselves to browsing in the depths of thick growth they would not come into contact with man at all. But sometimes they are said to raid cultivated places, where they can do great damage in a short time. Thus they arouse enmity.

Both these apes make nests to sleep in at night; chimpanzees and more rarely gorillas make day nests as well. Gorillas make a fresh nest each night, usually at the base of or low down in trees. Chimpanzees, more vulnerable to leopards, place their nests higher, from fifteen to thirty feet up, and, being cleaner than gorillas, will sometimes use the same nest for several nights. All this nest-making might seem to require much labor, but it takes only a few moments for a chimpanzee to bend and knit leafy branches together for a comfortable bed.

Like baboons, gorillas and chimpanzees often travel in troops—made up of an old male, several wives, and their young of various ages. Very old males become solitary. Infant gorillas and chimpanzees are born quite helpless and have to be carried about by their mothers for a long time. Observations on captive gorillas have shown that the mothers fondle and play with their babies very much the way human mothers do. The more one watches them the more human they seem.

The Tanzania chimpanzees that live in the savanna are more and more coming down out of the trees, and perhaps may be evolving toward an existence in the open, like baboons. Amongst their other food they sometimes kill and eat small or very young antelopes. They also like termites and will insert a stick into an active termite heap, draw it out when it is covered with termites, and lick off the insects with every evidence of enjoyment.

OTHER FOREST MONKEYS

Other forest monkeys range from small guenons *(Cercopithecus)* to large mangabeys *(Cercocebus)* and the long-haired, decorative colobus *(Colobus)*. Being smaller and lighter than chimpanzees, all of these are better climbers. They feed high up in the tallest trees—sometimes at an astonishing height. When they are alarmed they make a perilous passage, with a hundred-foot drop below, look easy. The colobus is an especially spectacular leaper, capable of clearing thirty feet.

Most monkeys feed upon fruit, especially wild figs. In the top of a big tree several species may congregate, and are sometimes difficult to distinguish from each other. Size is not a reliable guide; a young mangabey may be a good deal smaller than an old guenon. They can mostly be recognized by the length of their fur, their color, or the way they hold their tails.

The black and white colobus monkeys *(Colobus polykomos)* are absolutely unmistakable. They are widespread in forests from high mountains in East Africa to West Africa; a number of races are described according to the amount of white hair and other characters. In West Africa there is a jet-black colobus *(C. p. satanus)* locally held to be the devil's closest relative. The red colobus *(C. badius)* occurs in lower-lying forests.

Colobus are handsome, gentle, inoffensive creatures that feed on leaves. They may eat fruit as well, but they alone of forest monkeys do not worry man and his crops. But colobus monkeys, and especially the longhaired black and white East African and Ethiopian colobus, are hunted for their beautiful skins. Fortunately, in truly large forests, sharp-eyed monkeys can generally escape a man armed with anything but a high-powered rifle; and when hunted they quickly become shy.

Baboons are generally terrestrial animals of the savanna, but two species, the mandrill *(Papio sphinx)*, and the drill *(P. leucophaeus)* have adapted to forest life. They retain their terrestrial feeding habits, and live in troops. They inhabit the forest from the Cameroons to the Congo River but neither occurs on the left bank of the great stream. Little detail seems to be known about their habits in the wild state, but the mandrill is a favorite exhibit in zoos because of its extraordinary physical features. The center of the nose of the male mandrill is bright red, and the sides are fluted and bright blue. The drill has a black face and a red posterior. Such bright colors, common among baboons, may have a sexual function. The mandrill is probably the largest and most powerful of baboons, with relatively short hair and a solid muscular body. It is bigger than the olive baboons that also enter the edges of forests.

BROWSERS OF THE LOWER LEVELS

The animals that live on the forest floor are mostly browsers. The elephants that live in forests are smaller than the savanna elephants, and have small tusks and rounded ears. The buffalos are small red animals, very different from the great black beasts of East and South Africa. There are two unique, large browsing animals, the okapi *(Okapia johnstoni)* and the bongo *(Booceros euryceros)*, and there are a host of such smaller animals as bushbucks and duiker. In wet riverine forests the sitatunga *(Limnotragus spekei)* may be found, but it prefers to eat swamp grasses.

Okapi, retiring animals, living only in a small area in the depths of the Congo forest, are the nearest living relatives of giraffes. Very difficult to approach, they are very hard to study in the wild state. They do well in captivity, however, and in many zoos their beautiful plushlike dark-brown fur adorned with white stripes can be better appreciated than in the forest. No one knows how many okapi remain, but they are commoner than is often thought.

Some forest duiker are bright red. Their short horns, low forequarters and gait with the head hung low are probably adaptations to forest life. (Paul Popper)

The bongo sports the same broken color patterns as the okapi—dark red-brown with white stripes. Far more common and widespread than the okapi, it inhabits areas from Sierra Leone to Gabon and some mountain forests in Kenya. It is not found in every area suited to it and no one can say why. In some places it seems, like the okapi, to favor dense secondary growth—the tangled low forest that springs up after the big trees have been felled—but there is plenty of this sort of cover in Nigeria and Uganda, where it is unknown.

Bongos resemble eland in that both sexes have horns. They are large heavy animals but are nevertheless able to thread their way through dense growth in an almost miraculous manner. Their well-defined runs make them fairly easy to trap, but they are very difficult to see. They have one weakness—they are easily bayed by dogs. Courageous animals, they stand to defend themselves with their horns, thus allowing a hunter to approach without reacting. They run in small herds, and old bulls become solitary.

Neither bongos nor okapi are very numerous, and the commonest forest animals are the bushbuck and duiker. All these animals, probably originated from steppes or savannas, have colonized the forest and thrived there. For only one species of duiker that still lives in the savannas there are ten or twelve in the forest. They range from the large yellow-backed duiker, weighing 130 pounds, to the tiny Maxwell's duiker, weighing about ten pounds. Most are very difficult to watch, except at night, when they can—to their cost—be dazzled by a light. Only a few forest duiker emerge into savanna, and even there they are seldom far from dense cover. Yet I once saw a yellow-backed duiker, an animal one might seek fruitlessly for weeks in forest, out in the open on a burned stretch of the Niger flood plain.

One can often see forest antelopes by climbing an understory tree. Such a tree is the vantage point of the great forest eagle *(Stephanoaetus coronatus)*, which lives on monkeys and small antelopes.

A red river hog, the forest race of the widespread bushpig family. Bright orange red, with long ear tufts, it is one of the most handsome of wild pigs. (Paul Popper)

A PYGMY BUFFALO

In East and South Africa the buffalo *(Syncerus caffer)* is a huge black bovine weighing nearly a ton. But in the heartland of the Congo forest, the buffalo is a small, bright red, relatively slender animal weighing about six hundred pounds. Instead of the massive, wide-spreading horns of the Cape buffalo, these little red animals have short pointed horns running almost straight backward.

Forest buffalos look so different from those of the savanna that some call them dwarf buffalo *(Syncerus nanus)*. Yet between them and the great black beasts there is almost every form of intermediate variation, and it seems better to consider all as one highly variable species. In the wet West African savannas outside the forest there are buffalos that have larger and more massive horns, weigh about one thousand to twelve hundred pounds, and are sometimes black. Farther to the east, in the Congo savannas, there are black, brown or red buffalos described as marginal forest inhabitants. The buffalos of Queen Elizabeth Park in Uganda are large and black but their calves are reddish brown and some females are brown too.

The acid test of a species is whether it lives in the same area as a near relative without interbreeding. The large black buffalo and small red buffalo do not normally live in the same area so one cannot say whether they would interbreed or not. The little red buffalo would normally come into contact with one of the intermediate forms. Though pure herds of small red and intermediate black buffalos can be seen in some savannas, most herds on the forest-savanna boundary will contain both types.

Small as they are, the little red forest buffalos are as worthy of respect as their huge black relatives. Not normally dangerous, when wounded they retreat into thick cover where, if a hunter would follow, he must crawl; the animal may then charge with just as much determination as ever. Their little pointed horns are an unpleasantly sharp alternative to the widespread and crushing boss of a black savanna buffalo. Their calls, herd habits—everything about them but their color and size—is so similar to other buffalos that it is difficult to believe they are a separate species.

BUSHPIGS AND LEOPARDS

Two large species of wild pigs grub fallen fruits and dig up roots on the forest floor. They are the giant forest hog *(Hylochoerus meinertzhageni)*, discovered as recently as 1904 and also found in the montane forests, and the bushpig *(Potamochoerus porcus)*. Bushpigs are widespread, almost omnivorous animals and are found in every patch of thick bush in Africa; they are an appalling pest in farm areas. The West African race is often known as the red river hog, as it is bright orange-red, with long ear tufts. Bushpigs are found in small or large troops of up to a hundred or so and, though they are very common, are not often seen.

The only large predator of the forest, offering a serious threat to other animals, is the leopard. It is a very adaptable animal with a wide range in Africa and Asia, and is found in both

A young Congo gorilla, probably of the eastern or mountain race, which also occurs in lowland forests of the upper Congo basin. (Weldon King)

open bushland and forest. Solitary, cunning, and for its size immensely strong, a leopard can kill animals up to the size of a cow and is regarded as the chief killer of both baboons and bushpigs. As a result it is generally considered beneficial to man, though that does not stop people from hunting leopards for their beautiful skins.

I often wonder how many bushpigs a leopard kills, for they too are formidable animals. A full-grown male bushpig weighs two hundred pounds and is armed with sharp tusks. Once on hands and knees I encountered a huge red river hog boar in a tunnel in thick riverine bush; I was much relieved when at a range of two or three yards he decided that I was more dangerous than he. I believe such an animal would be a match for a leopard. Yet in areas where leopards are hunted out of existence, bushpigs, like baboons, seem to become more common and therefore more of a nuisance to man. Perhaps leopards kill young bushpigs when they can catch them unawares, or perhaps bushpigs are more cowardly creatures than I suppose. But I believe that forest leopards prey most on smaller animals, such as large rodents that feed on the forest floor at night, and even birds. I have often seen deep scratches about an inch apart on the trunks of trees, the claw marks of a leopard that has climbed after prey.

Leopards climb trees to rest on large limbs or to lie in wait for prey; there they also catch roosting monkeys at night. The fearful outcry of monkeys frequently betrays the nearby presence of a leopard. Although they are fairly common, leopards are so secretive that they are very seldom seen except on roads in the headlights of cars. I have known one to lie till I was within six feet of it before it moved away, and since then I have wondered how often I have been scrutinized by a leopard of whose presence I had no inkling.

COLOR AND SIZE IN FOREST ANIMALS

Some forest leopards are black, sharing a common tendency towards darker color among animals and birds that live in wet climates. This may take two forms. Either all the individuals of a species are rather dark, or there may be a higher than normal proportion of black mutants in the population. This latter seems to be true of several forest cats, and in the Augur buzzard *(Buteo rufofuscus)* black individuals are commoner in wet forested areas than in dry open country.

A bright red color may also be an adaptation to forest life. Small forest buffalos are bright red, their savanna counterparts black. Bushpigs and bushbucks are bright red in western forests, darker brown or black in relatively dry country further east. The bushbucks that live in the cold wet Ethiopian Highlands are the blackest of all, while those that live in the tropical forest are the reddest. Men who live in hot dry African steppes are darker skinned than those that live in moist tropical forests. The advantage of a red color in forest life is difficult to understand, for it makes all animals much more conspicuous than if they were black or dark brown.

The relation of melanism and erythrism to a forest environment may be difficult to understand, but the prevalence of pygmy forms is easier. Anyone who has worked his way through a dense tangle of creepers will appreciate what an advantage it is to be small. Forest elephants, buffalos, bushbucks, and human inhabitants of a forest are all smaller as a rule than their counterparts in open country. True pygmy species, however, are pretty rare. The small elephant and buffalo have been called pygmies, but there are intermediate forms connecting them to the larger open-country animals. And the pygmy men of the Ituri forest interbreed with tribes of ordinary size. A true pygmy species is one which lives in the same areas as a similar but much larger form, without interbreeding. On this basis elephants, buffalos, pygmy chimpanzees and men are all excluded and there is only one true pygmy in the whole of this forest—the pygmy hippopotamus *(Choeropsis liberiensis)*. Only a tenth of the weight of a normal hippo, it is often found near the same rivers.

Pygmy hippos are found only in the densest parts of the Guinea forests. Strangely enough, they do not occur in the Congo heartland, though this is the home of most species peculiar to forests. They have been recorded in the Niger delta, but their chief haunt is from Liberia to the Ivory Coast. They are less truly aquatic than the ordinary hippo, have their eyes placed lower on the head, and are less able to submerge for long periods. They tend to frequent the dense bush of river banks, behaving rather like an aquatic sort of pig. They live in pairs, not in herds, and are nocturnal.

FOREST WATERS

In most parts of the forest there are many small streams, and at intervals far from streams, small shallow pools. Some writers describe these as dew ponds, but since there is very little dew, as opposed to drip, on the forest floor this premise seems illogical. They consist of little hollows filled with water replenished by rain, and often made more watertight by the wallowing of elephants and buffalos. A few forest animals come to drink at them and leave tracks, but many do not need much water for they get it from succulent vegetation.

There are areas of forest without much water. On deep free-draining sandy soils there are places where, in the dry season, surface water is very hard to find. The Benin sands of Nigeria are so porous that a torrential downpour at the rate of six inches an hour sinks straight in. The ground surface is dry again within a few minutes of the rain's ceasing, and there are hardly any pools inside the forest in this area. The Benin sands may almost be described as a sedimentary rock rather than a soil. Water accumulates in them and emerges only at a layer of true rock two or three hundred feet below the surface. From here it gushes out in many clear springs and streams. In forests of this region one may suddenly come upon a crystal-clear river, running bank-high every day of the year, never flooding, and ten feet deep. To bathe in such streams is a glorious refreshment, but the acidity of the water keeps them free of all but a few fish.

In such environments lives the water chevrotain *(Hyemoschus aquaticus)*, a member of the family Tragulidae which also has representatives in Asia. Anatomically a link between pigs and ruminants, it has well-developed canine teeth in the male, and is red with white spots and stripes. It occurs from Sierra Leone to the Congo and is probably less rare than is supposed. An animal sometimes confused with it but not closely related is the tiny royal antelope *(Neotragus pygmaeus)*, the smallest of all ruminants. When disturbed this little animal, the size of a rabbit, disappears at astonishing speed in ten-foot bounds.

Much forest occurs on high ground, and the rivers draining it usually flow strong and clear. They rise in highland springs and swamps, and rush through steep gorges in turbulent rapids full of white water. Reaching flatter lowlands they slow down, and often grow deep and sluggish. Forest rivers fluctuate far less than rivers that drain open grasslands or subdeserts, because the forest forms an efficient protection from erosion in the catchment. Most rain sinks in and then seeps out slowly, even in such areas as the Cameroons where the rainfall averages an inch a day. In deep forest soils protected by leaf litter, the rain never beats on naked earth, and so water is stored at depth and is pumped out by the trees. Though there are seldom sudden floods, forest rivers swell and spread out over flood plains in the rainy season.

The major part of this forest region is drained by one huge river—the Congo. It draws its water from the Cameroon highlands in the west and from the mountains west of the Great Rift Valley to the east. Tributaries flow into it from the savannas to the north and the south, some rising in the highlands of Rhodesia and Angola. They all combine to produce a flow second only to that of the Amazon.

Several African rivers rush down from highlands, flow slowly over an elevated plateau, and later descend from this in waterfalls and rapids. On the plateau, inundation zones occur where the channel cannot drain the water quickly enough so that it spreads out in swamps. The Congo is somewhat different in that most of its valley is a broad shallow basin from which it eventually escapes, quite close to the coast, in a series of tremendous rapids. There are extensive areas of swamps and shallow lakes in this basin, superficially

The vervet monkey, commonest of all African species, is found in forest and woodland alike; here one is in a tangle of palm fronds. (Emil Schulthess)

rather like the inundation zones of other rivers but of different origin. They include the permanently flooded areas around Lake Leopold II and Tumba. Forest that grows in riverine swamps of this nature must be able to survive in poor drainage. Certain tall trees make a special type of aquatic forest, and there is often a tangle of raphia palms and wild canes difficult to penetrate. Here live the sitatunga and the red river hog.

It is very difficult to explore such swamps on foot. It is best to do so in a dugout canoe; as the tree branches sweep the water surface, one must duck and creep beneath them. After a passage through such a tunnel of dense growth it is always a relief to come out into an open backwater. Forest backwaters are usually still and beautiful pools in an old oxbow of the river's course and surrounded by long bright green grass. There may be hippos here and, as one works along the edge, lovely shining blue kingfishers *(Alcedo quadribrachys)* fly like cobalt streaks from stem to stem. There will also be miniature malachite kingfishers *(Corythornis cristata)*, sometimes large pied kingfishers *(Ceryle rudis)*, and the giant kingfishers *(Megaceryle maxima)*. These are fish-eaters, but in the forest there are kingfishers that have given up an aquatic life and have become insect-eaters, such as the blue-breasted kingfisher *(Halcyon malimbicus)*. Unlike the kingfishers that breed in earth banks these breed in holes in trees or in tree-termite nests. Along these lagoons one can see four or five different species of kingfishers of which some occur only in the forests; nowhere on earth can one see a greater variety of these beautiful birds.

LUNGFISH, CATFISH AND FISH EAGLES

In these African rivers no fish run from the sea to the source, but most of the rivers do have migratory fish. The genus *Barbus* is usually migratory and swims upriver with the rains till stopped by a waterfall. At the foot of such a fall, or at rapids, the fish can be seen jumping like salmon, and they can be caught easily. Stimulated by the rising water, the runs of migratory fish take place in the rains. Some breed on the flood plains or in the small river creeks that flow only in the rains but that provide good nurseries for fry.

Some species of fish live in flood plains or swamps most of the time. Here they survive drought in small pools or in backwaters, and some even become dormant in mud. Among these are the lungfish *(Protopterus* and *Polypterus)*—very primitive fishes that are virtually living fossils, related to the marine coelacanth and to the Rhipidistian fishes that emerged from the water to become the ancestors of all terrestrial vertebrates. Lungfish occur in Australia and South America as well as in Africa, and are a group that has led some scientists to believe that at one time the three continents were all connected. They have a form of lung derived from the air-bladder possessed by all fish, and can progress for a short distance on land. In dry areas they aestivate in mud; *Protopterus* makes a sort of cocoon, and when rain comes again they emerge, feed, and breed. In rivers like the Congo, however, they hardly ever need to aestivate, since the flow is perennially high.

Some, but not all, catfish of these rivers can also breathe air, but less efficiently than the lungfish and, unlike lungfish, they cannot aestivate in mud. Catfish can surface, take a gulp of air, and absorb the oxygen into the bloodstream while they are underwater. They have gills as well, and are not therefore wholly dependent on their "lungs."

Both lungfish and catfish are carnivorous and feed upon other fish, or even on young birds. Catfish are in the habit of visiting gill nets in which valuable food fish have been caught, and sometimes when the fisherman raises his net all he finds are remnants half bitten away. Lungfish have bony plates in their jaws which enable them to crush or chew their food. Catfish on the other hand have enormous mouths in which they simply engulf their prey.

Fish that come to the surface to breathe are vulnerable to aerial predators. The chief predator is the African fish eagle *(Haliaetus vocifer)*, a bird well known on all African waterways and lakes. Their snow-white heads and necks make them conspicuous as they perch on tall trees, and in flight they are impressive with broad dark wings. They will feed on dead fish when they can find them, but often take large live fish as well.

Their method of hunting is to make short sorties from their point of vantage, often seeming to fly straight to their prey; actually they have been guided by the slight ripple made by a catfish or lungfish, as it surfaces in order to breathe. Like the leopard, the fish eagle is carnivorous and can be considered beneficial to man. Even if it lived exclusively on valuable food fishes it could not seriously affect fishing interests. In one area it has been calculated that the local fish eagles ate the equivalent of 0.4 per cent of the annual catch by fishermen, and that was probably an over-estimate.

The fish eagle is sometimes confused with the palm nut vulture *(Gypohierax angolensis)*, which also has a white head. The latter is, however, much smaller and looks quite different in flight. It feeds principally on the fruits of the oil palm *(Elaeis guineensis)*, with which its range more or less coincides. It can also catch small fish on the surface and in the few places where there are no oil palms it eats freshwater crabs.

Crabs are also one of the main foods of the clawless otter *(Aonyx capensis* and several other species) that live in these rivers. They live outside the forests too, and along all big rivers in Africa they can sometimes be seen sitting upright on a sandbar or on a rock, holding a mussel or a crab in their paws and eating it as a man eats a slice of watermelon. Their droppings on rocks demonstrate that they live chiefly on crabs, and since they do not catch slippery fish they can do without claws.

SNORING OWLS, HORNBILLS, BAT HAWKS AND PEACOCKS

The fish of these forest rivers do not escape being preyed upon even by night. Pel's fishing owl *(Scotopelia peli)* is quite common along the flood plains of forest rivers, though it is very seldom seen. It is usually invisible by day, hiding in some dark tree overhanging the water, but at night it emits a loud, humming, snoring sort of call. This sound can sometimes be mistaken for the call of a leopard, but the owl also gives a loud hoot, ending in a terrifying wail. It feeds on fish and on frogs, occurs in pairs, and breeds in holes or other birds' nests.

On a river bank, or along a roadside, the forest generally presents an impenetrable green wall. Exposure to extra light

A young chimpanzee. Chimpanzees are more agile, noisy, and excitable than gorillas. They climb trees easily, but will descend to the ground to escape danger. (Pierre A. Pittet)

and air makes for an exuberant growth of creepers that form a dense screen. But the large crown canopy trees protrude above this screen, and one can see best what goes on in their tops from a river. Big forest hornbills and touracos are among the birds that can be seen in this way while in early morning and evening parrots fly over, screeching. Several African forest hornbills are very large, notably the wattled hornbill *(Ceratogymna atrata)* and some of the genus *Bycanistes*. These great black and white birds attract attention by their braying calls as they feed high up in trees, and when they fly from tree to tree their wings make a loud soughing sound.

Some of these big forest hornbills have very long nesting cycles. The female walls herself into a hole and stays there till the young are fully mature. The male must feed his mate and young for about six months, and must work very hard. He is able to get enough food because there is always a plant fruiting somewhere in the forest. There are no seasons of abundance followed by long droughts such as would force these big birds to cut short their breeding seasons.

Among some of the smaller forest hornbills of the genus *Tockus*, however, the female comes out of her stronghold before the young are full-grown. In this way they resemble hornbills that live in savanna and thornbush. One may conclude that the large hornbill's habit of walling up the females for the whole season, which probably helps to avoid predators, can succeed only in a forest environment where food is plentiful for long periods.

Touracos are relatives of the hornbills though they do not look much like them. Usually green with some white and red markings, they are the most beautiful of all the bigger birds of the forest. They go about in noisy groups, and hop over branches with extraordinary agility. They are fruit-eaters, and make flimsy nests high up in trees. The largest of them, the great blue touraco *(Corythaeola cristata)* is very common in all these western forests, yet it has been little studied.

At evening thousands of bats come out to fly over the river. They are relentlessly pursued by the bat hawk *(Machaerhamphus alcinus)*, a highly specialized kite that feeds almost exclusively on bats. Though it sometimes flies about by day it does all its hunting in about half an hour each evening. It needs a clear open space against which to sight bats, and a still river pool or backwater is ideal for this purpose. Bat hawks often live in towns, where bats are abundant, and they will then hunt over an open lawn or even a railway station platform. But they never look so formidable as when hunting bats and swallows over a tropical river at dusk.

The birds of the forest canopy are chiefly strong fliers with extensive ranges. Even among these there are some that are confined to the Upper Guinea forest, while others do not occur west of the Cameroons; they will not readily cross a ten-mile stretch of savanna. Some of the more local and remarkable forest birds are strictly inhabitants of the heart of deep rain forests. Let us look more closely at a few of the most interesting.

Most African game birds are either francolins or guineafowl. There are many species, and some are found in forests where they are exceedingly difficult to see. Forest francolins and guineafowl are, however, members of a group common in every type of country in tropical Africa. The Congo peacock *(Afropavo congensis)* is quite different from these.

This bird is the only representative of the large tribe of pheasants and peafowl common and widespread on the Asian mainland and islands. Its existence was deduced by the late Dr. J. P. Chapin, of the American Museum of Natural History, from feathers and old, incorrectly mounted museum specimens. He finally found the bird in 1937 in the deep forest of the Congo heartland. There it is not uncommon, but is heard more often than seen; its nest has never been found. It was one of the last major ornithological discoveries in Africa. What is remarkable about it is that it is separated by about four thousand miles of savanna or desert from any of its near relatives. Its presence in the Congo heartland proves that forest must have existed there for a very long time indeed, and that at one time it must have covered a very much larger area.

The bare-headed rock fowl *(Picathartes)* are extraordinary ground birds with bald heads of various colors. There are two species, one found in the Cameroons *(P. oreas)* and the other in Upper Guinea *(P. gymnocephalus)*. They too may be survivors from some remote, ancient Asian invasion, for they bear resemblance to some eastern genera. They breed under rocky overhangs, making a mud nest adorned with moss and lined with fiber.

The tree pangolin (Manis tricuspis) is one of many unusual animals found only in forests. Pangolins live chiefly on ants, but also eat termites. (C. A. W. Guggisberg)

ARMIES OF DRIVER ANTS

Although many of the forest birds are very difficult to see, a hunting army of driver ants will often bring them out. Driver ants are not confined to forests, but they are most common within them and are not found in very dry country. They are most active at night and in the rains. When they are on the move every living thing, including elephants, gives way before them.

They are usually seen marching in a long column about an inch wide. Close examination of this column will show that in its center are small individuals, traveling rapidly along, some carrying eggs. The outside of the column is guarded by inch-long soldiers with formidable pincers. If an obstacle is encountered in the line of march the ants instantly swarm all over it, biting viciously. Such columns are engaged in moving from nest to nest. When hunting in earnest the ants spread out over a wider area and devour whatever they can catch. Anything that cannot escape by flying or crawling is killed and carried away if small enough, or eaten alive if too large. Marching armies of driver ants can drive human beings out of their homes, and can only be diverted by hot ashes, or one of the potent modern insecticides.

The okapi (Okapia johnstoni), a unique giraffe-like animal of the deepest Congo forests, is commoner than is generally supposed. (Weldon King)

Parties of insectivorous birds follow the ants and snap up insects that emerge from hiding to escape the ants. Such bird parties are common in the forests, and are well enough known to Africans to have names, such as *"ejak"* in the Cameroons. A typical assembly would consist of a flycatcher or two, some shrikes, forest bulbuls, thrushes, barbets, and even one or two small hornbills.

When forcing my way through dense undergrowth I have once or twice had the misfortune to be badly bitten by driver ants. Once the attacks lasted intermittently for about half an hour and at the end of that time I felt ill, with a bad headache. I have always been careful to avoid a repetition of this experience and have since given these ants a wide berth. Young animals and small birds must suffer miserable deaths from such attacks, and one can well imagine that elephants could

Forest elephants are smaller, slighter, and have rounder ears and smaller tusks than their plains cousins; these are adaptations to existence in dense vegetation. (Henri Goldstein)

be driven mad with irritation should driver ants get into their trunks. Even after one has pulled off the bodies of these ants, their heads, jaws locked, will still remain attached to the flesh.

The male driver ant is an inoffensive looking insect known as the sausage fly, with a body half an inch to an inch long, rather like a fattish wasp. It flies at night and is attracted to lights. The queen is a grotesquely stout creature, seldom seen and jealously guarded by the ferocious soldiers.

MAMBAS AND VIPERS

Some forest snakes are extremely active and can climb to the tops of the highest trees. These include mambas, the most feared snakes in Africa, whose potent nerve venom induces unconsciousness and death in a few minutes. But mambas cannot really travel as fast as has sometimes been related, and are shy unless cornered. *Boiga blandingi,* a back-fanged snake, is another expert climber. It can reach colonies of weaver birds' nests suspended from the tips of branches a hundred feet from the ground and calmly eat the contents.

It is quite easy to understand how snakes reach the top of a creeper-covered tree, but even when the bole is relatively smooth a snake can often climb an almost vertical trunk with the help of rough places and fissures in the bark. The snakes are then exposed to attack by several birds, of which the most interesting is the Congo serpent eagle *(Dryotriorchis spectabilis).* It is a member of a group that normally inhabits open country, but with its very large eyes, this eagle is equipped for living in forest. It eats chameleons as well as snakes.

Neither this nor any other bird appears to attack the large vipers of the forest floor. The Gabon viper *(Bitis gabonica)* is widespread, and is the largest and most horrific of vipers. A large one measures six feet long and is as thick as a man's calf, with a triangular head armed with fangs over an inch long. When it strikes, it injects an enormous dose of highly virulent poison containing both blood and nerve toxins. A bite from a Gabon viper is likely to prove fatal to man unless serum is injected at once. Fortunately Gabon vipers are so sluggish that they are very reluctant to bite. In the open they have a bizarre and brilliant pattern of oblongs and zigzags, but are scarcely visible among the dead leaves of the forest floor.

The rhinoceros horned viper *(Bitis nasicornis)* is smaller but also secretes a very virulent venom. Why these snakes should require such deadly poison to kill the rodents and other small forest mammals on which they feed is something of a mystery. Normally when a viper strikes it lets go at once, the prey runs away, and the viper follows the trail slowly by scent, flicking out its tongue at intervals. The Gabon viper, however, retains its hold on the prey once it has struck, and perhaps the huge dose of virulent venom stills the victim's struggles almost at once.

MAN AND THE FOREST

The forest is in slow retreat before the forces of nature. Arguments are tossed to and fro as to whether Africa is slowly drying up, but there can be little doubt that the continent has grown drier in the last two thousand years, since elephants are known to have wandered in the neighborhood of ancient Carthage. This is only a very short time, geologically speaking, and it is only in the last fifty years or so that any part of the forest has been studied by scientists. Some recent evidence seems to show that in the forest-savanna mosaic of Nigeria the dry seasons are getting longer and more severe. Here, on the edge of the Togoland gap, is just where one would expect such an effect to show the most.

Vast areas of the forest are inhabited by man, and more of these areas are cleared for cultivation every year. On the boundary with savanna this permits the grassland to creep into what was once forest and, through fire, to prevent its revival. Other areas far inside the forest consist of secondary growth—the large trees all gone, and a tangle of vines and shrubs blocking the passage where one could once walk upright. In the very high rainfall of some forest areas this process inevitably leads to abandonment of the area by cultivating man, for the nutrients so slowly concentrated above ground by the large trees are washed quickly down through deep sandy soils, into the rivers, and away.

But immense areas of forest still stand in all their pristine magnificence. Some men will look upon these as good farming land that might yield subsistence for a year or two if the trees were cut down and burned. Others will look upon them as a source of commercial timber to be ravaged and left for a period before it is worth ravaging again. Yet there will be some who appreciate that these forests are among the richest and most fascinating tapestries in all the world of nature.

An Animal Paradise

The East African Grasslands

9

Let us follow for a while the trail of the travelers who walked inland from the East African coast at the end of the last century, before the Uganda railway was built. Having traversed a formidable barrier of thornbush known as the nyika (described in the next chapter) they gradually came to more pleasant areas. As they went inland they mounted an almost imperceptible incline in the great plain on which the nyika lies. The days became a shade less hot, the nights cooler and crisper. Isolated rocky mountains, some of them forming considerable ranges and giving rise to permanent rivers, as at

Right: Masai giraffe. The puffs of dust indicate that each stride in its gallop is about ten feet long. (E. S. Ross) Below: A secretary bird in grasslands performs the function of a terrestrial eagle. It nests on top of low but almost impregnable thorntrees. (Clem Haagner)

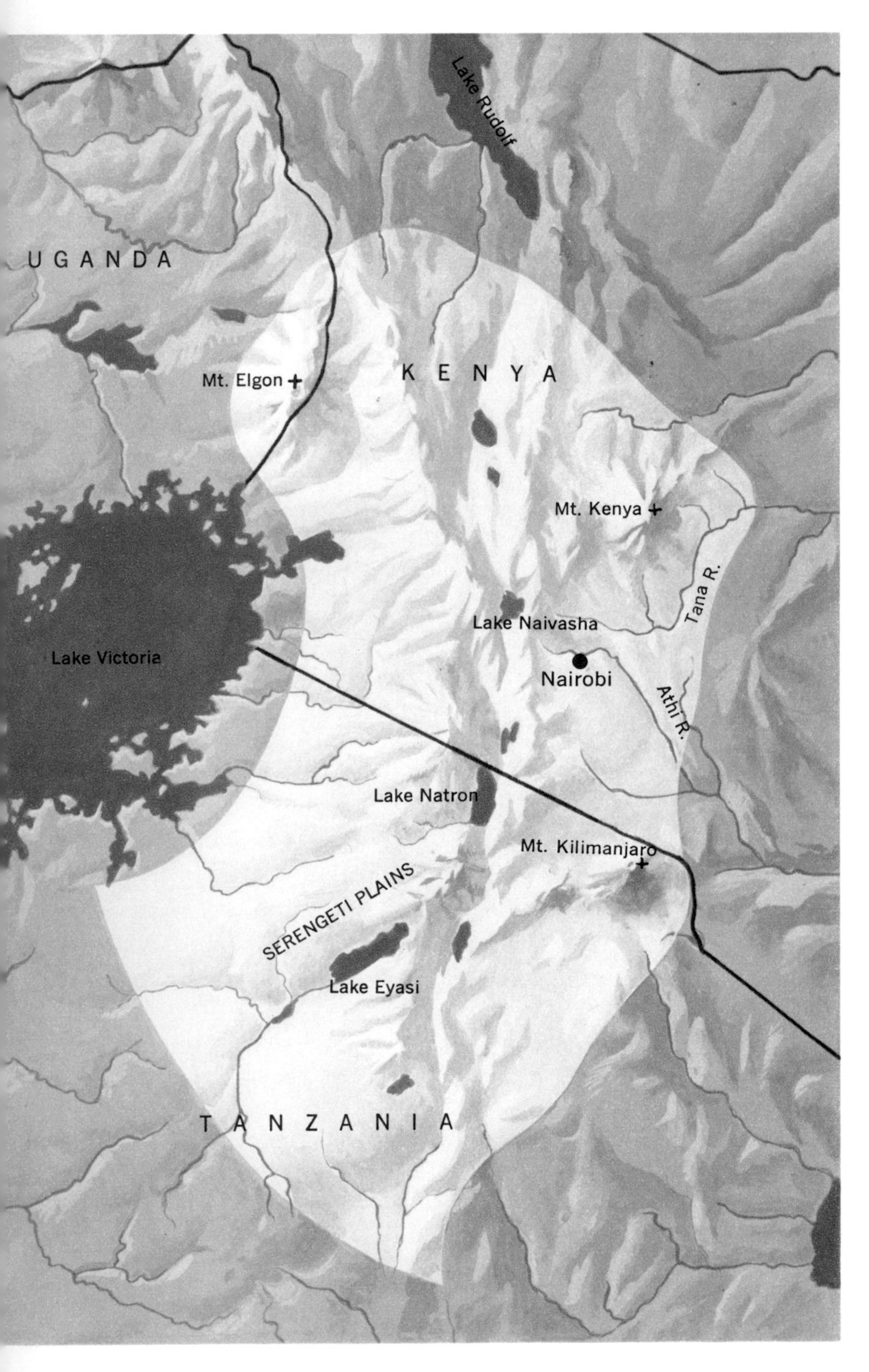

The East African grasslands, including parts of Kenya, Uganda and Tanzania, have long been known for their magnificent herds of wild animals.

Voi, became more frequent. Glimpses of Kilimanjaro, the highest mountain in Africa, generally cloud-encased but sometimes displaying the glistening snows of its summit, cheered the travelers as a foretaste of the land they knew lay in front.

At last, after twelve to fifteen days walk through the dense confining thornbush, they emerged into open grassland—in those days teeming with wild animals in almost infinite variety and numbers. To the tired travelers the huge golden and blue spaces, the invigorating breezes of open country and the sight of thousands of wild animals must have seemed, after the nyika, like emerging from hell into heaven.

In some cases the transition from bush to grassland was abrupt. The travelers would struggle up out of a bush-clad valley over a stony sill and there in front of them would be the lava plateau of the Kapiti Plains, covered with waving grass as far as the eye could see, with hardly a tree upon it. Or, as near Taveta, they would find the horizon retreating from fifty yards to fifty miles as the bush gave place to grassland. In either event there was, and still is, a striking change, and one may fairly wonder why it occurs.

GRASSLANDS

These abrupt changes from bush to grassland are not explained by rainfall. Although in East Africa there can be marked changes of rainfall within a few miles, these are usually caused by a nearby hill mass, and do not occur on flat plains. So another reason must be sought; it could be fire, animals, volcanos, or simply the soil itself.

Many believe that the world's grasslands are chiefly man-made, that the destruction of forest and savanna and repeated burning of the regrowth has led to the dominance of grass over trees. Beyond question some grasslands have been and are still created in this way, but such are generally found in areas of high rainfall where there is or has been a dense human population. Such a dense population is necessary to destroy substantial areas of tropical forest. In high-rainfall areas fire does not easily penetrate the edge of undisturbed rain forest, for the forest is protected by a screen of shrubs. But where rainfall is high enough for agriculture, and therefore in areas especially attractive to cultivators, forest may be destroyed. Fire, recurring annually, can then prevent any regrowth. In East Africa one may see great forest trees of a species called *mvule (Chlorophora excelsa)* standing alone in the midst of a sweep of grassland ten feet tall. These trees are the survivors of a forest that thrived hundreds of years ago but that now cannot regenerate because of fierce annual fires. After the fires comes erosion of the topsoil, which most affects the steeper slopes; in time this makes the soil too shallow for big trees to grow. Thus, through a combination of fire and of soil loss, grass supplants trees.

Animals can also assist the development of grasslands. Especially significant are elephants, which have turned large areas of former savanna into grassland by destroying arboreal vegetation and so opening the way to fire. Another theory holds that after man had first opened up the country by felling and burning, large herds of animals could follow and maintain the grassland by trampling, grazing, and browsing. But it seems a little unlikely that man, if in sufficient numbers to fell forest, would thereafter tolerate large herds of animals.

In other parts of the world some grasslands may be caused by burrowing animals that eat the roots of trees and thus encourage grass. But such animals require loose, friable soil in which they can burrow freely. There is no such soil in much of the East African grassland, and there are consequently no such large colonies of burrowing rodents as are found on the North American prairie. One burrowing animal,

A cheetah cautiously circles a big bull giraffe, which ignores the predator and could easily kill it with a kick. (Curt A. Moser)

a purblind stumpy little rodent, the mole rat *(Tachyoryctes sp.)* is common; but it eats the roots of grasses rather than those of trees and cannot therefore be said to encourage grassland.

None of these explanations, however, quite explains the large expanses of grassland in East Africa. The rainfall is on the whole too light to have encouraged large numbers of primitive cultivators. If primitive men lived there, they were probably hunters, food-gatherers, or pastoralists like the Masai. The domestic animals of pastoral man have come to Africa only within the last few thousand years, and in former times their numbers were checked by periodic outbreaks of disease or by droughts. Burrowing animals, elephants, or a mixed population of large herbivores are not proved causes for most of the grasslands in East Africa.

The most obvious explanation lies in the soil. The Kapiti Plains, and those of Laikipia, which are typical of much East African grassland, are flat or gently rolling volcanic plateaus. These were first formed by fluid lavas that welled out of many fissures and solidified as a nearly flat sheet of rock. Nearer the great volcanic mountains—Kilimanjaro, Mount Kenya, and others—successive lava flows ran down into the flatter country and solidified there. Often the soil overlying these lava flows is very shallow, and where there is little depth of soil big trees will not normally grow. And if the trees are not large or adapted to fire it is self-evident that they will not survive the periodic fires that sweep through natural grassland.

Shallow soil, or a layer of gravel close to the surface, is thus one of the main causes of grasslands. Heavy clay soils that become water-logged in the rains and crack deeply in the dry season, and can in the course of cracking damage tree roots while leaving grass tussocks unharmed, are another cause. The combination of these two causes, rather than animals or human interference, is probably the basic reason for much of East Africa's grassland.

ANCIENT LAKE BEDS AND VOLCANOS

Some grasslands developed on what were the beds of ancient swamps and lakes. In the floor of the Great Rift Valley, and in such neighboring areas as the Serengeti Plains, there are beautiful stretches of highly nutritious grassland on deep, freely drained soils. These old lake beds, laid down in times when sheets of water covered much of the floor of the Rift Valley, are sometimes associated with soil washed down from the slopes of the Rift or the volcanos that rise from its floor. But these lands are still grassland, despite fairly heavy grazing by domestic stock.

It does seem, however, that when heavily grazed by domestic stock the grasslands on these soils are more readily colonized by undesirable bush species than are poorly drained areas. Heavy grazing by relatively static domestic stock, as

opposed to nomadic wild animals is, in East Africa, a development of the last fifty years or so. In 1910 domestic animals were probably far less numerous than they are now, for cures and vaccines for many tropical diseases were then unknown, and there was far less water available. In the next half century these grasslands could well disappear under a blanket of bush unless greater care is taken of them.

Some experts also believe that volcanic activity alone may have caused grasslands, especially in and near the Rift Valley. East Africa is one of the great volcanic regions of the world, and during the Pleistocene epoch, which ended about a million years ago, there were large numbers of small volcanos all over the Rift floor. In such a period of intense volcanic activity the country must have been showered with hot ash and cinders at frequent intervals, and grassland could also be set afire by lava. Trees and their seedlings would have been destroyed, while grasses could occasionally have set seed and themselves survived.

Although volcanic activity has not yet ceased, it is now quiescent, and there have been few fires caused by showers of ash for probably several thousand years at least. It is difficult to believe that even if volcanos could have caused such grasslands in the first place, they would have persisted after volcanic activity stopped. Nor would this theory explain why the slopes of some volcanos are covered with dense bush while the flat plains at their foot are grassland.

THE LAST GREAT REFUGE OF WILD ANIMALS

Whatever produced the East African grasslands, they are still the home of the most spectacular concentrations of wild animals left on earth. Nowhere else can one stand on a minor elevation and see in every direction pristine grassland dotted with herds of the species that existed a thousand years ago. Nowhere else is there such an extraordinary variety of wild ungulates. Large areas of the grasslands have now been affected by the grazing herds of man; but there are still places where, striding through the grass on a dewy morning, one may share the delight of early explorers at the wild herds grazing on every side.

Walking through such grassland one does not at first appreciate that it is composed of a multiplicity of plants. The dominant grass species in several areas is red oat grass *(Themeda triandra)*. One may sit on a high point at sunset and see at certain seasons a solid sheet of russet grassland—an impression given by the color of the heads of the red oat grasses. Go down among it, however, and one discovers there are many other grasses and herbs. One of the most valuable of the grasses is star grass *(Cynodon)*, of which there are two species; this often grows on old termite hills where the work of termites has brought about greater fertility and better drainage. Indeed, the grasses growing on old or active termitaria are usually more nutritious than those found on the flatter land in between.

Left: Giraffes stalk from one clump of bush to another across the open plains; they do not feed on grass. (Weldon King)
Below: Two giraffes often swing their necks together and sometimes strike quite heavy blows. The action, called "neck-swaying" may have sexual significance. (Julius Behnke)

Some areas, such as the floor of the Ngorongoro crater, are rich in small clovers and other legumes. On areas of black cracking clays, different but still valuable grasses flourish. The impression throughout is that most of this huge sheet of vegetation is all good food for any large grazing animal. It is what the South Africans call sweet veld—grassland composed of species palatable to herbivores even when dry. It may well be that the high proportion of palatable grasses and herbs on East Africa's game plains is one of the keys to their great biological productivity.

Much of the huge area of grassland has been degraded and damaged by man's abuse of the land, coupled with his ability to control the diseases of domestic livestock, to provide water where there was none before, and by other measures which have altered the balance of nature. In other areas, where the grassland itself has not been damaged, it has been enclosed by ranchers for use by high-grade domestic stock. The wild animals are gone, or only a remnant remains. But fortunately, enough of the original grasslands, such as the Serengeti Plains and the Kapiti Plains between Nairobi and Kajiado, remains, enabling travelers to share the joy and wonder that early explorers must have experienced everywhere in this land.

The senseless destructiveness of man has never been better demonstrated than in his treatment of the wonderful assembly of animals on the East African grasslands. Early in the century these animals were undoubtedly appreciated by most who saw them. But the naturalists among them were chiefly hunters who took little heed of the many details essential to the proper management of wildlife. They knew the general habits of the game, but had neither the time nor the knowledge to go deeper into the subject.

Up to World War II the numbers of wild animals seemed virtually inexhaustible. But during that war they were slaughtered in thousands, sometimes inhumanely, to feed prisoners. And since the war there has been a rapid spread of human activities into lands formerly occupied only by wild animals. Between 1950 and 1960 the game in one area I know, once almost as well stocked as the Nairobi National Park, has dwindled to a twentieth of its former strength. And the reason for this was a ruthless extermination, sometimes to make way for domestic stock, but sometimes, where tsetse fly precluded stock-keeping, not even for that purpose. A unique biological asset that existed nowhere else in the world has been replaced by beef, mutton and wool, which can be produced in a hundred other places.

Only recently has there developed a realization that the East African grasslands are of supreme interest and cultural value to the world. But that may not prevent men from looking at them with covetous eyes. Tribes like the Masai, driven by their own population increase to seek new pastures may wish, for instance, to invade the Serengeti. And a far greater danger than such pastoral tribes to the relatively fertile western corridor of the Serengeti is the overflow of agricultural tribes from around the shore of Lake Victoria. It could happen that the efforts of conservationists will be ignored and that the wildlife will be destroyed for ephemeral gains that will in

Lion cubs at the age of these three litters cannot hunt for themselves and are fed by their mothers. They are very playful. (Clem Haagner)

Blue wildebeest are the commonest large antelopes of East African grasslands. Normally running in herds of ten to fifty, they sometimes migrate in herds of thousands. (Sven Gillsater: Tio)

the long run benefit no one. It is fair to add that at present these forseeable dangers are not acute, and the parks are being well maintained in East Africa.

WILDEBEEST AND OTHER GRAZING ANIMALS

The fauna of the plains is essentially grass-eating. Browsers, such as predominate in bushlands, are relatively few. Some animals, such as eland, gazelles and impala are both grazers and browsers. But since most of the area is covered with grass, ruminant grazing animals form the bulk of the fauna. This is true both in terms of numbers and in total biomass—the weight of living animals supported by any given area of ground.

The common large animals of the plains are wildebeest or gnus *(Connochaetes taurinus),* the wild horses known as zebras *(Equus burchelli),* and hartebeest—roughly in that order of numerical strength. Although wildebeest are ugly, ungainly-looking creatures they have a certain charm. They form the bulk of the herds which are still such a glorious spectacle in the Serengeti or Ngorongoro crater. Wildebeest go about in fair-sized or big herds; they mass together when disturbed, and, since they are black, they are the most conspicuous of all the plains game. In the Serengeti Plains, the Ngorongoro crater, and the Nairobi National Park, they far outnumber every other animal of comparable size; but they do not occur throughout the range of hartebeest and zebras.

Wildebeest have certain regular calving grounds in places such as the Ngorongoro crater and the Loita Plains in Kenya. To these calving grounds the herds migrate, following well-defined tracks and, where they pass across ridges, making deep gullies in the hillsides. Once at their calving grounds the wildebeest calve within a few weeks. For some weeks thereafter the area is alive with mothers and their young; grunting snorts are heard on every side, and the smell is often that of a farmyard.

Their characteristic breeding rhythm can, however, be upset by natural calamity and then seems difficult to restore. During 1960–61, for instance, there was a catastrophic drought in eastern Kenya and Tanzania in the course of which the wildebeest cows did not come into oestrus at the normal time. When those which had conceived before the drought calved, they abandoned their offspring at once, since they were without milk. One calf crop was thus lost, and the wildebeest cows did not conceive the calf crop that should have been due the following season. Although in the subsequent years there were heavy rains and unprecedented floods in East Africa, the calving rhythm of the wildebeest was not restored for several seasons.

Similar breeding rhythm is characteristic, to a less striking degree, of the hartebeest and zebra. They do not seem to calve simultaneously in the same area and in the same short period as do wildebeest, but their foals and calves are likely to be born when good grazing ensures plenty of milk for the mothers. A succession of good years builds up the numbers of all the plains game. Then, inevitably, comes a drought or an outbreak of disease and the numbers drop dramatically.

Such great variations in numbers, at the mercy of an erratic climate, could perhaps be avoided by culling the wild animals when numbers were high. It is evident that all plains game have a breeding capacity that enables them to increase quickly after a natural calamity. It may be that one of the best hopes for survival of the plains animals is regular culling of the large populations that build up in favorable years. To some this seems inhumane; but death from drought or disease is no kinder than that from a bullet.

THE GRAZING SUCCESSION

Zebras, wildebeest, and hartebeest all tend to eat grass at a slightly different stage of growth. Their effect on the grassland is complementary rather than competitive. Zebras first attack the long coarse growth, and are then followed by wildebeest, hartebeest, and gazelles. No species of animal subjects the grass to very heavy use. When the preferred stage of growth has passed they move on.

The succession of animals achieves efficient usage of the grassland without damage, an effect that cannot be duplicated by domestic stock. Cattle and sheep cannot replace the range of eight or ten different wild ungulates. The grassland evolved in association with the wild ungulates and where these have been replaced by domestic stock there is a deterioration in quality of pasture even under skilled management.

Some animals have rather specialized preferences. In relatively low-lying, often rather swampy grasslands we find the topi *(Damaliscus korrigum),* which we met in a distinct racial form in the northern savannas of West Africa and the Sudan. Topis are common only in certain areas, but they are of much importance in maintaining the quality of grassland. They tend to eat the dried-up stalks of older grass, ignored or disliked by wildebeest, zebras and kongonis. And they thus serve to keep down old growth that, unchecked, might feed a fire or choke new growths of more palatable seedlings. Topis are particularly common in the grasslands of parts of the Rift Valley, as at Lake Rukwa or Lake Edward, but are also numerous in the wetter parts of Masailand and the Mara. They are strictly animals of open grassland or light savanna woodland.

THE LOVELY GAZELLES

Of the smaller animals on the grasslands, the most numerous are the Grant's and Thomson's gazelle, both chiefly grazers though Grant's also browses. Grant's is one of the biggest and most splendid of gazelles in these grasslands. It is here that it is seen at its best, both in body size and in the length and form of its horns. In its various races it inhabits areas from southern Somali to northern Tanzania and Uganda, and it is a characteristic animal of the deserts of northeastern Kenya. Yet it is as much at home in the rich grasslands of the Mara which has as much as sixty inches of rainfall. All gazelles are proverbially graceful in motion, but a herd of mature Grant's gazelle bucks is supreme.

Thomson's gazelle, which is much smaller than the Grant's gazelle, formerly occurred in thousands upon thousands. It is still one of the most numerous of species in many parts of these grasslands, but it is less adaptable than Grant's gazelle and cannot endure desert conditions. It is not found commonly in areas with much less than twenty inches of rainfall per annum, and it avoids areas of thick bush. But where conditions suit it, as on the Serengeti, Thomson's gazelle is commoner than almost any other species. With zebra, it has often been accused by ranchers of reducing the fodder available for domestic stock. But since twenty Thomson's gazelles, each weighing about forty pounds, eat only as much grass as one steer, their damaging effect has been overrated.

Near water and on the fringes of bushy watercourses are found waterbucks and impala. The waterbuck feeds chiefly on grass whereas the impala also browses bushes. These two species, together with the warthog, the large inoffensive eland and, where good cover is found, the African buffalo, complete the main stock of animals that feed on the grassland. Others, such as the steinbuck and oribi, are insignificant in relation to the larger species.

WILD VERSUS DOMESTIC GRAZERS

The best replacement that man can find for this wide variety of wild animals is a combination of cattle, goats, and sheep. The effect of this combination on grasslands is adverse. Domestic stock are more selective, and prefer to eat certain species of grass. They avoid certain other coarse, stemmy, and unpalatable grasses of, for instance, the genus *Pennisetum.* At every level of grassland from two thousand feet in lowlands to eight thousand feet on the edge of mountain forest there is a species of pennisetum. Under heavy usage by domestic stock, sweeter grasses tend to die out and pennisetum becomes dominant, making the pasture almost worthless. Yet where wild animals occur, pennisetum is also eaten down. I believe that zebras, which tend to feed on coarse grasses, play a major part in this. Unlike antelopes, they have incisor teeth in both jaws and can effectively graze coarse grass with stiff wiry stems. But wildebeest also eat pennisetum, and where a succession of

A rare photo of the birth of a wildebeest calf. The event is attended by a hungry jackal, which will quickly consume the afterbirth. (Alan Root)

wild animals has fed, the pasture is, not selectively, but evenly mown.

The fact, too, that herds of domestic animals generally move over the plain in fairly close-knit groups means that they trample the grassland heavily; they also cause gullying by continually following the same route to water. By contrast, a mixed herd of wild animals—wildebeest, hartebeest, zebras and gazelles—spreads out over a wide area and does not constantly return to the same place. Also, when they have eaten down the grass in one area wild animals move on, whereas a herdsman will keep his herd in one area because he is unwilling to move his own dwelling place.

Recent studies of the anatomy and carcasses of some of the main species of plains game have shown that they are better able to make use of what they eat than are domestic stock. Through a combination of their grazing habits and their more efficient digestive systems, the wild animals can make more effective use of the pasture and so are able to produce more meat per acre than can domestic stock. Moreover, they cost nothing to keep, require no fencing, and are immune to many diseases that afflict domestic stock. The only genuine difficulty is in harvesting and marketing the crop.

The low water requirement of wild animals is another point in their favor. Some, notably the larger species, require water regularly, but no one knows how much they drink in the wild state. Other animals, such as gazelles, impala, or even the huge eland scarcely need to drink at all. They can extract enough water from the grasses and shrubs that they eat. This advantage is even more clearly displayed by wild animals that live in true desert country. Providing adequate water is one of the most costly aspects of keeping domestic stock in dry country; if given water wild animals will drink it, but they do not need so much of it to survive.

RHINOS AND GIRAFFES

Thus far we have concentrated on the grazing animals of the plains; but there are also browsers that feed chiefly on bushes and trees. Rhinos live in thickets along watercourses and among rocky outcrops on hillsides. Giraffes often walk over grassland but hardly ever eat grass. When they seem to be feeding in grass they are actually eating herbs and creepers. One of their favorite foods is the shrubby ant-gall acacia *(Acacia drepanolobium),* which grows on heavy clay soils.

Standing as tall as eighteen feet, giraffes are the only animals in the whole complex of plains and bushland game that can nibble the leaves of tall trees without seriously damaging the trees. Elephants also eat the leaves of trees, but they smash the trees in doing so. Giraffes can feed on vegetation at any height from eighteen feet to ground level, but they most often feed at from four to ten feet above ground. To reach plants at ground level they have to straddle their legs and bury their heads in the grass; when they do this, they lose the protection against predators that their superior height otherwise affords. It is probable that giraffes feed upon vegetation with a regular protein content of fifteen to twenty

Thomson's gazelle occurs in hundreds of thousands on the Serengeti Plain. They can run at over forty miles an hour and dodge nimbly. (Alan Root)

per cent—similar to good alfalfa hay; such a diet could give them a rapid growth rate, and may explain why they look fit and sleek even in times of drought.

Undeterred by fearsome thorns, giraffes commonly feed upon the leaves of various species of acacias. They do this by utilizing their long, prehensile and rather sticky tongues to grip selected bunches of leaves, by which they avoid having to thrust their muzzles amidst the thorns. Moreover, the young tips of acacia branches, including the thorns, are soft. The thorns of other trees are also soft when growing—for example desert date *(Balanites aegyptiaca)*, which is pruned by giraffes into a semblance of topiary work and forms an impenetrable tangle of two-inch spikes at its center.

THE KING OF BEASTS

Almost needless to say, the herbivores are preyed upon by several flesh-eaters. Those important on the plains are the lion, cheetah, hyena, wild dog and, to a lesser extent, the leopard. Of these the lion is the most fabled and famous; and certainly a big-maned lion, such as may be seen in the crater of Ngorongoro and on the Serengeti or Mara Plains, is a superb animal. Personally I do not think that the lion is as splendid an animal as the Asian tiger—and even the largest lion is not quite so powerful as a tiger—but the lion's mane

Right: Zebras play a vital role in grasslands by eating coarser growth rejected by other animals. Each zebra has its own stripe pattern. The dome of Kibo towers 15,000 feet above these plains. Below: Zebras at a pool in the Ngorongoro crater. Although common, they are always a striking spectacle. (Both by Alan Root)

gives him a nobility of aspect which the tiger does not have.

Lions generally go about in family groups which have been given the fanciful name of prides. The main biological advantage of these groups is that when a big animal is killed, it can either be devoured then and there by several lions together, or it can be guarded by some while others go to water. By contrast the leopard has to hide its kill in a tree if it wants to leave it for safe keeping, and the Asian tiger must either lie up near its kill, to guard it from intruders, or hide it in a dense jungle. If tigers, which are solitary animals, lived on the East African plains, they would inevitably lose their kills to vultures or hyenas, since they could neither hide the prey in deep jungle nor protect it when they themselves went to water.

Lions kill all plains animals from gazelles to bull buffalos, but they usually kill one of the larger antelopes or a zebra, since these are the easiest to catch and they provide a truly substantial meal. They are also said to relish wart hogs, to wait outside wart hog burrows for hours, and even to dig the pigs out.

A wildebeest can provide a human being with 200 to 250 pounds of meat, but lions often eat parts we would disdain. I have seen a lioness eat her way into the carcass of a wildebeest from the rear, consuming the intestines in the process. They may eat intestines for the vitamins. Often, however, they will disembowel their prey and drag the intestines to one side. After killing they neatly bite out a strip of skin about an inch wide along the middle line of the belly; they can then easily open the body cavity.

A pride of lions may vary from two or three adults and their cubs to twenty or more. A lion eats about ten pounds of meat a day on average, and a pride of ten would have to kill a wildebeest every second day to satisfy their needs. After eating all that is worth while of a wildebeest at a sitting, they may well abandon the remnants to vultures and hyenas, but sometimes they eat everything. I watched one Ngorongoro pride of twenty-three adults that had killed and completely eaten an eland. I calculated that on this occasion each adult lion must have eaten between forty and fifty pounds of meat, about a sixth of his own weight, in one meal lasting several hours. Thereafter they lay around gorged, hardly moving, for four days, their distended stomachs visibly shrinking a little each day. On the fifth day they became more active and they were ready to kill again on the sixth or seventh day.

Such facts make one wonder whether predators like lions have any marked effect upon the number of their prey in places where the latter greatly outnumber them. In Nairobi National Park there are about twenty lions and from four to five thousand large herbivores. If the lions killed a large antelope each day they would still only have killed about one in fifteen of the population in the course of a year. At

Facing: Lions in some areas do climb trees, and sleep soundly aloft, perhaps to avoid too-numerous flies. (Alan Root)

Above: Young male lions and those that live in thick thornbush do not carry a full mane like their elders. (Julius Behnke) Center: A black-maned lion stretching. His belly is full and he is content. (Alan Root) Below: A young lioness, more agile in trees than the larger and heavier male, playfully curls her tail over her back. (C. A. W. Guggisberg)

Lion kills are cleaned up by scavengers such as vultures and jackals. A gorged vulture retreats before the attack of a hungry jackal. (Alan Root)

Ngorongoro and in the Serengeti the proportion of lions to herbivores is still lower. It therefore seems likely that as is common in other predatory species, the lions alone cannot effectively control the numbers of their prey, but merely take a proportion of surplus animals that might otherwise die in the next bad drought.

One may well ask why lions do not become more numerous when their food is abundant and easy to catch. The answer seems to be that the lion is a territorial animal and will not permit other lions to enter what he considers to be his home ground. There is a Swahili saying that when the lion roars so magnificently he is saying, *"Nchi ya nani, yangu, yangu, yangu,"* meaning, "Whose is this land—mine, mine, mine." This interpretation is not far from the truth since when lions roar they are probably advertising their position to other lions, so that the others may know and keep away. But lions probably roar for more than one reason.

Lions are even reputed to kill young elephants, especially bulls that break away from the maternal herds of cows in search of independence. With smaller animals the kill is usually very swift, and needs to be, for otherwise the lion itself could be injured and perhaps incapacitated for hunting and die of hunger. But the kill is not always quick: I have seen pictures of a bull buffalo being slowly eaten alive by lions that had mauled him to exhaustion but still would not face his formidably horned head. Young lions may sometimes bungle their early kills, but they soon master the technique, which is to bring the prey down and then finish it by strangulation or by biting the neck. I have even known a lion bite the thick neck of a buffalo, though it seems barely credible that its jaws could open so wide.

Lions and other predators of the plains hunt chiefly by sight, although lions have at least sufficient sense of smell to be able to follow a trail. The lion lacks full color vision and it may be that animals such as zebras, which appear very conspicuous to humans, are not conspicuous to a lion. On a moonlit night, when colors cannot be clearly distinguished, it is less easy for a human being to see a zebra than a wildebeest. A human being may then be seeing the zebra somewhat as a lion sees it, that is, in different neutral shades.

HYENAS, WILD DOGS AND OTHER HUNTERS

Hyenas are chiefly scavengers, and they have exceptionally powerful jaws which enable them to crush the largest bones. But they are also killers of living prey, and will even kill and eat old and weak lions. Hyenas may actually kill more animals than lions, for they kill the newborn calves or the helpless young of many plains animals, and especially those of wildebeest and gazelles. When a wildebeest calves she is often attended by hyenas, and despite her efforts to drive them away, hyenas will kill her calf a few minutes after it is born. But hyenas probably get much of their food by scavenging the remains of lion kills, or by eating animals which have died from disease or drought.

Hyenas are not gentle killers: they eat their victims alive. So do wild dogs *(Lycaon pictus)*. Wild dogs run in packs, and pursue an animal relentlessly until it is exhausted; they then tear it apart within seconds. An area through which wild dogs have passed remains disturbed for some time. To us they seem cruel beasts, but they are interesting creatures, deserving closer study.

Hyenas hunt by smell for carrion at night, and by sight for living prey by day. Wild dogs hunt by day and by sight—so do cheetahs; and cheetahs are the cleanest killers on the plain. They single an animal out, pursue it at astonishing speed for a short distance, bring it down and kill it by biting its neck. As the lion feeds on the larger animals by choice, so the cheetah is the natural predator of smaller animals, the swift gazelles and impala. Cheetahs in some areas are becoming rare; no one knows why.

On the plains, leopards are of secondary importance as killers. And there are a whole host of other smaller predators—jackals, bat-eared foxes, many birds, and such snakes as the puff adder. A large puff adder is capable of eating a springhaas *(Pedetes capensis)*. Nothing that is killed on the plains is wasted: if it is not eaten by a nocturnal scavenger, it will

Right above: Black-backed jackals (Canis mesomelas), the commoner East African species, congregate near the remains of a dead giraffe. (Len Young) Right: The Cape hunting dog (Lycaon pictus) is a rangy, relentless predator that pursues antelopes for miles at over forty miles per hour and eventually eats them alive. (C. A. Spinage) Far right: Spotted hyenas live in burrows and can crack all but the very largest bones with their enormously strong jaws. (Alan Root)

Ostriches (Struthio camelus massaicus) are common on the grass plains. Three males display near a female by waving their white wing plumes. The erect tail of the center male denotes aggressive dominance. (C. A. W. Guggisberg)

be eaten by vultures by day, the remains of a lion's kill being cleaned up in a few hours by jackals, hyenas and vultures. Only in times of drought or disease, when the death rate is such that the predators and scavengers cannot consume all that is available, do carcasses lie about on the plains for any length of time. And even then they rot away and are eaten by ants and other insects in a surprisingly short time.

Modern research in these grasslands, even if inadequate, is beginning to demonstrate that they form a harmonious whole, controlled by a set of principles which ensure a beautiful dovetailing of the functions of the individual animals and plants that make up the whole grassland complex.

Among the large mammals of the grass plains, what strikes one most is the way each herbivore or predator occupies a particular niche in the ecology of the region, and is complementary in its activities to those around it. The grassland is an area of high biological productivity in terms of palatable herbage. The big herbivores make use of the grass and herbs, even the small trees, that grow in the grassland. The carnivores in turn take from the herbivores a proportion of the animals that they can kill, and any remains are eaten by scavengers. Only in times of catastrophic drought or after an outbreak of disease does there appear to be any waste, and even then the carcass returns to the soil, and is not exported like beef.

LESSER CREATURES OF THE PLAINS

There are of course innumerable smaller creatures on these plains. Birds range from the world's largest, the ostrich, great and small bustards, plovers and sand grouse, to larks, pipits and a variety of seed-eaters. There are bird predators too, of which the secretary bird is the most characteristic of grassland; it is a sort of terrestrial eagle, and it alone of the predatory birds walks about in the grass. Other resident hawks are the augur buzzard *(Buteo rufofuscus)*, the black-shouldered kite *(Elanus caeruleus)*, the bateleur *(Terathopius ecaudatus)*, the white-eyed kestrel *(Falco rupicoloides)* and the marsh owl *(Asio capensis)*.

In winter the plains swarm with harriers, kestrels and eagles—migrants from Europe. And four or five species of vultures, which seldom or never kill for themselves, but nevertheless subsist entirely on flesh, are able to find a living there. The two commonest are the white-backed vulture *(Gyps africanus)* and Rüppell's griffon *(Gyps rueppellii)*. Both nest in colonies, one in trees, the other in rocky crags, and both are likely to congregate by any carcass, thus often betraying the whereabouts of greater predators such as lions.

Of the smaller mammals of the plain much remains to be learned. No one has yet made a detailed study of the habits of the bat-eared fox *(Otocyon megalotis)*, a fascinating, endearing little creature that lives in burrows and is partly insectivorous, varying its diet with eggs, small birds and mammals, and vegetable matter. The springhaas, or jumping hare—but not a true hare at all—is a nocturnal burrowing animal, seldom seen by most visitors to the grasslands, but common enough in certain areas. Rats and mice of the grasslands have been studied in so far as they are likely to affect man's interests, as when they multiply and damage crops, or if they are likely to carry bubonic plague.

RESEARCH STATIONS

Several of the more important areas of East African grassland have now been set aside as national parks and, provided these are permanent, long-term research and investigation can be done in them. But expediency and lack of knowledge have already led to some major blunders. Only a few years' work has demonstrated that the Serengeti National Park, the most remarkable remaining area of faunal interest on the globe, is not a self-contained ecological unit. Animals spend much of their lives outside the park, and they then run the risk of being killed by meat-hungry Africans. In the long run they are also in danger of being hampered in their seasonal movements by the development of ranches or similar projects. This danger is acute in the case of the celebrated Nairobi National Park, an area of only 44,000 acres surrounded by plains owned, but scarcely used, by the Masai. The Nairobi Park brings in far more money per acre than could possibly be obtained from the most efficient ranch husbandry. But it could be irreparably damaged by development of ranches on its boundaries.

The American prairie once swarmed with large herbivores even more numerous than the herds once found in the East African grasslands. In America the wild animals have now gone, except in very small areas. It should be possible to prevent such a catastrophe in East Africa. But grasslands have always been an attractive habitat for agricultural man because they can be ploughed more easily than can bushland or forest, and for pastoral man because to him they mean food for the animals on which he himself depends. Pastoral men have already ravaged—in some cases irreparably—huge areas of East Africa's grasslands, and the process is continuing, to the benefit of no one, not even of pastoral man. Let us hope that research may be done in time to demonstrate the value of retaining the wild areas as they now are. Since there is no other area on the earth where wild animals can be seen in such numbers and variety, these grasslands are a priceless asset for all mankind.

Baboons are widespread in savannas and grasslands alike. This race (Papio anubis cynocephalus) has a shorter muzzle than the dog-faced baboon. One female is grooming another who carries a young baby. (C. A. Spinage)

Elephants, Baobabs and Rocks

The East African Thornbush

10

When bygone travelers entered East Africa through the port of Mombasa they landed in a lush tropical paradise with an adequate rainfall, coconut palms, and a thriving agricultural community. Since their object was to press on to the highlands of Kenya or to Lake Victoria, and since there were no railways or roads and the tsetse fly precluded the use of horses, they had to walk, their goods carried by porters. The trail from Mombasa rises rapidly over a succession of ancient sand dunes, shales and sandstone beds, part of the old coast of the African continent, here only a few miles from the present coastline. In less than twenty miles as the crow flies they had gained several hundred feet in altitude, had left behind the moist coastal strip and were about to enter the nyika.

Nyika is an African word meaning, roughly, wilderness. Certainly no ecological feature on the continent's surface better expresses the idea of wilderness, where a man could well go round in circles until he dies of thirst. The nyika, as typified by the bushlands of east Tanzania and Kenya, is a dense growth of small trees, often succulent or semisucculent, almost always thorny and sometimes poisonous. Along a path it can be penetrated quite easily. Once off the trail, the traveler cannot go far before the claws of an acacia reach out to catch his shirt or hat. In bending and twisting to get free of these he is likely to spike himself on the thorns of some other tree, or he may grasp at a green front and find it spurting a poisonous milky sap. The overwhelming impression is of vegetation hostile to intruders.

A HOSTILE BUT ATTRACTIVE LAND

Technically, the nyika is a bush thicket covering thousands of square miles. During brief rainy seasons it produces a flush

Leafless acacia thornbush and sparse grass await the life-giving rain from the hills. (Weldon King)

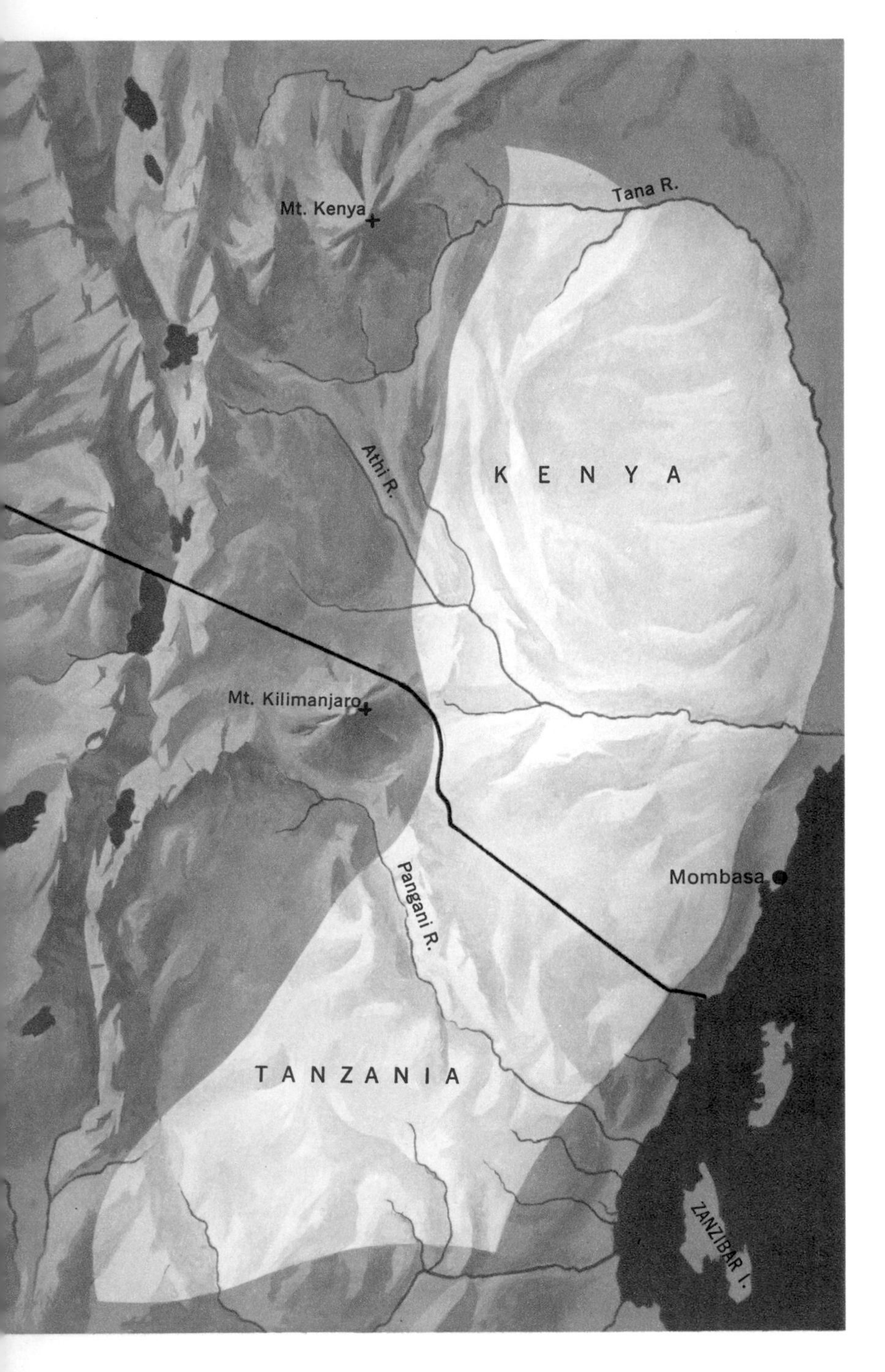

The nyika, covering the drier, eastern parts of Kenya and Tanzania, consists of extensive thorn thickets, the favored haunt of elephants, rhinos and many birds.

of green leaf and flowers, but during most of the year it is leafless and gray—apparently dead. Then the trees, with contorted scaly-barked branches, the coils of grayish-green creepers and the hornlike fronds of prickly euphorbias give it an almost reptilian aspect. In the dry season the heat is great and the sensation of drought is real. Water is scarce and frequently bad, either saline or fouled by large animals, except in a few large springs and widely spaced permanent rivers. In the wet season tropical rains pour down and generate a steamy heat which light breezes barely alleviate. Dry sandy beds of rivers become for a brief space raging torrents, bearing along trees and dead animals, often so thick with mud that deep, potentially fatal holes in the river bed are undetectable. This is not country for a weakling, whether animal, vegetable or human.

The nyika may be hostile, but it has one redeeming quality: remoteness, which at times brings a sense of peace. One may sit in the shade of a spreading green-leaved acacia tree and watch elephants and rhinoceroses digging for water in the sand; or in the still of a moonlit night the grunting of a lion, more menacing here than in open grassland, may echo over the bush. And if one climbs one of the rocky hills that dot the plains, he will find perhaps a cool patch of forest at the base of a precipice, where only the winds of the heavens and birds and the leopard that bedded down there yesterday may keep one company. For those who love wild country, the nyika has a quality that stimulates the imagination.

The nyika bushland generally develops on undulating sandy plains dissected by river beds, most of which are now dry, but in which smooth rocks bear witness that they once carried much more water. The ancient parent rocks outcrop above the general level of the plain as small rocky hills, larger whaleback ridges of stone, or sometimes even as large ranges of forested mountains. At intervals there may be an escarpment where the plain's level is sharply altered.

In more recent times volcanic ridges and mountains have risen on the plains. Some of these ranges, such as the Chyulu Hills in eastern Kenya, are, in geological terms, of very recent origin. Others, such as the great mass of Kilimanjaro and Mawenzi, are older. These volcanic rocks and hills overlie much older rocks and, where the two join, some remarkable springs appear. Recent volcanic rocks and soils are usually very porous, and the rain which falls upon them sinks straight in. It percolates through cracks and fissures until it reaches relatively impervious underlying rocks and then bursts out clear as crystal, sometimes in such volume as immediately to form a considerable river.

There are many such springs in the nyika of eastern Kenya and northern Tanzania. The most famous is the Mzima Springs in the Tsavo National Park—the main source of the permanent Tsavo River—whose flow creates a wonderful oasis in an arid land. These springs contain fish and other aquatic life sometimes cut off from any other permanent water supply, for often the water does not travel far before it is absorbed in a sandy bed. Crocodiles and hippos are found in some of these springs. The hippos in the Mzima Springs are resident, but they have access to the Tsavo River. The crocodiles may in times of flood travel up narrow river valleys and find in such springs a desirable home. Were it not for the more recent and high volcanic ranges of mountains which attract high rainfall, these springs would not exist at all.

THE DELICATE BALANCE OF TREES AND GRASS

The vegetation of the nyika develops in a particular complex of relationships—between climate, soil, and water. In this land astride the equator the rain falls in two seasons, each beginning a little after the equinox, that is, in April and in early November. Since the total rainfall is about twenty inches

Leopards climb trees to ambush prey, to rest by day, and to hang their kills out of reach of other predators. (Bernhard Grzimek)

Black rhinoceros cow and calf. Such enormously long horns, worn thin at the tip by constant rubbing on the ground, are exceptional. (Len Young)

per annum and since the two rainy seasons are separated by long periods of drought, the rain available in any one season suffices only for a brief, luxuriant flush of such short-lived plants as exist here. Longer-lived perennials, such as the thorny trees and euphorbias, can only survive if they adopt one of nature's methods of preventing water loss or of storing the precious fluid. The commonest is the shedding of leaves at the onset of drought, but some plants develop a huge storage bulb, or have a waxy cuticle enclosing masses of watery tissues. Few trees in the nyika can ever grow large unless they have access to some underground water supply.

An exception to this rule is the extraordinary baobab tree *(Adansonia digitata),* sometimes known as the upside-down tree, since, when leafless, it looks as if its roots, not its branches, were pointing at the sky. Perhaps two thousand years old, some baobabs are now thought to be among the oldest living plants. They doubtless have achieved this great age through close adaptation to their environment. Their huge swollen gray boles, often as much as ten feet thick, are so soft that a rifle bullet can travel through them. They are semisucculent, contain a woody tissue, but no hard wood, and they are also protected by a thick, glossy, gray bark, smooth in texture and effective in preventing water loss.

The huge bole rises in a tapering column for fifteen or twenty feet, then splits into a number of big branches. In the rains the baobab bursts into leaf, providing welcome shade for the traveler and a fair substitute for spinach. The bark, rich in calcium, provides food for elephants and a useful fiber for man. Great waxy flowers, lasting only for a day, give rise to large, oval, hard-shelled fruits containing edible pulp and seeds. In the nyika, baobabs are focal points, not only for the human eye, but for large and small wildlife.

In the nyika the contest between trees and grass for life-giving water is delicately balanced. As has been illustrated, trees survive the dry seasons by storing or saving water. Grasses, on the other hand, die back and are seldom thick enough or tall enough to carry a fierce fire, so that trees do not have to withstand that scourge to which arboreal vegetation in regions of heavier rainfall is subjected. Usually just before the rain the trees come into new leaf and flower, and the grass is partly shaded. Should little rain fall, the trees simply shed their leaves again, and, although grasses may sprout, they wither before they can produce seed. Only in unusually wet years does the grass grow luxuriantly, but then quantities of surplus seed are produced that lie dormant in the soil and can germinate with rain for years afterward. Conditions on the whole favor the trees more than the grasses.

BUSH CLEARING BY BIG GAME

Sporadically, animals upset the natural balance of vegetation. The typical big animals of the nyika are the elephant and the black rhinoceros; the giraffe is also not uncommon. Other characteristic animals are the lesser kudu, considered by some to be the most beautiful of all antelopes, and the gerenuk, less common here than farther north. Around permanent water there are also large herds of impala. Impala are basically browsers on bush and trees though they may sometimes eat grass too. The smaller species, gerenuk and lesser kudu, are too small to have much destructive effect on the bush. It is otherwise with the giraffe, the black rhinoceros and, especially, the elephant.

Most people probably associate elephants with lush tropical forests and swamps, and it may seem a little incongruous to see elephants, their bodies plastered with red dust, in sparse thorn bushland where there is apparently little to eat and no water. But there are many elephants in such territory. They can walk fast enough to cross great waterless stretches without hardship. Their thick skins enable them to break through thornbushes, which would be agonizing for thin-skinned creatures; and with their trunks they can pull up and feed upon the succulent, if spiky, plants of the bayonet aloe *(Sansevieria)*, which provides a part of their water needs. So, after all, it is not so surprising to find elephants in this hostile land. And nowhere in the whole of their wide habitat do elephants have a greater effect upon the vegetation, or upon the lives of other beasts and birds.

If one watches a herd of elephants feeding in thornbush, it is evident that the small gnarled thorny trees are defenseless against them. The trees are smashed to pieces, torn out by the roots or, if too big to uproot, pushed over with the forehead; their branches are then stripped of leaves and partly eaten. One can see where elephants have been feeding by the tangle of fallen trunks and branches, and roots sticking into the air, strewn about in a jumble as impenetrable as was the original bush. In riverside strips of forest the elephants uproot or smash seedling vegetation that might otherwise form a dense thicket.

Other great browsers, the giraffe and the rhinoceros, are not so destructive. Giraffes are, as has already been described, highly selective nibblers of green leaves, chiefly acacias. They are not numerous enough, however, to have a great effect on the vegetation of the nyika. But rhinos chew and browse bushy vegetation to a lower level than do elephants. Elephants normally crop bush down to four or six feet above ground, but rhinos feed at one to three feet from the ground; rhinos have the same effect on shrub-like bush as cows in pasture. In areas where elephants are numerous, rhinos can get only what the elephants leave or neglect. They cannot, like elephants, smash or uproot the larger vegetation, nor uproot succulents. In hard times they are likely to suffer by competition with elephants for the available food, though they sometimes feed on the branches of trees pushed over by elephants that would otherwise be inaccessible to them. Their effect on the bush is considerable but still secondary.

AFTER THE ELEPHANTS—FIRE

The trees, smashed and broken by elephants, lie on the ground; their canopy of leaves no longer shades the grass; their roots, which could have sucked up all the moisture of the early rains, are twisted or point forlornly at the sky. The grass now has its chance. It germinates in the torn-up soil and it grows dense and thick. After a year or two what was once dense bush is covered with a mass of broken branches, stumps, and long dry grass. Then fire comes and consumes all—grass, dead branches, even the boles of bigger trees. The latter smolder for days before collapsing into a pattern of white ash. In this way elephants unwittingly convert whole stretches of dense bush into open grassland.

The converse pattern now begins: grazing animals come in after the fire and eat the grass. Over the years they suppress the grass so that what remains will not carry a raging fire; seedling trees are thus enabled to survive, and their thorns protect them from animals with sensitive muzzles. Little by little, as once again the grass is kept down by grazing or through shading by trees, the trees regain their ascendancy. The cycle may take many years to reach a stage when a good stand of elephant fodder is once again available. It is of course not quite so simple a process as this. But the main lesson to be emphasized is that an essential function of the elephant in the nyika bush is to break up the thickets and so provide grazing for other creatures.

THE ELEPHANT AS WELL-DIGGER AND ROAD-BUILDER

Destruction of the bush is not the only effect of elephants in this country. They also provide water, not only for themselves but for most other animals. Permanent pools and rivers with running water are hard to find in the nyika, but there are plenty of sand-filled watercourses where, behind rock bars or similar obstructions, water collects in the sand. Here the

The black rhinoceros bull is unpredictable and dangerous when suddenly met in thick cover. The tick bird or oxpecker on his back warns him of danger and rids him of parasites, but also lacerates his open sores. (Curt A. Moser)

elephants use their feet to dig a series of holes; these soon fill up with water. The elephants dig the holes deep enough to avoid filling their trunks with sand when they drink. When they have gone, other creatures, from the rhino to myriads of small birds, and even bees, benefit from the elephant's spade work.

During the rains too, the elephants help to spread water supplies. After a storm, water lies in many shallow muddy depressions, where it sinks in or evaporates in a few days. But along comes an elephant; the water is cool, so he goes into the pool and squirts it over himself. The mud is refreshing, so he lies down and rolls in it; so, for that matter, does the rhino. Over many seasons the great beasts deepen these pans and, by compression of the soil under their enormous weight, render them less likely to leak. The pans so enlarged will not last long once the heat of the dry season strikes them, but they will last longer than without the aid of elephants. Elephants in this way help to prolong the life of outlying water supplies, permitting available feed to be more completely eaten by other animals.

Finally, the elephant is roadmaker-in-chief. In the nyika one can see these roads, especially from the air, extending for miles—nearly dead-straight and going from one good water hole to another. On their roads elephants do not tolerate fallen trees or other obstructions, but simply push them out of the way. The surface of the road they make is often smooth enough for a bicycle, and most animals make use of them.

THE APOLLO OF ANTELOPES

If the largest creatures of this hostile land attract the most attention, the smaller are no less entertaining and they are frequently far more beautiful. The lesser kudu, for example, has been called the Apollo of antelopes. It occurs all through the nyika thornbush, from the edges of the northern deserts in north Kenya and Somali to where, with increasing rainfall, it merges with the broad-leaved savanna. Shy, cover-loving animals, the lesser kudus are most at home in areas of moderately dense thorn and thickets to which they can retreat during the heat of the day. They are browsers and, like many other permanent dwellers of the nyika, rarely need to drink. Lesser kudus, given a suitable vegetative habitat, are not much influenced by the changes of seasons or the success or failure of the rains. They do not move in dry seasons to permanent water but stay out in the plains in the wastes of thin *Commiphora* thorn.

The other truly characteristic animal of the nyika thornbush in all its several forms is the dikdik, just as common here as in the dry Horn of Africa. I have the idea that when someone makes a special study of the dikdiks they will be found to be intensely interesting creatures. They live solitarily or in pairs, and at the end of the breeding season the pairs are accompanied by their young. The adult dikdik is a delicate creature, with limpid dark eyes and legs only a little thicker than a pencil. A baby dikdik is exquisite: its little legs are almost as slender as knitting needles, but they have perfectly formed hooves at their tips. To watch such a baby tripping through a tangle of sticks and thorns is to see miniature perfection in action. The dikdik may look delicate and weak, but woe betide you if you catch one and it kicks you: the razor-sharp little hooves will slash your skin, and a careless person is as likely to be badly wounded by this little animal as by a rhinoceros.

LIONS IN THE BUSH

Lions and leopards both occur in the nyika, but they usually live near good water sources. Although nyika lions are not the splendid full-maned creatures of the highland plains of East Africa, they are just as big and powerful. It is in their habits that they chiefly differ from plains lions.

As has been described earlier, plains lions go around in fairly large groups, or prides. Having killed a big animal such a pride may leave the carcass after one meal as though saying, "There are plenty more where that came from." But in the nyika the lions cannot afford this prodigality. Big animals are relatively scarce and it is not easy to find suitable prey. Thus when lions kill in the nyika they are inclined to stay by the carcass, keeping vultures and other competition at bay, and to devour it more completely than plains lions. The behavior of a group of lions near the Aruba Dam in the Tsavo Park during the drought of 1961 illustrates this trait. Because the lions stayed close to the water, they were easy to observe. A daily record of their kills showed that the length of time between kills varied according to whether the victim was a buffalo or an impala. They lay up beside their kills and went to water in relays. They wasted nothing and neither vulture nor hyena was able to scavenge much from their leavings.

BIRDS AND BAOBABS

In the nyika the greater animals are sometimes elusive and during the heat of the day are usually inactive. Many people complain that one can drive for days through this country and see nothing but dikdiks and an occasional elephant. One may grow bored looking for only the bigger creatures, but one cannot possibly be bored if instead one starts watching smaller mammals, birds, or insects that infest the bush.

The multitude and variety of birds found in the nyika always astonishes me. It seems hardly possible that this hostile land could support so many. Yet the quantity of birds here is far more apparent than in many tropical forest areas where, with abundant fruits and insects, one would expect to find many more. In part this is due to the fact that few trees in the nyika are much more than thirty feet high. Birds must here forage, often among bare branches, within ten to fifteen feet of the ground, or even on the ground itself. Hence they are more easily seen than in high forest, where they may be two hundred feet up in a dense, leafy canopy. Nyika birds have been fairly extensively collected and the eggs of many are known; a few have been photographed. But little detailed work has been done on many of the species, and for ornithologists there is a potentially rich field of discovery here.

There is no better place to watch the nyika birds than under a baobab tree, where even in drought there will be some shade. Within the many hollows of its vast trunk a baobab provides nesting places for such birds as rollers and hornbills.

A bull elephant, standing ten feet at the shoulder, can feed on branches eighteen feet above the ground. (C. A. Spinage)

Its upper branches, standing perhaps fifty feet above the rest of the vegetation, offer commanding perches and safe nesting sites for large birds of prey, and the lower branches are commonly festooned with various sorts of nests.

The most prominent of all nests are the large stick masses built at the ends of branches by buffalo weavers. There are two sorts, the commoner being the white-headed buffalo weaver *(Dinemellia dinemelli)*, a very conspicuous brown and white bird with a harsh chattering call. The male has a bright red rump, which shows as a brilliant signal when it flies away. This is one of the birds that almost every visitor to the nyika remarks upon.

Possibly buffalo weavers are as successful as they are because they construct what must be, for a small predator, one of the most formidable nests known. Like those of many weaver birds, its nest has an entrance tube and a nesting chamber but, unlike most weavers' nests, it is made of loosely interwoven thorny sticks and is balanced along, and not pendent from, the upper part of a branch. To reach the entrance a small predator must push past not only the nest but also a tangled mass of thorns placed on the branches by the birds. I have never been able to handle any part of a buffalo weaver's nest without being scratched.

Buffalo weavers inhabit their homes only during the rains; when the nest is not in use several other birds take over. Among these are the superb starling *(Spreo superbus)* and the pygmy falcon *(Poliohierax semitorquatus)*. The former is a gaudy bird, very common in the thornbush country. It comes to every camp and is easily attracted to a bird table. Although in most European countries the brilliance of its coloring would attract attention, in Africa it is taken for granted. It normally builds its nest in thorny bushes and is not above taking over an empty buffalo weaver's nest and filling it with its own rudely-made ball of straw.

The pygmy falcon, the smallest African bird of prey, is a delightful little creature. It weighs about two ounces and at first sight looks more like a shrike than a falcon. Chiefly insectivorous, it can also kill small birds and small reptiles. To a casual observer it is remarkably like the white-headed bush shrike *(Eurocephalus anguitimeus)*—also very common in the nyika—but in flight it can be distinguished from the shrike by the white spots on its tail and wing feathers.

FALCONS AND STARLINGS

Falcons do not make nests, but breed instead in natural ledges or cavities, or in the nests of other birds. The pygmy falcon uses the old nests of buffalo weavers, or, in South Africa, the huge nest masses of the sociable weaver *(Philetairus socius)*. The association is apparently amicable; the buffalo weavers do not seem to resent the falcon and the latter does not kill them or eat their eggs or young. Whether pygmy falcons use buffalo weavers' nests in their original thorny state, or whether they take them over when they have been relined by some other bird such as a superb starling, I do not know; I suspect the latter, for I have seen pygmy falcons going in and out of straw-filled buffalo weavers' nests.

Falcons' eggs are generally a dark red, the paler ground color being wholly obscured by rich-colored rufous freckles. The pygmy falcon, which breeds in a sort of artificial hole formed by the nest of the weaver bird, lays dull white eggs. Safe within its hole, the little falcon has no need for the reddish coloring of most falcons' eggs; one would therefore conclude that pygmy falcons have been associating with buffalo and social weaver birds for a very long time. This surmise would be supported by the pygmy falcon's nearest relative, Fielden's falconet *(Poliohierax insignis)*, found only in the woodlands of Burma and Thailand. What is fascinating is that it is not really known whether Fielden's falconet uses the nests of other birds for breeding. It is said to use a stick nest, which it almost certainly does not build itself. It seems likely that these two scions of one parent stock have been separated for a long time, and that the nesting habits of the African pygmy falcon in association with buffalo weavers have developed since the separation.

Superficially like the nests of buffalo weavers, but more often built in thorn trees than in baobabs, are the packed masses of the nests of wattled starlings. This is a nomadic species that seems peculiarly responsive to changes in the weather. I have an idea that close observation of wattled starlings—rather dull brown birds that travel in large flocks—might yield clues about air currents which are the precursors of rain. It has sometimes seemed to me that they know beforehand when rain is coming or, conversely, when there is likely to be a drought. To employ such apparently unscientific methods in our statistically-minded age might well arouse skepticism, but it is certainly not impossible that witch doctors of old made use, in their predictions, of such portents as the movements of wattled starlings. During the rains wattled starlings appear in numbers in the nyika to breed, and at this season the male grows curious black wattles on his bald yellow head.

A number of very colorful starlings frequent the nyika. The superb starling, already mentioned, is outshone by the long-tailed royal starling, which could well be Africa's most beautiful bird. Rich blue above, yellow below, graceful of form and iridescent at close range, this starling is brilliant looking but it is a shy bird and usually slips away before one can get close to it.

THE WAYS OF HORNBILLS

Hornbills are among the other common nyika birds. The bushland hornbills *(Tockus* spp.) are usually small, white-spotted, rather dull-looking birds by comparison with the big casqued hornbills *(Bycanistes* spp.) of tropical forests. They are more insectivorous than fruit-eating, and they catch much of their food on the ground. They have an undulating flight and their monotonous sobbing calls are heard in the heat of the day when little else stirs.

It is well known that in the nesting season female hornbills remain shut in their nests, but it is less well known that this is usually of their own choice and not because they are imprisoned by their mates. Thus the female of Von der Decken's hornbill *(Tockus deckeni)*, one of the commonest species,

Right above: Yellow-billed hornbill. An abundant bird of the thornbush, it feeds mainly on the ground. (Emil Schulthess)
Right: Agama lizards, a distinctively African family of reptiles, are common in most parts of the continent. They like to bask on rocks. (Bernhard Grzimek)

builds herself into her hole at egg-laying time with a mixture of earth and saliva brought in pellets by the male. A small slit is left through which the male feeds her, and far from objecting to being walled in, the female will quickly rebuild the wall if the entrance is enlarged. She sits inside for about six weeks and in that time hatches her young and sheds her feathers. Far from being the persecuted female, she is cosseted—the male doing the active, outside work during which he is exposed to the accompanying dangers.

Toward the end of the rains the female breaks out, and the hole is at once sealed again by the young inside. The female can now share in providing food for the growing brood. Three weeks later the young break their way out and join their parents. Feeding by both sexes in the later stages probably means that better use is made of available food supplies late in the rains, and that the young can fledge more quickly than if they had to rely for nourishment on the male alone. The females of some large forest hornbills remain in their nest holes from before egg-laying till after the young leave. The bush hornbills have modified these habits, presumably because of the relatively short period of abundant food in the nyika.

THE REMARKABLE BATELEUR

In the upper branches of baobabs one may find the nests of chanting goshawks and larger eagles, especially the bateleur eagle. Familiar throughout all savanna, plains and thornbush country in Africa, bateleurs are without doubt the commonest large eagle in the nyika country.

The bateleur is a truly extraordinary bird. The adult's coloring is coal black with a chestnut back and brilliant red bare skin on face and legs. In flight, the underside of the wings show pure white with a black trailing edge; males and females can be distinguished from one another by the pattern of black and white on the underwing. Adult bateleurs have a small stumpy tail and their feet project beyond it; they are nature's prototype of the delta-wing aircraft. When in flight the wings are usually angled backward and the bird travels at a steady air speed of about thirty to fifty miles an hour, usually at one to two hundred feet above ground. They do perch, but they spend nearly all day on the wing and they may very well travel two to three hundred miles on most days of their lives, almost all of it planing to and fro over their nesting territory, minutely searching the ground below for something edible. They are basically eaters of carrion and reptiles; sometimes they will even attack the deadly puff adder, whereupon they may themselves be killed. They are also pirates, using a violent diving attack to take kills away from other raptors, and they sometimes actually strike other birds.

To me the strangest thing about the bateleur—a bird that has been a special study of mine—is its apparent intelligence and its ability to express an almost human wrath. In a vast expanse of featureless bush a bateleur frequently chooses to nest close to a man-made path or road. This can hardly be pure coincidence, and the sitting eagle can often be seen by dozens of passers-by. As long as the human beings keep to the road they pass unmolested, but let them leave it and come close to the nest and an outburst of furious protest will result. The bateleurs—for the male usually appears as if by magic when the nest is disturbed—dive at the intruder, and the noise of their wings can be heard a mile or more away. They give the impression of being beside themselves with fury; no other eagle I have watched behaves in this way.

HYRAX: THE ELEPHANT'S NEAREST RELATIVE

In most of the bush one can scarcely see fifty yards in any direction. But an excellent vantage point is provided by one of the many small rocky hills that dot the bushland. These range from a mere pile of rocks atop a whaleback of stone, to huge, smooth humps rearing many hundreds of feet out of a tangle of vegetation and boulders to a cloud forest at the summit. These hills known as inselbergs or kopjes are formed of hard ancient rock left behind after the surrounding softer material was eroded away. At the foot of such hills are generally a jumble of rock and boulders. These stone piles are favorite homes of an interesting little animal, the rock hyrax.

Rock hyraxes, of which there are several species, are very adaptable animals and are found in Africa from sea level to fifteen thousand feet. It is virtually impossible to sit for long on a kopje without either seeing or hearing a hyrax. Colonies of fifty or more live among the boulders and they like to come out and bask in the sun. Their high-pitched, screeching call

Left: Rock hyraxes are abundant among piles of boulders. Superficially rabbit-like, they are the nearest living relatives of elephants. (C. A. Spinage)   Right above: Red-billed quelea or dioch. A pest of grain crops, it has benefited through the spread of agriculture. Males assume bright colors only in the breeding season. (D. C. H. Plowes)

Right: Bushbaby (Galago senegalensis). A nocturnal member of the family Lorisidae, it is a link with Asian and Madagascan faunas. Bushbabies make delightful pets, live in holes in trees by day, and at night move about in springy leaps. (Alan Root)

A baobab or "upside-down tree." Its huge bole and stunted branches resemble some grotesque inverted root vegetable. (Emil Schulthess)

may echo from some lonely rock tower at any hour of the day or night.

Rock hyraxes bear a vague resemblance to rabbits or guinea pigs. But a hyrax has a sharply pointed face with long whiskers and a most unrabbitlike acuity of expression. It can clamber over boulders with astonishing ease because its feet have horny pads which enable it to grip firmly the smoothest surface. On close examination the feet give a clue to the family relationships of *Hyrax*. They reveal that the animal belongs to the order *Hyracoidea* of the super-order *Paenungulata,* or near ungulates. The next order in this super-order is the *Proboscoidea* to which the elephant belongs. Strange as it may seem, the little hyrax weighing about two pounds is the nearest living relative of the elephant, which weighs up to six tons. It therefore seems right and proper that they should both be mammals characteristic of the nyika.

Hyraxes are browsers and can evidently subsist for long periods without water. At times, in semi-arid country, when the trees have shed all their leaves and the grass is dry, the hyrax must be hard put to it to find any green matter. Hyraxes do not eat the euphorbias, the commonest large succulents on these rocky hills, no doubt because of the acid sap of the plants, but they do eat the leaves of latex-bearing figs that are shunned by most animals. Hyrax colonies can be found in the depths of the desert, where no rain falls for eleven months out of twelve. They are able to survive in such environments because their kidneys are highly efficient and extract most of the water from their urine. Their urine is thus viscous and dries quickly on the rocks, leaving telltale white streaks.

Unfortunately for the hyrax, its size makes it suitable prey for a variety of large raptorial birds; nor does the leopard disdain to eat it. Generally, however, in their rocky hiding places, they are secure from mammalian predators. But not from eagles. Hyraxes have a habit of basking in the sun on flat pinnacles and ledges, and they are, unlike most animals, able to stare straight into the sun. This has given rise to the fable that they are blind, but the habit probably indicates only a different eye structure from that of most mammals. Ability to stare up at the sky might be thought advantageous in preserving hyraxes from their winged foes, but in fact birds catch them just the same, sometimes when they are asleep. In particular Verreaux's eagle, a splendid coal black and white bird found on most rocky hills in dry country in East and North Africa, lives on little else but hyraxes.

CLOUD FORESTS

If the hill is very large, the jumble of boulders at its foot will at some point give way to a smooth face or a whalebone ridge of rock, often so steep as to be unscalable but sometimes with bush-choked gullies where a man may scramble up. These precipices, sometimes more than a thousand feet high, may start almost vertically and then curve gradually backward. Or they may rear up in fantastic overhangs, quite smooth, apart from little ledges where a little grass, a variety of aloes and other small succulent plants grow. Such ledges may be the nesting places of falcons, eagles and vultures, while narrow crannies will harbor colonies of swifts.

The torrential storms which burst over the nyika during the rainy season rush down these sloping rock faces, scouring them clean of vegetation. At the foot of the cliff there will be a rich necklace of trees, sometimes representative of true forest. Here it is cool and quiet. There are fruits and forest birds, and beneath big boulders there are caves dim and dry, with powdery earth on their floors. Here, too, one may rest and, if there is a leopard living on the hill, traces of it will probably be found. These cool strips of forest below the precipices are also beloved of the black rhinoceros; he likes to lie up for the day in them and the visitor should be careful not to take any chances.

The tops of these hills are frequently quite bare of vegetation other than lichens and a few small succulents. But if there is a pocket of soil and stones, there will be forest, generally more luxuriant than the dwarfish forest at the foot of the crag.

The forest survives here on low rainfall because there is enough other moisture, chiefly from clouds which periodically straddle the tops of the hills. These cloud forests are always delightful places. They are generally free of heavy undergrowth and a breeze blows through them. They may be festooned with hanging lichens and orchids and harbor many species of animals and plants characteristic of much larger and wetter forests. They are in fact relics from an age when the whole land was much wetter than it is now. They are able to survive, although constantly assailed by fires running up the slopes, solely because of the moister climate up here. Relics of vegetation usually only to be found at high altitudes occur on these inselbergs. In East Africa, for instance, giant heath grows on some such mountains at an altitude of six thousand feet, stunted it is true, but as hardy as that found on Mount Kenya and Kilimanjaro at ten thousand feet and above. But the bamboo and *Hagenia* forests, however, which on higher mountains form an intermediate belt between the heath and temperate rain forest on the larger mountains, have died out.

Some of these mountaintops have been isolated sufficiently long for new races to develop, especially among the smaller forms of life. New species will doubtless be found on some of the higher hills when these are more closely examined. Among the small forest birds is the white-eye *Zosterops,* many races of which have been described from such isolated rocky hills. But because of the dangers of fire and destruction of vegetation by man, the existing forest remnants may disappear before such isolated races can evolve into full species.

The relict mountaintop forests are cold and dank, dripping with mist in the rains, but in all Africa there is hardly a more delightful experience than to look down from them on a fine evening in the dry season and watch the sunset flood over the plains. If you keep still, with your back against a slab of rock, you will be accepted as part of the landscape by the animals emerging for their evening feed. A bushbuck may mince daintily out over the bare rock searching for the small succulent plants that supply water in these arid places. On a more open ridge below, a rhino may be seen browsing along a favorite feeding track; at the foot of the precipice an outcry from baboons may signal the appearance of a leopard that has spent the day in a cave; perhaps a hyrax will be heard shrieking and a party of swifts will whizz exuberantly by. Below lies the plain of the nyika stretching to far horizons. As the sun sinks, the dry leafless bush turns first to orange red, then to a crimson shot with gold, and finally fades into mysterious purple before the blackness of night envelopes it. There it is hot and dry and the elephants will be making for water. But on the mountaintops it is cool and peaceful, and as remote as it is possible to be from human beings on this planet.

The Great Southern Savannas

The Miombo Woodlands

11

The Congo forest, the Nile basin, the East African grasslands and the nyika thornbush all bound on the south one of the greatest expanses of uniform vegetation in all Africa, or in the world. Stretching sixteen hundred miles from east to west, and from eight hundred to twelve hundred miles from north to south, is a huge belt of savanna. It is separated from the west coast only by a narrow strip of desert and from the east coast by a thin band of coastal plain and forests. It fills all of southern Tanzania, most of the southern Congo, Angola, Zambia, Rhodesia, and Nyasaland. For hundreds of monotonous miles it stretches, seemingly with little change in the basic vegetation.

In southern Tanzania, where we enter this region, the country is called *miombo,* and, although there are other local names, we will use this one. The miombo usually occurs on the ancient elevated inland plateaus of southern Central Africa, sometimes descending to lower levels. It may be luxuriant woodland fifty or sixty feet high on hot plains two thousand feet above the sea or it may, on cool ridge tops at six thousand feet, be stunted and gnarled, moss-grown, and reminiscent of montane forest. But even a glance will reveal essential similarities among these varieties of miombo in vegetative composition and sandy soil. It is the utter monotony of the miombo that is striking—and to some, oppressive.

With minor exceptions the inland plateaus in these regions consist of ancient pre-Cambrian rocks. They weather into deep sandy soils which, under heavy tropical storms for six months of the year, are leached of most of their nutrients. Some areas of this kind are almost white, acid, devoid of humus, and highly infertile. Consequently they are of little use for cultivation, and the miombo is generally thinly inhabited.

The woodland grows on the ridges, hills and uplands. Along the valleys and drainage lines there are water-logged strips called *dambos.* In very flat areas these are broad, and the vegetation they support, thin growths of acacias and tall sour grasses, is quite different from that on the ridges. In smaller dambos in steeper country the acacias may be missing, but the water-logged grassland is present. Trees grow along the edges of the drainage streams, or on raised hummocks and termite heaps, and purple flowering shrubs and tall fibrous *Hibiscus* are found there.

Anyone who has lived in the savannas of Guinea would at once feel at home here. The soil is basically similar to much of Guinea, and so is the climate, since it rains for half of the year and is dry for the other half. There is the same regular succession of sandy upland and soggy, sour swamp. Along the streams one finds a very closely related species of waterside tree, *Syzygium,* which shades every little savanna stream in central Nigeria. The two belts of savanna may be more than a thousand miles apart, with one fairly dissimilar connection through the Nile basin, but they look very much alike. There are, however, some essential differences too, and these differences set the miombo apart.

SPRING: A PERSIAN CARPET

The miombo is a type of savanna—defined as an area of tall grass with scattered small trees. But it is really a type of woodland with grass beneath, and "savanna" is used here only because it is an accepted term. In many places the trees are tall and almost contiguous, and they largely suppress the grass. In such conditions fires are not fierce and woodland dominates.

However, the climate giving rise to the miombo is the same as that of the northern savannas, and the annual cycle is much the same. The leaves of the trees die and fall, the grass withers, and fire creeps or sweeps through it. For a time the woodland is black beneath and bare above—depressing in the extreme. All this is just like Guinea. But before the rains come again there occurs in the miombo a miraculous change that is unlike any other in Africa.

The beautiful flush of new leaves that heralds the rain in the Guinea savannas is dull beside that in the miombo. The dominant trees in this region belong to the genera *Brachystegia* and *Julbernadia* (closely related to the *Isoberlinia* of northern Guinea savannas). In season, they break into glorious bright red, crimson, or copper leafage that turns gradually bronze, olive, and finally glossy bright green. It is as if the whole countryside were covered in copper beeches. The new growth is almost as spectacular as the great sheets of color that deck northern woodlands in autumn. But it has a lightness and life with bright tropical sunlight glinting from every wind-shaken leaf, that is entrancing. This is not death, but new exuberant life springing in all the hues of a Persian carpet.

There are true autumnal tints here too. When drought comes in these parts it comes sharply and water reserves are quickly reduced in deep sandy soils. Clear, cloudless skies herald the end of the rains and there is no haze brought by a dust-charged harmattan to obscure the sun. The flow of sap is quickly cut off, and the change from full leaf to dead yellow and red tints is rapid. Then the leaves fall or are blown off, the grass fires come, and the woodland is inexpressibly glum and black.

Victoria Falls is the world's greatest sheet of falling water, visible as a whole from the opposite side of this narrow chasm. In flood the chasm is filled with spray. (Tad Nichols)

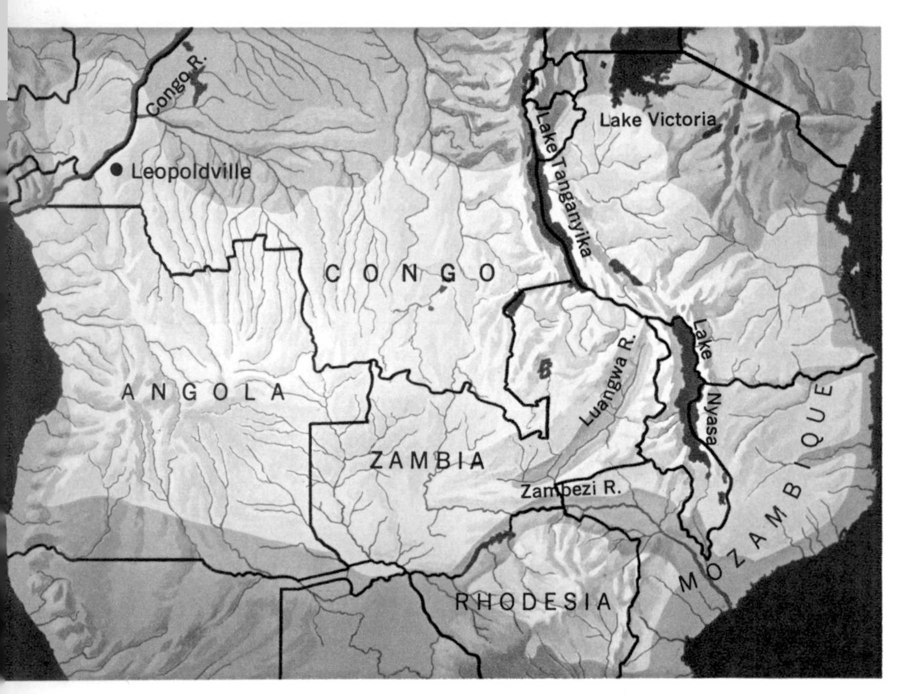

The miombo, a vast block of monotonous savanna stretching from coast to coast and from the Congo to the Zambezi. It is penetrated by Rift valleys and enriched by flood plains teeming with game.

The miombo may appear to be composed of only a few species of trees, but is florally much richer than the Guinea savannas. This is partly because it occupies a much larger, and especially a much broader, area. The Guinea savanna area is much narrower from north to south, and in past dry periods the encroaching Sahara has compressed it still further. It is always easier for a multitude of species of plants or animals to survive or evolve in a large area than in a small or narrow one. The miombo was probably always a fairly solid block of homogeneous vegetation even though it too has been reduced in area in dry periods. It has been a more effective home and refuge for a larger variety of life than the northern savannas.

But the most significant difference of all between the miombo and the northern savannas is the time of the year at which the rain falls. The oscillation of the earth brings the sun overhead in December, not in June. Rain therefore falls in the miombo country from November to May, rather than from April to October. This single circumstance results in an area of lush growth and plentiful feeding south of the equator during the northern winter, an area larger than any other similar one on earth, and it brings a flood of northern migrant birds into the miombo.

A GREAT UNSPOILED WILDERNESS

The miombo is one of the great areas of relatively unspoiled wilderness in Africa. Vast parts of it are still practically untouched by man. It is unspoiled because, in the main, its soil is infertile and cannot support large numbers of agricultural man. The tsetse fly, which excludes the herds of pastoral man because of the disease it carries, has also acted to prevent damage to habitat through overgrazing. Even now, despite potent anti-tsetse measures, the fly still has a grip on large areas of country, and soon returns once such measures are relaxed.

In the miombo one is very conscious of its wilderness character. In flat country it is as easy to get lost as in the equatorial forest. The trees are all about the same size and kind, and what looks like a distinctive clump soon repeats itself not far away. In the dry season much of the miombo is almost waterless, so that it is a country in which to be cautious until one is familiar with it. Even in hilly areas it is difficult to be quite certain where one is going because most of the hills are wooded to their tops. But occasionally there are prominent bosses of hard black rock that afford a good vantage point.

Such rocky hills are called inselbergs (or bornhardts, after the German geologist who first studied them), that is, island mountains. They are characteristic of Africa and other tropical countries. Typically they occur in rather flat country composed of gneiss and schists which have been intruded from below by an igneous rock, granite. Since inselbergs are not found outside the tropics, it is clearly some feature of the tropical climate that is responsible for their formation.

Actually it is probably a combination of the rapid rock decay that takes place in a moist tropical climate and the hard, chemically resistant nature of granite that makes an inselberg. Rock decay penetrates only to the level of ground water. As large tropical rivers cut their valleys deeper and deeper, so the water table recedes and more and more of the overlying gneiss and schists decay and erode away. But the granite intrusion, chemically resistant to decay, remains, protruding above the surface. At the base of an inselberg one can pick up slabs of rock that crumble in the hand while the rock of the summit seems perdurably hard.

I find inselbergs very interesting. They support a characteristic flora and fauna that varies little from one ecological zone to another. Leopards and baboons live on them, as well as hyraxes and klipspringers *(Oreotragus oreotragus)*, and there are usually interesting birds of prey to be seen on them. From their tops one may watch the sunset glowing over the woods, and the coming of dusk. And wherever the inselberg is, I know that the freckled nightjar *(Caprimulgus tristigma)* will then begin to call. Other birds are also associated with inselbergs, but their constant inhabitant is this nightjar. The association with the black rocks must be very ancient, for the bird, which is a member of a generally brown genus, has not only become unusually dark itself, but its eggs are also spotted with dark gray, rather than the usual buff. I have found the nests of this nightjar right out on the bare black rock, without a vestige of shelter from the sun. The bird sits so still and is so nearly invisible that one can pass as close as six feet without seeing it. As one walks around her she closes one eye slowly, presumably so that its telltale reflections will not give her

Right above: Male lesser masked weaver (Ploceus intermedius) building his nest. He has nearly completed the loop in which he will stand for all subsequent work. Right: Black-bordered charaxes (Charaxes pollux). This genus of butterflies is as characteristic of Africa as are lions. Far right: False acraea butterfly (Pseudacraea boisduvali). It escapes predation by mimicking a highly unpalatable species of acraea. (All by D. C. H. Plowes)

Overleaf: Burchell's or common zebra and blue wildebeest at a waterhole. Once reassured by the presence of other animals, the whole herd drinks greedily. (Clem Haagner)

Giraffes must straddle their long legs to drink from the water. (Clem Haagner)

away. And when she does flush, the eggs are so hard to see that one has to look closely to make certain they are there.

WOODLAND ANIMALS

The large fauna of the miombo shares some animals with the Guinea savanna, but it is much richer and it includes some species that occur only here. The northern hartebeest is replaced by another species, Lichtenstein's hartebeest *(Alcelaphus lichtensteinii),* and the western kob is replaced along river valleys by the puku *(Kobus vardoni).* Although this seems almost unbelievable in such an adaptable animal, some even regard the yellow baboon *(Papio cynocephalus),* the characteristic baboon of the miombo, as a species distinct from its northern and southern cousins. Buffalo and reedbuck, common in northern savannas, occur here, and the roan antelope, almost completely absent in intervening equatorial belts, is also common. But there are several other animals, including zebras, that do not occur in the Guinea savanna. The finest of these are the greater kudu *(Strepsiceros strepsiceros)* and the sable antelope *(Hippotragus niger).*

It is generally agreed that the most impressive of all antelopes is either the greater kudu or the sable. Only these two ideally combine stature and beauty. The Derby eland might be a contender, but the roan, large and handsome enough, is coarse and colorless beside the sable. And the beautiful lesser kudu, or the bigger gazelles, lack the greater kudu's magnificent sweep of spiral horns. To me, each has at some special moment seemed to be the most glorious beast that ever stepped. But on the whole I choose the sable, less retiring, easier to see, and more erect of bearing than the slender kudu. The utter blackness of a sable bull, the splendid curve of his horns, and the sharp white marking on face and belly set him apart.

The roan and sable both belong to the Hippotraginae (horse-like antelopes), and are both woodland animals, though they will sometimes graze in open country, even treeless plains. Of the two, sable are more difficult to see and more likely to stick to woodland. Both spread into other vegetation belts but are most at home in the miombo. The roan is the largest of its family, with sable a close second. It is remarkable that these two closely related antelopes, each formidably armed, should occur together throughout most of this great area. But when more is known about their feeding habits it will probably be found that they are sufficiently different to avoid competition with one another.

Kudus, though widespread in the miombo, are less common here than in drier country farther to the south. They are always rather difficult to see. It is astonishing how animals of this size can escape observation even in relatively open country. The kudu is aided by white vertical stripes which break up the outline of the body, but it depends chiefly on unusual vigilance.

In the network of dambos that intersect the miombo there often used to be herds of zebra, though in many places these have now been wiped out. Eland were also fairly widespread, but are now much reduced. The same is true of Lichtenstein's hartebeest. Bushbucks are to be found in strips of forest along watercourses, duiker are common throughout, and klipspringers occur on rocky hills. Lions, leopards, and cheetahs prey upon these animals, but are chary of the formidable horns of the roan and sable.

The miombo woodland supports about twice as many species as the Guinea savannas. But even in the past it never supported the vast herds that were found on open East African plains. This is chiefly because of the poor quality of the grass, which is all, in woodland and dambos alike, "sourveld"—that is, grass which is not palatable when dry.

The protein content of such grasses can fall to less than one per cent for three or four months of the year, and will only be above ten per cent in one or two months, in the first flush following rain. Since a ruminant animal requires food with an average of seven per cent protein to maintain body weight, it follows that the great bulk of low protein dry grass is inadequate for this purpose. The protein content in the diet must be made up with small quantities of more tender grasses, leaves, shoots, seeds and pods obtained by nibbling and browsing.

Wild animals manage better than cattle because they have a more efficient digestive system. They do not, like cattle, lose as much as a third of their body weight each dry season. But even so, the number that can survive the dry season in the miombo woodland is low, since most of the bulk of dry herbage is of little use as food.

WASTEFUL SLAUGHTER

The wealth of wild animals in the miombo has been slaughtered on an unprecedented scale for two reasons. First, it has been deliberately exterminated in campaigns to try to reduce or eliminate the tsetse fly. Second, and probably more destructive in the long run, has been the steady slaughter by local Africans. This has been greatly accelerated by the development of industrial cities hungry for meat. Over great areas where woodland animals were once common, there are now none. And since the tsetse often continues to exclude cattle from such areas, the country is sterile and produces nothing.

The tsetse control operations in parts of the miombo have become known as "operation butcher," and have been vigorously condemned as brutal, unnecessary, ineffective, and wasteful of natural resource. They seem to have been a clumsy, costly and wasteful method of controlling the tsetse fly, adopted in the absence of anything better. Yet they still continue despite public outcry against them. Even game reserves may not be inviolate.

There are many different kinds of tsetse fly, but the most important one in the miombo is *Glossina morsitans*. This is a widespread species, occurring also in northern savannas. Most tsetses have their vulnerable points, and can be eliminated by selective clearing, or by spraying insecticides along watercourses. But *morsitans* is more widespread in the woodland, so that its elimination through the destruction of small areas of bush is impossible. Hence, since tsetse feeds on wild animals, it has been argued that wild animals must be destroyed and replaced by cattle less efficient at making use of the herbage, more susceptible to disease, and much less beautiful.

Modern methods of research, however, give a glimmer of hope, at least for some wild animals. The tsetse prefers to feed on certain species; man is one of its favorite "hosts." Among wild animals wart hogs are the favorite, and buffalos, elephants and kudus are also fancied. The fly seems to prefer blackish animals and to avoid pale-colored beasts. Zebra and hartebeest need not have been killed in the attempts to keep out the tsetse. Zebras are apparently avoided because of their black and white striped pattern; tsetse also avoid fly traps striped like zebras.

Through ignorance of the fly's preferences, tsetse control operations have meant the unnecessary killing of tens of thousands of animals. The fly often returns, and since empty land attracts wild animals from other areas, the fly's hosts return too. The slaughter goes on and on, and is very costly over a long period of years. And the end is often an area denuded of wildlife with a residual population of tsetse flies sufficient to be able to infect cattle.

The land itself is often too poor to stand the cost of wholesale bush clearing for cattle ranching. Moreover, it is inevitably impoverished by such an act. In the miombo, deep-rooted trees have the function of drawing upon stores of nutrients too deep in the soil to be reached by shallow-rooted grasses. Their leaf fall restores some of these salts to the surface. If the trees are removed, the shallow-rooted grasses flourish more luxuriantly for a time, but they cannot reach the deeper soil layers. Hence, in time, the nutrients are partly lost by leaching, the grass itself suffers for lack of them, and the whole environment is impoverished.

In this part of Africa above all, it would be more realistic to recognize that, except in limited areas of good soil, the wild animals of the miombo are a better and cheaper source of meat for human beings than are domestic cattle. The policy of slaughtering to hold back the tsetse fly, and the killing by Africans at all seasons of old and young, male and female alike (which has been the most destructive aspect of the slaughter policy), has rendered sterile and useless large areas of country that had some potential through wildlife.

MANY CLEAR WATERS

Most of the miombo is drained by a multitude of little rivers collecting in a single great river system—the Zambezi. The deep sandy soils absorb the rain water, filter it, and release it more gently than in many other regions of Africa. Repeatedly one comes upon streams of clear blue water running over a bed of smooth rocks, so different from the turbid brown floods from the East African volcanic regions or Ethiopia. It is most refreshing to bathe in a clear pool in one of these streams in the heat of the day, and in uninhabited country there is little fear of disease.

The network of dambos among the miombo maintains the level of the little streams. In the rains the dambos are soggy, running with water, yet the soil is gritty to the touch and the water is seepage rather than clay swamp. In these dambos the wattled crane *(Bugeranus carunculatus),* which we last described in a swamp in Ethiopia, at 11,700 feet, sometimes breeds. Here it does not seem to be the excessively shy bird that it is in Ethiopia, and one may conclude that this is its true home and that the Ethiopian population is a remnant. The ground-scraper thrush *(Psophocichla litsipsirupa)* also reappears in this region, after a fifteen-hundred-mile gap. And there are several other links with Ethiopia.

The Zambezi itself is to my mind much the most attractive of all the big rivers of Africa. In the rains it does become turbid and brown, but in the dry season it flows clear and blue. It has a wealth of fish, and the bird life along its banks is at least as interesting as on other rivers, with innumerable plovers, herons, storks, and kingfishers. The southern carmine bee eater *(Merops nubicoides)* fills the place of the carmine bee eater of the Niger and other northern streams, but is as a whole less numerous.

The fish fauna of the Zambezi system is distinct from that of the Nile, Niger and Congo. It lacks the perchlike predatory genus *Lates;* the chief predatory fish of the Zambezi is the tiger fish *(Hydrocyon lineatus),* a lithe silver fish with black longitudinal stripes and savage-looking teeth. It exists in other river systems as far north as Lake Rudolf and is technically a nilotic fish. Yet one associates it most with the clear waters of the Zambezi and its tributaries. Those who angle for tiger fish must beware of crocodiles, which seem to be particularly dangerous in the Zambezi system.

THE ZAMBEZI GORGE

The Zambezi and other rivers of this region rise in mountains and flow out onto a plateau. When they descend from the plateau the result is often spectacular. On the Zambezi it is one of the wonders of the world.

The Victoria Falls at Livingstone drop nearly 400 feet into a fissure in basalt about a mile wide. Their form is almost exactly similar, but on a much grander scale, to the falls of the Blue Nile at Tisisat in Ethiopia. Below the falls, which are the largest sheet of falling water in the world, the great river has cut itself a narrow gorge—a deep ditch running for a hundred miles.

The trough has been cut through four horizontal lava flows which can plainly be seen on the sides of the gorge. Over the ages the river has found a succession of fractures in the basalt into which it could cut more easily than elsewhere. A succession of earlier falls can be traced in the gorge. Even now the river is beginning to wear a new passage at the western end of the Devil's Cataract; here a small gully is slowly working eastwards along a new line of weakness. Eventually this will carry the main flow of the river, but the form of the falls will remain basically unchanged during our lifetime.

It is an exciting experience here to put on a bathing suit and climb out onto the rocky promontory on the Zambian side, where constant spray drenches the soil and produces a lush patch of tropical rain forest. The roar of the water is stupefying, and everything is wet and slimy. Another impressive experience is that of climbing down a weak point in the crag to the bottom of the gorge. Here there is no roar of the falls, but the power of the mighty river surging swiftly along is tremendous. If one were to fall in, one would be battered to death in the rapids, and would eventually be eaten by a crocodile.

Sitting on the rocks near the water one is in a strange world. Screes of volcanic boulders are homes for hundreds of rock hyraxes that live here safe from leopards and other predators. They come out and gaze curiously at the intruder, their cries of alarm inaudible above the dull thunder of the rapids. The air is oppressive and hot, and above one sees birds like trumpeter hornbills *(Bycanistes bucinator)* passing from one side of the river to the other.

This gorge is the breeding place of the small, very rare Teita falcon *(Falco fasciinucha).* First known from the Teita district of Kenya, it has only recently been seen in Rhodesia. It made a spectacular entrance before assembled ornithologists at the Pan African Ornithologists' Congress at Livingstone in 1957. Never has a rarity (known by less than a dozen specimens) appeared at a more auspicious moment.

One may wonder, with reason, why such a bird should be rare. Later study has indicated that it is a typical falcon, a bird-killer like a small peregrine. Its avian prey, bulbuls, doves and the like, abound in large areas of tropical Africa, and there are plenty of suitable nesting crags between Teita and Livingstone. Yet the little falcon is absent from the intervening area, another of those mysteries of distribution for which there is no easy explanation.

THE FERTILE FLOOD PLAINS

Each of the big rivers, the Kafue, the Luangwa, the Zambezi itself, have flat stretches of valley with extensive flood plains. These are fertile strips of alluvium a mile or more wide, with the river meandering about in a trough whose banks are higher than the land on either side. When in flood, the rivers spill over at numerous places and inundate vast areas on either side.

In some cases the inundation is gentle. The Kafue simply rises gradually and the water, which is quite clear, spreads out silently all over the flood plain getting deeper and deeper. In others the flood is more violent. The Luangwa River runs an erratic course, continually tearing away new chunks of

Right above: The arboreal boomslang (Dispholidus typus), which lives largely on birds and chameleons, varies greatly in color. Its venom is extremely toxic, but as a back-fanged snake, it is not normally dangerous to man. (Sally Anne Thompson) Right: Southern carmine bee eaters (Merops nubicoides) are among Africa's most beautiful birds. They breed in colonies on steep banks of large rivers. (D. C. H. Plowes)

The piglike snout of an aardvark (Orycteropus afer) and its long tongue exploring the broken-up mass of a termite mound. (Paul Popper)

bank to burst into an old bed. Arms of the river may be cut off for two or three centuries, and may form placid lagoons fringed with large forest trees. But in time the river returns and tears them out again.

These flood plains support the main concentrations of wild animals in this region and are vital for the survival of many species. Pukus, for instance, and waterbucks, seldom occur away from them. They are also the main area of concentration of big herds of buffalos, and of elephants in the dry season. Hippos formerly abounded in these rivers and, under protection, have recovered in the Luangwa and now number about twenty per mile of river. They feed out on the flood plains too.

Elephants are much less numerous in much of the miombo than they are farther north. But buffalos are very common, and on these flood plains there are the same features that lead to the huge biomass of living creatures per square mile found in some of the grasslands and savannas of the Nile basin. The total population is difficult to estimate in this rather heavily-wooded country, but it would not surprise me to learn that the biomass of elephants, buffalos, and hippos on such flood plains rivals the 100,000 pounds per square mile of the Nile basin.

Over a wider area, however, the weight of animals carried would be far less. The flood plains are backed, not by relatively green savannas containing a fair proportion of palatable grasses, but by a forest of mopane *(Colophospermum mopane)* or miombo with very much poorer grass.

The mopane forest is found on heavy clay soils, and reminds one of a wood of ancient oaks. It is clean underfoot, and in the dry season the leaves turn dark red; moreover, since the leaves often remain attached to the trees for a long time, the forest resembles an oak wood or forest in autumn. Elephants are very fond of mopane and they push over the big trees and browse the smaller ones down to about six feet. They thus aerate and disturb the soil, and provide bushy browse of good protein value for animals that cannot reach the top of the big mopane trees. Impala reappear commonly on these plains, though they are rather rare in the *Brachystegia* woodland.

Bird life along the flood plains is spectacular. In the dry season there are many little swamps and pools decked with water lilies and fringed with tall reeds and succulent grasses. There may be an old hippo bull wallowing contentedly among jacanas *(Actophilornis africanus)* and pygmy geese *(Nettapus auritus)*. Open-bill storks *(Anastomus lamelligerus)* feed on snails with their curious forceps-like beaks, open in the middle and closing only at the tip. Yellow-billed storks *(Ibis ibis)*, marabous, and three or four species of herons and egrets may be seen. The most spectacular of all is the saddle-billed stork or Jabiru *(Ephippiorynchus senegalensis)*, black and white, as big and heavy as a marabou, but much neater-looking and more handsome, with a huge black, yellow and red pickaxe of a bill. Jabirus are not common over most of Africa, but in these flood plains they are more numerous than elsewhere.

THE RED LECHWE

Some of the riverine flood plains and some other swamps, such as the extensive inundation area of Lake Bangweulu, support herds of a unique animal, the red lechwe *(Kobus leche)*. Of the several local races, those from Lake Bangweulu are blacker and are known as black lechwes. The last lechwes we described were in the Sudd of the Middle Nile, and the animal is a classic example of a species with a once continuous distribution which has been split in two by the eastward advance, in wetter times, of the Congo forest.

The red lechwe is far better known than the lechwe of the Nile, but they have essentially the same habits. They live in shallow water on inundated grasslands, taking to deeper water to escape pursuit, and resting on anthills or other raised dry places. Their hooves are splayed and longer than those of their nearest relatives, and they can travel over wet ground at a fair speed. But in this area lions, for lack of other prey, have been forced to learn to catch lechwes and have overcome their normal dislike of wet areas.

Lechwes are intensely gregarious animals and formerly were seen in huge herds. Thirty years ago they numbered perhaps 250,000 on the Kafue flats and 150,000 at Lake Bangweulu. There are other smaller herds elsewhere. These great herds have been reduced by wasteful commercial slaughter to about fifty thousand on the Kafue and sixteen thousand at Bangweulu. The method of killing was often by communal hunts involving almost indescribable brutality which tended to eliminate more females and young than adult males, and thus took toll of the breeding stock which should have been preserved. Fortunately this communal killing has been stopped, but it has done its damage, and it will take many years before the herds can recover.

The lechwe does not compete in any way with domestic stock, and could be a valuable meat resource if properly and selectively cropped. Lechwes will probably produce a greater weight of meat per acre than will any cattle in these parts, for a female reproduces her own weight in about two-and-a-half years, as against three or four for cattle. Even if one argues that the most important reason for allowing an animal to live is so that it can be useful to man, preservation and

Aardvarks, strangely helpless-looking creatures, are enormously strong and can break open cement-hard termite hills with their powerful digging claws; they live almost wholly on termites. (Paul Popper)

cropping of the lechwe is a sensible course. In at least a few places smaller herds of lechwes are preserved for their beauty and interest alone.

On flood plain grasslands drier than the lechwe flats is found another animal, the tsessebe *(Damaliscus lunatus)*. It is the southern representative of the topi-korrigum group, or bastard hartebeest, and has the reputation of being the world's fastest antelope. Formerly common locally, the tsessebe, like the lechwe, has been reduced to remnants by senseless commercial shooting for meat, and the grasslands it once inhabited, still tsetse-infested, are now without animal life.

THE HAVEN OF MIGRANTS

These southern savannas are the greatest continuous area of country that is warm and wet during the winter in the northern hemisphere. Consequently they provide abundant insect food at a time when it is not normally to be had, even in the northern tropics. Insectivorous birds that wish to feed well must make the journey from the huge landmass of Eurasia to southern Africa. In the rains, from October to May, the country swarms with swallows, bee eaters, rollers and several migrant hawks.

Hobbies *(Falco subbuteo)* are insectivorous falcons that breed all through the northern deciduous forest belt, from Great Britain to China. In October they move southward through tropical Africa, meeting the rainy season at the equator in October and November. But in December the rains stop here, so the birds move on and live in the miombo country during the wet weather there. By the time they move north again in April, the rains in the miombo are tailing off, but have begun once again at the equator and in northern tropical Africa. So the hobby has an easy passage northward too.

Hobbies in Africa feed largely on flying termites that swarm out of their holes in millions at the beginning of the rainy seasons. When a rainstorm brings out the termites, it is then likely that hobbies, whose presence was hitherto quite

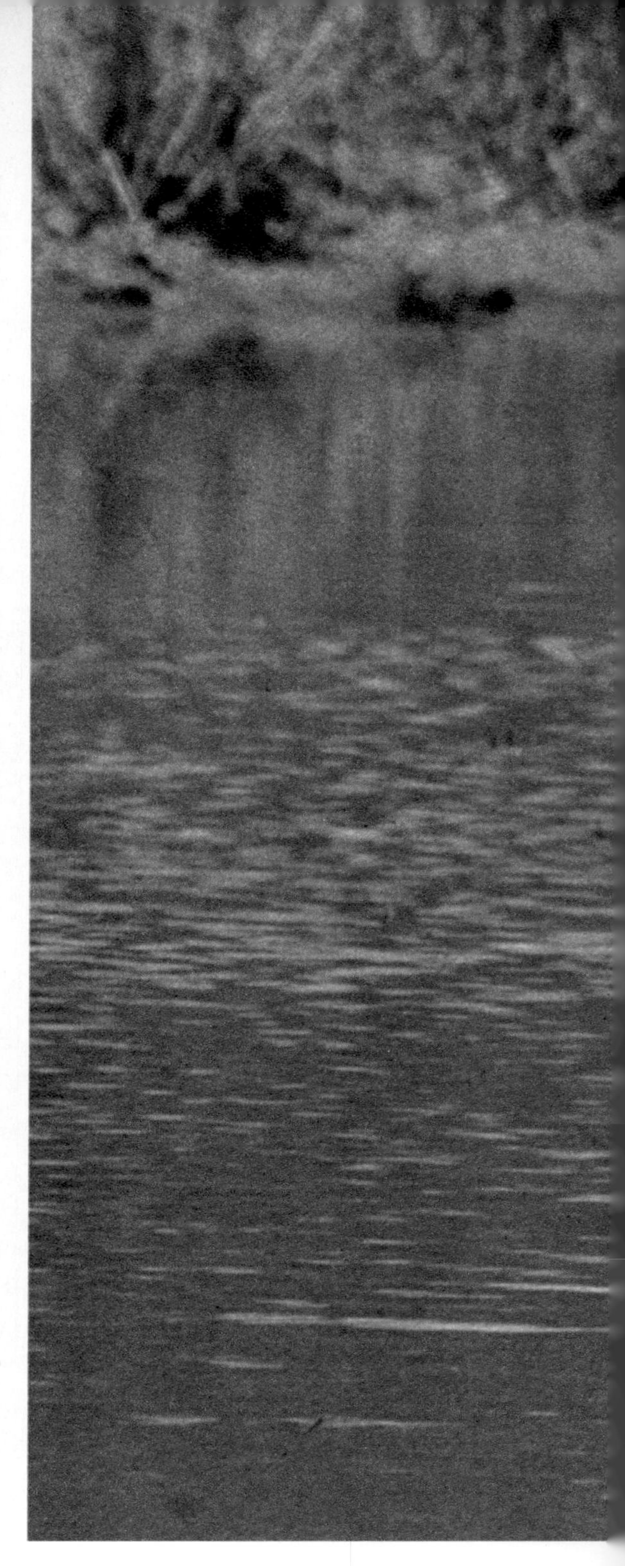

Left above: The Gloriosa or flame lily is common in most parts of tropical Africa. (Emil Schulthess) Left: Chameleons are noted for their ability to change color. This specimen of Chamelaeo isabellinus has picked up not only the leaf green but also the yellow of the cassia flowers. (W. T. Miller)

Above: The saddlebill (Ephippiorynchus senegalensis), Africa's most spectacular stork, is widespread but nowhere common in tropical Africa. (Clem Haagner)
Right: Grasshoppers assume many bizarre and beautiful forms and colors, but all share a destructive appetite for vegetation. (E. S. Ross)

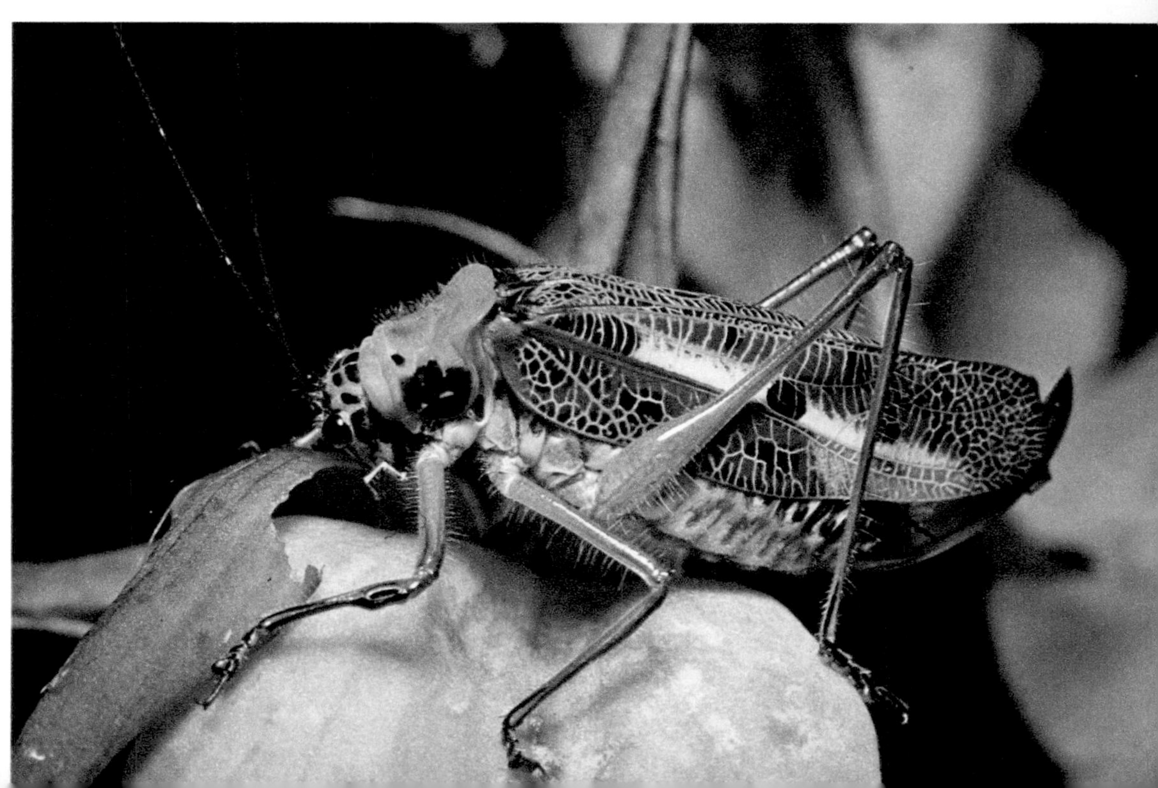

Mopane forest (Colophospermum mopane), an open, clean-floored woodland, with baboons drinking in a puddle. (D. C. H. Plowes)

unsuspected, will descend in hundreds to gobble them up. They catch the termites on the wing, sailing easily to and fro through the flying column of insects, and are not deterred by heavy rain.

A still more remarkable migration is that of the red-footed falcon *(Falco vespertinus)*. The eastern red-footed falcon *(F. v. amurensis)* breeds in China and migrates south into Assam in great numbers. But it differs from hobbies in that from then on its movements are unobserved until it reappears in the miombo in October. It could feed en route like the hobby, but apparently does not do so. The same type of migration occurs in the lesser cuckoo *(Cuculus poliocephalus)*.

Red-footed falcons collect in huge communal roosts before departure again for the north. They then move off northward and can be seen as far as Tanzania, where they again disappear. Do they make the flight at so great a height that they are invisible, and do they fly four thousand miles from Assam to Nyasaland nonstop? No one knows.

The miombo is also a haven for winter migrants from the south. During the South African winter, which can locally be quite sharp, many birds spend the months from June to October farther north. Among them are kites *(Milvus migrans)*, one of the most adaptable and successful birds of prey in the Old World. At different times of the year in the miombo there may be found migrant kites from southern Africa, kites that come in the dry season to breed, and migrant kites from Europe. This is a crucially important wintering area for migrants from both Eurasia and South Africa.

THE SOUTHERN FRINGES

The mopane forests of the Zambezi and Luangwa valleys are extensions of a belt of this woodland that runs right across Africa from Angola to the Transvaal, separating the true miombo from southern thorn bushveld. In the Luangwa or Zambezi valleys one drops off an escarpment from the miombo straight into mopane woodland. But on the flat, wind-blown Kalahari sands at the southern fringe of the region the transition from the miombo to mopane is more gradual. Mopane trees gradually become dominant as one travels toward the south.

In mopane regions several animals that are rare or absent in the miombo but present in East African grasslands and thornbush reappear. The giraffe and the impala are two of the more obvious ones, but there are many others. If exactly the same species does not reappear, a close relative will often replace it.

For wild animals mopane is potentially better country than the miombo itself. It is a local form of dry savanna, and the herbage floor is of "sweet" grasses, which are fairly palatable even when dry. The increase in the number of wild animals as soon as one enters an uninhabited stretch of mopane forest is obvious. Elephants in particular are very fond of mopane. If they were not common in some northern parts of the miombo one might think, on these southern fringes, that they have rejected the *Brachystegia* and are almost confined to mopane.

A strip of mopane and dry bush follows the Zambezi Valley inland for eight hundred miles, separating the plateau of Rhodesia from the much greater area of the miombo north and west of it. A similar finger runs northeast along the Luangwa Valley to within two hundred miles of the Ruaha trough in Tanzania. This too supports a drier type of woodland that connects directly with the drier parts of Tanzania to the northeast. Although the miombo today presents a solid barrier to the north-south movement of animals, it is easy to see how animals could have moved north and south in a climate only a little drier than at present. In such times these two long finger valleys would have made a corridor between northern and southern grasslands and thornbush.

Even in more arid times the miombo would still have been a very solid block of homogeneous woodland covering a large area of southern Africa. An imaginary map, drawn to show what the vegetation might have been like in one of the arid interpluvial spells of the Quaternary Epoch would indicate the miombo filling much of the present Congo basin and connected to the Guinea savannas by the Nile Valley and the western Rift. At such times the roan, white rhino, lechwe and kob would have had a continuous range. Since then the forest has again extended eastward and has divided the northern populations of animals from the southern. Among more specialized animals this split has led to the formation of new species, the puku from the kob, and the Nile lechwe from the lechwe. Today the miombo itself, with its own peculiar beasts, aids the forest in the segregation of northern and southern semi-arid faunas.

In other respects the miombo must have been a continuous environmental factor of great importance. The migration patterns of long-distance fliers like red-footed falcons, hobbies, and lesser cuckoos, and of transequatorial migrants like Abdim's stork and the pennant-winged nightjar have been evolved while the miombo existed. When their breeding range is inhospitable, these migrants take advantage of this great block of suitable habitat south of the equator.

Like the Sahara, the miombo has probably been present in Africa for a very long time; and like the Sahara it is likely to remain a wilderness for a long time yet. It may even be one area of African wilderness that will resist utilization and destruction by man, since in utilizing parts of it man so upsets the balance that he cannot himself survive.

Big Game, Kopjes and Salt Pans

The Southern Bushveld

12

South of the Brachystegia woodland and mopane a great belt of semi-arid country runs right across the continent. On the north and south its boundaries are rather indeterminate, being in the nature of transition zones from mopane woodland to acacia bushland in the north and from bushland to low desert scrub in the south. On the east and west this belt is quite clearly defined by physical features: the low chain of the Lebombo Hills separates it from the coastal plains of Mozambique, and the South West African plateau escarpment divides it from the Namib Desert.

This region is divided into two fairly distinct parts by an irregular broken chain of mountains running northward from the Natal Drakensberg through the Transvaal to the eastern escarpments of Rhodesia. There are gaps in this chain through which characteristic fauna and flora run uninterruptedly from west to east. But in Swaziland, for instance, there is a northward extension of high, cold, wet mountain grassland similar to the Natal Drakensberg and utterly different from the lowveld to the east and the dry, cool plains of the inland plateau to the west. Although the latter areas are in turn rather different from each other, they are a part of this same region. The eastern lowveld is characteristically dense bush in a hot climate. The western acacia steppe or bushveld running across from the Transvaal and Rhodesia to South West Africa is more akin to the Sudanese transition zone described in Chapter 4, and has a cool or cold winter.

The differences between these two main areas are emphasized by geological and physical features. The eastern lowveld is founded on ancient basement complex soils or old sediment of the Karroo system. Gouged out by erosion after continental uplift, it is traversed by numerous large permanent rivers running east to the coast from the high broken chain of mountains; the largest of these rivers is the Limpopo. The harder rocks of the Lebombo chain impede the course of most of these rivers, which break through it in spectacular gorges. This section is relatively fertile and well watered. By contrast, much of the western part lies on the Kalahari sands, where there is practically no surface water, and even large rivers vanish before reaching the sea.

Despite these differences, several features occur throughout this zone. The rainfall is too low for agriculture, and much of the land is infested with the tsetse fly; hence only parts of the zone have been developed as grazing land. The amount of rainfall is also erratic, and years of plenty alternate with severe droughts. In these conditions grass does not grow very tall and fires are not very intense. The rainfall is also inadequate for big trees, so that most of the acacias and other trees are no more than twenty feet tall.

At first glance this zone looks very much like the nyika in the east or the Sudanese or Somali subdeserts. It is only upon closer examination, however, that differences become apparent. The most important overall difference between this bushland and the nyika is that the rain falls in one season—from November to April. On the high western plains and to a lesser extent in the eastern lowveld, a cool dry winter, with many months of cloudless skies, is characteristic.

LIFE OF THE BUSHVELD

In this southern bushveld one is struck by the fact that some species of animals and plants are either very closely related to or identical with those of the nyika or the Somali subdeserts. The number of species of plants, birds and insects is generally lower. But this is not true of the large mammals, of which there is as fine a variety in this bushveld zone as anywhere in Africa. The distribution of mammals often upsets zoogeographic theories based on the number of species of plants or insects.

The bushveld is now separated from similar country in the north by the broad belt of the miombo, and by coastal savannas and forests. But, as we saw in the last chapter, a climate only a little drier is needed to create a continuous corridor running north and south right through the miombo; another corridor would also then develop near the coast. The pluvial periods of the ice ages separated northern and southern semi-arid areas and these are still separated. But in the last arid interpluvial period—only about twenty thousand years ago—they were probably joined.

Any differences in fauna and flora must chiefly have occurred since that time, and it is not at all surprising that these regions are so closely akin. In most cases the plants or animals probably had their centers of abundance in the north and moved south. In some cases new species have evolved; in others they have remained identical.

Among the trees and shrubs there are some notable absentees. Euphorbias, for instance, which are extremely common through the bush in northeast Africa, are rather rare or altogether absent in the southern bushveld. *Commiphora,* the dominant vegetation over thousands of square miles of the nyika and Somali, grows much less extensively in the south though common in places. But the rivers of the eastern bushveld are set about with the same green- or yellow-barked fever trees *(Acacia xanthophloea)* that border every large river in

A fine symmetrical baobab flourishes at the base of a rocky hill, where it benefits from the run-off water. (R. D. K. Hadden: Rhodesia Information Service)

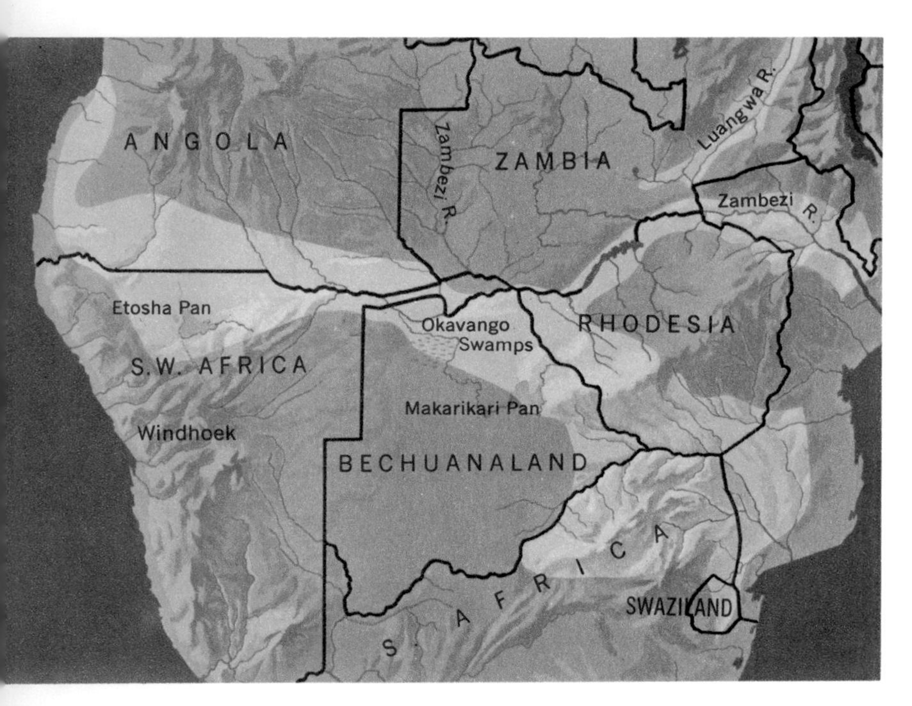

Southern bushveld comprises the dry thornbush of south Angola, Bechuanaland, and South Africa.

the nyika, and *Acacia detinens,* the true wait-a-bit thorn, is so like the *Acacia mellifera* of the north that some now consider it only a variety of *A. mellifera.*

Birds tell a similar story. Both yellow-billed and red-billed hornbills are very common in the bushveld, as they are in the north. But Von der Decken's and Jackson's hornbills do not occur here, nor do two very characteristic nyika birds—the white-headed buffalo weaver and the superb starling. On the other hand, common buffalo weavers occur, as do white-crowned shrikes *(Eurocephalus anguitimens),* two species of oxpeckers, wattled starlings, and many other birds that are also found in the nyika. Along big rivers the southern carmine bee eater *(Merops nupicoides)* replaces the northern species, *(M. nubicus).*

The similarities in the bird life seem to be more numerous than the differences. Of course there are also species which are to be found in the bushveld and not in the nyika, like the striking magpie shrike *(Urolestes melanoleucus)* and the crimson-breasted shrike *(Laniarius atro-coccineus).* One could sit in the shade of a baobab tree in the eastern lowveld, and hear and see many birds found further north but absent from a great belt in between.

MAMMALS OF THE EASTERN LOWVELD

Large wild animals still abound in several parts of this zone. Much of the land east of the mountain chain has been preserved in the famed Kruger National Park, and here the fauna is both abundant and varied. The park stretches from the eastern foothills of the Transvaal Mountains to the Lebombo range and it is one of the few national parks in Africa that forms a full ecological unit. The animals need not migrate out of the park at any time, though naturally some do move across its boundaries.

The Kruger Park, like several other parks in Africa, owes its existence largely to the human and animal diseases that made it difficult for early settlers or African tribes to inhabit the territory. Before the rinderpest epidemic of 1896, parts of it were infested with the tsetse fly, which kept out African pastoralists, and, when malaria was still a dread disease, European settlers avoided it. Even so, the wild inhabitants of the lowveld were greatly reduced before they were given protection. Transport drivers and hunters from the high plains of the Transvaal used to visit the lowveld during the cool dry winters when the area was relatively healthy. They killed great numbers of wild animals, and some species became very rare. The recovery of the animals from surviving remnants to their present abundance is one of the great success stories of wildlife conservation. At the same time this recovery illustrates the resilience of wild animals, when they are left unmolested.

What strikes one most about the big animals of this region is their variety. In few other parks of Africa is there the same mixture of large grazing animals and large browsing beasts. In both the East African grasslands, and in the nyika or Somali, grazers or browsers tend to predominate. But in the eastern lowveld, species which are largely confined to open plains farther north are found in relatively thick woodland, and the fauna is further enriched by a southward extension of the range of such characteristic miombo animals as the roan and sable. The bushveld is the true home of the greater kudu, one of the most widespread of all species throughout this region.

In Kruger Park one finds large browsers like the elephant, giraffe, eland and greater kudu. Both black and white rhinoceroses existed here in the past, died out, and have been reintroduced. Impala are extremely abundant, and in parts a rather rare browsing animal, the Zululand nyala *(Tragelaphus angasii)* is found. Large grazers include hippos near rivers, the buffalo, zebra, roan, sable, wildebeest, hartebeest, and tsessebe *(Damaliscus lunatus).* Grazing animals, like the wildebeest or tsessebe, may keep to more open parts from choice, but even the tsessebe will enter thick cover on occasion. There is a striking absence of any form of gazelle, which is not really filled by small grazing animals of more solitary habits like the stembuck or oribi. And there is no counterpart of the gerenuk, or the extremely abundant dikdik of northern bushlands.

All the major predators—lions, leopards, cheetahs, hyenas and wild dogs—inhabit the lowveld. In the early years, when attempts were being made to restore the former abundance of herbivores, many lions were shot; because of this, antelopes were able to multiply. But in this thick bush country lion hunting had to be done on foot, and was much more laborious than on the East African plains. Once their numbers had been reduced, the lions also produced larger litters and bred more often so that in the end the attempt at control largely nullified itself. Carnivores and herbivores all thrived together, and lions are quite abundant though some control may still be necessary. The relatively dense bush and the concentration of wild animals near water in the dry season probably makes it easier for lions to kill here than in completely open short-grass plains like the Serengeti.

Rounded boulders like these often crown castle kopjes in the bushveld. (A. Ehrhardt)

CASTLE KOPJES

A feature of landscape in the lowveld is the numerous small hills or kopjes composed of masses of almost square boulders piled on top of each other. Because of their resemblance to the crenelated walls and towers of medieval castles, they have been called castle kopjes. These rock piles are almost all that breaks the horizon in much of this bushveld, and like those in the nyika they abound in rock hyraxes and baboons.

Castle kopjes are akin to inselbergs in that they are hard blocks of rock that have resisted the forces of weathering, decay and erosion. They are often composed of plutonic rocks—rocks that have been pushed upward from below and have then solidified beneath a mantle of other rock or soil. Such rocks cool slowly and are usually crystalline and jointed like a masonry wall. The joints weather more rapidly than the hard centers of each block, and so the characteristic rectangular, perched blocks result.

A wonderful group of these kopjes on the northern edge of the bushveld is found in the Matopos Hills in Rhodesia. Here one drives for miles in and out among rock piles of fantastic shapes, with sometimes a rounded whaleback ridge. The hills support dense woodland and must once have been forested, for several forest birds, such as turacos and forest flycatchers, survive here in an environment rather different from their normal habitats.

Ground squirrels live in holes in the ground and are chiefly terrestrial. Ubiquitous in tropical Africa, they are very agile and are difficult for a predator to catch. (South African Information Service)

In the Matopos there is an extraordinarily dense population of black eagles *(Aquila verreauxi)*. Sometimes two pairs nest within a mile of each other, which is not a normal habit of this species. Eagles are usually supposed to be intolerant, aggressive birds, ready to drive any intruder from the neighborhood of their nests, and in most parts of the world, pairs keep themselves far enough apart to avoid any likelihood of direct competition or fighting. But in the Matopos the black eagles constantly fly close to neighboring pairs apparently without arousing enmity. One can only conclude that the food supply, in the shape of the hyrax, is so abundant that there is no need for one pair of eagles to resent another's intrusion on its home range. It is nonetheless remarkable that a habit which may be necessary for the survival of the species in one area does not hold in another area.

LITTLE-KNOWN BECHUANALAND

West of the Transvaal mountain chain the country is nearly flat plateau, descending gradually westward to the Kalahari basin. The Kalahari sands extend northward well into the fringe of the bushveld, and even beyond into the miombo. This is very different country from the eastern lowveld. Here the mopane woodland that borders the miombo in the south degenerates first into low scrub and then gives place to shrubby acacias and grass. The country is much more open than the lowveld as a whole, but there are dense thickets in places.

If there is any part of Africa that rivals the Serengeti Plains in its great game concentrations, this is it. Wildebeest, springbok, and gemsbok are very numerous, and eland, hartebeest and kudus are also common. No accurate figures exist, but it is estimated that at least a quarter of a million wildebeest are found on these sandy plains. In the dry season they are forced to concentrate on the few permanent sources of water near the Makarikari pans and the Okovango River, and it is then that their numbers are appreciated. In the time of rains they disperse over a vast area to the south into the Kalahari Desert proper.

The huge herds have not survived here because they have received careful protection. Far from it. A heavy toll is taken annually by biltong hunters, and the African inhabitants of this area kill animals whenever they can. However, they are rather few in relation to the number of wild animals and perhaps after independence a more responsible attempt will be made to preserve this valuable resource.

This great haven of wildlife remains little known because it is so inaccessible. In the old days the shortage of water made exploration difficult and the few tracks found there today are in deep sand and very difficult to use. But in the last few years the area has attracted many big-game hunters who find it increasingly difficult to obtain trophies elsewhere. Biltong hunters, whose only interest is dried meat and hides, come from the neighboring parts of South Africa, where most of the formerly abundant wildlife has been wiped out. The vulnerable point of the nomadic animals of Bechuanaland is that they tend to concentrate on certain water sources in time of drought; there they can easily be killed.

Careful cropping of the stock could do no harm, and indeed would be beneficial, for without it the animals of this area

Impala, abundant in the bushveld, are among the most beautiful of African antelopes. (Clem Haagner)

can increase to the point where a drastic reduction in numbers may result from lack of food. Such tragedies can be forecast without strict accuracy, by analyzing the proportions of young and old animals in the population and studying their condition. When very large numbers die in a drought it is probable that the population has become too great, a situation that can be avoided, at least in part, by careful management.

In neighboring areas of Rhodesia it has been proved beyond doubt that this bushveld country is certainly capable of producing more usable meat from wild than from domestic animals in a given area. This is what one would expect, considering the variety of animals that utilize the vegetation in the bushveld very efficiently. And, as elsewhere, they need no veterinary care, are immune to diseases caused by the tsetse fly and several other diseases, and can live with less water than domestic cattle. The difficulty is to cull the stock in remote areas and persuade people accustomed to prime beefsteak to eat the meat of wild animals.

THE OKOVANGO DELTA

The highlands of Angola to the west, a high rainfall area, give birth to the Zambezi, Cuanda, and Okovango rivers. The Cuanda eventually flows into the Zambezi, but all of these rivers spread out over vast flat flood plains above the Victoria Falls. This is actually the continental divide, but the drainage pattern is so confused that one would hardly realize it. One may be traveling through open dry bush and suddenly meet with a slowly advancing sheet of shallow water. At some remote period in the future the strong-flowing Zambezi will doubtless capture all these waters. Meantime those of the Okovango flow out onto flat Kalahari sands and limestone and produce a huge swamp, similar in general to Chad or the inundation zone of the Niger, and supporting vast herds of wild animals.

Here is a meeting ground of typical flood plain grazing animals like the hippo, buffalo, lechwe, waterbuck, and even sitatunga, with bush and woodland animals like the sable, roan, wildebeest, zebra, kudu and hartebeest. Sables and roans, normally animals that stay inside fairly dense woodland, can here be seen grazing in the open. Even the bushbuck, lover of thickets, emerges onto the lush grazing of the flood plains. Gemsbok and springbok, nomadic animals of the Kalahari sands, also come to the fringes of the swamps. Elephants are fairly numerous, but nowhere in this area do their present numbers approach those of some of the great East African herds. This situation may change, and in time elephants may become far more common.

In the rivers very large crocodiles formerly abounded, but these have been killed for their skins and their numbers have dwindled. Crocodiles here seem to be more dangerous to men than in some other parts of Africa; in the rivers, and in the Zambezi in particular, they devour a few people each year.

A magnificent kudu bull. Despite its large size, the kudu is often very difficult to see. The white side stripes help to break up its outline. (R. D. K. Hadden: Rhodesia Information Service)

Perhaps this is because they feed on mammals as well as fish.

Water birds abound here, just as they do on the flood plains of rivers in the miombo country to the north; for storks, herons, ibises, ducks, geese and fish eagles, one flood plain is as good as another. The meandering of the rivers in past ages has produced many enclosed lagoons which in the dry season are ideal secluded haunts for water birds. Spurwing geese *(Plectropterus gambensis)* are unusually common among these lagoons.

The swamps, and some other large pans of water in northern Bechuanaland, are the wintering area of numbers of migrant ducks from southern Africa. Cattle egrets *(Bubulcus ibis)* ringed in South Africa have also been recovered in this region. The southern water birds must migrate north to avoid the winter, just as the Palearctic population of ducks, geese and waders must go south. The former are much fewer, because the landmass to the south is far smaller than the great expanse of Europe and Asia. Probably, also, a smaller proportion of the total population migrates since the winters are not so severe. But the same general principles that govern the migration in the northern hemisphere apply here in the reverse direction.

In the South African summer these migrants leave, but there is then a big influx of other Palearctic migrants besides the water birds. The lesser spotted eagle *(Aquila pomarina)*, a bird that breeds in swampy northern woodlands, comes this far south. And Abdim's stork *(Spenorynchus abdimii)*, which breeds in the tropical Sudan, "winters" as far south as the Northern Transvaal.

TWO GREAT DRY LAKES

In this region there are two enormous flat expanses of mud, known as the Etosha and Makarikari pans, each of them covering many thousands of square miles. There are lesser expanses at Lake Ngami and Lake Dow. These are lakes only in name; they dry up in all years but those of exceptional rainfall.

Such "pans" are a feature of the northern Kalahari and the southern part of this bushveld zone. They are dead flat, and absolutely featureless. Mirage distorts and magnifies little irregularities of the surface, and from a few miles out the shoreline is quite invisible. These pans are, in fact, expanses of mud desert, analogous to the great flat salt plains or "sebkhas" in the Sahara. Such pans are produced by a combination of water and wind. When a rapidly flowing stream slows down, the first material to be deposited is coarse sand and gravel. Fine silt and mud is carried on. When the river eventually fills a huge, nearly flat basin, it kills much of the vegetation and deposits a layer of fine silt. When the basin has no outlet, as in the Makarikari and Etosha pans, it also becomes saline, so preventing plant growth.

The silt beds of these pans were deposited at a time when the rivers flowing into them were much larger. Now that they are almost continually dry the winds can get to work. In such hot dry areas small whirlwinds, known as dust devils, are continually generated. These pick up the fine silt dust and carry it far away. Thus, over the ages, the silt brought down by the rivers is carried off and the pan is gradually deepened.

Flamingos, both lesser and greater, occur in great numbers on these pans; estimates of the number range from a quarter

Impala are famous leapers, capable of clearing thirty feet or more in one bound. (Sven Gillsater: Tio)

million to a half million flamingos—far fewer than in East Africa. It is probable that this is a distinct population that does not move away from this general area, for there do not seem to be many records of sick and stranded flamingos on dams or swamps to the north, as there would be if migration were regular.

Flamingos breed on the Etosha Pan, and a fair number have recently been ringed there, so that a more detailed knowledge of their movements should emerge. They were formerly reputed to breed on Lake Ngami, but examination of the old records has shown that those birds were pelicans. This is a good example of how an erroneous record can be repeated from book to book.

The Makarikari Pan is filled from time to time by the overflow from the Okovango delta, through the Botletle channel. This first flows into Lake Dow, and only reaches the Makarikari Pan in times of flood. But there is evidently much subterranean drainage, for many fresh and saline springs occur around the margins of the pan. These are the main permanent waters around which the great herds of wildebeest, eland, gemsbok, springbok, and other nomadic animals of the sandy Kalahari Desert congregate in times of drought. Around the pans is nutritious, short grass pasture.

The Etosha Pan, in a large game reserve, contains in an area of about six thousand square miles about as many large ungulates as the Ngorongoro crater, which is only fourteen miles across. But among these there are believed to be ten times as many (360) lions at Etosha as in Ngorongoro. The Etosha lions must therefore have a far greater controlling effect than those of Ngorongoro on the numbers of their favorite prey. The difference in relative populations is probably due to the territorial habits of the lion. In a small area of about 150 square miles like Ngorongoro only a certain number of lions can live, no matter how abundant the herbivores or the water supply. But in the vast flat expanse of the Etosha Pan each widely separated spring can support a pride of lions that does not need to compete directly with its neighbor. One cannot safely generalize on the number of herbivores required to support a pride of lions, for it varies greatly from place to place, according to the cover available, the size of the area, and the amount of water supplies. Even at Etosha, however, the lions must barely be able to control the numbers of their prey.

THE WESTERN SCARP

West of the Etosha Pan there is a mountainous area known as the Kaokoveld, a wild country of rocky hills and bushed

Overleaf: A scene that epitomizes the African dry season: thirsty giraffes tower over zebras against a background of leafless bush. (Clem Haagner)

valleys, rising to nearly six thousand feet in the north. In these mountains there are a fair number of elephants, some black rhinoceroses, and some mountain zebras. A species of dikdik is also found here, further pointing the relation to northern bushlands. The local race of mountain zebra *(Equus zebra hartmanni)* has survived here in far greater numbers than has the nominate race *(E. z. zebra)* on the Cape; there are perhaps ten thousand of them. At one time the range of this animal must have included much of the South West African plateau; but it has been greatly reduced in settled country, though it extends south to the Orange now.

To the west of the mountains lies an area of more arid bushlands on a terrace intermediate between the high plateau and the northern tail of the Namib Desert. Here also there are some elephants, giraffes, rhinos and many other animals. This area too was formerly included in the Etosha Pan reserve, but this reserve is threatened for political reasons, and the Kaokoveld may be removed from it. It is a rather barren area, lacking in water, poorly vegetated, and in parts eroded.

Nature's weathered masonry. The joints between these blocks of granite have worn away more rapidly than the cores of the blocks themselves, producing fantastic shapes. (Rhodesia Information Service)

Much wildlife still exists on the farms of South West Africa. The farmers have wiped out predatory beasts, greatly improved the water supplies, and thus unconsciously provided an improved environment for some of the bushveld animals. The greater kudu especially thrives on farms, and the eland, red hartebeest *(Alcelaphus buselaphus caama)*, gemsbok, and springbok are also fairly common. Wildebeest, which only occurred in parts of the farmed land, have been almost exterminated.

MAN'S INFLUENCE

This region is one which has been less affected by the activities of man than many in Africa. Much of it has been regarded as useless because of the prevalence of human or animal diseases like malaria or trypanosomiasis, and such natural drawbacks as lack of water. Even in the developed parts the impact of civilization has fallen chiefly upon the larger mammals; smaller creatures—birds, reptiles, and insects—are often hardly affected at all. There are probably just as many geckos and agama lizards in the inhabited areas as ever there were, perhaps more, because certain of the predators have been destroyed.

Man's effect upon an environment depends largely on whether he is a cultivator or a pastoralist. If cultivation is his way of life, the natural vegetation must be destroyed before crops can be planted. Stock-keeping, however, means only the modification of the vegetation by grazing. By and large it is climate that dictates the choice between pastoralism and farming. A man may choose to be a pastoralist in an area of good rainfall, but in an area of low rainfall the choice is made for him, for crops will not succeed there. Thus, in a semi-arid belt such as this region, man has in general modified rather than destroyed the vegetation.

The effects of overgrazing have been very carefully studied in this part of Africa. The natural vegetation is a mixture of trees and grass which compete for the available water. In low-rainfall areas grass naturally tends to be dominant, since the dense shallow mat of fibrous grass roots is better able to make use of the scanty rainfall than the widespreading roots of trees. When drought comes the leaves of the grasses die, and only the roots and growing points remain alive. Trees and shrubs, on the other hand, must maintain the water content of their twigs, and continue to use a certain amount of water through the long dry season, though they reduce their water loss by such means as shedding their leaves.

In natural conditions in this region a mixture of browsing and grazing animals feeds on both trees and grass, but never uses either to excess. The first act of pastoral man is to bring cattle and sheep into the area, and these are chiefly grazers. Even goats prefer to eat grass, though they browse as well. They have generally been maligned as makers of desert when in fact they merely utilize shrubs better than do cattle or sheep. It is the latter that causes the initial deterioration; goats are a later stage in the succession.

The impact of grazing cattle and sheep destroys the natural balance, and helps trees and bush to dominate the grass. The suppression of fires in order to preserve the grass also helps trees to flourish. Thus, under heavy use by cattle and sheep in semi-arid country, the bush becomes thicker and eventually the value of the pasture land is much reduced. As described

Stapeliads are succulents common in most dry parts of tropical Africa. They often have a repulsive smell that attracts flies. This is Stapelia gettleffii. (D. C. H. Plowes)

Huernia zebrina. A striking stapeliad with dark red center and striped surrounding leaves. (D. C. H. Plowes)

in the chapter on the nyika, heavy use by elephants and giraffes has exactly the opposite effect, turning bushland into grassland.

The increase of bush, together with the destruction of lions and leopards, is probably the main reason why the impala and the kudu often thrive so well on farms. Eland too can do well but some other animals such as the appealing springbok compete directly with sheep for available grass, but they produce no wool.

There is a growing realization that wild animals that prefer to feed on bush can thrive together with domestic cattle and sheep, and that they complement the grazing effect of the latter. The day is still distant when a rancher will encourage elephants to take up residence and perform the function of a bulldozer, but that too may come in time. Meantime, one may take heart that in many parts of this bushveld zone the senseless total destruction of wild animals, which is responsible for such a tragic picture in most parts of Africa, has largely ceased. Indeed the process has been reversed, at least among more enlightened people, and many ranches are being restocked with selected wild animals, as much for their usefulness as their beauty.

Red Sands, Gemsbok and Dune Beetles

The Southern Deserts and Subdeserts

13

All the western part of southern Africa is desert or semidesert. The basic reasons for this are the same as those for the Sahara: an arid zone girdles the world in these latitudes. The Kalahari Desert and other deserts here are smaller and less severe than the Sahara for the most part because the continental landmass is much narrower at this point. The prevailing easterly rain-bearing winds affect more of the continent in its narrow southern portion than in the great northern expanse.

The deserts of this region make up three fairly distinct units. The largest is the Kalahari, a huge, sand-filled basin stretching from northern Bechuanaland to the Molopo River and beyond, and from the high plateau of South West Africa in the west to the bushveld and plains of the Transvaal in the east. The Namib is a narrow strip, about a hundred miles wide, running up the west coast from the Orange River to beyond Mossamedes in Angola. It is defined on the east by a sharp escarpment, the edge of the South West African plateau. It is a much more extreme desert than any other in this part of the world, with less than five inches of rain a year, and in many areas less than one inch.

The Karroo is rather different from either the Kalahari or Namib deserts. It fills its own great basin of ancient sediments south of the Orange River, and is rather flat except where later volcanic rocks provide relief. It is covered with a peculiar type of low bush that is related more to the subtropical Cape maquis or *fynbos* than to the tropical grasses and bush plants that have colonized the Kalahari and Namib. And it gets more rain in winter (that is, from April to September) than the others.

These deserts share the character of the northern deserts in that there is scanty and irregular rain; this feature, in fact, is found throughout South West Africa, little of which is far removed from desert. Strong winds are frequent, and there are large variations in temperature from day to night. Many of the same adaptions to the conditions found among the animals of the Sahara occur here too. But there is one rather important difference. These deserts are on the whole cooler than the Sahara. Even the low-lying Namib, which has no frost and can be very hot, is classed as one of the cooler deserts of the world. In the Kalahari and the Karroo, long cold periods in winter, and sharp frosts, are the rule rather than the exception.

A SEA OF RED SAND

Except for the fact that there is practically no surface water, the Kalahari is not a true desert. It is a subdesert steppe, with a fairly good cover of vegetation in most parts; and consequently it supports large numbers of nomadic animals. A man can die of thirst almost as easily in the Kalahari as in other deserts, but the desert beasts manage to obtain an adequate diet from the vegetation.

The reason for this is that whatever rain falls on the Kalahari sinks into the sand, and is then available to plants. The whole expanse consists of dunes that roll over the landscape like great waves, one hundred to five hundred feet apart, and often run almost straight for many miles. There are no big areas of rock, nothing like the hamadas of the Sahara, from which nearly all the rainfall runs off and collects elsewhere. An area in which a rainstorm falls will provide relatively abundant grazing for some time thereafter. The water is stored in the sand at depth, and the deeper-rooted shrubs and big acacia trees suck up and utilize whatever the grasses cannot reach.

The dunes of the Kalahari are a beautiful rich pink, red, or almost maroon, the color coming from iron oxide. Each dune has along its crest a growth of stiff grasses, chiefly *Eragrostis* and *Aristida*. Green when there are rains, these grasses dry to a whitish color in drought. For limited periods they provide good feeding for animals. On the sides of the dunes there are low, evenly spaced spiny shrubs; standing a few feet apart and among these shrubs grow small strongly-rooted tufts of stiff grass. Generally low on the dunes, but sometimes quite high up, there are big trees, notably *Acacia giraffae* and *A. haematoxylon*, of a very hard, heavy red wood. In the flat valley bottoms between the dunes there are more succulent plants.

One can travel for many miles across the Kalahari and find no extensive bare areas. In places the effect is parklike. The trees, grass and bushes protect the desert from the wind, and though the sand does blow on the dune tops, this bears little resemblance to Saharan sandstorms or the smoking dunes of the Namib. The bushes produce leaves, and the big acacias yield pods that are eaten by animals. By comparison with various other deserts of the world there is no shortage of food, but animals obtain most of their water from sappy plants.

The rim of the Kalahari is from four to five thousand feet above sea level on the west, and is still higher in the east; its

A white-backed vulture perched on a dead acacia in a barren but beautiful landscape of dry river bed, dunes, and spectacular sky. (Laurence K. Marshall)

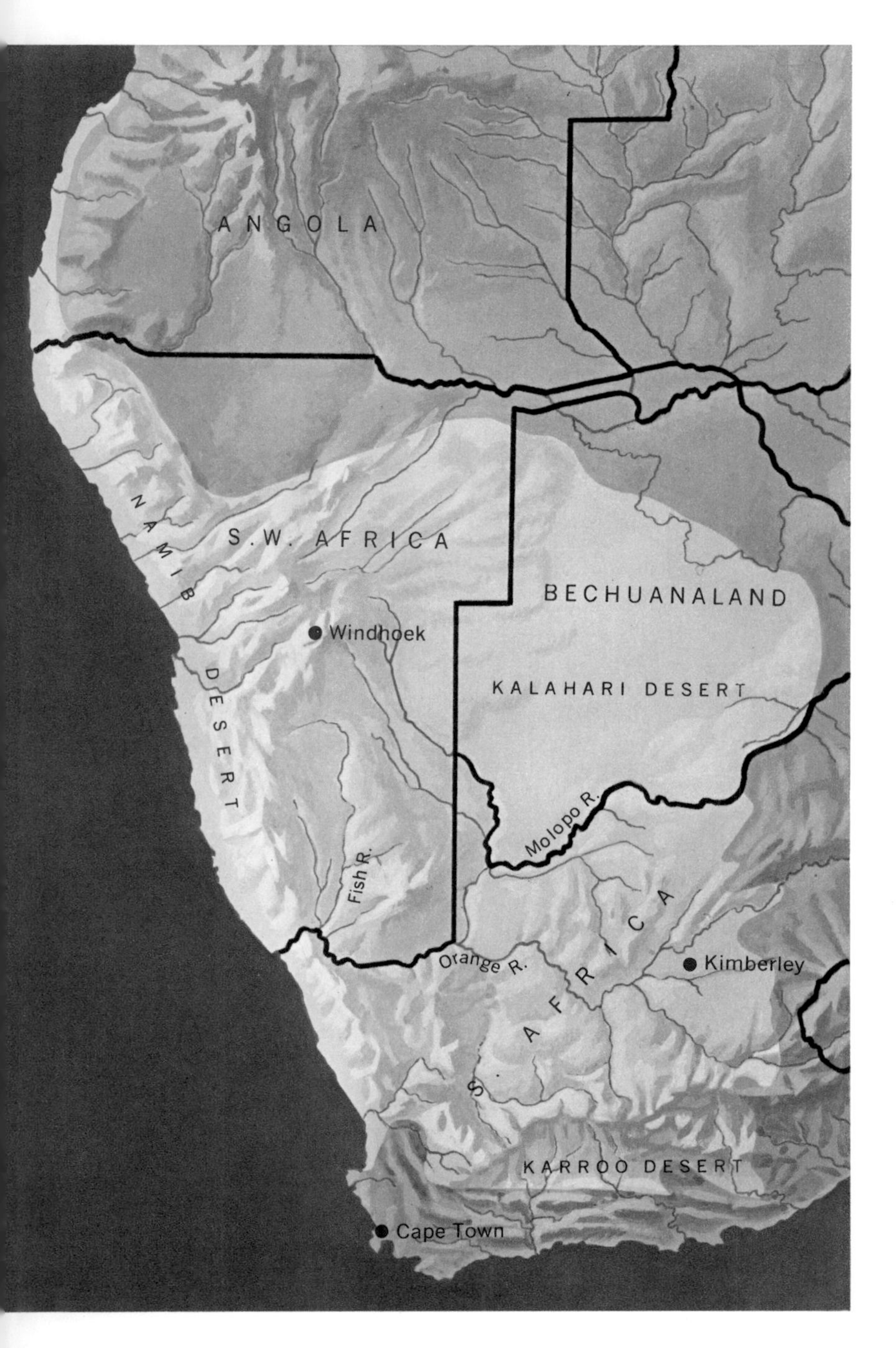

The Kalahari and Namib deserts cover a large tract in Bechuanaland and South Africa, varying from cold dry uplands to huge sand dunes.

lowest point is about 2,800 feet. In this huge hollow the Kalahari dunes were presumably formed in a more arid period. The prevailing wind could not then have been what it is today, for in many areas the dunes do not lie at right angles to the wind, as they normally would. Since that more arid period the dunes have been stabilized by vegetation and they cannot be moved by the wind unless the vegetation is grazed away.

Like the Sahara, the Kalahari is ancient. Its primary sands are of the Pliocene age, and have been formed by the decay of rock fragments within the basin. They are entirely continental, not marine. But in the last two million years they have been shifted about again, and as little as eighteen thousand years ago arid conditions may have extended far to the north in what is now the miombo woodland of the Congo and Angola. Although the desert is for the most part of ancient origin, it has experienced rather sharp changes of climate in relatively recent times.

GEMSBOK AND SPRINGBOK

The typical nomadic animals of this desert are the gemsbok *(Oryx g. gazella)* and the springbok *(Antidorcas marsupialis)*. The gemsbok is a magnificent beast, similar to the northern beisa oryx, but much larger, with horns up to four feet long. It has the same black facial stripes as the northern oryx, a black line separating the white belly from the brown body, and a black patch at the base of its long, flowing tail. Whether or not one regards the northern and southern oryx as one species, the gemsbok can be considered a clear link with northern desert fauna.

The springbok is a single, widely-distributed species that here replaces the large variety of northern gazelles. They are like gazelles except that they have a white patch on the back enclosed in a pouch which is expanded when the animal is excited. The name derives from their habit of jumping when excited or frightened. Although they jump much higher than gazelles, their action is essentially similar to the movement known as "pronking" in gazelles, a series of stiff-legged bounds that act as an alarm signal. Springbok are fundamentally gazelles. Like northern gazelles they are primarily grazers that also browse shrubs.

Since both gazelles and oryx have more representatives in northern arid areas than in the south, it is likely that both these animals at some time entered this region from the north. They could have come down an arid eastern corridor that must have existed in former dry periods. Presumably the gazelle ancestor of the springbok was one of many species. Springbok are like the Thompson's gazelle in body shape and color, but are larger and have horns of a different shape. They have diverged more sharply from the northern gazelle stock than has the gemsbok from the oryx.

In this area, besides these true desert animals there are wildebeest, eland, occasional kudus, and red hartebeest. These all inhabit much drier country here than they do farther north. In Kenya and Tanzania neither wildebeest nor hartebeest would be found in country with as little rain as the Kalahari. It may be that the relatively more luxuriant vegetation, and the fairly cold climate both combine to allow them to survive here in conditions that would be too harsh for them farther north.

These animals are apparently not nomadic from choice but rather from necessity. In areas where water is easily obtained by pumping from the substrata, they drink regularly and therefore tend to become more settled. Many gemsbok and springbok live on farmland in this area. In fact in South West Africa there are two to three animals on farmland for every one in a game reserve. The same is true of the hartebeest and

The Kalahari black-maned lion is perhaps the finest lion in all Africa. Two females display curiosity but the great male is sleepy and indifferent. (Clem Haagner)

the eland; however, wildebeest seem to be more naturally nomadic.

HONEY BADGERS AND AARDWOLFS

In the Kalahari one can sometimes get a good view of animals that may have a wide range but are very seldom seen elsewhere in Africa. One of these is the honey badger *(Mellivora capensis),* which is found from the southern end of the Atlas Mountains throughout the Ethiopian Region except for extreme deserts and deep forest. In twenty-five years I have had only a few glimpses of honey badgers elsewhere in Africa, yet in the Kalahari I have watched one for nearly three hours in broad daylight.

For their size, honey badgers are perhaps the most powerful animals on earth, with the possible exception of the northern wolverine. About three feet long, they have immensely thick skins to withstand the stings of bees, and extremely strong jaws. Their long hair is gray above, blackish beneath, and the end of their short tail is bare. They are supposed to use this bare patch to attract angry bees, but it probably has some other function. Bee stings would in any case make little impression on their long hair and thick skin.

A honey badger goes about its business with no regard for any other creature. Anything that attacks it will probably be worsted, for it can twist and turn inside its thick skin like an otter, and fasten a vicelike bite on its assailant. Honey badgers are credited with killing even big animals like wildebeest, though not for food. They travel in a rolling lope, occasionally stopping to dig with the long curved claws of their forefeet or climb a tree, and they pay practically no attention to a human being. Indeed it would be unwise to provoke the animal; it might bite, and this would certainly be a thing to regret.

Honey badgers live chiefly on the contents of bees' nests—the comb, grubs, honey and all. But nothing comes amiss: birds' eggs, insects, small mammals, and probably carrion are all eaten. In the Kalahari I would think that honey badgers live less on honey and grubs than elsewhere, and spend more time digging in soft sand for young ground squirrels or gerbils. One that I watched traveled about four miles in three hours, digging at intervals. It appeared to depend a good deal more on its sense of smell than on its sight to locate possible prey.

Honey badgers are sometimes led to honey by a bird, the honey guide *(Indicator indicator).* This bird will also guide men to honey, but it seems to have abandoned the habit in some parts of Africa since civilized men replaced primitive honey-gatherers. The bird flies along in front, chattering, and the badger or man follows. It is believed that men learned to follow the honey guide by observing its association with the badger. The bird itself eats wax. In the Kalahari, chanting goshawks *(Melierax canorus)* and eagle owls *(Bubo africanus)* sometimes watch the honey badger and probably catch animals it disturbs.

The aardwolf *(Proteles cristatus)* is another queer beast occasionally seen in the Kalahari. Normally solitary, it is sometimes found here in small packs. The aardwolf is a long-legged, long-haired, doglike animal that lives by day in a burrow. It vaguely resembles a hyena, but its teeth are adapted only for eating insects. Probably it lives largely on termites. But in deserts, animals that show a preference for certain foods in lands of relative plenty cannot afford to be particular. Predatory birds, honey badgers, and aardwolfs may all have a more varied diet in the Kalahari than in other parts of Africa.

THE SMOKING DUNES

The Namib is a very different place from the Kalahari. Its rainfall is very low, and most of its surface is bare of vegetation. It is composed in part of flat gravelly plains and, over much larger areas, of some of the biggest sand dunes to be found in the world. Individual dunes are often more than five hundred feet high, and some approach a height of one thousand feet.

The Namib exists for two reasons: first, the rain-bearing easterly winds that reach it have already crossed the continent, and the last of their moisture falls on the high South West African plateau. Secondly, a cold antarctic current, the Benguella current, starts near the Cape of Good Hope and runs northward up the coast. This means that the sea off the west coast is very cold, and therefore does not generate rain, though it often does produce fog. Thus the Namib gets hardly any rain either from the east or from the west. However, arid as it may be, it is relatively cool compared to the Sahara, and within twenty miles of the coast it receives some moisture from fog. But it is one of the more extreme deserts in the world.

The huge dunes of the Namib are called barkans. These are

Left: Springbok resemble the gazelles of North Africa in their slim forms and black side stripes. Right: The red dunes of the Kalahari are a fitting setting for the finest of all oryx, the gemsbok (Oryx g. gazella). (Both by Clem Haagner)

individual dunes that often stand on their own base but may join with others to form confused masses, as in the ergs of the Sahara. Each dune moves before the wind, but its thin, outflung extremities travel faster than the massive center and summit; thus the dunes tend to be crescent-shaped, with the horns of their crescents pointing in the direction of the prevailing wind.

A big Namib barkan rises like a little mountain range of sand from a stony base, and it takes a great effort to reach the crest. The sand is red, the darker colors deriving from garnet, a very common mineral in this area. The sand blows off the tops all the time, and from a distance the dunes appear to be smoking. At close range the blowing sand is seen to form vortices in the shape of a rotating coil on the leeward side of the dune.

The dunes cover all of the stony substratum from the Kuiseb River to the Orange River. They reach a maximum altitude above the sea of about four thousand feet, and engulf small mountains and rock outcrops. Lines of dunes occur again south of the Orange River and in the northern extremity of the Namib toward Angola. But for a long way north from the Kuiseb River to beyond the Swakop River the ground is of gravel or stones, almost completely bare of vegetation and forming a habitat like the ergs of the Sahara. Here and there there are salt pans similar to those in northern deserts and the Kalahari.

The dunes are gradually pushing the Kuiseb River northward. Where its valley is relatively steep the flow is still sufficiently strong to clean the bed at rare intervals. But near its mouth the dunes have blocked the outflow, jumped the mouth, and are marching north across the gravel flats. This has also happened at the mouth of several other rivers; at the mouth of the strong perennial Kunene River one can see how dune sand has a sort of blind life of its own. The sand there is washed out to sea as soon as it reaches the river, and is again cast up north of the river mouth. There the dunes reform and start their northward march once more to the Coroca River in Angola, which finally halts them.

STRANGE DESERT PLANTS

Along the Kuiseb and other river valleys there is quite luxuriant vegetation of big trees *(Acacia giraffae* and *A. albida)* together with tamarisks *(Tamarix austro-africana)* and a thorn tree *Parkinsonia africana*. These last two trees are the southern counterparts of the tamarisk and Jerusalem thorn of northern deserts. A leafless member of the cucumber family, *Acanthosicyos horrida,* forms its own little dunes. Most of this plant is below the sand, with only harsh fronds protruding. For protection from animals plants have evolved the same protective means here as in the northern deserts: they are either spiny, exude poisonous sap, or are otherwise repellent to man and beast.

The vegetation on the river beds was formerly sufficient to support small herds of elephants. Nowadays baboons live there, and jackals (which are far more omnivorous than most people suppose) feed on various berries. These relatively lush strips are not really part of the desert, and they occur only because the Namib is a narrow band between the escarpment and the coast. If the desert were broader or flatter the rivers would lose themselves in it, as some of the smaller streams actually do.

Some stiff grasses manage to grow on the lower slopes of some dunes and these grasses are sometimes remarkably green, but much the larger part of each dune is bare of all vegetation. The vegetation on the dunes, however, may be more luxuriant in parts than that on the flat gravelly plains. At the foot of the escarpment these bear a fuzz of ephemeral grasses like *Aristida,* depending on occasional rains, but near the coast they are almost devoid of vegetation. A few small shrubs, *Zygophyllum stapfii* and *Arthraema leubnitzii,* are all that break the monotony of the expanse.

But on these flats grows one of the most extraordinary of all plants. It is a monstrous-looking thing with broad strap-shaped leaves writhing out from a short central trunk like the arms of an octopus. The central portion produces flowers and fruit. This is the *Welwitschia bainesi* called *mirabilis* by its discoverer, the German botanist Welwitsch, who was so overcome with excitement on seeing it that he fell on his knees beside it.

The Welwitschia starts life as two ordinary-looking leaves, rather like those of a big lily. As it grows, a short trunk forms, and the leaf bases are expanded and split. The plant then looks as if it had more than two of the straplike leaves, but actually the same two leaves last the whole of its life, for perhaps a thousand years. No other plant in the world behaves in this way.

Each Welwitschia has only an insignificant tap root, and probably could not survive at all in a truly hot dry desert. The key to its survival is apparently the nightly cold sea fog. The broad writhing leaves condense the fog, which then drips to the ground, enabling the plant to survive in an almost rainless area.

Left: A Suricate meerkat is a small, active predator that lives on insects and small mammals. (Satour) Right: Naked mountains of granite or gneiss protrude here and there from the engulfing sea of red desert sand. They are the basement complex, or skeleton of Africa, showing through later deposits. (Odo Willscher)

Welwitschia is frequented by sap-sucking bugs, *Probergrothius sexpunctalis,* that live on it, and on it alone. Yet these bugs seem to have nothing to do with pollinating the flowers, and no one has yet solved the mystery of how the abundant seed crop is produced. It is not altogether surprising that the first botanist to come upon this extraordinary vegetable was so excited.

BEETLES, GECKOS, AND SIDEWINDERS

In most deserts, dunes are a habitat hostile to all but very primitive forms of life. The same condition might have been expected in the Namib, for here the dunes are not only very large but are constantly being blown and shifted. However, by comparison with areas of dunes in other deserts, the Namib supports an astonishingly rich fauna, especially of beetles and reptiles.

Tenebrionid beetles are a group of this very large order of insects that live largely on vegetable remains. They are not unknown in other deserts, but in the Namib they have specialized in an extraordinary way. Several hundred species and at least thirty-five genera are found only in the Namib. The fauna of tenebrionid beetles here is many times richer than that of similar dune areas in the Sahara, North America, or Somali.

All these beetles appear to have evolved from a few basic genera that inhabited South West Africa. Life in dunes involves traveling about in loose, shifting sand, and the beetles have become specialized in response to the habitat by, for instance, acquiring spurs and snowshoe-like structures of hair on their legs for better traction, and often by developing bodies that enable them literally to swim into the sand. On a single dune, four species can be found: one inhabiting the blowing sand of the dune top, two more the shifting sand of the lee side, and a fourth the more compact sand at the dune base. Some species are diurnal, others nocturnal. Some emerge consistently at one particular time of night, others later. Thus an extraordinary number of species manage to live together without competition. They include the only known white beetles, the white color being caused by the reflection of light from innumerable small trapped air bubbles. But whiteness does not seem to be especially advantageous, for there are plenty of shiny black, diurnal beetles that must endure greater heat than the white ones.

The source of their food is surprising; it seems to come from a combination of wind and fog. The easterly winds blowing fiercely across the deserts of the interior transport organic matter which drops in the Namib dunes. Plant fragments, insects and even large birds like hornbills are sometimes blown into the Namib and die there. All these are scavenged by the beetles. Both the sand itself and the dead fragments of vegetation among it tend to attract some moisture from the almost nightly sea fog. Thus the beetles live in a habitat that apparently should support no life.

There is other life too. There are scorpions, silverfish *(Lepisma),* spiders, and a remarkable variety of reptiles. There are several lizards that burrow in the sand by day, a nocturnal gecko *(Palmatocecko)* with webbed feet which help it to run over the loose sand, and even a large sand-colored chameleon—a creature that one would usually associate with tropical forest. There are also three species of vipers, and a dwarf python as well, though this last does not normally live in the dunes.

At night a large, swift-moving spider, known as the "White Lady of the Namib," comes out and may even prey upon geckos. It belongs to the genus *Cerbalus*—that also frequents North Africa. No one has ever seen a spider catch a gecko, but observers have noted that their tracks sometimes converge, with only the tracks of the spider continuing onward. The White Lady of the Namib is plainly a somewhat sinister creature.

The lizards of the Namib virtually swim in the sand. Some dive into it head first, others submerge by lateral movements of the body. They must submerge, not only to hide from avian predators, but to avoid the extreme heat of the surface, which may reach 160° F.; a lizard cannot tolerate temperatures above 107–114° F.

The vipers of the Namib progress in loose sand by sidewinding. A snake normally moves forward in what is called a serpentine glide, thrusting in alternate directions on the outside of the curves of its body. A sidewinder moves sideways, raising and shifting first one part of its body and then another. It shifts first its neck and an area about two-thirds the way along its body, then the center of its body and tail. In this way it can progress up the deep shifting sand on the steep leeward slope of a dune where a human being would flounder and struggle.

Left: The honey badger (Mellivora capensis) is nearly omnivorous but prefers the nests of bees and wasps. For its size it is probably the most formidable animal in Africa. (Bob Campbell: Armand Denis) Right: The astonishing nest of the sociable weaver (Philetairus socius) consists of a cartload of thorny sticks with grass on the underside of nest chambers. Such colonies are used for many years by a succession of different birds. (Clem Haagner)

The whistling rat of the Kalahari lives in burrows. Its population cycle builds up slowly to abundance followed by a sudden decrease. (Clem Haagner)

THE LIFE OF THE COLD CURRENT

The cold Benguella current of the South Atlantic both creates the Namib and supplies it with moisture. The pounding surf continually throws up new deposits of sand which are blown inland. The whole coast is waterless, except for some seepage lagoons of brackish water at the mouth of the Kuiseb and other usually dry rivers where there are huge gatherings of flamingos and other water birds. Yet just offshore there is abundant life.

As also happens off the coast of Peru and Chile, the cold upwelling waters, rich in salts, mean abundant microscopic life, and through this, abundant fish, which in turn support a large fishing industry. But long before man came, the multitudes of fish were the food of hundred of thousands of cormorants *(Phalacrocorax capensis* and *P. lucidus),* and many pelicans, gulls, terns and other sea birds. They also enabled the Cape fur seal *(Arctocephalus pusillus)* to live on this coast as far north as Cape Cross, well within the tropics. These seals, more properly called sea lions, are much the most numerous seals on any African coast.

There are between 300,000 and 600,000 fur seals along the African coast. They breed at certain localities, chiefly islands, and on the mainland at Cape Cross. Their breeding place at Cape Cross was formerly a rocky island in a lagoon, but the sand has encroached and joined the island to the mainland. Probably the seals would desert it if they were not carefully husbanded by sealers who harvest an annual crop of pups, at a level which maintains the stock.

The seals are highly polygamous, and throng the beaches and surf in packed, roaring herds. They mate in December-January and the calves are born at the same time. As often happens among seals, the cows are ready to mate a few days after calving. Bulls may weigh up to 475 pounds, but they eat only about four pounds of fish a day, or about one per cent of their body weight. As a result they do not really constitute a hazard to fishing industries, provided their numbers are kept within bounds.

The cormorants of this coast breed and rest on islands and on large wooden platforms that have been built for them. They too are useful in that they produce guano, a valuable agricultural manure. One guano company went out of business because the sand encroached on a lagoon; and therefore an island, where the cormorants bred, was no longer attractive to the birds.

Off these coasts there are a few jackass penguins—truly antarctic birds. At sea, albatrosses *(Diomedea* and *Phoebetria)* demonstrate that the origins of this bountiful supply of fish are in south polar waters. Yet tropical elements appear in the shape of numbers of lesser flamingos that feed in the lagoons in Walvis Bay and Sandwich Bay; and in the winter the coast is thronged with migrant waders from Europe. It is called the Skeleton Coast by mariners, who go in fear of it, but there is abundant other life along it.

ENORMOUS BIRDS' NESTS

Wherever there are acacia trees growing along drainage lines all through this dry country, some of them bear huge masses of sticks and straw. The largest may be twelve feet or more across and five feet thick and are occasionally so heavy that the tree gives way under the weight. These are the nests of the sociable weaver *(Philetairus socius),* among the most remarkable birds' nests in the world.

Sociable weavers are small birds, and each nest is actually a colony. A nest starts with only two or three pairs, but a very big one may contain fifty to seventy, even a hundred. The birds first build a roof of thorny sticks, beneath which they place a mass of grass. Individual nests are fashioned in this layer of grass, each having an entrance spout and a chamber warmly lined with feathers. Though similar in shape to other weavers' nests, they are apparently made differently; most weavers' nests are suspended from a support, but those of social weavers are excavated within the mass of grass by nipping off stems. The sharp ends of the grass stems point downwards, and may well help to discourage the intrusion of predators.

In time, more and more sticks are added to the top of the nest and there may be three or four feet of sticks above the individual nest chambers. The colonies are occupied for many years by a succession of different birds. Before and after the breeding season the nests are used for roosting. In some nests little change has been observed even after a period of over thirty years.

No one has satisfactorily explained why the sociable weaver should build this complex structure, when other weavers seem

Right above: Evening light against a leaden sky briefly makes the desert beautiful. (G. G. Collins) Right: The wedge-shaped nose of this sand lizard (Meroles cuneirostris) enables it to dive quickly under the sand. Its habitat is semi-stable sand among grass tufts near the base of dunes. Far right: Long toes and flattened bodies enable these shovel-nosed sand lizards (Aporosaura anchietae) to run swiftly, and literally to swim into the loose sand of the leeward slopes of dunes. (Both by W. D. Haacke)

to thrive without constructing anything comparable. One would think that the nesting chambers would be fairly safe from predators such as honey badgers, for they are situated on the underside of the pile, often several feet from the outside edge. Yet they are said to harbor snakes, even sluggish snakes like puff adders that do not normally climb, though how a snake could reach one of those nest chambers is a mystery. These great haystack colonies must also be warm and well insulated against the heat and cold, which might be an advantage in an environment where both extremes occur.

In the Cape Province, where large acacia trees are lacking, the birds have taken to building on telegraph poles. They also sometimes build on the tree aloe *(Aloe dichotoma),* one of the larger trees in the open plains country. The pygmy falcon that we described in the nyika as breeding in the nests of buffalo weavers breeds in these nests also. Apparently these intrusions are not resented by the weaver birds; but the falcon abuses their hospitality and will kill them when it can.

TOWARD THE KARROO

The southern parts of these deserts are less sandy and more stony and rocky. For great stretches the ground is covered with slabs of shale or sandstone, overgrown with thin thorny scrub. Where hills rise from the plain, tree aloes grow among jumbles of shattered boulders. Through this country the Fish River has cut itself an impressive gorge, like the Grand Canyon in miniature, and with the same strange sandstone shapes on its sides. The Fish River rarely flows now except in times of violent flood, when it may rise as much as fifty feet. Such floods, over ages, have been sufficient to cut this deep gorge in a low-rainfall area.

The largest river in South Africa, the Orange River, drains westward to the Atlantic from the spine of highlands that bounds these deserts on the east. It too has cut itself a deep gorge, with impressive crags, and at Aughrabies there is a splendid waterfall 470 feet high, an African spectacle that is eclipsed only by the Victoria Falls. Beyond the Orange River one enters Karroo country.

The true Karroo is a great basin of very ancient sedimentary rocks of continental origin; many fossil dinosaurs have been found in the ancient lagoon and lake beds. The enormous length of time needed to deposit these rocks can be guessed from the fact that their combined thickness is more than seven miles. The lowest of the Karroo rocks is a tillite, which is composed of compacted glacial till, a term denoting the mass of earth and small boulders carried along by a glacier. Thus at a very remote period, before the formation of the vast lagoons and swamps in which the Karroo sediments were laid down, glaciers must have existed in this part of Africa. They probably lay to the north of the present Karroo basin, while the main movement of the ice sheet was to the south.

The end stages of the Karroo formation were volcanic. Huge masses of basaltic lavas welled up, forming, among other structures, the highlands of Basutoland and the Drakensberg escarpments; numerous volcanic "pipes" pushed through the deep sedimentary rocks and formed flat-topped lava flows. The remains of these pipes, seen as caps of rock on flat-topped hills from which all the softer sediments have eroded away, are characteristic features of the Karroo landscape today.

The rainfall here is five to fifteen inches a year, and in some parts as much as half of it falls in winter. As we noted in the north, where there is a low average rainfall, it is more advantageous if it is restricted to one season than if it is spread over two seasons or composed of small storms all the year round. Combined with long cold periods in winter the distribution of rainfall makes the Karroo a harsher desert than its total rainfall would seem to indicate.

The Karroo is characterized by a type of vegetation known as Karroo bush. This is a link between and a mixture of tropical plants from the north and the subtropical Cape bush, or maquis. It varies from place to place, and sometimes consists largely of succulent plants, when it is known as succulent Karroo. It is generally composed of low shrubs such as *Pentzia* spp. *Chrysocona tenuifolia,* and *Rhigozum trichotomum,* with a scattering of grasses among them. There are hardly any trees except for acacias *(Acacia karroo)* along the bigger river valleys. This is a land that has been described as a multitude of bushes, each growing in its own little desert.

The southern fringe of the Karroo abuts on the folded mountain ranges of the Cape. There a gradual but distinct transition from Karroo vegetation to the Cape maquis occurs. The Little Karroo is a small subdesert area enclosed between the Steenkamps and Swartberg Mountains. It has its own special vegetation, notably a large number of the beautiful South African Mesembryanthemums.

PAST AND PRESENT IN THE KARROO

When man first knew the Karroo it was still a desert, but undoubtedly a more attractive one, than it is today. There was

Left: Welwitschia (Welwitschia mirabilis) have two strap-like leaves that last the life of the plant. The leaves condense the nightly fog, enabling the plant, which has no large root system, to live in the desert. (R. J. Rodin) Right: The Fish River canyon, dug through sedimentary rocks by rare, violent floods, is a thousand feet deep. (G. G. Collins)

a fair amount of grass and an abundance of wild animals like springbok, wildebeest, gemsbok, and the now extinct quagga *(Equus quagga)*, pronounced "Kwaha" as in Afrikaans. But almost all the wild animals have gone, to be replaced by sheep farms. This development has led to great changes in the composition of the vegetation, changes which are, as usual, for the worse.

It seems scarcely possible for man's domestic animals to duplicate the effect of nomadic wild animals. This is not so much because man tries to keep a greater total number of animals, but because the nomadic habit of desert animals is lacking. In a desert environment, over a period of years, continuous grazing inevitably kills off the preferred species of vegetation. Nomadic wild animals do not graze the same area continuously, but man's herds do, especially when the water supplies are improved by boring. Thus it comes about that land on which cattle once could thrive soon supports sheep only. Sheep graze out the little grass that remains, and the more unpalatable shrubs then begin to dominate the vegetation. In the end, an area which was once potentially productive and supported large numbers of wild animals, can no longer support an equivalent biomass of domestic stock.

This process has occurred in North America, and in all other semi-arid areas of the world that have been colonized by pastoral man. The typical Karroo bush has now spread far to the east of its original range, while the desert is creeping in from the west. Such processes can be checked, but only at some cost, and they have not been checked in the Karroo.

Stock farmers, after they have driven away or killed off the wild animals that formerly lived on their farms, will not

Right: The Namib dunes, arid as they may be, support more vegetation than black hills of rubble such as those in the background. Here a harsh grass, Aristida sabulicola, grows rather luxuriantly. Below: The nocturnal Palmatogecko rangei has webbed feet which help it to run on loose sand. Nevertheless, it is sometimes caught and killed by a large spider. (Both by W. D. Haacke)

tolerate the carnivores like jackals that formerly preyed upon them. So they poison and trap the jackals out of existence, and try to reduce eagles and other predatory birds and beasts. This in turn leads to other problems. Hyraxes, the natural prey of Verreaux's eagle, have increased so much in some places that they have moved down from their normal rocky fastnesses and now live on the plains. And plagues of rats and ground squirrels have become more frequent. Unless the farmer learns to live with and make use of nature's natural checks, he will ultimately be forced to use more and more costly pest control measures and his enterprises will eventually defeat their own ends.

No large part of the Karroo can now be seen in its natural state. It is a sadder spectacle than either the Kalahari or the Namib, parts of which have been preserved in reserves or national parks. Admittedly much of the Namib is so useless to pastoral man that few people cast covetous eyes upon it unless they are interested in Tenebrionid beetles or side-winders. But there would seem to be a good case for making a large section of the Karroo into a reserve in which the natural regenerative processes of wild creatures could be allowed full scope, and where the natural effects of the former population of wild animals could be studied over a long period.

West of the Fish River the layers of sedimentary rocks have eroded into forms of an almost unnatural symmetry. (G. G. Collins)

A Ruined Paradise

The Basutoland and Natal Highlands and the Highveld

14

Most of the interior of the South African subcontinent is a basin with raised edges, enclosing the Kalahari and Karroo desert regions, and drained toward the west coast by the Orange River. The rim of this basin, which runs with scarcely an interruption from South West Africa to Rhodesia and varies from five thousand to ten thousand feet above sea level, is known as the Great Escarpment. Sometimes one is almost unaware of its existence, as for instance, when one climbs northward to the Karroo through the series of folded mountain ranges of the Cape. But in other places it is clear and sharp, dividing high plains on one side from steeply sloping or desert lowlands on the other. Thus it divides the Namib

Right: The grasslands of Natal are largely the result of destruction of forests by too-frequent fires. (Emil Schulthess)
Below: Blesbok, so called because of the white face blaze, have made a good comeback from near-extinction. (W. T. Miller)

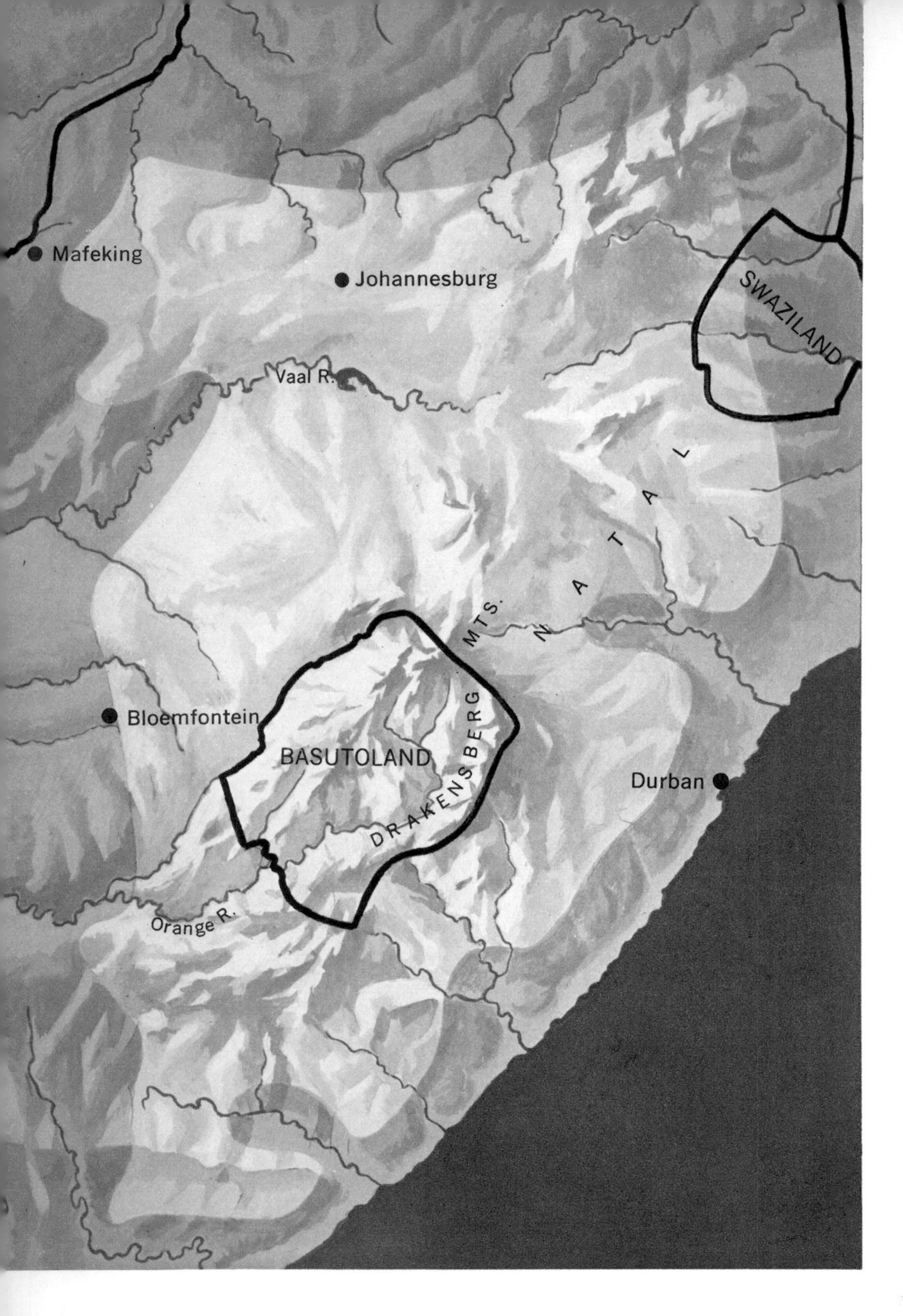

Basutoland and Natal, including the "roof" of South Africa, the highveld, and the grasslands of Natal.

Desert from the plateau of South Africa, and the lowveld from the rest of the southern bushveld zone.

In Natal, Basutoland, the Orange Free State and in southern Transvaal the escarpment rises to its magnificent crest in the Drakensberg Mountains. Altitude and rainfall combine to make this a distinctive region of southern Africa. As in the southern bushveld zone the escarpment divides it into two parts: the rolling grasslands of Natal, and the inland highveld of the Orange Free State and southern Transvaal. On the crest of the escarpment itself there is a block of country in Basutoland which is so high and cold that it stands out—a region similar to the high grasslands of Ethiopia and unlike anything else in Africa south of the equator.

It is really unsound to include in one region a large and varied stretch of country that ranges from two thousand to ten thousand feet in height and from lush subtropical forest to dry plains. Studies of the veld of South Africa define over seventy types; but many ecologists would regard that as an oversimplification. There are, moreover, cliffs, gorges and other small but specialized habitats essential for the survival of certain plants and animals. But most of the land in this region is essentially open grassland, not thornbushveld or shrubby country like the Karroo and Cape maquis. It is therefore convenient to include all these varied habitats in one region of surpassing beauty.

It is essential to realize that in this region, man has seriously affected the wildlife and the vegetation. There are hardly any parts of it that remain in their pristine condition. Even the small areas that have belatedly been preserved as parks or game reserves were subjected to the destructive activities of man before they were saved. The destructive activity had begun with the native tribes that inhabited parts of the area before the early white settlers came. But it was greatly accelerated by these settlers, and it still continues. The effects of mankind on the natural conditions of the area are still incalculable, but will in the long run probably be more damaging than beneficial.

THE ROOF OF SOUTH AFRICA

This region may be likened to a roof with a steep pitch on one side and a gentle slope on the other. The steep pitch is short and descends to three thousand feet in about half the distance the gentle slope requires to reach approximately the same level. Moreover, the rain-bearing winds from the Indian Ocean strike against the steep pitch and drop most of their moisture there, so that many short, swift-flowing rivers run eastward to the sea. On the gentle western slope the rainfall is much less, and almost all the water that runs off collects in one great river, the Orange, which flows westward to the Atlantic. Its valley is the only large break in the Great Escarpment.

The underlying rocks of the whole of this region are of the Karroo series—chiefly sandstones of varying degrees of hardness, and many thousands of feet thick. But at the end of the Karroo period there was a tremendous outbreak of volcanic activity. Great masses of fluid basaltic lavas emerged from vents to form flat plateaus in much the same way as the plateaus of Ethiopia and East Africa were formed in more recent times. The lava flows followed so closely on one another that the top layers of one had no time to weather before the next ran over it. These successive lava flows can now be seen on the crest of the Drakensberg, where they are about four thousand feet thick. At one time they were much thicker, but the top layers have been eroded away in the course of the ages.

The short, steep rivers carrying off the heavy rainfall to the east have far more erosive power than the westward-flowing rivers draining areas of comparatively low rainfall. The power of water to carry away silt increases far more rapidly than

Towers and buttresses of the Great Escarpment in the Natal Drakensberg. Four thousand feet of successive lava flows overlie softer sandstones that outcrop in the foreground. (Satour)

mere increase in velocity. A sluggish stream traveling at one eighth of a mile per hour will just move fine silt. If its velocity increases to half a mile an hour it will carry sand, and at one and a half miles per hour it will easily move pea-sized gravel. At ten miles an hour—not an unusual speed for a mountain river in flood—it will move rocks weighing one and a half tons.

Thus the rivers of the east have swiftly cut their way downward and backward into the lava and sandstone of the escarpment. At one time the lava flows, now ending at the Drakensberg crest, must have extended far beyond the present coastline of Africa. All this huge mass has been worn away back to the present escarpment, more than a hundred miles inland. Beneath the lavas is sandstone of varying hardness. One of the softer layers is a wind-blown sandstone, laid down in an arid period, which weathers into large shallow caves. Bushmen used to live in these caves and decorated the walls with their paintings.

Water erodes the softer material faster than the harder, and hard sandstone layers form tabular spurs far above the course of the rivers themselves. Natal can be divided in this way into three broad terraces, each cut by deep valleys. At the end of each terrace spur there are steep cliffs, and where the river is still eroding its way inland there is a waterfall. Here the stream flows almost flat along the top of the hard layer, then plunges over a sill and cuts a deep gorge in the softer material beneath. The twisting, meandering course of the streams shows that they were formed first on gentle gradients, but cut their way deeper and deeper as continental uplift increased the slope.

To the west of the escarpment the rivers are neither so large nor so steep, and consequently have much less erosive power. This results in country of flat or gently-sloping plains dissected by shallow valleys, often with swamps or "vleis" in them. But the over-all climate creates a grass cover, so that despite differences in the activity of the rivers the area as a whole is similar in character.

A MIGHTY PRECIPICE

The plateau of Basutoland drops off into nothingness in one of the most stupendous crags in Africa, rivalled only by the Semien escarpment in Ethiopia. There is a striking likeness between the two. This Drakensberg crag also has been eroded over the ages into bays separated by long castellated razorback spurs that jut out into the lowlands. But there is a difference. This crag has been formed by a series of flat lava flows from plateau fissure eruptions whereas the Semien crag is the remains of huge shield volcano of the Hawaiian type. Thus there are no *ambas* or volcanic plugs adorning the foothills of the Drakensberg precipice.

The summit crags of the precipice at Mont-aux-Sources, or in

Left above: Zantedeschia tropicalis, a showy aroid that grows in swampy places. Left: Christmas bells (Sandersonia aurantiaca), a delicately beautiful lily often found in sheltered places near streams. (Both by D. C. H. Plowes) Right: Dry red oat grass (Themeda triandra) glows with color below rocky bluffs in the Drakensberg foothills. (E. H. Errington)

the Giant's Castle area, fall about a thousand feet sheer before they break into grassy ledges. These ledges continue downward, broken by rock steps, for another three thousand feet before basalt gives way to sandstone strata. The rivers, where they tumble over the lip in waterfalls and dissipate into spray before they reach the base, are small, for they drain only a small part of the Basutoland summit plateau. But one, the Tugela, has captured a headwater stream of the Orange River. If there is no further change in the lie of the land, the faster-flowing lowland rivers of Natal will, in the course of the ages, eat farther back into the escarpment and capture the main drainage of Basutoland.

The high plateau of Basutoland above the crags is an expanse of montane or subalpine grassland. The winters are severe there and the ground is frozen for long periods, but snow cover is intermittent. Slopes become waterlogged and hillsides are seamed with small arc-shaped scars where the sodden ground has slipped. In summer the ground remains boggy and resembles alpine meadows in north temperate latitudes. Apart from certain areas in the Atlas this is the only large area of this type in the whole of Africa.

Part of the Basutoland plateau is a very ancient land surface, the last segments of the huge ancient continent of Gondwanaland. This included Africa, South America, Australia, Antarctica and Peninsular India, all fitting together like the pieces of a jigsaw puzzle. The theory of continental drift suggests that in the remote past the pieces of this vast continent broke apart and gradually drifted away from each other and to their present locations. The Gondwanaland surface can still be detected in various parts of Africa, but in Basutoland it is raised far higher than elsewhere and has been dissected by rivers till only a few remnant ridges remain. Only an expert can recognize what these ridges represent, for they are covered with the same highland grassland as the rest of the plateau.

Undoubtedly this area would carry more snow in winter but for the fact that it lies in the summer rainfall area of South Africa. Hence snowfalls are light, but frosts are keen on clear nights. Half the beds of running rivers freeze over, and melt again in the day's sunshine. Unlike the highlands of Ethiopia or the East African mountains, the plateau seems not to have been glaciated in any recent geological period, though long, long ago great glaciers occurred here and most of them moved southward.

LAMMERGEIERS AND BALD IBISES

On these heights there is a remnant population of the lammergeier *(Gypaetus barbatus),* a European and Asiatic bird common in Ethiopia but rare elsewhere in Africa. The nearest relatives of the Basutoland lammergeiers are in the Crater Highland of Tanzania, two thousand miles to the north. But the lammergeiers here are not racially distinct from those of East Africa or Ethiopia, although there can have been no intermingling for many millennia.

Partly because it is rare here, and so attracts special attention, the lammergeier has been more closely studied at its nest in Basutoland than elsewhere. The nests are large, flat structures of sticks placed in a cave or the overhung ledges of cliffs, but not necessarily on the highest precipices. They are lined with wool, hair, and other such remnants of the lammergeier's food. Observers in this region have found that both male and female lammergeiers take turns at incubating their single egg and tending the chick, and that a large part of the food given to the chick is pieces of bone up to eight inches long. The parents drop the bones on neighboring rocks to break them, and then bring the fragments to the nest. The young one is hardly ever given any red meat.

There are perhaps twenty pairs of lammergeiers left in Basutoland and Natal. Formerly the birds also occurred in other mountain ranges of the Karroo and the Cape. The Cape mountains have always been covered by maquis, and are not a favorable habitat for lammergeiers, which are usually associated with ready supplies of carrion. The overgrazed highland pasture of Basutoland provides many dead sheep, and the lammergeier can live better on these than on dead wild animals.

Another remnant bird of this area, possibly in greater danger of extinction than the lammergeier, is the bald ibis *(Geronticus calvus).* This is a large, glossy-green bird with an extraordinary bald patch of bright red skin on its crown. It is probably most closely related to the North African and Arabian waldrapp *(Comatibis eremita).*

All ibises normally feed by probing in wet or soggy ground, so it comes as a surprise to find them nesting in rock cliffs like eagles. But the bald ibis does this and so does the waldrapp and the Ethiopian wattled ibis. The nesting colonies of the bald ibis have been occupied by a succession of different birds that have used the favored nest ledges year after year for centuries.

If the bald ibises stayed constantly near their remote nesting colonies they would not be in great danger. But they fly down to lowlands to obtain food, and in winter they leave their breeding area for milder climates. They then leave the limited breeding areas where they can be protected, unlike the lammergeier, which remains in the mountain fastnesses. Of the two the lammergeier is unquestionably the rarer bird, and it is the more likely to be exterminated in due course by careless and irresponsible use of poison bait for jackals. The plight of these two remnant birds shows how difficult it is to give protection where the areas protected are not large enough to form a full ecological unit covering both winter and summer feeding and breeding ranges.

PITIFUL REMNANTS

East of the escarpment, only very small remnants of the original life of this area remain more or less untouched by man. Some of the more splendid scenic areas at the foot of the Drakensberg are nature reserves or parks, and here one can get a glimpse of what the country was like before man came upon it. But even in these areas nature is not as it originally was. Various animals such as wildebeest and blesbok *(Damaliscus dorcas phillipsi)* have been reintroduced, but they often must be pampered for a time, since they are brought from flat country and are unaccustomed to cliffs and rocks. In time—like the eland, that most adaptable of all big antelopes—they will build up into populations which are familiar with the areas from birth.

Formerly, wild animals swarmed in much of the grasslands of Natal, but in many areas Africans had greatly reduced them before the arrival of white settlers. It is not possible to restore this former abundance, since this is land of good agricultural potential and man will not relinquish it unless circumstances force him to do so. Here too the over-all destructive effect of man's occupation is all too apparent. Entire hillsides, once covered with a dense protective mat of grass, have now been exposed to erosion and are seamed with gullies that eat back from streams into the land surface. Small streams, trickling in an excessively wide bed, testify to the increasing violence of floods from denuded uplands. In many cases this erosion has gone so far that it cannot be repaired without very costly engineering. It is fairly certain that man has started a new cycle of rapid erosion that he cannot or will not now stop.

The only wildlife remaining in these Natal grasslands—usually a pitiful remnant—is what is tolerated by man. In the open grasslands of the African Transkei area it is extraordinary how little life remains. Even the young and eggs of larks and buntings are likely to be eaten by small boys. Elsewhere many enlightened farmers regret the total disappearance of the original wild fauna and seek to restore it by introducing a few wild animals. Such animals as impala and eland can often thrive on land which has been rendered more or less useless for domestic stock.

Man has affected birds much less than he has the larger mammals; and the smaller mammals, reptiles and insects have hardly been affected except where special habitats have actually been destroyed. In this region one can observe yet another form of bird migration, one that is altitudinal and according to the seasons, a phenomenon common in some other mountain areas.

In the uplands at the foot of the Drakensberg the winters are fairly hard, so many of the birds, large and small, migrate downhill toward the coast. Among the most conspicuous are blue cranes *(Tetrapteryx paradisea)* and Stanley bustards *(Neotis denhami stanleyi),* but many small singing birds also migrate. In spring the Stanley bustards and blue cranes can be seen flying up the hill, pausing at intervals to perform their courtship display. The blue cranes of this area breed on the tops of bare grassy ridges in the protected areas, but where they are liable to disturbance by domestic stock they tend to nest in swamps. Wattled and, more rarely, crowned cranes also breed in swamps. Blue cranes, South Africa's national bird, are exceptionally beautiful, of a delicate blue-gray color with a long trailing train of black feathers—the elongated secondaries of the wings. They occur in other parts of South Africa and in some areas are so numerous as to be a pest.

Formerly, large wild animals must undoubtedly have made this journey in winter to warmer climates, but now they cannot, because they soon come up against a wire fence. The former population of wild animals in the foothills of the Drakensberg can never be restored in full, for only those species able to withstand a rather sharp winter without migrating can survive. It is not likely that these very high grasslands ever supported very large herds of ungulates permanently.

OPEN GRASSLAND AND RELICT FORESTS

The original vegetation on these eastern slopes was grassland with patches of forest in the heads of valleys and with a fair amount of acacia bush lower down. The tree cover has been greatly reduced in parts by the excessive use of fire in winter to encourage green grass, a practice the white settlers learned from the Africans. The use of fire in grasslands is a highly controversial subject, one on which ecologists and pastoralists will seldom agree. If fire is used to burn off old growth and enable new grass shoots to appear, it certainly increases the erosion hazard on steep slopes, while all the valuable nitrogen and most of the organic matter in the grass goes up in smoke. But if it is not burned, the grass is apt to become a senile inedible mass of dead stalks and fiber, of very low grazing value either for domestic stock or wild animals. Hence an uneasy compromise is usually reached, where fire is used to a limited extent when it can do least harm. Even then, its inevitable long-term effects are increased erosion.

The fires that sweep the grasslands of Natal in winter and spring are driven before very strong winds and are extremely violent. A fire may leap down from the crest of a high crag through the medium of tussocks of burning material blown over the edge by the wind. Little of this grassland can escape fire unless it is protected by firebreaks, and on steep hillsides these are costly to make and difficult to maintain. All the vegetation in these grasslands is thus subject to fire, and the grass has by this means probably taken over from what was once more widespread forest.

The little patches of forest that are found in steep valleys

The Cape vulture (Gyps coprotheres) at its nest on a cliff. Formerly abundant, their numbers have been greatly reduced by lack of available carrion and by poisoning. (Peter Steyn)

and beneath crags are being steadily reduced by fires. The smaller a patch of forest becomes, the less is its chance of survival. Once it has been reduced to a certain size, it can no longer produce a typical forest microclimate within itself and will die out, whether fires attack it or not. Rock hyraxes are also playing a part in reducing the patches of forest; with the total extermination of leopards, wild cats, jackals, and other terrestrial enemies, they have multiplied and can safely feed on the ground away from protective rocks. They eat down the soft plants of the forest floor, such as lilies and grasses, and so expose the leaf litter to increased desiccation and erosion by heavy summer storms, for trees break the force of falling rain but do not stop erosion altogether.

In places the relict forests have been encircled by the planting of other trees, such as pines or eucalyptus, and here they are fairly safe. Very large areas of steep hillsides have been covered with these introduced trees, and there is an extraordinary contrast between the life they support and that of the indigenous forest. Few of the indigenous forest birds make any attempt to colonize this new environment, though some sunbirds feed on the blossoms of eucalyptus, and one or two very adaptable species that occur in both forest and savannas, like the black drongo *(Dicrurus adsimilis)*, have learned to make use of them.

The relicts of indigenous forest are similar to the small patches that occur from sea level up to three thousand feet in the Cape, and on mountain ranges in East Africa up to eight thousand feet. Here they occupy intermediate altitudes from two thousand to six thousand feet. They are the remains of a great forest that once must have been almost unbroken along the mountain spine of South Africa from the Cape to Rhodesia, and to the higher plateaus of East Africa even as far as Ethiopia. Inside one of these patches of forest one finds many trees, such as podocarpus and olive, that are also found thousands of miles away to the north or south, but not for any distance east or west of this mountain chain.

Likewise the mountain chain supports many heaths and other flowers typical of the Cape maquis. On the slopes of the Drakensberg, *Watsonia* and *Scylla* are abundant. In spring, after the fires have passed and early rains have fallen, the hillsides are bright with them. But I have noticed that almost every budding scylla bulb had been eaten down by some animal, probably hyraxes; the Watsonia had been similarly nipped. On the whole it is surprising how little there is of tree heaths on these high mountains. Dry winters, vigorous growth of grass in summer, and fires, are doubtless responsible.

THE HIGHVELD

West of the escarpment there is a broad nearly flat plateau of grassland sinking slowly toward the west and becoming gradually more arid till it merges into the border of the Karroo. The rainfall on this plateau is uniformly less than in the eastern uplands, and rivers are smaller with more gentle gradients. Consequently, except in the headwaters near Basutoland, the region has not been cut into deep valleys by the erosive effect of the streams. About four to six thousand feet above the sea, the plateau consists of very broad valleys and low intermediate ridges, with only a few small hills to break the monotony of the horizon. Trees are rare, and largely confined to the banks of rivers and streams.

This highveld country is dominated by tall bunch grasses, especially the red oat grass *(Themeda triandra)* characteristic of great areas of the East African grasslands thousands of miles to the north. This grass is also dominant on the uplands east of the escarpment, but on the plateau it forms a true prairie climax, whereas in the east it is an invader following the destruction of forest by fires. Themeda is a sweet grass, palatable to herbivores even when dry. But under excessive grazing it tends to be replaced by sour grasses such as *Hyparrhenia* and *Cymbopogon*. This replacement leads man to burn the grassland more and more often to obtain young palatable herbage, and the themeda tends to die out, to be replaced by inferior grasses such as *Aristida* and *Eragrostis*.

Characteristic animals of this highveld are the vaal rhebok *(Pelea capreolus)* and the common reedbuck *(Redunca arundinum)*. Reedbuck are not confined to swampy areas and, though they often like to retreat into a swamp by day, they can be found grazing out on high, open slopes. The common reedbuck is a red animal about the size of the impala, that lives in pairs and small herds. It emits a sharp whistle and when alarmed goes off with a bounding, rocking-horse motion, throwing its hind legs high into the air and displaying a prominent white tail. It has been allowed to survive in fair numbers; it also occurs far to the north, as far as the East African grasslands.

The vaal rhebok is a unique animal found only in South Africa. It is closely related to the reedbuck, but quite distinct, having hooves more like those of a goat. It lives in small herds, but fifteen or more may sometimes be seen together. The vaal rhebok remains fairly common partly because it is considered inedible as a result of the fact that bot flies lay their eggs and hatch large grubs beneath its skin. One rhebok may harbor a dozen or more of these parasites, especially in dry weather. This curious accident of natural preference by a fly has saved the rhebok from excessive shooting, but sentiment has played a part too, for the rhebok reminded the early settlers of home.

The name "rhebok" has nothing to do with the animal's similarity to the reedbuck. The old settlers were apt to name animals after European beasts with which they were familiar; thus "wildebeest" for wild cattle, and "hartebeest" for a deerlike cow. "Gemsbok," the name of the southern oryx, is cleary an aberration; it is neither related to nor resembles the chamois. But in build and general appearance the vaal rhebok is strikingly similar to a roe deer or "reh," as it is called on the Continent. When a male stands at gaze, his straight, upright horns and general posture are strongly reminiscent of the roebuck of European forests: the only difference is that the vaal rhebok is gray, not red. The name "vaal rhebok" is a derivative of "gray roebuck," though the former is not closely related to the roebuck.

VANISHED AND VANISHING BEASTS

Formerly this highveld supported incredible numbers of wild animals. The spectacle of great herds probably had no equal

Spring rains bring up the bright green grass on recently burned slopes, and a protea catches the light in the foothills of the Drakensberg near Cathedral Peak. (E. H. Errington)

The crowned eagle (Stephanoaetus coronatus) sometimes nests in the forested parts of Natal. Living on such mammals as hyraxes, small antelopes and young monkeys, it feeds a fledgling for up to eleven months after the first flight. (Leslie Brown)

on the African continent, not even in the East African grasslands. The characteristic plains animals, all grazers, were the white-tailed gnu *(Connochaetes gnu)*, hartebeest, zebra *(Equus burchelli burchelli)*, quagga *(Equus quagga)*, and blesbok *(Damaliscus dorcas phillipsi)*. Formerly springbok occurred here in enormous numbers, migrating in fabulous herds in search of new pastures. The last known large-scale migration was in 1896, and nothing like it has been seen since.

These animals also inhabited the Karroo south of the Orange River, and were the characteristic grazing animals of South Africa. In the early days of settlement, the wild animals were slaughtered unmercifully for their hides or for meat—though the settlers were far too few to eat all that they slaughtered. The spectacle provided by these enormous herds has gone forever. It might never have been practicable to save the animals without setting aside a very large area of land, for it seems that they were all strongly nomadic, and probably migrated between the more arid Karroo and the highveld according to the availability of pasture. It would have been natural for the animals to graze the sweet themeda pastures of the highveld in the dry winter and to move into the Karroo to avoid the cold wet rains in the highveld. But no one can now say what actually happened.

Despite the slaughter of all these animals, only one, the quagga, actually became extinct. The quagga was a zebra-like animal distinguished from the common zebra or *bonte-quagga* (meaning pied quagga) by having few indistinct stripes, chiefly on its legs. The quagga (its pronunciation, "kwaha," as in Afrikaans or Hottentot, is a fair rendering of the barking bray of the zebra tribe) was principally an inhabitant of the more arid western plains and the Karroo, and despite rumors to the contrary it has unquestionably gone for good.

The white-tailed gnu was nearly exterminated in the same way. When at the end of the last century, it was reduced to about five hundred animals scattered on farms, a few enlightened farmers realized that this animal was on the verge of extinction, and made efforts to preserve it. Naturally gregarious beasts, the small remnant herds of them did not breed well. But attempts to increase the size of herds by introducing females from other areas were almost frustrated by the gnu's curious habits: bulls will actually kill strange cows, and cows will combine to kill bulls. But through care and effort the small remnants have been maintained, and the species is now out of danger and is being reintroduced to many localities. The case of the white-tailed gnu, a species so nearly lost altogether, is a warning that no wild animals should be reduced to the point where their essential herd habits are disrupted, as a result of which they cannot breed successfully.

Blesbok, once almost incredibly abundant, were also slaughtered to the verge of extinction for their skins, which fetched about a shilling each. Perhaps two thousand of them were alive at the beginning of the century. The recovery of the blesbok, however, has since been far more spectacular than that of the gnu, and more than fifty thousand now exist on farm preserves. Both blesbok and gnus can be seen on the Somerville reserve in the Orange Free State and in the Transvaal, but both have become extinct as truly wild animals and owe their survival only to belated attempts by man to preserve the remnants.

The horrible slaughter that exterminated the quagga and all but exterminated the blesbok and gnu parallels the destruction of the bison in the American West. It is very likely that the wild animals that formerly grazed the highveld made more efficient use of the pasture than could domestic stock. Similarly, in the American West the numbers and biomass of bison were probably two and a half times as great as those of the domestic animals that now graze the deteriorated grass plains. By replacing the wild creatures with selective grazing sheep and cattle, man has caused grave deterioration in the pasture, particularly in the drier areas west of Basutoland, where the typical shrubby Karroo bush has made major thrusts into the grassland in the last two centuries.

MAN AS A BENEFICIAL FORCE

Even the remnant wild areas that have been preserved in this region are affected by man because of the extermination of predatory beasts and birds. Farmers will not tolerate in their midst a small reserve containing lions or leopards that might break out to kill stock, and they would regard any remnant population of jackals simply as a breeding reservoir that could reinfest their own properties. Thus none of the predators of this region have escaped man's influence.

Still, as we have seen in other parts of South Africa, many smaller animals and birds have scarcely been affected and may even have benefitted from the elimination of their predators. Larks and other ground-breeding birds on the highveld are doubtless freer from potential attack, now that jackals, wild cats and birds of prey have been nearly wiped out. And in some ways man has improved the habitat for certain birds and beasts—notably in the construction of very many small dams to store water in the dry season where there was no permanent water before. This has led to a great increase in waterfowl: thousands of ducks and geese now live in the highveld where previously there were none, or only a few small, widely separated colonies in favorable spots. The characteristic ducks of this region are the yellowbill *(Anas undulata),* the redbill *(Anan erythrorhyncha),* Cape shoveller *(Spatula capensis),* African sheldduck *(Tadorna cana),* Cape teal *(Anas capensis),* South African pochard *(Netta erythropthalma)* and hottentot teal *(Anas punctata).* Larger than these are the Egyptian geese *(Alopochen aegyptiacus)* and spurwing geese *(Plectropterus gambensis).* There are other ducks and geese, but these are the commonest. Most are also found in eastern Africa as far north as Ethiopia, but not in such numbers as here, and the shoveller and shelduck are southern representatives of Palearctic species.

Naturally, other water birds like herons, egrets, grebes, cormorants, ibises, coots and rails, have also increased. Several large breeding colonies of herons, darters, sacred ibises, and other water birds have developed for the first time. Migrant Paleartic waders, such as sandpipers *(Tringa* spp.), stints *(Erolia),* and greenshanks *(Tringa nebularia)* also find these waters to their liking in the northern winter.

However, even the good that man does can boomerang. Egyptian geese, less tasty, more wary and so less often shot than some ducks, have in some areas become so numerous that they are a threat to wheat fields. This is another area in which that avian plague, the dioch *(Quelea quelea lathami),* occurs. In recent years it has spread enormously, probably through a combination of increased food in wheat fields and increased water supplies. A costly control program has become necessary, and millions of diochs are being killed annually.

If this region is a tragic example of the destructive effect of mankind on wildlife, it is also one in which naturalists can find abundant interest in the secondary effects of man's activities. No other large animals are likely to become extinct here, though the same could not be said of some other regions of Africa where indigenous man is still the cardinal destructive force that the earlier Dutch settlers were in the highveld and Natal. The wheel has come full circle, and perhaps the extinction of the quagga is a small price to pay for an attitude of more enlightened cooperation between man and his environment.

Seabirds and Flowering Coasts

The Cape Subtropical Region

15

At the southern tip of Africa is a small but very remarkable region with a subtropical climate essentially similar to the Mediterranean climate of northwest Africa. The rain falls in winter, which occurs here between April and September, and the summer is hot and dry. The country is covered with dense shrubbery strikingly like that of North Africa. Some of the plants are in fact identical to those in North Africa: for instance the tree heather *(Erica arborea),* which is found in the Mediterranean region and on the tops of high mountains between the Mediterranean and the Cape of Good Hope. This type of vegetation is known as *maquis, macchia* or locally as *fynbos.*

Approaching this region from the northwest through Namaqualand, soon after crossing the Orange River, one is aware of a change in the vegetation: many shrubs that indicate a transition to the Cape maquis appear. After rain in Namaqualand the ground is truly carpeted with beautiful flowers—also like those of the coastal plains of Morocco and Algeria in spring. The flowers are chiefly Compositae, and they are usually yellow or orange, sometimes white. There are many species of *Mesembryanthemum,* succulents with flowers like asters but actually of a different family, the Aizoaceae. In fact the whole brilliant assembly is far more varied than the spring flowers that cover the fields of North Africa.

Farther east the change is still more obvious. Coming from the Karroo, a traveler crosses the Hex River pass and in a few miles moves from shrubby desert vegetation to a relatively lush valley with purple mesembryanthemum flowering along the roadside. Or, coming along the coast from Natal one crosses the Kouga River south of Port Elizabeth, where the tropical coastal vegetation disappears and is replaced within a few miles by maquis.

This region consists of the coastal plains of the southern and western seaboards from near Humansdorp to Namaqualand, and a series of magnificent ranges that rear steeply upward, broken by rock faces and often cloud-capped. The winters are quite severe on these mountains and the snow lies fairly deep. But there is no permanent snow here, and apart from periods of strong winds the climate is mostly rather mild and pleasant.

FOLDED MOUNTAINS

The ranges inland from the Cape are like the Atlas and Algerian mountains in that they result, not from vulcanism (like the high mountains of East Africa and Ethiopia) but from the buckling or folding of the earth's crust. Apart from the Atlas they are the only mountains in Africa that are formed into true mountain ranges by folding, comparable in a small way to the Himalayas or the Andes. Most of the mountains are formed of sedimentary rocks—rocks laid down by the action of erosion in long past ages in flat layers or strata. There are also metamorphic rocks, which are rocks changed by violent pressures resulting from the movement of the earth's crust. Although ancient, these sedimentary formations are not as old as the basement complex rocks that underlie most of the eastern half of Africa.

The sedimentary rocks have been folded both in North Africa and in the Cape through the proximity of another continent—in this case Antarctica. We may suppose that at some remote period, after the rocks had been deposited in flat layers like a sandwich, great pressure from the south buckled these layers till they resembled a corrugated roof. On one side of a mountain range the layers of rock are bent upward and on the other side downward. In many places the once horizontal layers of rock have been pushed into a vertical position. This can be seen for instance in the jaws of the magnificent Swartberg pass, on the borders of the Karroo. Here one drives through a narrow entrance like a doorway to find oneself surrounded by frowning precipices in which the strata now lie vertically.

There are two main groups of ranges in the Cape. To the west the mountains have been folded so that the line of each range is roughly northwest to southeast. In the east a series of ranges run roughly from east to west, nearly parallel with the south coast. Where the two groups come into contact, the contortions of the once flat layers of the "sandwich" are extreme. The cracking and slipping down of segments of the earth's crust, called faulting, has in places accentuated the contortions of folding. The end result is splendid mountain scenery.

In between the mountain ranges there are broad flat valleys, nowadays cultivated or planted with orchards. These broadly resemble the intermontane basins of the Atlas or the Rockies. Traveling through fields of wheat one is struck by the likeness to landscape in North Africa. But instead of European finches among the grain there are flocks of bishop birds *(Euplectes),* the red males looking strangely incongruous in spring and early summer. And on pastures the crowned lapwing *(Stephanibyx coronatus)* replaces the European lapwing.

WONDERLAND OF FLOWERS

The outstanding feature of this region is its extraordinarily varied flora. There are thought to be between fifteen and

Aloes growing above a beach on the wild South African coast. (Carl Frank)

Cape subtropical, a part of the southern tip of Africa, is formed of folded mountain ranges covered with extraordinarily rich flora and washed by the Antarctic seas.

twenty-five thousand species of flowering plants here—about as many as in the vast expanse of the tropical African forest. Many of these flowers are grown in private gardens all over the world. *Gladiolus, Agapanthus* and *Freesia,* for instance, are three South African lilies that have been extensively planted, as have many beautiful flowering heaths. The succulent mesembryanthemum, with its radiant starlike flowers of many colors, has also been used as an ornamental in dry climates elsewhere.

The astonishing number of species found in this relatively small region indicates that at one time flora of this type grew over a very much larger area. Now this area has been reduced by the development of arid conditions in the interior, which have pushed the remaining plants into the mountains of the Cape. Here, in a multiplicity of different habitats, further evolution could take place. There is every variety of terrain from sea level to 7,600 feet, in rainfall from ten inches per year to sixty or seventy inches, and in aspect from dry, sunny slopes above the Karroo to mist-shrouded mountains that look more like the landscape of the west of Scotland than a part of Africa. In these circumstances many small local populations of species can develop. But the variety remains astonishing, and is far greater, for instance, than in the Atlas, where one could expect a similar range of ecological conditions. Table Mountain alone has as many varieties of flowering plants as in the whole of the British Isles.

Typical Cape maquis consists of shrubs in several layers or stories, but each has small stiff or shiny leaves, adapted to withstand conditions of summer drought. The tallest or climax layer consists generally of proteas, small trees up to twenty feet high that bear extraordinary compound circular flowers as much as six inches across. There are many genera of the Protea family, and several may grow together in one place. Beneath the proteas are smaller shrubs with thin stems, many of them heaths. Grasses are few, but reedlike plants of the family Restionaceae are very abundant. The whole assembly gives a brownish-green cast to a hillside, and bears more resemblance to the dense, soaking wet heathlands of the Bale Mountains in Ethiopia, or the giant heath zone on the Aberdares or Mount Kenya than to other places in Africa. But again it is the extraordinary variety of plant species that is unique.

This maquis persists, with variations, from the coast to the mountaintops. It varies locally, and in some more favorable areas plants with softer leaves may appear. On the mountaintops the shrubs are small and stunted from exposure. Despite such exposure, introduced pines and eucalyptus attain a far greater size, even at high altitudes, than do any of the typical plants of the maquis.

Most of the maquis at lower levels has been destroyed or altered by cultivation. Where cultivation has been abandoned, or along river valleys, there is often an inextricable mixture of introduced trees and shrubs from other parts of the world with similar climates. Australian acacias thrive, and a Mediterranean pine, *Pinus pinaster,* is in some places regenerating like a native tree. One Australian member of the Protea family, *Hakea,* is so well suited here that it forms impenetrable thickets that crowd out the natural vegetation.

In the days before settlement, fire periodically swept through the maquis, and since then burning has become so much more

On the Cape of Good Hope, reached by a spectacular scenic road, one may see animals typical of Africa as well as birds of the Antarctic seas.

frequent that it is now difficult to find climax growths. To human beings this mass of shrubbery must always have seemed wholly useless, either to themselves or as fodder for stock. But after burning, limited poor-quality pasture could be obtained and Hottentots and early settlers alike set the maquis on fire. The Portuguese mariners who first rounded the Cape of Good Hope remarked on the number and extent of fires on shore.

But even without human interference, it is easy to see how the maquis, tinder-dry in summer, is subject to fires caused by lightning or other natural means. Such fires can burn for weeks until they reach a river or the sea. Fires of this type, probably fiercer than those that occur nowadays, were also less frequent, and consequently had a less drastic effect on the vegetation as a whole.

NECTAR-EATING BIRDS

The abundance of flowers has meant that birds feeding on nectar are among the commonest in this region. There are several sunbirds, including the very beautiful, metallic-green malachite sunbird *(Nectarinia famosa),* as well as the larger and the smaller double-collared sunbirds *(Cinnyris afer* and *C. chalybaens)* and the orange-breasted sunbird *(Antobaphes violacea).* Careful counts have shown that these are among the most numerous of all birds in the maquis. Among them are a unique group of nectar-eating birds found only in the Cape region—the sugarbirds *(Promerops* spp.)

Sunbirds are very common throughout most of Africa, and they are also found in Asia, though in less variety. Although not closely related they have evolved much like the neotropical hummingbirds, with long curved bills and tongues that can be thrust deep into the heart of a flower. But they are generally much larger than hummingbirds, and though they can hover, they do not usually feed while hovering. Most species are partly insectivorous, and it seems likely that they have evolved from an insectivorous group of passerine birds. Like hummingbirds they are often brilliantly colored, but they are not so jewel-like. Their nests are beautifully made, domed structures suspended from a twig or leaf. Sometimes they are adorned with lichen, bound with cobwebs and lined with either feathers or plant down.

Sugarbirds resemble large sunbirds and also have long curved bills. They are, however, larger and lack metallic colors. The males have long tails of many feathers, unlike several sunbirds whose central tail feathers only are elongated. Their nests are open, not domed, and much more coarsely made than those of sunbirds. Sugarbirds are very closely associated with proteas, and they usually nest in a protea bush.

One wonders whether these birds may, like insects, sometimes pollinate flowers. Birds have been credited with pollination in several parts of Africa and elsewhere, but it is probable that such birds visit flowers as much for the insects living in the corolla as for the nectar. Though both sunbirds and sugarbirds may have some effect on pollination, probably this is largely accidental. As a matter of fact, in these flowers special structures have evolved which permit pollination by insects but not by birds.

One remarkable flower of these parts, the bird of paradise flower *(Strelitzia),* seems at first specially adapted for pollination by sunbirds. The flower bud is a green-pointed sheath from which several pointed orange petals emerge upward one after another, like the fingers of an outspread hand. Each of these petals has a remarkable, blue spear-shaped structure rising at an angle from the center, with a gland at the base secreting a copious flow of nectar. In the center of the blade of the "spear" is the pollen store, while the sticky female stigma protrudes beyond the tip. One would think that a sunbird would perch on the spear, lean forward to reach the nectar-bearing gland, and bedaub its breast with pollen; at the next flower, the protruding stigma would be fertilized by pollen from the bird's breast. But it does not work that way. Instead, the sunbird alights on the sheath at the side, pushes its bill into the nectar-bearing organs, and takes its fill without touching any of the flower's reproductive organs. Sunbirds bore holes into many tubular flowers, and damage them rather than improve their chances of pollination.

Left above: The waves of the restless southern ocean crash against rocks near Plettenburg Bay. (W. T. Miller) Left: Banks of glorious flowers adorn the sandhills above the wide beaches of the Cape Province. (Emil Schulthess)

REMNANT FORESTS

Natural forests are rare in this region. The repeated fires in the maquis make it a habitat that trees cannot easily colonize, while, of course, it cannot of itself develop into forest. If fire could be absolutely excluded, forest patches could spread, but it is very difficult to exclude fire from maquis. Moreover, forest can only spread slowly from areas of existing forest; if there were no forest at all, the maquis would remain indefinitely as it is.

Two types of indigenous forest occur in this region. On some of the western mountain ranges, notably the Cedarberg, there are stands of two species of an indigenous conifer, *Widdringtonia.* Although called a cedar it is not a true cedar, resembling rather the East African cedar which is a giant juniper. Widdringtonia also grows farther to the north, on Mount Mlanje in Malawi, which gives an indication of the former extent of the Cape flora.

In the eastern part of this region there are forests of a different sort, made up of *Podocarpus* and several broad-leaved trees including olives *(Olea capensis),* stinkwood *(Ocotea capensis)* and the very beautiful Cape chestnut *(Calodendron capense).* These forests, which grow on the lower slopes of the mountains and in the submontane shelf a few hundred feet above sea level, are remarkably like mountain forests of East Africa at six to eight thousand feet. They demonstrate a characteristic feature from here northward—the recurrence of certain types of forest at greater and greater altitudes the nearer one approaches the equator. Such forests as these, from the Cape to Ethiopia, tend to harbor species which are either related or identical.

The finest remnants of this tropical type of forest are at Knysna and Tzitzikamma. Here they are surrounded by luxuriant growths of maquis in a climate wetter than much of the Cape region. They may have been able to survive here because the fires in the maquis are less severe and frequent than on drier mountain ranges. Although very much like East African forests, they are not so luxuriant. The trees are much smaller, and even a very old podocarpus does not compare with some of the big specimens on Mount Kenya. Inside, the forests are damp, cool and moss-grown, with a floor of leaf mould and ferns.

There are typical tropical African birds here, including a touraco, *Turacus corythaix,* and a parrot, *Poicephalus robustus.* This is also the present southward limit of the elephant, which formerly extended to the Cape. Elephants were once more numerous here, but now there are only about ten left in the Knysna and Tzitzikamma forests. They are rumored to be abnormally large, but this is probably not the case. The forests are so thick that it is very difficult to get a good view of these elephants. Since most of them are bulls they do not increase, though recently one cow elephant was said to have had a calf. While in the old days the elephants were slaughtered without compunction, sentiment would now forbid the culling of some of the excess bulls to make room for cows.

An elephant has approximately the same life span as a human being, and cows start to breed when they are about fourteen or fifteen years old. If there were a few more cows in the area, the numbers could slowly recover over the next century or so. But in any case this habitat, cold, wet, and with a very limited area of suitable food supply, may be marginal for elephants.

ANIMALS OF THE MOUNTAINS

On the coastal plains practically nothing remains of the once abundant wildlife. The Cape lion, reputed to be the largest and most magnificent of all races of the lion, is gone for good. Place names, like Elandskloof, are all that now indicate where wildlife once flourished. Yet a surprising number of antelopes survive in the mountain ranges, where in the dense maquis they

Right: Jackass penguins ashore on one of their breeding islands. They follow the cold current far up the west coast. (L. J. Milne) Below: The black-backed gull (Larus dominicanus) is a southern species that also breeds in New Zealand. (W. T. Miller)

are too difficult to hunt to extinction. There are mountain reedbuck *(Redunca fulvorufula)*, common duiker *(Silvicapra grimmia)* vaal rhebok and grysbok *(Rhapiceros melanotis)*. Grysbok and duiker live in the dense cover, and reedbuck in more open situations. The common duiker is probably the most adaptable and widely distributed animal in Africa, inhabiting regions from the Cape to Senegal and Ethiopia, and from sea level to fourteen thousand feet, near the limits of vegetation on high East African mountains. It is a species that is practically impossible to exterminate, for it breeds more freely when its numbers are low and, being small, is difficult to find in thick cover.

Mountain reedbuck are rather different; one would not imagine they could survive continual persecution. They frequent open grassy hillsides elsewhere in Africa, but here they live in the more open parts of the maquis. They are gray-brown in color and run in pairs or in small herds. Occasionally up to fifteen may be seen in one herd. When alarmed they run off with a motion like a rocking horse, a characteristic of all reedbuck.

Besides these there are baboons and innumerable rock hyraxes *(Procavia capensis)*. The hyrax is a larger, stouter animal than the smaller *Heterohyrax* that is common on rocky hills in tropical Africa, but it is essentially the same in habits, living and basking on rock piles in colonies, and feeding chiefly at night.

The baboons are of a species that is found all over Africa—the olive baboon *(Papio anubis)*. Formerly they were classified as a different species, the chacma baboon *(P. ursinus)*, but another and probably sounder view is that all baboons are of one species with local variations. The mountain baboons of the Cape thrive despite some persecution. There are four troops in the Cape of Good Hope Nature Reserve, one of which has lately taken to a beachcombing life—picking shellfish off the rocks at low tide.

Leopards survive in the mountains despite relentless hunting, probably because they too are extremely difficult to exterminate in such thick growth. They feed chiefly on baboons and hyraxes and, less often, on duiker and reedbuck. Despite the stock farmers' animosity toward them, leopards probably benefit the farmer by keeping hyraxes in check. But it is always a little doubtful whether leopards control the number of baboons, or whether the latter are controlled by some other factor such as competition for feeding areas or disease.

VANISHED ANIMALS

Probably there never were as many animals in this part of Africa as farther north, where good grazing encouraged the almost incredible numbers mentioned in early travelers' tales. The Cape had some peculiar species, notably bontebok *(Damaliscus dorcas dorcas)*, the mountain zebra *(Equus zebra zebra)* and the blaauwbok *(Hippotragus leucophaeus)*. There were also eland, as many place names testify, and hartebeest, both of which have now disappeared from this region. Of these three, only one species, the blaauwbok, became extinct. It was a relative of the roan antelope, but lacked the mane of the roan and sable, and was smaller than either. It was always local and therefore vulnerable to extinction; its fate was sealed before the end of the eighteenth century.

The bontebok was also brought very near to extinction. It has become extinct as a wild animal, but a few were saved on farms and these have multiplied so that the species is no longer in danger. It is now on several reserves. It too seems to have been an animal of restricted haunts, dependent on a few plants. It proved difficult to reestablish the species until the remaining animals were moved into a reserve on their original habitat. The mountain zebra was less of an animal of the southern Cape plains than of the mountains, frequenting terrain avoided by most zebra species. It still survives, and has been reintroduced in several small reserves.

All these animals were grazers turned browsers. Had there been much grass among the Cape maquis they would have fed on it, but as there was little or none they had to feed on heath, reedlike Restionaceae, or rhenosterbush *(Elytropappus rhinocerotis)*. It would seem that they were tropical, grassland animals starting to colonize a different environment, not always very successfully. The blaauwbok had evolved into a separate species, but the others were only races of more widespread species.

Eland could surely be reintroduced advantageously in many mountain areas. These great antelopes thrive in the heath zones of East African mountains, and should therefore do well on maquis. They should be able to live in it without the need for the constant, ultimately destructive burning needed to produce sheep pasture.

NORTHERN MIGRANTS

Many species of birds from northern Europe winter in the Cape where they enjoy the southern summer. The European swallow *(Hirundo rustica)* arrives in numbers around mid-November, and stays till April. When present it is by far the commonest swallow in the area.

Apart from other places in the Union of South Africa this is the only part of Africa where large numbers of birds have been ringed and where many observers watch for ringed birds from other areas. Ringing has shown that birds not only return in the northern spring to their breeding quarters there, but like to winter in the same spot. Indeed ringed waders have been recaptured in several successive years in the vicinity of Cape Town.

Some of these northern migrant species even breed in the Cape area. There have been several records of breeding by the European stork *(Ciconia ciconia)*, while the black stork *(Ciconia nigra)* is a more common breeder in South Africa than it is in Europe. The European bee eater *(Merops apiaster)* also breeds in thousands in the Cape. What is not clear is whether these bee eaters are birds which have already bred in summer in Europe and breed a second time here within a year, or whether they breed only in South Africa. There is no reason why birds that breed in the northern hemisphere and arrive in the south in the summertime should not breed again. But most migrant species do not, so perhaps the birds that breed here do so only in South Africa.

Ringers sometimes have astonishing luck. One of three ringed nestlings of a pair of European storks (very rare breeders in South Africa) which nested in the Bredasdorp area, the

Beauty in search of sweetness. A Malachite sunbird (Nectarinia famosa) about to feed on a protea bloom. (W. T. Miller)

most southern tip of the continent, was recovered a few months later just north of Zambia. The recovery was the more remarkable since rather a low percentage of birds ringed in South Africa was ever subsequently traced.

SAND DUNES AND SEABIRDS

The virgin coastal plain between mountains and seashore is now largely unrecognizable, since it has all been cultivated or otherwise altered by man within the last few hundred years. But in the bays along the seacoast there are great expanses of sand dunes and magnificent beaches. Along the Namaqualand coast the sand dunes are so extensive that they form a miniature desert.

The dune sand was originally carried down by the many rivers that drain the mountains. It is cast up by the rough seas and frequently dams the mouths of small streams so that lagoons are formed behind the line of dunes. When the first settlers came, these lagoons were the haunt of hippos, but even today these areas are excellent for sea and water birds. They are often alive with red-knobbed coots *(Fulica cristata)*, several species of ducks, such as the yellow-billed duck and Cape teal, while gray herons and little egrets *(Egretta garzetta)* stalk in the shallows. Here again the general scene is not at all typical of tropical Africa but resembles rather some estuary in northwest Africa or southern Europe. The channels of slightly brackish water are fringed with reeds *(Phragmites)*, and both local and introduced willows thrive along the rivers in fresh water.

In 1962, the greater flamingo *(Phoenicopterus ruber)* bred in the Cape for the first time in recorded history. That was a great breeding year for flamingos all over Africa, a vintage year so to speak. They were able to breed because of special water conditions in one such lagoon; this demonstrated the opportunism of flamingos in their nesting habits.

Two species of terns that breed in Europe, the Caspian tern *(Hydroprogne caspia)* and roseate tern *(Sterna dougallii)*, are found here. With them are seen common and arctic terns—migrants from Europe—and several resident species of terns found only in South Africa. But South African terns do not migrate far northward, so that one can never see the same varied assembly in North Africa.

The black oystercatcher *(Haematopus moquini)* is common along the south coast. Its only close relative is the European oystercatcher *(Haematopus ostralegus)*, which visits South Africa occasionally and, while there, consorts with its cousin. There are no resident oystercatchers in tropical Africa. The local breeding black-backed gull *(Larus dominicanus)* is very like the European lesser black-backed gull, but is actually the same species as breeds in New Zealand. On offshore islands there are large colonies of Cape gannets *(Morus capensis)*, while jackass penguins *(Spheniscus demersus)*, so called because of their braying call, breed in burrows or hollows on these islands. There is a remarkable similarity between the sea and shore birds of the Cape and those of Europe. If the same

Wilderness beach in Cape Province. The great seas throw up masses of sand which are bound by the plants in the foreground and are later colonized by bushes and trees. (Emil Schulthess)

species do not actually breed both in Europe and the Cape there are often very close relations that do. This further emphasizes the likeness between this little subtropical region and Mediterranean Africa.

But any such likeness stops at the Cape of Good Hope itself. Here a stark peninsula of rock juts out into the ocean with magnificent cliffs descending abruptly into blue, crashing seas. This is the spectacular southern tip of Africa, and from here one can see many of the oceanic sea birds of Antarctica. Seven species of albatrosses are recorded from waters off the Cape, and two of these, the wandering albatross *(Diomedea exulans)* and the black-browed albatross *(D. melanophris)* often come close inshore. Also to be seen inshore are the giant petrel *(Macronectes giganteus)*, the Cape pigeon *(Daption capensis)* and the Cape hen *(Procellaria aequinoctialis)*. A trip in a trawler out to sea would reveal many more species of petrels, shearwaters, and albatrosses. None of these birds breeds on South African shores but they come to inshore waters; they are a link between Africa and more southern lands.

The Cape of Good Hope has been called the fairest cape in all the world. It is also remarkable as a place where one can watch such contrasts as a tropical African baboon gathering shellfish among the rocks while out to sea there soars an Antarctic albatross.

Left above: The yellow-billed duck (Anas undulata) is Africa's representative of the mallard tribe. It is common from Ethiopia to the Cape. Left: The hoopoe (Upupa africana) is very widespread from Europe and Asia to the Cape, but it seldom finds such a beautiful cranny in which to breed. (Both by W. T. Miller)

Volcanos, Flamingos and Great Lakes

The Great Rift Valley

16

At a place called Losiolo, in the Samburu district of Kenya, one may sit on a rock slab and look down on one of the greatest views in Africa. One comes to Losiolo over downs of short grass dotted with ancient cedar and Podocarpus trees, in the pristine beauty of the high East African grasslands; one drops into a little patch of highland forest and emerges onto a rocky promontory jutting from an escarpment. Here, at eight thousand feet, and with a fresh wind blowing, it is like being on the prow of a ship that is thrusting into a boundless ocean. An occasional eagle or vulture sails past, but there is little other life to be seen.

Below, a series of steps and terraces leads down into an horrific land of contorted rock and scrub, cut by deep gorges. The heat shimmer from this lower landscape tells one that it is scorching hot. A few zebras graze on the nearer terraces, and in the scrub there may be elephants, looking like big reddish boulders as they idle in the morning sun. In the dense bush of the lower slopes there are shy, bush-loving kudus and gerenuks as well.

Five thousand feet below, the gorges run out onto an immense plain of whitish grass with open patches of dry gray mud shimmering in the heat. This is the Suguta Valley, where it is just as unpleasantly hot as it is pleasantly cool on the top of Losiolo. One looks right across a range of ecological zones, from well-watered forest to desert, where life, as in other such regions, is precarious and grim.

Beyond the plain rises a group of rocky hills, jagged masses of recent lava, sharp and starkly outlined. And far beyond them, on a clear day one can see the great escarpment of the Cherangani Hills, rising to eleven thousand feet. About a hundred miles away, they form the western boundary of this section of the Great Rift Valley. What one sees from this point is not an ordinary plain, but the floor of a huge trench cut

The groundwater forest under the Rift wall at Lake Manyara. The product of many seepage springs and streams, it resembles the western lowland forest rather than adjacent mountain forests. (Sven Gillsater: Tio)

through a great section of East and Central Africa. The Rift Valley has a character quite distinct from that of the hill masses on either side of it.

FROM THE LEBANON TO MOZAMBIQUE

It has been said of the Rift Valley that, although it may have its counterpart on another planet, there is nothing like it on earth. There are other rift valleys, but none of these is so great in extent and variety, nor can they be so easily studied, for other rift valleys of comparable size lie far below the oceans. Rift valleys, of course, differ from the other valleys in that they are the result of movements and fractures in the earth's crust rather than erosion by water or occurring by ice.

The Rift Valley begins in the lower spurs of the Taurus Mountains in Turkey and runs south from there through the Jordan Valley to the Gulf of Aqaba. It includes the natural wonder of the Dead Sea, the shore of which is the lowest land in the world, 1,286 feet below the surface of the Mediterranean. At Aqaba the Rift is submerged beneath the waters of the Red Sea, to reappear on the African Continent in the Afar depression of northeast Ethiopia. At this point three rift valleys—the Red Sea, the Gulf of Aden and the African Rift converge. The African Rift runs through the Ethiopian Highlands and right through the highlands of Kenya and Tanzania to a point in south Tanzania where it seems to disappear. Much of this part is studded with both old and recent volcanos, alkaline lakes, and hot springs.

Another branch of the Rift begins at Lake Albert in Uganda. This western branch curves in a great arc to the Kivu Highlands, where it is blocked by an impressive group of high volcanic mountains, some of them still active. It continues, however, into the deep trough containing Lake Tanganyika, one of the largest lakes in the world and the second deepest. Here the floor of the Rift is 2,300 feet below sea level, and 4,730 feet under water.

At the head of Lake Nyasa the main lines of the eastern and western branch join. The western branch is now dominant and it continues through the Lake Nyasa trough, which is similar to Lake Tanganyika but not so deep. The subsidiary trough of the Luangwa Valley runs southwestward, connecting the main Rift with the valley of the Zambezi about as far as the Kafue-Zambezi confluence. The Ruaha trough runs northeast, and nearby is the small but perfect Rukwa Rift, an isolated branch of the main system. The Shire Valley leads out of Lake Nyasa to the sea and the lowlands of Mozambique.

The Mozambique channel, between Madagascar and the mainland of Africa, may be the last notable part of the Rift Valley system. About seventy-five million years ago the formation of this deep and impassable ocean-filled trench cut

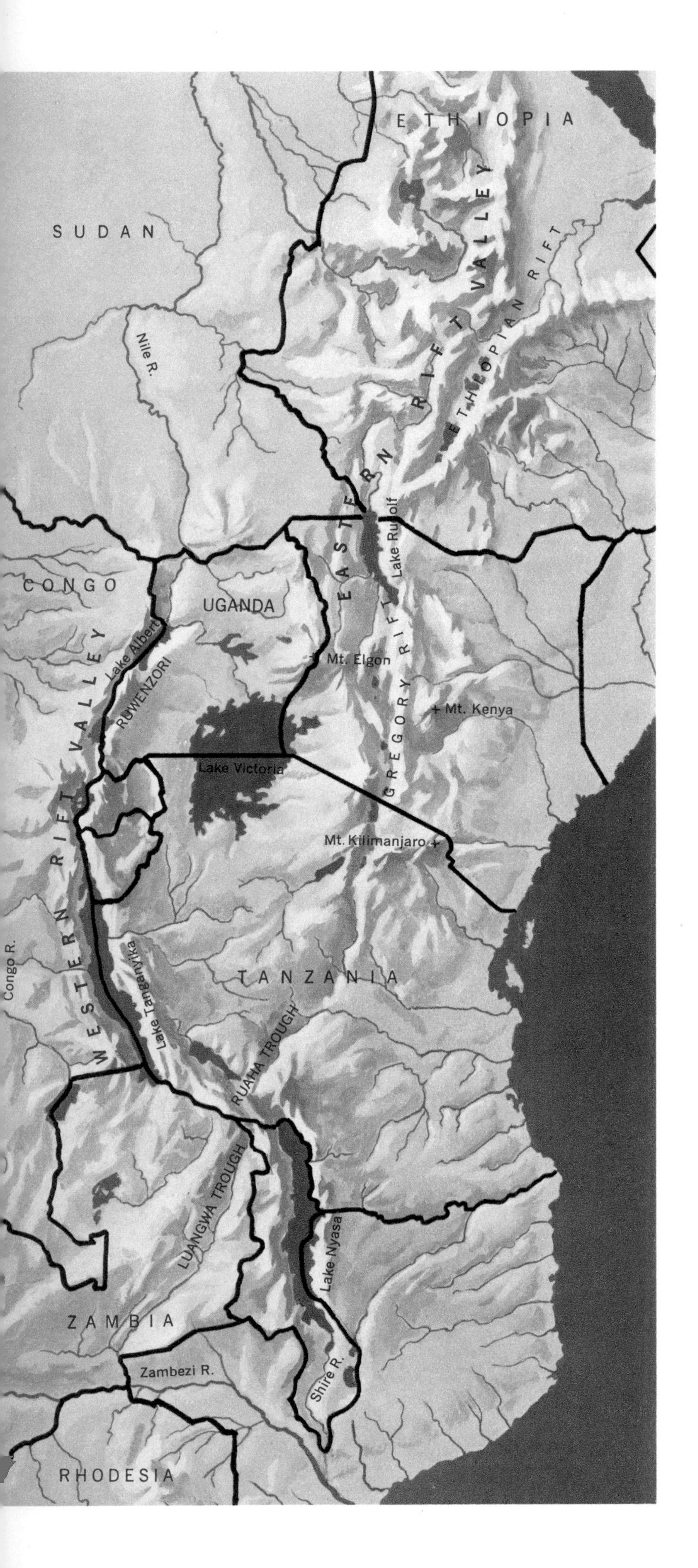

The Rift Valley, the outstanding geological feature of its kind on earth, is a huge trough slicing through Africa from Ethiopia to Mozambique. It is known for its volcanos, lakes and flamingos.

At Lake Assal in the desert near the Red Sea, a salt content of forty per cent results in beautiful crystalline growths where waves wash over the rocks. (R. Michaud: Rapho-Guillumette)

off Madagascar from Africa. The island's unique flora and fauna, of supreme interest to naturalists, was crystallized there, and has only had relatively minor introductions since that time.

Some question whether this great system of trenches and troughs running from the Lebanon to Mozambique is truly a unit. But a close look at a topographical relief map of the eastern half of Africa convinces most people that the Rift Valley can scarcely be the result of isolated and haphazard earth movements, but must be part of one great system. This impression is heightened by a study of the life on the floor of the Rift, which is often unlike that on the flanking hills and plateaus, but like that in other localities on the Rift floor a thousand miles to the north or south. Moreover recent research in the Indian Ocean has shown that the continental Rift is only a part of a greater system of valleys and ridges that run right round Eastern Africa under the sea.

RIFT AND RIVER VALLEYS

A rift valley is not really a valley at all; it only looks like one. Ordinary valleys are cut by rivers in their descent from mountains toward the sea; they may be steep-sided and narrow, but a big, old river valley often has a large flat alluvial plain on its floor and steep escarpments some distance back on either side.

Opinions still differ as to how rift valleys are formed, but the consensus is that they are sections of the earth's crust which have dropped to a lower level between two lines of cracks or faults. In dropping, these sections have often been shattered and formed into smaller steps and escarpments. Sometimes the minor cracks can still be seen running parallel to the main fault lines. Technically a rift valley may be called a graben, a term applied to any place on earth where a section of the surface has dropped into a hollow beneath the surrounding level. Volcanic craters are often grabens.

The difference of opinion arises over what caused the fall. Why should a great slice of the earth's crust drop to a lower level? Were the mountains on either side pushed upward, with the floor of the valley representing the original level of the land? Or did parallel yawning cracks appear on the surface to allow the area between to slide downward? The answer is probably that a combination of uplift and downthrust produced the phenomena we see today.

In Kenya and Ethiopia at least, the gradual uplift of sections of the continent have resulted in great domes in the earth's crust. The surface of such domes consists of hard rock resting on a more fluid interior. The shrinkage accompanying gradual cooling of the surface caused parallel cracks in the domes, running roughly north and south. Sections of the crust then subsided between these cracks, forming the Rift Valley. The process may be likened to the dropping of the keystone of an arch that has been weakened by horizontal tension. The molten interior of the dome would ooze or explode out of the cracks, forming sheets of lava or explosive volcanos, and with each fresh phase of cracking further eruptions would follow.

Some believe, however, that the Rift Valley is the result less of cracking and subsidence in the earth's crust as of downward suction caused by convection currents in the molten interior. Such currents could result from the gradual uplift of plateaus, and could drag down sections of the crust between lines of cracks. This theory is perhaps more attractive in those parts of the Rift that are not essentially volcanic. Yet another theory holds that parts of the Rift Valley were formed by lateral compression just as the crest of an arch can be thrust downward by great pressure from the flanks.

The faulting and sinking that made the Rift Valley must have occurred in distinct alternations of activity and quiescence over a period of twelve or fifteen million years. Movements have intensified during the last million years, but have temporarily subsided. Even today earthquakes and minor subsidences are common features of life at Addis Ababa and in the Kenya Rift. Since the earth's crust is rigid it tends to split or fracture in spasms, and these are the cause of earthquakes. It is sobering to stand on the lip of the Rift Valley near Nairobi and reflect that the solid rocks beneath you are liable to move again at any time, and that in terms of geological time the strange and splendid prospect of parallel troughs and ridges is only a temporary phase.

A CRUEL DESERT

The Rift Valley can best be surveyed in a journey from north to south, from the Red Sea to Mozambique. Even today much of this journey can be made only on foot; large tracts are inaccessible by road. This difficulty would face an explorer as soon as he stepped into the Rift at its northern end, for the Afar depression of Ethiopia is one of the harshest deserts in the world. It is, moreover, inhabited by tribes with an unsurpassed reputation for bloodthirstiness. Anyone who passes the Afar and Danakil deserts can be certain that nothing he will meet in the Rift thereafter will have quite as unpleasant prospects.

The Afar depression and the Danakil deserts form a huge, roughly triangular funnel leading the Rift Valley into a narrow neck that runs right through Ethiopia. The Awash River, rising in the Ethiopian Highlands, drains through this neck into the deserts, and eventually loses itself in salt lakes and marshes. The plains of dry grassland in the upper part of the Awash Valley are still an important wildlife area. As regards fauna, the Awash Valley and the Danakil and Afar belong to the Horn of Africa. There are oryx, gazelles, Grevy's zebras, and small remaining populations of the wild ass.

Located about 250 feet below sea level, the Afar is one of the hottest places on earth. Travelers there have recorded up to 165° F. in the shade. These temperatures were not, however, recorded with proper meteorological equipment, and they may not be hotter than the hottest known spot on earth, El Azizia in Libya, with shade temperatures of 136.7° F. A temperature of 165° F., if long continued, is insupportable to living creatures. It means that everything one touches, and even the air is hotter than an average person could bear in his bath or for his tea.

Left above: On the Rift wall at Losiolo. The fault scarp, grass-clad in the foreground, descends through many zones from remnant highland forest to the subdesert bush in the distance. (Leslie Brown) Left: Steaming rubble in the broad crater of Nyamlagira, the most active of the Virunga volcanos; it has erupted several times in this century. (Kai Curry-Lindahl)

In the Afar, signs of recent vulcanism are everywhere. Several active volcanic cones still spout smoke and ashes, if not molten lava. The floor of the depression consists in many places of fields of clinker and lava, still knife-sharp and unsoftened by any weathering in this desert climate. These black and purple rocks absorb the heat of the sun by day and retain it by night. A passage across the flat mud of an old lake bed or a stretch of sand seems cool and easy by comparison.

There are also remarkable salt and alkaline lakes here. The Awash River runs into a depression with no outlet. Its waters, born of the alkaline lavas of the Ethiopian plateau, and continuously concentrated by a scorching sun, end in alkaline lakes. In the Afar, salt springs have resulted in huge deposits of natural salt and of potash. The salt deposits cover perhaps two thousand square miles, in places two thousand feet deep, and are as hard and compact as marble. The whole deposit looks like a solidified sea. It is mined by local people, who cut it into bars that have for centuries been a standard form of currency on the Ethiopian plateau.

Scientific study in this area is difficult because of the ferocious nature of the tribesmen. Bloodthirstiness or a warlike nature is a common feature of desert tribes, and it is not difficult to understand the reason. Such people are entirely dependent on the produce of their stock, and a certain number of human beings must have a certain number of cattle, camels, sheep or goats to keep themselves alive. These animals, in turn, require a certain area of desert in which to forage. If the human population rises, the people try to keep more and more stock, the area available per animal is reduced and eventually overgrazed and damaged. The animals then starve and die, and the human beings dependent on their milk and meat suffer from famine. It is therefore vital for desert tribes to maintain a sufficient area for their herds in whatever way they can.

SHRINKING LAKES

Along the Ethiopian Rift and continuing into Kenya, the Rift floor is usually a hot dry plain in strong contrast to the cool, forested heights on either side. Underfoot, volcanic rubble gives place in parts to plains of fine white or red powdery dust that rises in choking clouds. These flat plains of dust are the remains of lakes and swamps that existed in wetter ages or were formed by damming by, for instance, the rise of a volcano. The most recent deposits were laid down in pluvial periods that probably corresponded to the temperate ice ages, but some of the larger and more extensive plains of white dust are much older. They consist of a great layer of fine silt on the bottom of big, dry lakes, with, in places, beds of the skeletons of tiny animals, called diatoms, whose descendants still flourish abundantly in alkaline waters on the Rift floor. In past times some lakes were very much larger, and must have been fringed with great swamps.

Some of the existing lakes, especially those in Kenya and

Temporary lakes such as this form during the rains in flat parts of the Rift floor but dry up again in a few months. They are all that remains of much larger lakes on the same site. (James R. Simon)

Tanzania, have now been studied for fifty years or more. Even during that time they have shrunk in size and depth, and have evidently been shrinking steadily during recent prehistorical times. About 2,800 years ago Lake Naivasha, in Kenya, was about 125 feet above its present level. A large river ran out of it through what is now a dry gorge. Lake Rudolf has sunk about six hundred feet below its original outlet to the Nile. When flying over the deserts of Turkana one may see its old beaches curving incongruously over the parched landscape.

The shrinkage of the last fifty years can be correlated with such worldwide climatic features as the retreat of most of the glaciers in the mountain chains of the temperate world. But in the last few years there has been exceptional rainfall and some lakes are now higher than they have been for a very long time. In 1964, for instance, Lake Rukwa inundated baobab trees thought to be five hundred years old, and Lake Naivasha and Nakuru are now as high as anyone living can remember them. If they rise any higher they will probably kill the encircling forests of huge feverthorn trees *(Acacia xanthophlaea),* which must be several hundred years old. This is probably only a temporary fluctuation in the rainfall pattern rather than a herald of a new pluvial period.

The black-winged stilt is typically associated with alkaline or saline waters. (Julius Behnke)

When these lakes shrink they generally become more alkaline. Sodium salts, chiefly sodium carbonate and its derivatives, increase in concentration until the water becomes so bitter that it is lethal to animals that drink it. If the shrinkage continues the lake eventually dries into a smooth expanse of acrid yellowish earth that blows away in a strong wind. About ten years ago Lake Nakuru and Lake Elmenteita were practically dry, and everyone living near them had sore throats from the dust. In recent years they have refilled, and the main discomfort now is the mosquitos that breed in the relatively fresh water of the swamps around their shores.

Some lakes, even when the level falls, do not become much more alkaline. Lake Naivasha is one of these, and Lake Baringo another. In such cases there must be subterranean outlets enabling the water to percolate through the shattered, porous rocks of the Rift and emerge elsewhere. When such waters do emerge they may be boiling hot and highly alkaline. While underground they have passed among rocks heated by the volcanic fires still close to the surface, and have been impregnated with salts.

THE MARVELLOUS PINK HORDES

Increased alkalinity spells death to fish or to zebras and hippos, but to some other creatures it brings life. The high carbonate content, the abundant sunlight, and the high temperatures of the floor of the Rift combine to make these waters an ideal habitat for certain minute plants—the diatoms and blue-green algae. These multiply till they turn the slimy waters of alkaline lakes into a rich, pea-soup green. This is wonderful food for any animal that can extract it from the water without swallowing the lethal fluid itself. The millions of flamingos that live in the Rift do just this.

There may be throughout the world about six million flamingos of four or five species. At least half of these, about three million, live in the East African–Ethiopian Rift Valley. The more numerous species is the lesser flamingo *(Phoeniconaias minor),* but the greater flamingo *(Phoenicopterus ruber)* also inhabits this area. It is the hordes of the lesser flamingo that create a matchless spectacle on some Rift lakes.

Millions of lesser flamingos are sometimes seen together. A lake which is, for the time being, specially favorable, harbors half, or more of the total population. On Lake Nakuru there is often a band fifty yards wide, extending for two or three miles along the shore, packed solid with the rich pink of flamingos. Off the hot springs of Lake Hannington I once saw a flock that contained about 720,000 flamingos. Even at rest such a flock is a superb spectacle, but when all the birds suddenly take wing together, the scene is breathtaking in its movement and color.

Lesser flamingos' beaks are highly specialized to extract the blue-green algae and diatoms from water. The inside of both mandibles is covered with fine hairs arranged in lines that

Lesser flamingos feed with their bills submerged, upside down, in the top two inches of water. They gather blue-green algae as they walk forward, continually sweeping their heads from side to side with a scything motion. (Arthur Christiansen)

rise and fall as the water passes in and out of the beak. A lesser flamingo feeds with its head upside down and its lower mandible uppermost. The tongue works to and fro in a groove in the lower mandible like the piston in a pump, causing a pulsing flow of water within the beak. The hairs, alternately erect and flat, filter the blue-green algae from the water. Other movements of the beak act like a pair of wool carders, and roll masses of algae down onto the tongue. Backward-pointing processes on the tongue then automatically pull the algae into the gullet.

This extraordinarily efficient method of filter feeding enables lesser flamingos to extract all the food they need from the top inch or so of water. They prefer to feed in shallow water where they can walk about, but can also feed while swimming in calm water. Their curving necks move from side to side with a scything motion as they skim the surface. From the murky water of Lake Nakuru a million or so flamingos can extract about two tons per acre annually of blue-green algae. But the total amount of algae present is scarcely affected by their activities, and at times this strange aquatic pasture could probably support far more flamingos than feed on it. Greater flamingos, much rarer, feed in fresher water, sieving the bottom mud for insect larvae and other small animals.

A HARSH BREEDING GROUND

The nesting place of all these multitudes of flamingos was unknown until 1954, when I discovered it in the middle of Lake Natron. Since then regular checks have shown that both greater and lesser flamingos breed here. The lesser flamingos breed in enormous colonies on an alkaline mudflat seven or eight miles from the shore. The mirage over the lake had hidden them from sight until I flew over the lake in an airplane.

Lake Natron is one of two alkaline lakes in this part of the Rift Valley. But this lake and the smaller Lake Magadi are largely dry, and consist of layers of crystalline sodium carbonates overlying foul black mud. Perennial springs, some of

Left above: The red-knobbed coot (Fulica cristata) is an inhabitant of the less alkaline lakes of the Rift. (Alan Root)
Left below: The little grebe or dabchick (Poliocephalus ruficollis), a widespread Old World water bird, is very numerous on Rift Valley lakes. Here a parent on a floating nest incubates one egg while a youngster returns to shelter. (Alan Root: Okapia)

Above: Lesser flamingos taking flight before a coming storm. They avoid rough water which hampers their mode of feeding. (Jacques Verschuren)

them large, create lagoons of strongly alkaline water that are good feeding grounds for flamingos. In particular, the south lagoon of Lake Natron is their regular home at present, and this lake is never entirely without them.

The crystalline crust of Lake Natron is white, sometimes tinged with pink, and the shallow water is often wine red, or coffee colored. This water becomes as hot as the average person would like his bath to be, and the surface of the soda flat at midday is about 150° F. The stinking mud where flamingos build their conical nest mounds is still hotter. Yet in this noisome place, amid the scorching heat and blinding glare, the flamingos rear their young. Flamingos are attacked and eaten by everything from the ratel or honey badger to lions, and by several species of eagles and vultures. In the center of Lake Natron they escape all but a few bird predators, an advantage that outweighs the disadvantages of high temperature and blinding glare.

The flamingos have a rather neat adaptation that helps the chicks to withstand conditions that would kill any ordinary young bird. Although the surface of the mud is very hot, the temperature of the top of the nest mound is only about blood heat. After hatching, the young flamingo can thus spend the first few days on top of the relatively cool mound, and will always return to the mound if it is somehow scared away. When it is a little stronger it descends and joins with others to form great flocks. These flocks then walk, sometimes for miles, to the nearest open water. But they do not move to the shore of Lake Natron till they are nearly ready to fly; they remain out in the middle of the lake, visible as a large brownish patch on the white soda.

Flamingos do not normally breed in Lake Magadi. But in 1962 Lake Natron was full of water, and about 1,200,000 pairs of flamingos, nearly all the lesser species, bred on Lake Magadi. Great numbers of young were reared, but large numbers were lost to predators, especially hyenas. Others were stricken by a curious malady; walking in the soda-saturated water they developed hard, ball-like masses of soda around their legs. These shackles eventually grew too heavy for them and dragged them down in the mud. Many died, but most were saved when they were driven into an area of less saturated water, and about 25,000 had their unwanted fetters knocked off by a team of volunteers.

After ten years of observation it appears that neither lesser nor greater flamingos breed every year. On the average, about 130,000 young are reared annually. No other major breeding ground is known, though one may exist. From these figures the average life of a wild flamingo must be over twenty years—astonishingly long for any bird.

A SUMP OF SODA

Lake Magadi is the second largest expanse of solid sodium carbonates in the world. Like several other lakes in the Rift, it was once forty feet deeper. Through desiccation and evaporation it has become a solid deposit like the salt beds in the Afar depression. But the deposit is chiefly soda, not salt, and Lake Magadi is well above sea level.

Lake Magadi, which is slightly lower than Lake Natron or the Uaso Nyiro River, is the sump of this part of the Rift Valley. The crystalline deposits are continually renewed by springs of alkaline water. Since the lake has no outlet, the water of these springs never escapes from it, and the great heat of this area results in intense evaporation. The contents of the springs quickly solidify into layers of crystalline salts, so that the inflow of salts is actually greater than the present rate of commercial exploitation.

Between Magadi and the Ngong escarpment is a contorted stretch of country called the Sykes Grid. Here parallel ridges of hard, blackish lava separate a series of flat valleys grown over with long grass. One may assume that at one time these valleys were lake beds, an assumption that is evidenced by fossils. But one may reasonably ask how such an extraordinary stretch of country was formed in the first place.

The explanation apparently is that the ridges and valleys are formed of wedge-shaped masses of lava "floating" on more plastic underlying material. If wedge-shaped pieces of wood are arranged alternately with the narrow end and the broad end uppermost, they will float in water in a manner resembling the rock formations of this part of the Rift. The center of gravity of each wedge is nearer the broad base than the narrow apex; when floating, the centers of gravity all seek the same level. Hence if the broad base is uppermost the wedge floats low, and vice versa.

The supposition is that the Sykes Grid is a very thin part of the earth's crust and this is easy to believe for there are many hot springs and sulphurous steam jets. The volcanic fires are not far below. Ol Donyo Lengai, a conical volcano at the south end of Lake Natron, is still active, spouting ashes and smoke from time to time. However, volcanic activity hereabouts is at the present time slight.

THE BIRTHPLACE OF MANKIND?

This part of the Rift is at present dry and harsh. The vegetation consists of sparse pasture and thorns, and it supports only rather small numbers of wildebeest, rhinos, oryx, gerenuks, giraffes, and zebras. Buffalos and hippos live in the Uaso Nyiro swamp, but in the main the wildlife is that of subdesert steppe. But it was not always so.

Much fossil evidence has recently been unearthed in this area, at Olorgesaile and Olduvai Gorge. Although Olduvai is in the northern Serengeti Plains, it once was part of a big lake or swamp associated with the Rift Valley lakes. The fossils give evidence of a fauna that, if alive, would make the present wildlife of the Serengeti seem insignificant. It is apparent that there were sheep as big as oxen, pigs as big as rhinos, hippos twice the size of a present-day hippo, and many other animals. Today the pigs and hippos here are no bigger than pigs and hippos elsewhere in Africa, and the huge sheep have altogether gone.

This astonishing assembly of animals existed in fairly recent times. During the pluvial periods of the Pleistocene the pastures on the floor of the Rift must have been incredibly rich, and the whole area must have been dotted with lakes and swamps. Some of the richest assemblies of present-day animals exist on flood plains in the Rift Valley, so it is not difficult to imagine how a much richer fauna could have lived at a time when most of the Rift floor was lush pasture or swamp. In these favorable circumstances the animals grew so big that when harder times came, with increasing desiccation, they died out. Early man must have seen the decline of these animals.

Ethiopian Rift Valley lakes support the same sort of birds found on other lakes a thousand miles to the south; here are cormorants, pelicans, and migrant Palearctic ducks. (Anna Riwkin)

Man may be described as a primate who *makes* tools—as opposed to merely using them. At Olduvai, in the last few years, remains of very early men have been found. One of these, *Zinjanthropus boisei,* appears to have been very large. The evidence is increasing that this part of Africa may have been the origin of mankind.

That there is a dearth of remains of manlike animals is easily explained. There were hyenas in the past as there are now, and hyenas are very efficient undertakers. Any bone that is not too big for them they crush and break to pieces, and except in a few places the relatively small bones of early men would thus have all been consumed. Even at the beginning of this century one standard method of disposing of human bodies in Africa was to leave them out for the hyenas to eat—a very sanitary method of disposal too.

Early man had no means of carrying much water. This meant that he had to live near rivers, streams, or lakes, where fish, turtles, frogs, and the like were easily caught. These earliest known men were, however, toolmakers, for numerous obsidian axe-heads have been found in this region. Big-game hunters of today who set forth in trepidation, although equipped with powerful rifles, to hunt rhinos, might well salute their primitive ancestors who, armed only with clubs and stone axes, attacked much larger beasts.

HOT-WATER FISH

The larger ancient lakes must have contained abundant fish, but in several of the present lakes the water is too alkaline to support fish life. The freshwater lakes, Naivasha, Baringo, and part of Lake Manyara, however, still contain numbers of tilapia. But in Lake Natron and Lake Magadi the tilapia have been forced to adapt themselves to the only comparatively fresh water available—the hot springs that run into the lakes.

One may sit in one of these hot springs and have a bath in the gentle current of dilute soda. As one bathes, a tickling sensation makes one aware of hundreds of little fish around one's body. These little fish are *Tilapia grahami,* a dwarf species that can live only in the hot springs. If they are taken out and placed in cool, fresh water they die.

Usually, *Tilapia grahami* is confined to these springs and

cannot live in the more alkaline waters of the lakes. But in time of exceptional rain these waters are diluted and then there is a population explosion of the little fish: the shallow water at the outlet of the springs ripples with millions of them. They are preyed on by every variety of fish-eating bird, from thousands of little grebes *(Poliocephalus ruficollis)* to the great white pelicans *(Pelecanus onocrotalus)*.

Great white pelicans regularly migrate down the Rift from north to south. Their splendid soaring flight enables them to rise on thermals to great altitudes, and they then glide from lake to lake, occasionally flapping their wings to maintain height. They descend at evening, when the air cools, and, since they often settle in places where there are no fish, they must sometimes go to sleep hungry. One place in the Rift where they are known to breed regularly is at Lake Rukwa, in southern Tanzania, where there is regularly enough fish to feed them.

In 1962, a population explosion of *Tilapia grahami* in exceptionally high water in Lake Natron induced a large number of pelicans to try to breed there. For this purpose they used volcanic rocks, normally surrounded by dry mud, that became islands in the unusually high water. Possibly twenty thousand pairs of pelicans attempted to breed there, attracted by the myriads of small fish. Their daily food need must have been about thirty tons of *Tilapia grahami,* so that the extent of the multiplication of these fish, from the initially small numbers in the springs, can be imagined.

The pelicans did not succeed. Either the lake became too alkaline, or the supply of oxygen dissolved in the water failed, and all the fish died. Tidelines of dead fish, yards wide, were formed all round Lake Natron, especially near the outlets of springs. The pelicans, their food supply cut off, simply abandoned their attempt to breed.

Many thousands of pelicans migrate annually down the Rift, but they do not seem to breed very successfully there, not even at Lake Rukwa. They lay their eggs on flat swampy islands in the flood plain at the north end of the lake, and there they are frequently stranded by receding water. At first the young pelicans cannot fly far, and most are lost in their attempts to reach the lake through great areas of swampy grassland. That so many pelicans continue to survive at all is surely evidence that they are very long-lived birds that do not need to rear many young each year to maintain their population.

ANOTHER GREAT TROUGH

The pelicans at Lake Rukwa have brought us very close to the western arm of the Rift Valley, which begins at Lake Albert in Uganda about six hundred miles to the north. This western arm has, near Lake Albert, possibly been formed in a rather different way from the Ethiopian and Kenyan rift valleys and it does not look nearly so new as these, though some recent movements have occurred. The contours of the Rift scarps are much softer than near Nairobi, and there are few abrupt vertical precipices.

The glowing lava pool in the crater of Nyiragongo, in the Virunga volcanos. This mountain has been more active recently than when it was first discovered. (Alan Root: Okapia)

Yet this is the part of the Rift where some of the most violent of recent volcanic activity has taken place, and where eruptions with flowing lava have occurred within the last fifty years or so. The fearful explosions that formed the craters in the Queen Elizabeth National Park have been described in the chapter on the Nile Valley. There are, moreover, a group of volcanos here, one of which is still vigorously active.

These mountains, namely the Virunga volcanos, are of varying ages and three distinct groups. Except for Mount Sabinio, which is a cone formed by a continuous flow of lava, and the active Nyamlagira, which is a shield volcano, they are all conical volcanos of the explosive type, with a crater at the top. Only the western group is still active, and of these Nyamlagira is the only one that still spouts lava. This volcano erupted in 1938 and again in 1948, and it is probably the most active of all the cones the whole length of the Rift.

Both Nyamlagira and its nearest neighbor, Nyiragongo, have typical craters in their summits. Nyamlagira's crater is over a mile across, but that of Nyiragongo is more perfectly formed and more easily examined: about two-thirds of a mile across, its steep walls drop to an almost level floor of rock. This latter volcano was still active at the end of the last century, but had become dormant by 1908. However, when Nyamlagira erupted in 1938, Nyiragongo also became active, though only inside its crater.

The three groups of the Virunga volcanos evidently lie along an east-west transverse fault in the Rift floor. Such faults are probably the origin of many small and large volcanos—such as Mount Longonot, still gently fizzing, near Nairobi—found all along the floor of the Rift. As the floor of the Rift subsides over the ages, new cracks are formed, and out of these spout new volcanos that are active for a period and then lie extinct, ever present reminders of the volcanic nature of the area.

The highest of the Virunga volcanos, Karissimbi, over fourteen thousand feet high, is one of the most remarkable volcanic cones in the world. The Virunga volcanic group constitutes an area of exceptional beauty and is of much biological interest with its mountain gorillas *(G. g. beringei)*.

DROWNED RIVER VALLEYS

Volcanic activity frequently blocks the course of a river and results in lakes; several lakes in the western Rift region have been produced in this way. The most famous and the largest of these is Lake Kivu, generally considered the most beautiful of all the great lakes of Africa. Lake Bunyonyi in Uganda is another.

Lava flows from the Virunga volcanos have dammed a section of the Rift Valley that once drained northward to the Nile, so producing the deeply indented Lake Kivu. The fjord-like bays of Lake Kivu were formerly the deep river valleys draining the highlands of Ruanda into the Rift. In this high-rainfall area, where the very high Virunga volcanos probably increased the over-all rainfall, the space behind the dam filled up until the water escaped through another river course. Lake Kivu now drains via the Ruzizi River into Lake Tanganyika. Lake Tanganyika probably had no outlet when the overflow began, but the added water from the Ruzizi was enough to raise the level and allow it to flow out through the Lukuga creek to the Congo. Thus the direction of the flow of rivers in this area, once toward the Mediterranean, was shifted toward the Atlantic by volcanic eruptions.

Lava still flows into Lake Kivu from Mount Nyamlagira. The lava of this volcano is rich in potassium and is very fluid. When in 1938 and 1948 strong eruptions sent masses of lava running down the hillside—at up to twenty-two miles per hour—water in the lake became very hot and great clouds of steam arose. One can clearly imagine how the earlier eruptions must have killed most of the fish in the river that was dammed to form Lake Kivu.

Fish that inhabited lakes formed in such drowned valleys could at first be only of the species existing in the river before it was dammed. Any others have evolved in the course of time or have somehow entered the lake after the blockage. Both in Lake Kivu and in Lake Bunyonyi there are few species of fish. Although Lake Kivu is now connected to the Congo system through Lake Tanganyika, its fish fauna still evidences its early connection with the Nile and Lake Edward. Most fish cannot surmount the Ruzizi River rapids, but one species, *Barilius moorei,* has somehow managed to enter Lake Kivu.

Lake Kivu is a deep lake, averaging about six hundred feet in depth and reaching a maximum of about thirteen hundred feet. But only the upper layers of the water—that is, no deeper than two hundred feet—are suitable for fish. The lower depths are charged with dissolved salts and contain much sulphuretted hydrogen, making the water an impossible environment except for some microorganisms. The water in the lake does not circulate, so that the nutrient-rich lower water never reaches the top. Only the shoreline shallows support large numbers of fish.

TWO GREAT LAKES

Thus far in our journey down the Rift we have been almost entirely in country of a volcanic nature. But we now come to parts of the Rift that are formed in much older rocks than the lava of either Ethiopia, Uganda, or Kenya. Lake Tanganyika and Lake Nyasa lie in very deep troughs that cut through rocks of the basement complex, or old sandstone.

The Cape wigeon (Anas capensis) can live, unlike other ducks, on alkaline waters thick with green algal slime. (Arthur Christiansen)

Lake Tanganyika receives all the drainage from Lake Kivu through the Ruzizi River, and from many other streams, but it has no outlet other than the small, reed-choked Lukuga creek that connects it with the Congo basin. Once the Malagarasy River drained west from Tanganyika straight into the Congo basin. Then the plateaus and mountain ranges on either side of Lake Tanganyika were gradually uplifted, and a huge trough formed between them. Thereafter, the Malagarasy River could no longer flow into the Congo, but filled the hollow instead, helping to form Lake Tanganyika. But the traces of its old course remain in the lowly Lukuga creek. This creek only flows into the Congo basin when, as at present, the lake is very high.

Lake Tanganyika is enormously deep. If the height of the mountains on either side is taken into account, the trough in which it lies is almost ten thousand feet from top to bottom. It looks more like a fjord than a part of the Rift Valley. Lake Nyasa is not quite so deep, but its bottom is still well below sea level. It has a strong outlet through the Shire River. It seems strange that this river should flow out so strongly when Lake Tanganyika has no real outflow. Apparently the evaporation rate relative to the inflow and rainfall is greater in Lake Tanganyika.

The main interest in these two great lakes is their extraordinary fish fauna. Especially among the cichlid fish, or mouth-breeders, there is a remarkable development of species found only in these waters. Eighty-nine out of ninety cichlid species are endemic in Tanganyika, and 171 out of 175 in Lake Nyasa, while Lake Albert, which has long been connected to the Nile, has only two endemics out of seven species. Ninety-eight and ninety-nine per cent of the cichlid species in Lake Nyasa and Lake Tanganyika are peculiar to their home lakes, as compared with twenty-nine per cent in Lake Albert.

The extraordinary proliferation of mouth-breeding fish has been explained on two grounds—the absence of powerful predatory fish, and long isolation. In Lake Rudolf and Lake Albert, which have nilotic fish faunas, the predatory Nile perch is common. Both perch and tiger fish are absent in Lake Nyasa, which has the richest cichlid fauna. But both are present in Lake Tanganyika, where the number of endemic mouth-breeding fish is still very high. It might therefore seem that their long isolation, depth, and size, are better reasons for the elaboration of cichlid species in these lakes than the absence of fierce predatory fishes.

Nor are fish the only creatures that have produced endemic forms in Lake Tanganyika. There are numerous snails and bivalves peculiar to the lake, an endemic subfamily of water bugs, and many peculiar crustacea. A caddis fly, *Limnoecetis tanganyikae,* has so far departed from the ordinary habits of caddis flies as to lose its powers of flight and skate upon the surface like a water boatman. Finally, there is a water cobra, *Boulengeria annulata stormsi,* that has abandoned the land habits of most cobras and become completely aquatic.

The majority of African lakes are murky, but Lake Tanganyika is almost entirely clear. Most of the streams that run into it drain sandy soils and so do not carry much silt. Moreover, they come from acid soils and rocks, so that microscopic life does not multiply in the water and make it opaque.

The waves form clean shingle beaches, and it is delightful to swim in this water, provided one is not disturbed by how deep it is.

As in Lake Kivu, all but the upper two hundred feet of Lake Tanganyika is lifeless—and never circulates to the surface. It is full of accumulated salts but devoid of oxygen, so that no fish life can exist in it. In the deepest parts of the lake the top layer overlies about four thousand feet of this dead, useless fossil water. It is indeed remarkable that such an extraordinary fish and mollusk fauna has developed in it. One of the most interesting of the fish is a small member of the herring family, the dagaa *(Stolothrissa tanganyikae)*. These fish come to the surface at night in schools and fishermen attract them with lights. They can be seen darting about in water that is like pellucid, greenish glass thousands of feet deep.

Lake Nyasa too has a deep layer of dead water at its bed. Since its formation perhaps two million years ago, it has never been fully connected to the Zambezi River system, from which tiger fish could have entered it. The Shire River flows into the Zambezi, but the Murchison Rapids are a sufficient obstacle to prevent the upstream migration of tiger fish. There are carnivorous catfish in Lake Nyasa, but they probably have not been as effective as tiger fish and predatory perch in reducing the number of species of small mouth-breeding fish.

THE LIFE OF THE RIFT

At Lake Nyasa we come to the last spectacular part of the Rift Valley system. Here the line of the eastern arm of the Rift, which seems to peter out in Tanzania, crosses the western arm and strikes westward into the Luangwa and Zambezi valleys. From the map in this chapter one can see that the western branch now runs southeast at the end of its great sickle-shaped curve from Lake Albert.

The clear, parallel lines of scarps, with steps and terraces on their sides, that marked the northern part of the Rift Valley, now disappear. Some have considered that these deep valleys are not true rift valleys but are produced, like many lower escarpments, by downwarping or buckling of a part of the earth's crust. Yet it is difficult to believe, when one looks at a map, that this complex of similar troughs is not all part of one great system with two main branches.

This feeling is strengthened by common features that exist the length of the Rift from Danakil to the Luangwa Valley. The floor of the Rift is always hotter and always has less rainfall than its sides; the western scarps are usually higher than the eastern; and the valley bottoms are often flat flood plains of rich grazing, which support a far greater concentration of wild animals than the mountains and plateaus on either side.

Whether it is all one system or not, the Rift acts like a single system and has its own way of life. Millions of migrant birds pour down it each year. It is probably one of the more important migration routes in Africa, though these are little known. The birds vary from myriads of European swallows to big eagles that soar along the mountainous scarps and feed on the abundant rodents and water birds on the plains and lakes. The most spectacular of all the migrants are the soaring cohorts of pelicans, that come south each year to Lake Rukwa but so seldom succeed in breeding there.

This life of the Rift, as a great pathway through the eastern half of Africa, may have evolved in wetter times when the high hills on either side must have been forested and the plains of the floor were probably rich pasture land with far more abundant water than there is now. Enormous herds of animals, of which only a remnant remains here and there, could have used this pathway. In dry periods there would also have been corridors along these rift valleys that enabled the fauna of dry areas in South and North Africa to meet.

Thus the Rift system, whether or not it is all of similar geological origin, has probably performed a vital function in the movement of African fauna—and still does so for migrants. In this respect, as well as in its remarkable physical features, it is unique. And a final touch of strangeness is added by the huge lakes at its floor, each one different from the next and each supporting forms of life that occur there alone.

Glaciers and Giant Plants

The East African Mountains

17

The highlands of East Africa are not truly a mountain block like those in Ethiopia. They are plains at four to seven thousand feet, chiefly covered with grasslands, and with a bracing and rather dry climate. If these highlands lacked higher points than the general level of the plain, the rain-bearing winds would sweep over them unimpeded and the climate would probably be drier than it is. There would therefore be no areas of intense rainfall, and few forests, major rivers, or deep valleys.

But rising from the plains are a number of isolated mountains of great height. They include the highest mountain in Africa, Kilimanjaro (19,321 feet), as well as Mount Kenya and the Ruwenzori range, both around seventeen thousand feet. Besides these great peaks there are many others—Elgon, the Aberdares, Meru, and the Virunga volcanos. Among a host of lesser mountains, many of them well over ten thousand feet high and relatively unknown, are Mount Hanang, the Crater Highlands of Tanzania, and the Cherangani range; and there are others of whose existence hardly anyone is aware.

These mountains deserve recognition, for they compose a unique area of Africa. Indeed it was once proposed that along with the thirteen-thousand-foot Mount Cameroon of West Africa they should be known as the Cameroonian Region Kilimanjaro, Kenya, and Ruwenzori are the only African peaks that bear ice and snow all the year round and give birth to small but genuine glaciers. Although there are permanent snowfields on the Atlas, there are no glaciers, despite these mountains' majestic height. Snow also lies from time to time on the Ethiopian heights and on the higher South African peaks, but it melts away in warm weather.

The East African mountains stand well isolated from each other, each of them like a towering island on the plains. This isolation makes each one subtly different with species peculiar

The glaciers of snowy Kilimanjaro are gradually disintegrating, since evaporation exceeds the eight-inch rainfall on the summit. (Emil Schulthess)

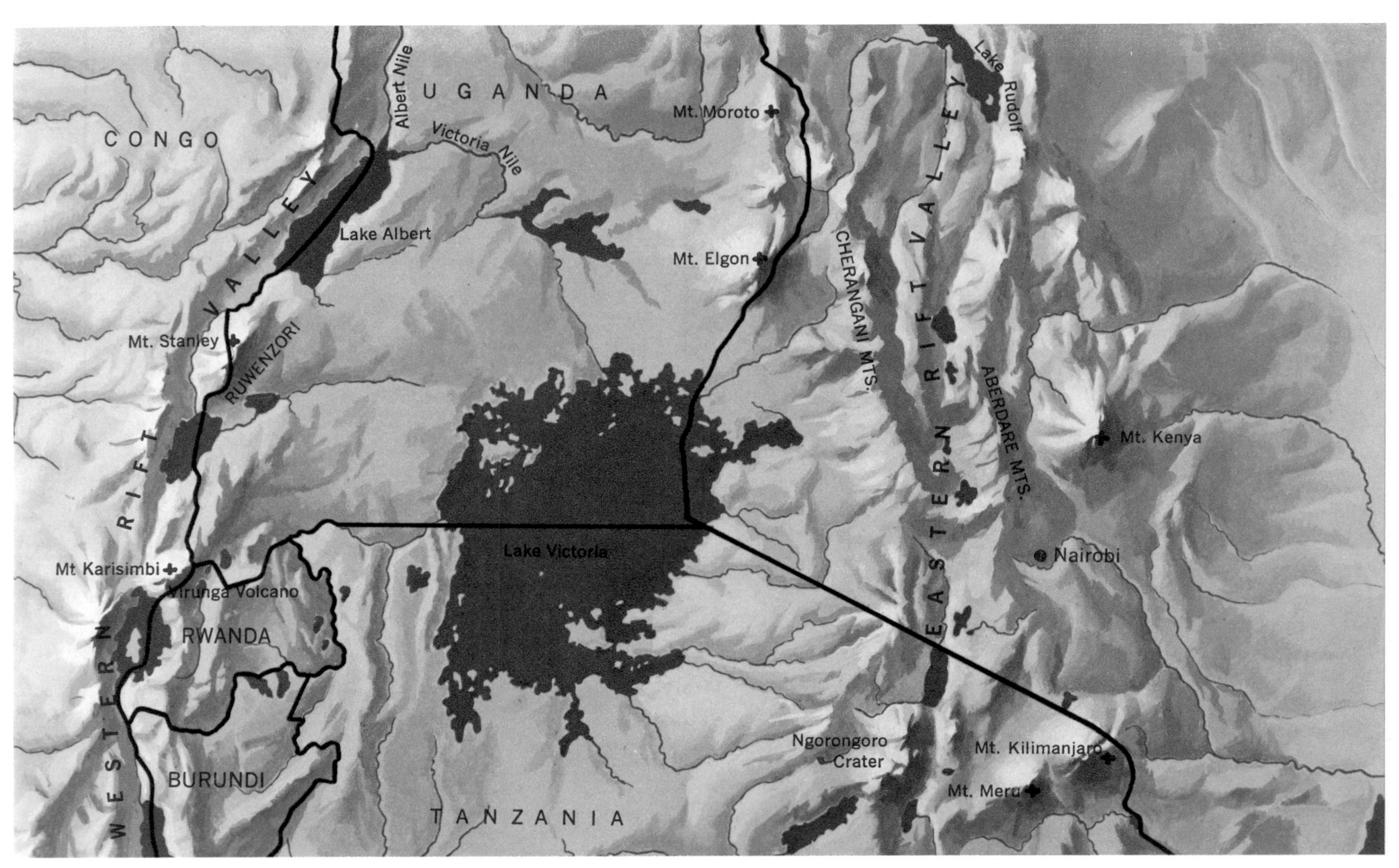

The East African mountains are magnificent isolated peaks, usually old volcanos crowned with the only glaciers in Africa and covered with astonishing vegetation.

to single peaks or groups. And they bear upon their summits some of the most extraordinary vegetation in the world—monstrous arborescent growths of plants that are normally no more than small herbs. Best of all, perhaps, they are unspoiled areas of transcendent beauty, too cold to attract tropical man, and too high for man to live on in any comfort.

SNOW ON THE EQUATOR

Despite the oft-repeated statement that there is snow on the equator in Africa, there is actually none. Only three of the high mountains, Kilimanjaro, Mount Kenya, and Ruwenzori, have permanent snow and ice and, except for Mount Kenya, they are all well south of the line. Meru, Elgon, and the lower of Kilimanjaro's two peaks, Mawenzi, bear transient snowfields with patches that never entirely melt. The equator does pass through minor peaks just to the north of the summit of Mount Kenya, but there are no permanent glaciers or snow on these. The largest of Mount Kenya's glaciers, the Lewis Glacier on the east side of Point Lenana, is just south of the equator. So, though snow falls on the equator occasionally, it does not lie.

However, not very long ago in geological time, during the last of the ice ages, there was permanent snow on the equator. The glaciers on these mountains came much lower and were much larger then. Mount Kenya, for instance, was covered with a complete icecap. Some peaks now without snow then had glaciers. Ancient moraines, the piles of rock pushed in front of a glacier and left behind like a tide line when it retreats, prove that the glaciers on Mount Kenya came down to about ten thousand feet, and on Ruwenzori to seven thousand five hundred feet.

Like glaciers elsewhere in the world, those on the East African mountains have been retreating during this century. Old photographs show these glaciers as lying much farther down than they do now. The small Tyndall Glacier on Mount Kenya has probably retreated four hundred and fifteen feet in the last forty years and the Lewis Glacier, the largest, has retreated one thousand five hundred and fifty feet since 1893, at a rate varying from twenty-one to thirty-seven feet per year.

The retreat of most of the glaciers is probably due to the same worldwide influences that are causing other glaciers to shrink. On Kilimanjaro, which still has larger glaciers than any other of the peaks, the ice sheet is disintegrating. The rainfall on the summit of Kilimanjaro is only about eight inches a year, quite insufficient to balance the annual loss of ice by evaporation. It has been calculated that if present trends continue, Kilimanjaro will have no ice two hundred years hence. Some also believe that increased volcanic activity may be raising the mountain's temperature and so accelerating the shrinkage of the icecap.

The giant heath zone, Ruwenzori. The constant damp festoons the growth with usnea lichens and carpets the ground with luxuriant mosses. (E. S. Ross)

OLD AND NEW VOLCANOS

Volcanic eruptions can take several forms. The lava can flow gently out of fissures and vents, spread out over great areas, and form flat plateaus, as has happened in Ethiopia and East Africa; or it can build up a huge rock dome by flowing gently out of large vents, producing a Hawaiian or shield type of volcano. Or it can, in the classic manner of Vesuvius, gush through a narrow pipe, throwing up clouds of ash, rocks, steam and smoke with such force as to produce violent explosions. This is the traditional idea of a volcanic eruption. Most of the East African mountains are classic, conical volcanos of explosive origin.

Characteristically, a volcano of this type is a steep-sided cone, with a crater at the top, discharging smoke, pieces of red-hot rock, and at times streams of molten lava that run down its sides and solidify in layers. When such a volcano starts on a level plain it is likely to rise quickly in a series of eruptions. But the eruptions raise the height of the cone, so that the lava has farther to rise before it can escape and at the same time release the intense pressure in the underlying layers. A time comes when the mountain erupts less often and less violently. Finally a mild eruption pushes a mass of lava up the vent, but not high enough to escape from the top. This cools where it is, and forms a hard plug in the vent.

Sometimes when this happens the pressure beneath becomes so great that the mountain blows off its top in a gigantic explosion, leaving a jagged summit with a deep crater; such explosions have formed Mount Meru, Mount Hanang and one of Kilimanjaro's summits. More often a new vent opens on the side of the mountain and forms what is called a parasitic cone. But often parasitic cones do not equal the height of the original volcano. The violent pressure underneath may have been largely released in building the main mountain. Many high volcanic peaks are dead at summits, but they have fuming vents and active craters lower down on their sides.

Many stages of this process can be seen among the East African mountains. Nyamlagira, one of the Virunga volcanos, is still very active. Nyiragongo, its next-door neighbor, has become dormant only within the last century. Kilimanjaro is still gently active and may be warming up again; Kibo (the name of its highest peak) is a parasite cone between two older, and now lower, eruptive centers. Elgon, a huge, gently sloping volcano, is dead except for a few hot springs, and vegetation covers the floor of its large crater. The high peaks of Kenya and Mawenzi are both plugs formed in the vents of cooling volcanos. The ash and soft rocks of their sloping sides have been eroded away and the peaks that once ringed their craters have likewise disintegrated, so that finally the plug, harder than the rocks around it, stands forth like a cork upside down. These plugs show that both Mount Kenya and Mawenzi were once higher than Kibo. Mount Kenya was about twenty-three thousand feet high.

THE MOUNTAINS OF THE MOON

There are several exceptions to the general rule of vulcanism in the formation of mountains. The major one is the great Ruwenzori range, the famed Mountains of the Moon and one source of the Nile. Here there are six groups of snowy summits above fifteen thousand feet, culminating in Mount Stanley at sixteen thousand eight hundred feet. Certainly the Nile waters that originate in the glaciers of Ruwenzori come from a greater height than those coming from anywhere else.

When one can see Ruwenzori—which is rare, for it is usually shrouded in dense cloud—it is at once obvious that it is not an isolated conical peak like Mount Kenya or Mount Elgon, but a range. It is actually about sixty-five miles long by thirty wide, and a series of peaks form a chain along its crest. Its formation has been entirely different from that of other high mountains.

Ruwenzori is actually composed of very ancient rocks that are not of volcanic nature. It is what is called a fault block of the ancient basement rocks of Africa, on top of which all other rocks are normally found. Although it is not a volcano, volcanic eruptions and the formation of the Rift Valley are probably part of the reason for its existence. The faulting and sinking that formed the Rift Valley possibly resulted in powerful counter-movements that thrust up at an angle this block of the underlying rocks. It stands now on a line separating the Albert Rift from the plains of Lake George and Lake Edward.

Although Ruwenzori is formed of much older material, it was uplifted to its present height more recently than some of the other East African mountains. Its history is not fully known, but it may not be more than two million years old whereas some of the older volcanos are at least fifteen million years old. Ruwenzori is eroding comparatively fast. The rock of which it is composed breaks up easily, and it has the highest rainfall of any of the East African peaks, which results in great rushing rivers that have cut deep gorges. In the ice ages, glaciers came down to about seven thousand five hundred feet on the western side, lower than elsewhere in East Africa.

The eleven-thousand-foot Cherangani range in western Kenya is another major example of a high mountain group which is not volcanic. It too is of ancient rocks, and it lies along the same general line as a group of high mountains on the borders of Kenya and Uganda—Sekerr, the Karasuk Hills, and Mount Moroto—that form the western escarpment of the Rift Valley in this area. Although much lower than some volcanic peaks, the Cheranganis have some of the features of the greater volcanos. But one walks there on gritty gravel, not on volcanic dust or pumice.

CLEAR COLD HEIGHTS

Whether they are volcanos, or whether they have been formed in some other way, all these great isolated mountains have strong similarities. On their summits one has the feeling of being perched on a spike at an immense height above the surrounding country. Even on a gently sloping mountain like Mount Elgon, one can always climb one of the pinnacles surrounding the crater whence the ground drops away very steeply to plains far, far below. The impression of height is especially striking on Mount Meru, a jagged tooth of rock from which one looks down three thousand feet vertically into a heath-filled crater. From this airy spire it is ten thousand feet to the plains below, and from the dome of Kilimanjaro to the plains it is fourteen thousand feet. This makes these mountains quite unlike the high peaks of Ethiopia or the Atlas, where one is often surrounded by other peaks nearly as high.

I know of no places on earth that give so strong a feeling

Mount Kenya from the Teleki Valley. The most shapely of East African mountains, it is the plug that solidified in the throat of a long extinct volcano. Giant groundsel and lobelias are scattered over the slopes. (Len Young)

of being out of this world. I recall once climbing Point Lenana (a subsidiary peak of Mount Kenya, 16,400 feet high) in the moonlight. In the piercing cold and the rarefied air I felt slightly light-headed, though I had been up there a week and should have become acclimatized to the altitude. At the top of the long grind up the screes I turned to look over my shoulder. The moon was setting, and over the plains of Laikipia was a huge blanket of cloud, shimmering like mother-of-pearl. Out of it, fifty miles away, rose the Aberdare range. Nearly ten thousand feet below, the clouds shrouded another world in warm slumber while I stood shivering beneath the firmament of stars.

The climate of the alpine zones of the mountains is like summer by day and winter by night. When the sun rises, the temperature climbs quickly, and the sunshine dispels the bitter frost of the night in a few minutes. Then for a few hours, and on rare occasions for most of the day, this mountain world enjoys clear sunshine. So fierce is the sun that it will skin the face of the most hardened mountaineer. Usually in mid-morning, mists begin to form on the lower slopes and gradually creep up toward the top. By midday one is usually enveloped by them, and in the afternoon snow or hail often turns the slopes to porridge-like slush that runs in streams down the hill at every footfall. This sequence of weather normally occurs on all the higher mountains.

At evening the peaks usually clear. From the plains below one sees the dome of Kilimanjaro emerge from its blanket of cloud, glowing pink in the sunset. It looks lovely, but anyone up there is hurrying to eat his evening meal and to get into his sleeping bag. When the sun finally dips behind a ridge, the cold grips like a vice. The temperature between midday and midnight can vary by sixty to seventy degrees Fahrenheit. Outside a hut or tent it is exceedingly uncomfortable, but that does not detract from the frozen beauty of the night. The stars, undimmed by haze, shine here with an extraordinary brightness and there is a feeling of remoteness and great peace.

RINGS OF VEGETATION

The similarities between these mountains extend to their lower slopes. Each is surrounded by more or less regular zones of vegetation at different altitudes. These vary somewhat according to aspect and the direction of the prevailing wind, and one side of the mountain is usually wetter than the other. But whichever is the wet or dry side, rather similar vegetation will be found at about the same altitude on all the peaks.

Starting from the bottom, there is first a belt of rain forest. The width of this depends largely on how far Africans had cut into it before it was protected. On Mount Kenya, for instance, forest once came down to about 4,500 feet, but now begins at six thousand feet.

The rain forests are almost as fine as the true tropical rain forest, and on the whole more beautiful. But they are usually composed of different species of trees, and in general they support fewer species of plants, animals and birds. On Mount Kenya there is an area of splendid camphor *(Ocotea usambarensis)* forest above Chogoria that is among the finest I have ever seen. The huge trees rise from a clear floor of leaf mould, and most lean slightly as they grow older. Many have been bored into in their youth by elephants seeking bark to eat, and as a result are hollow. When the weight of the leaning trunk becomes more than the roots can support, the tree crashes and lies, undecayed for many years, on the forest floor.

Camphor and other forest trees give way in time to a more open sort of forest composed largely of a primitive conifer, *Podocarpus*. This is a magnificent tree that hardly looks like a conifer, for it has a great spreading crown and a huge bole. The berries of podocarpus are relished by mountain parrots and other birds. Elephants and other heavy animals like the buffalo and rhino formerly abounded at this level, and are still very common there. They keep the forest fairly open, so that one can walk about with ease.

Mixed with the podocarpus, and occurring as pure stands on the drier sides of the mountains, are forests of cedar *(Juniperus procera)*. This is the tree that is so common in Ethiopia. It is a giant form of a plant that is normally no taller than a big bush in temperate latitudes. Cedars look very ancient, and are often stagheaded and festooned with lichen *(Usnea)*. But they do not compare in age with truly old trees like big baobabs and some of the huge old conifers of North America. Underfoot there is a carpet of moss, shrubs, and sometimes grass, and great creepers climb up and hang over the cedars.

In river valleys, and where rock is near the surface, there are many little glades. These are usually carpeted with good pasture of Kikuyu grass *(Pennisetum clandestinum)*. Around the glades there is St.-John's-wort, and in the middle there may be a reed swamp. Clear streams, ice cold, run through these glades, but they support no fish except introduced trout. Farther down the mountain the waterfalls on successive lava flows prevent lowland fish from adapting to these streams.

THE HOME OF THE BUFFALO

This upper forest is splendid country for big animals. Elephants and rhinos inhabit it, but above all this is the home of buffalos. They are exceedingly numerous and here they live an easy life. With good grazing in the glades, shade when they want it, and abundant water, they do not need to move far for their daily needs.

Although buffalos are easier to watch in the great herds of some tropical flood plains, they always seem to me more at ease in these high forests than elsewhere. Groups of old bulls will settle in a little glade for weeks together, and will scarcely move a hundred yards during the day. When the sun grows warm they move into the shade of a bush on the edge of the glade, and unless something disturbs them they will not appear again until the evening. The buffalo of these forests, especially on the western side of Mount Kenya, is bigger than any other buffalo in Africa.

Buffalos have the reputation of being dangerous animals, but this is not borne out unless they are hunted and wounded. If they have been wounded, or are afflicted with some disease such as rinderpest, they can be exceedingly dangerous. Once they have made up their mind to charge, they are the only animals that cannot be distracted from their purpose. A charging buffalo will mangle its adversary or die in the attempt. It charges with its head up, eyes fixed upon the enemy all the

Left: A female mountain gorilla and her infant. Compare these long-haired animals with the lowland gorilla shown on page 126. Right: The slopes of Mount Kenya at 14,000 feet are dotted with the flower spikes of giant lobelias and the cabbage-like growths of giant groundsels. (Both by Alan Root: Okapia)

time, and must be brought down if one is to escape. It is no use trying to run away or climb a tree unless one has a very good start.

Fortunately, in most of these forests, it is rare to meet a buffalo that is ill or wounded. But in remote parts one sometimes meets herds that have little fear of man. They are curious beasts, and unless familiar with man's evil ways they will not readily run away. I have known herds to come trotting toward me in an alarming solid phalanx until, their curiosity satisfied, they turned and rushed away with tails flailing the air. By that time I was usually up a good-sized tree.

There is no better place to see buffalos than in the Ngourdoto crater, a natural gem lying in forest between Mount Meru and Kilimanjaro. There, there is a herd of about five hundred that never seems to move very far. They lie out on the open grass floor of the crater and can be viewed from vantage points along the rim. If one watches them there, one may find it difficult to think of them as dangerous beasts.

Besides the buffalos, there are always bushbucks in these glades. The bushbucks of East African mountains are also larger and bear finer horns than any other race of bushbuck, though the black Ethiopian bushbuck may be more beautiful. Bushbucks too have their regular haunts, and come out in the same glade to graze each evening.

GIANT GRASS

A zone of mountain bamboo *(Arundinaria alpina)* circles most of these mountains at about eight to ten thousand feet. Sometimes, on smaller peaks, the bamboo is stunted and the zone is compressed, but during an ascent of the higher mountains one struggles through it for the better part of the day. From a distance it shows as a pale, dull-green belt resembling grassland above the dark forest and below the moorlands. It is indeed a towering grass, but up close it is very different from the pasture that it resembles from far away.

The bamboo grows to a height of thirty or forty feet, and excludes almost all other vegetation. Beneath, there is a carpet of dead, spiky leaves, small ferns, fine grasses, and mosses. The bamboo grows for a number of years, and then seeds. The seed head is an open panicle, like that of many other grasses, and it produces great quantities of grain. This sometimes carpets the forest floor and one would think that myriads of grain-eating birds would be attracted to it. But there are only a few small seed-eaters and rather rare large francolins *(Francolinus jacksoni* and others).

The bamboo dies after seeding and stands like a forest of dead, rotting stems. Insects bore into the stems whose tops snap off in the wind, leaving a hollow. Walking through these dead stalks one feels constantly uneasy, for the banging and rattling of the stems against each other resembles the sound made by feeding elephants. More eerie still is the noise of the wind howling and moaning through the holes and hollow tops of this skeletal growth. And when the whole zone is also shrouded in cold dense dripping mist it is really extremely unpleasant.

Seedling bamboo is even more daunting to walk through. It grows in dense masses, and when it is six or eight feet high it is all one can do to force a passage through it. One has to stick to the trails made by elephants and other heavy animals, and one constantly wonders what will happen if by chance one were to meet a herd of such beasts. Elephants feed on the seedling bamboo, browsing off the tops. In the dense mass of canes they would be invisible to a man except at very close range. Even were they only seeking escape, they could come crashing along the track one was trying to follow. I have always felt relief when I have passed through a growth of seedling bamboo without incident.

Other than elephants, little wildlife lives in or makes use of bamboo. Buffalos live in it if there are glades where they can graze, and there are a few duiker, but birds are rare, in this strange world of hollow rattling stems and eerie moaning sounds.

Left: In the bamboo. The tangled thirty-foot stems of the giant grass permit little but a few ferns and mosses to grow beneath them. (U. Rahm) Right: Mountain forest near a waterfall. The successive lava flows of East African mountains creates waterfalls at frequent intervals along each stream. (Weldon King)

HAGENIA AND HEATH

Above the bamboo territory one comes again to gloriously beautiful country, where there are large glades carpeted with Kikuyu grass and lady's mantle *(Alchemilla)*, a half-prostrate, bushy growth similar to that found on the high mountains of Ethiopia. These glades are shaded by huge hagenia trees *(Hagenia abyssinica)*, ancient of aspect and often half-reclining on the turf. The hagenia zone is less luxuriant than in Ethiopia, and gives way soon to tree heath *(Erica arborea* and *Philippia)*.

These upper glades are once more alive with buffalos, bushbucks, and often waterbucks too. On some mountains they are even frequented by eland. Bongos are found on several mountain ranges in Kenya, but not in Tanzania or Uganda. They sometimes come out in these glades but are commoner in the forest lower down. Giant forest hogs *(Hylochoerus meinertzhageni)* are quite common but not easy to see.

The giant heath that fringes these glades is the start of the true moorland vegetation of the mountaintops. Here it grows as much as sixty feet high, and forms open forests with fine grasses and succulent herbs beneath—good pasture for animals. At about this level nightly frosts become regular, and for that reason the apparently rich pasture is probably less productive than it seems.

The heath is festooned with lichen, and this is probably about the moistest level on all the mountains. The total rainfall is not as high as in the rain forest farther down, but light rain falls here nearly every day. The ground is constantly soggy underfoot, and the heath zone is often shrouded in cloud even when the peaks above stand clear. Mosses, liverworts, ferns, and lichens that flourish in cold wet places thrive here and assume fantastic forms, especially on Ruwenzori.

Leopards are very common at these upper levels of the forest, and they are often very dark or almost black. The same is true of serval cats, especially on Ruwenzori. This is the result of an increased tendency to melanism in cold wet climates. A race of spotted lions was formerly said to exist on the moorlands and in the giant heath. There are lions, but these generally seem to be ordinary lions that have wandered up from the plains. But that spotted lions do exist is a persistent belief among Africans on all these high mountains. I have heard tales of them myself, on Mount Kenya and the Aberdares, and such beasts are also said to inhabit the Virunga volcanos. It is a little difficult to believe that *all* these accounts refer to subadult lions that have retained the spots that all lions have as cubs.

WANDERING ANIMALS

The zone of giant heath is the normal upper limit of most big animals. Above, there are normally only duiker, steinbok *(Rhapiceros campestris)*, and some leopards. But on the open moorlands small rodents abound, and in rock piles the hyrax *(Procavia capensis jacksoni)* is often very common.

Forest animals occasionally wander up onto the heights. Even plains animals, especially eland, may occur on the moorlands. A herd of eland is often seen on the fourteen-thousand-foot plateau between Kibo and Mawenzi, and there are about seven hundred of them on the Aberdares. Elephants sometimes cross the mountains to reach another feeding ground, but they do not stay.

Some of these cases of wandering can quite easily be accounted for. The leopards that have been found entombed in ice on Mount Kilimanjaro and Mount Kenya, for instance, present no mystery, despite Hemingway's often reported observation that "no one has explained what the leopard was seeking at that altitude." Leopards prowl the mountains regularly, and I have found their droppings up to thirteen thousand feet. They seem to live on small rodents and on the abundant hyraxes that come out at night from their rock piles to feed on the leaves of giant lobelias.

More difficult to explain are the odd buffalos that have wandered up to sixteen thousand feet and died there. On Mount Kenya there are several skeletons of buffalos, the existence of which has been known about for many years—including one from the time that Sir Halford Mackinder first climbed the mountain in 1896. These animals may possibly have been blind. It is an established fact that there are blind buffalos. Perhaps they wandered up one of the valleys, could not find a way out, and died when they reached inhospitable heights.

In the ice of the Lewis Glacier there was formerly a dead colobus monkey—a species normally inhabiting the cedar and podocarpus forest. It has been suggested that this animal was carried up there by a large bird of prey, but the only bird likely to kill a colobus is the crowned eagle *(Stephanoaetus coronatus)*. This eagle occurs up to eleven thousand feet, but it could not possibly carry a colobus to sixteen thousand feet. So the colobus must have reached the Lewis Glacier by its own efforts.

But by far the most remarkable of all these wanderers was a small group of wild dogs *(Lycaon pictus)*, seen and photographed by a mountaineer on the summit of Kilimanjaro, at over nineteen thousand feet. Wild dogs normally live on the grass plains, sometimes entering the lower fringe of the forest. Normally their highest altitude would be high plains at about eight thousand feet, but on Kilimanjaro the plains merge into forest at about 4,500 feet. Hence the dogs must have climbed almost fifteen thousand feet through forest and moorland, and finally up barren scree and snowfields to reach the top. The mountaineer reported that they eyed him curiously, but were not aggressive or desperate with hunger. No one can reasonably explain why they climbed Kilimanjaro.

GIANT PLANTS

It is not surprising that large wild animals are lacking above eleven thousand feet. Above that height one enters levels where the daily variation of temperature is extreme, where all living things have to face the alternation between sunshine by day and piercing frost at night. The extremes grow worse as one climbs, till at the snow line the climate is too severe for anything but a few lichens.

Yet at moderate levels, from an altitude of eleven to fourteen thousand feet, certain groups of plants have flourished and have evolved rampant growths of monstrous forms. These are the giant heaths, giant lobelias, and giant groundsels

Giant groundsels in the Ruwenzori Mountains. The strangest of all mountains plants, they grow up to almost 15,000 feet. (Bernard Pierre)

(Senecio). Everlastings *(Helichrysum)* are also very common. The everlastings and heaths form a link with South African floras, but the lobelias and especially the groundsels are truly unique. *Adenocarpus manni* is a link with the Cameroon Highlands, and was first found on Fernando Po island at a height of 6,500 feet.

The lobelias here are not usually so big as those in northern Ethiopia, but far more varied. They all have a similar growth habit, with a spike of flower emerging from a rosette of elongated leaves. When the lobelia is young it is a low, rounded hump of leaves, and at this stage on Mount Kenya is heavily browsed by hyraxes. In time it grows tall enough to escape their attention, and in flower it may stand seven or eight feet tall. The flower spikes are extraordinary rather than beautiful. Some are bearded with long, hanging bracts, others are nearly plain, with the corollas open to the air. Beneath the flower spike is the leaf rosette, connected to the ground by a naked hollow stem of varying length, marked in a reticulate pattern where old leaf bases have fallen off.

The giant groundsels are still more extraordinary. Some of them are trees up to thirty feet high. In the crater of Mount Elgon there is a forest of giant groundsels several miles across. These, *Senecio barbatipes*, and similar species on Mount Kenya, Ruwenzori and Kilimanjaro, are trees with a thick, corky bark and a rosette of fleshy leaves at the end of each branch. The undersides of the leaves are soft and downy, and the young plants look vaguely like cabbages.

At intervals, tree groundsels produce large spikes of rather dull flowers, and when this happens several new branches emerge below the flowering point. Lobelias, on the other hand, die altogether after flowering. Since they do not flower for a good many years, their life cycle is a long one. A brilliantly beautiful green sunbird, *Nectarinia johnstoni*, constantly feeds on lobelia flowers and may have some part in pollinating them.

Both lobelias and groundsels on the East African mountains have undergone very rapid evolution into endemic species. Mount Kenya has *Lobelia keniensis*, Ruwenzori and the Virunga volcanos, *L. bequaerti*, Meru, Loolmalasin and Hanang, *L. burttii*, and Kilimanjaro, *L. deckenii*. These all belong to a closely related group known as the *"deckenii"* group. Other lobelias, of the species *L. wollastonii* and *L. telekii*, are more widely spread over several mountains. *L. wollastonii* is found on Ruwenzori and the Virunga volcanos, and *L. telekii* on Kenya, the Aberdares, and Elgon. Much the same is seen in groundsels. The tree groundsel of Kenya is *S. keniodendron*, that of Elgon, *S. barbatipes*, and that of Kilimanjaro, *S. kilimanjari*. One groundsel, *S. adnivalis*, has different varieties on Ruwenzori and the adjacent Virunga volcanos, showing that further speciation is in progress.

These mountains can only have been isolated one from another since the last ice age, which ended about ten thousand years ago. When glaciers came down to 7,500 feet on Ruwenzori, this monstrous alpine flora must have extended over much greater areas, connecting the mountain groups. The upward retreat of the ice, and with it the zone of alpine vegetation, has led to the formation of the many new species, not only in groundsels and lobelias but also to a lesser extent among everlastings and heaths. Some other families of plants, however, such as rushes and Cruciferae, have not to the same extent evolved new forms.

No entirely satisfactory explanation for the prevalence of these extraordinary plant forms has been propounded. The only other area in the world with similar climates is the Andes near the equator. There too the plants of the pineapple family (Bromeliaciae) have produced some queer forms. Some of these even resemble giant lobelias, with a spike of flower rising from a rosette of leaves supported on a naked stem. Therefore the most likely explanation would seem to be the curious climate of summer during the day alternating with winter by night.

The tussocky grasses and sedges that cover these mountains, and those of the Andes, resemble the grasses that occur in Patagonia and New Zealand. The daily frost-thaw climate is rather like that of Kerguelen Island, in the South Pacific, at sea level. Though the effect of the climate seems the most likely explanation, intense radiation is another possibility. Another reason for the survival of these growths may be that they are primitive groundsels and lobelias that have never had to withstand aggressive competition for space from more highly evolved plants.

BONGOS, GORILLAS AND GIANT PIGS

During the ice ages the glaciers pushed the alpine zones of vegetation to lower altitudes till they covered much larger areas. At the same time the equatorial forest spread eastward over a much larger area. The distribution of some birds and animals shows that the forest came as far east as Kilimanjaro, where perhaps it merged with a belt of coastal forest of a

Left: Crested rat and young. Living in mountain forests they are seldom seen by day. The hair parts to produce black and white striped effects. (Alan Root) Right above: Mountain gorillas feed among succulent herbage. They sometimes climb to 12,000 feet. Where not molested they may soon become used to and ignore an observer. (Alan Root: Okapia) Right: This bizarre mantid (Pseudocreobotia wahlbergi) is an inhabitant of the lower mountain forests. (F. G. H. Allen)

Colobus monkeys are gentle, leaf-eating beasts. They are entirely harmless but are cruelly persecuted in some places for their long black and white fur. (Weldon King)

rather different nature. Almost all of the center of Africa, from Liberia to Mombasa, was once covered with forest. This allowed some of the typical forest animals to spread eastward, and others to spread west from the east coast.

One would expect, therefore, to find isolated communities of some of the forest animals in all these mountain groups. But of the likely species the only one that does occur widely is the giant forest hog *(Hylochoerus meinertzhageni)*. It is found on Kilimanjaro, Kenya, the Mau, Aberdares, Elgon, and Ruwenzori, and northward to the southern Sudan, Mount Nyiro, and Ethiopia. This hog was first found in the forests of western Kenya in 1904 and was only later found in the tropical forests of the Congo.

Giant forest hogs are impressive beasts. A big boar weighs up to four hundred pounds and has long black glistening hair. They live in dense cover and are far more common than is usually supposed. Visitors to Treetops, near Nyeri, usually see them, but mostly they are difficult to find. I once crept up to an indeterminate black mass at the base of a tree on Mount Kenya, thinking it was a buffalo. But it proved to be a herd of giant forest hogs lying in one heap; when at close range they became aware of my presence, they sprang out in all directions.

Bongos and gorillas may once have had a similarly wide distribution. But they survive now only in certain mountain forests. The bongo is common on Mount Kenya, the Aberdares, the Mau range and the Cheranganis, but not on Elgon, Kilimanjaro, Meru, or Ruwenzori. Why they are not found on Elgon, in particular, is very hard to explain, for this mountain is only forty miles or so from the Cherangani range. Bongos could even have moved from one mountain pass to another along forested river valleys in the last century. But it seems they did not do so.

Mountain gorillas *(G. g. beringei)* have a still more restricted distribution. They are found only on certain of the Virunga volcanos and some adjacent lowland forests. These gorillas are larger than lowland gorillas and are long-haired. They are shy retiring animals that live in the densest forest, and are especially fond of wild celery. The very wet climate of the Virunga volcanos is only part of the reason for their distribution. Gorillas will not cross a river too large to be bridged by a fallen tree, and may originally have reached the Virunga volcanos at a time when the tropical forest was more extensive to the north of the long curve of the Uelle River. With the retreat of forest in drier times they have thus been isolated far to the east of their lowland relatives.

THE TREE HYRAX, BUSHBABY AND GIANT RAT

The mountain forests abound with other interesting life, some of which make their presence known chiefly by night. Of the night animals the tree hyrax *(Dendrohyrax)* is the most obvious. These hyraxes are not exclusively confined to mountain forests, but are more often heard there than anywhere else. Soon after dark one will always hear their loud harsh rattling call coming from the trees above. The call is extraordinary for so small an animal, and carries for miles. It resembles the sound of a heavy wooden ratchet being turned irregularly. The tree hyrax calls most on moonlit nights; its call probably has some territorial or display function.

The presence of bushbabies *(Galago)* also becomes very evident as night falls. They make a rather harsh sobbing call or screech. Once the call is located it is quite easy, if one uses a flashlight, to watch the bushbabies going about their nightly business. If one keeps quiet they are not disturbed, but once alarmed they make off in a series of elastic bounds. They too are not confined to mountain forests, but inhabit woodland, bushland and forest over much of Africa.

Bushbabies belong to a group of primitive primates related to the lemurs of Madagascar, the potto of West African forests, and the loris of Ceylon. In past times animals like bushbabies were probably much more common than they are now, and there may have been diurnal as well as nocturnal species. But while lemurs have survived in Madagascar, both as diurnal and nocturnal animals, their relatives, the bushbabies, have been forced by stronger and more highly evolved diurnal monkeys to live a nocturnal existence. They remain common by night, when monkeys are roosting.

The most common forest monkey is the beautiful long-haired black and white colobus. Blue monkeys *(Cercopithecus mitis)*, one of the most handsome of the guenons, are often found in bamboo forest. Here they sometimes come to ground to escape, though where there are large forest trees they are very arboreal. The deep crowing call of the colobus salutes the dawn; at night it probably marks the passage of a leopard below.

Crested rats, large rodents with long black and white hair, are found only in these mountain forests. When alarmed, their hair, revealing a large amount of white, stands erect. It seems likely that this is an effort on the part of a rather helpless mammal to mimic a more dangerous creature, for the pattern thus displayed is like that of a badger and similar to the black and white warning patterns of skunks. Little is known about crested rats in their wild state, and one would be lucky to see one in the forest.

MOUNTAIN PARKS

Fortunately several of these magnificent mountain areas have been included in national parks. Mount Kenya and the Aberdares above the forest line are both national parks; it is to be hoped that Kilimanjaro will become one too. The Virunga volcanos are included in the Parc National Albert. Even today most of the mountain parks can only be visited on foot, but one can drive across the Aberdares and see a typical moorland of heath and tussock grass. There is no other place in the world where one could catch a two-pound trout while watching elephants, buffalos, bushbucks and possibly giant forest hogs and bongos as well.

Several other mountain areas, although not national parks, have been effectively protected by other means. Many have been made into forest reserves to conserve the flow of vitally important rivers. One area of unique interest, ranging from grasslands through forest to alpine flora on twelve-thousand-foot mountains, and containing a big-game spectacle second to none, is the Crater Highlands of Tanzania. Here, at Ngorongoro is the largest volcanic crater in the world, with luxuriant pasture on its floor and lovely forests on its rim. This area is protected by a special authority that endeavors to reconcile the possibly conflicting interests of the few Masai who live there and the wildlife, while preserving the outstanding natural beauty and interest of the area.

It is well that many of these mountains have been protected; otherwise there was real danger that they would have shared the ruin that has overtaken some similar heights in Ethiopia. There are some who would cover these unique mountaintops with sheep that would destroy or damage much of the remarkable alpine vegetation, and whose owners would demand the destruction of predatory animals such as leopards. It is just not necessary to use these heights as sheep pasture.

These parks and areas should be—and some of them are—centers of research and exploration. They still afford scientists a rewarding field of discovery in surroundings of surpassing interest and beauty. And the visitor will not long be satisfied by a few roads posted with notices telling him not to get out of his car, for these moorlands cannot be fully appreciated from a vehicle. One must walk, in the cold clear sunshine and the keen thin air, to know these mountains.

Manatees, Coral Reefs and Lemurs

Africa's Coasts and Islands

18

The seacoasts of a continent are habitats that tend to be similar, whatever the local variations in climate and vegetation inland. In all these areas certain features recur. Temperatures are generally more equable than even a short distance inland, and rainfall is usually higher than in the continental hinterland. Certain forms of life are always evident, among the most familiar being seabirds such as gulls and terns, and the abundant shells of marine mollusks.

Along some parts of tropical coastlines there are mangroves, and along others, coral reefs. Each of these habitats requires a warm climate if it is to flourish, and for reefs warm water is essential. A cold-water current from the Antarctic flows north along the western coasts of Africa, preventing the growth of corals—which thrive in equivalent latitudes on the east coast. In coastal areas mangroves grow wherever wave action is slight, and tides are not too extreme; thus they flourish in the deltas of large rivers.

Of the many islands off the coast of Africa, some groups are far enough out to be considered oceanic. Among those fairly near the coast are the volcanic peaks of Fernando Po, Sao Thome, Annobon and Principe, off Cameroon; and Socotra, Madagascar and the Comoros, off the east coast. Madagascar, which is by far the most remarkable of these islands, is a subcontinent in itself. Generally, many of the plants and animals of offshore islands are the same as those on the nearby mainland, but often there are also unique forms. This is especially true of Madagascar and its neighboring islands.

STILT ROOTS AND MUDSKIPPERS

Mangrove swamps cover great areas of the West African tropical coast, and much smaller areas of the east coast. The most important mangrove areas are in the deltas and creeks of rivers from Gambia to Liberia, and around the Niger delta. In the east, mangroves grow from Somali to Mozambique, the largest areas being at the deltas of the Rufiji and Zambezi rivers.

The West African mangroves are of the same Atlantic species as occur on the tropical coasts of eastern South America—for instance, *Rhizophora mangle* and *Avicennia nitida.* The species on the East African coast and on Madagascar have strong tropical Asian affinities—for instance, *Rhizophora mucronata.* And *Avicennia marina* grows in established swamps on the landward side. The species of mangrove found in mangrove swamps thus depend on the ocean that washes them rather than on the continent on which they grow.

The different trees growing in mangrove swamps do not all belong to the same families of plants, and they have different requirements. A succession of different species traps silt brought down by the rivers and thereby perform a continuous land-building function.

All mangrove swamps are much alike. They form dense forests of small to medium-sized evergreen trees with bright-green glossy leaves. Each tree is supported partly on stilt roots that curve out from the stem several feet from the base and enter the mud some distance from the taproot. Often the only practicable way to traverse a mangrove swamp is by walking carefully over these stilt roots. Among the trees it is gloomy, hot and steamy, and birdlife is notably scarce. On the west coast, mangroves usually merge inland with fearful tangles of raffia palms, but in the east they often border savanna or even desert.

A mangrove swamp is generally a rather limited habitat for animals. Barnacles, sponges and various small shellfish attach themselves to the stilt roots, and crabs are usually abundant. But there are few birds, mammals or reptiles. Some crab-eating clawless otters *(Aonyx capensis)* occur, and one may see a genet cat, *Genetta,* soundly asleep at midday in the fork of a mangrove. But there is a striking contrast between the interior of the swamp and the open channels and mudflats.

The water in the channels is usually murky and consequently it is difficult to observe what goes on beneath the surface. But many fish, and especially various mullet *(Mugil* and other genera), come into the channels to breed. On the west coast the Atlantic tarpon can sometimes be seen jumping. An interesting little fish of the mud between channels on the west coast is the mudskipper. It has eyes on top of its head, and can crawl out of the water for considerable periods.

The channels are excellent places for migrant birds escaping the northern winter. Here one constantly hears the calls of whimbrels *(Numenius phaeopus)* and curlews *(N. arquata),* and many smaller waders. Characteristic resident birds of the mangroves are little green herons *(Butorides striatus),* several insectivorous kingfishers *(Halcyon senegalensis* and *H. malimbicus* in the west, and *H. senegaloides* in the east). Vulturine fish eagles *(Gypohierax angolensis)* normally feed on oil palm fruits, but in mangroves they live well on crabs, mollusks, and small stranded fish. Where mangroves border on deserts, large land birds like vultures and kites often breed in them.

THE UGLY MERMAIDS

Sea cows (Sirenia) are large, sluggish, vaguely walrus-like mammals that live in or near the mouths of rivers and creeks

Borassus palms (Borassus flabellifer) form almost pure stands in some parts of the rather swampy coastal savannas. (Henri Goldstein)

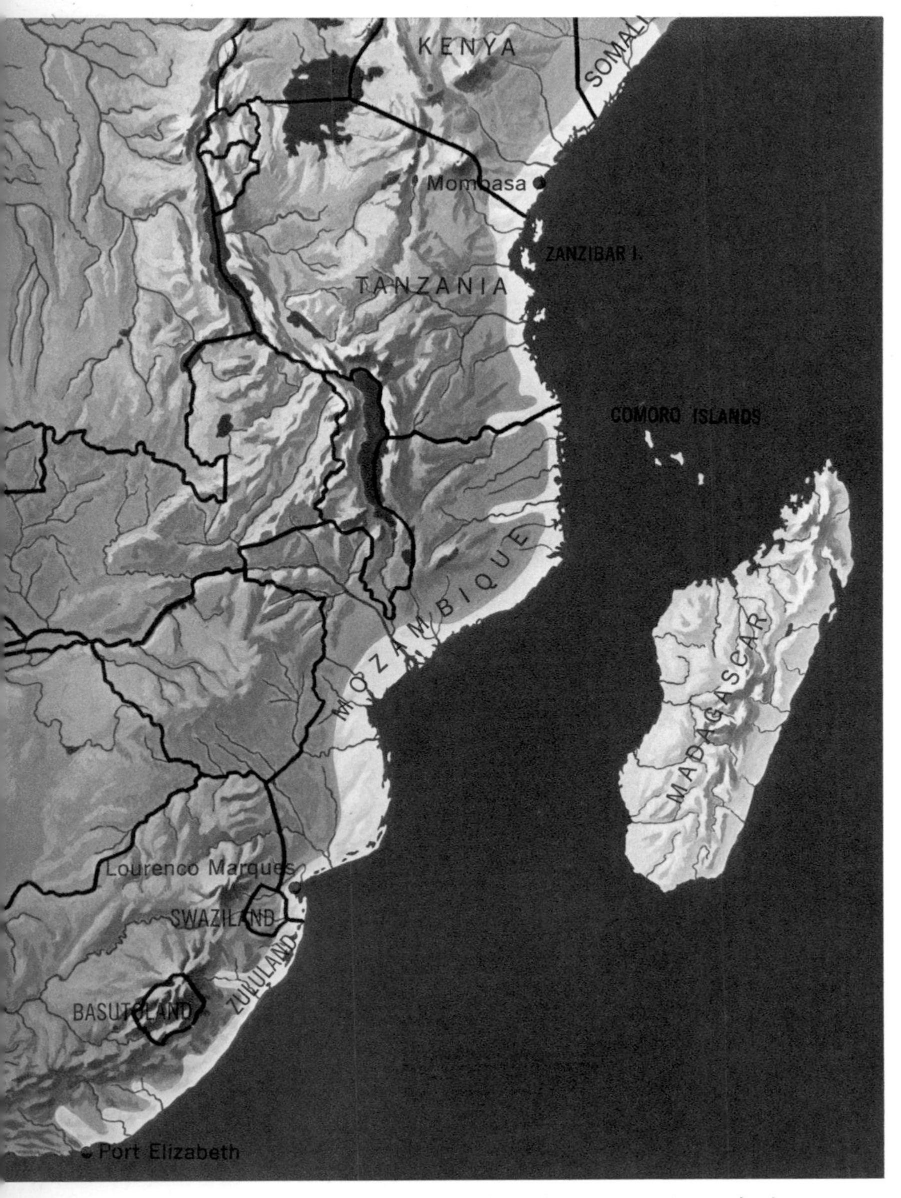

Coasts and offshore islands. The vegetation of the coasts, differing from that of inland regions, forms a narrow strip around Africa. A number of offshore islands, such as Madagascar, are of surpassing interest.

in tropical seas. There are two species in Africa: the African manatee *(Trichechus senegalensis)* and the dugong *(Dugong dugon)*. They inhabit the deltas and creeks of the west and east coasts respectively.

Sea cows are supposed to be the source of fables about mermaids. They are said to float upright in the water, holding their young between their flipper-like forelimbs. Anything less like a beautiful water maiden than these ungainly creatures is hard to imagine. Like walruses they have large bewhiskered muzzles, but no tusks; their teeth are adapted to a vegetarian diet. In old age, a variety of marine animals attach themselves to their thick skin. Sea cows can weigh up to two thousand pounds, and when taken out of the water they are liable to suffocate because the muscles of their chests are unequal to the effort of raising the body at each intake of breath.

The biology of wild sea cows is little-known because they are extremely retiring animals. By day they normally rest in some overgrown creek, with only their domelike snouts and nostrils above the water. They are wholly vegetarian, feeding on weeds that grow on the bottom or sometimes float on the surface. Their large muzzles, like the hippo's, are well fitted for cropping vegetable growth.

Although dugongs in the last century have decreased throughout their range, they are still quite common. They are sometimes caught in fishermen's nets in east-coast creeks, but if they are trapped too long beneath the surface they drown like any other mammal. Their flesh is like veal, and it is probably only their very retiring habits, or in some cases the religious prejudice of certain tribes, that has saved them from extermination by man.

MAKERS OF LIMESTONE

Coral reefs occur on the east coast of Africa from the Red Sea to Madagascar and Zululand, but they are not continuous throughout this area. The main concentration of reefs is on the Kenya-Tanzania coast, off Madagascar and the Comoros. But even there they are not as extensive as in the eastern Indian Ocean and the South Pacific.

True corals are very primitive colonial animals of the phylum Coelenterata, which also includes sea anemones and jellyfish. They have no bony structure, but form coral by secreting calcium carbonate (lime) beneath their living tissues. Corals can only flourish in warm seas, where the temperature range is 77° to 84° F. They grow at depths down to one hundred fifty feet—different species occurring at each level. They are usually associated with algae, which either live in the coral polyps themselves, or inhabit the interstices of the coral growths. Many algae also secrete carbonate of lime, and much of the structure of such reefs consists of lime that was not produced by corals alone.

All these animals are marine, so that the upper limit of a living coral reef is that of the low tides. At this level the coral polyps still go on secreting lime when they are submerged (sometimes as much as one inch a year), but in due course they inevitably raise their basal skeletons far enough to protrude from the surface of the sea at low tide; when this happens they die. The surface of a reef at low tide thus consists of dead coral; the living coral is under the crashing surf on the outside or on the edges of the inshore lagoon.

The coral reefs of East Africa are all of the commonest type: fringing reefs. These are formed around the edges of a landmass that for the time being is neither sinking nor rising. When slow subsidence of a continent or island takes place, the reef goes on growing, but it will then be farther and farther from land. In this way barrier reefs are formed. The continued subsidence of an island leads to an atoll—a circular reef enclosing a lagoon.

All along the East African coasts there are old reefs. These old reefs, resulting from continental uplift or varying sea level, form low cliffs, fretted and carved into razor-edged crenelations by the sea. Where a huge area of the continent has

Right above: Coral "mushrooms" and sculptured cliffs are formed by the ceaseless action of waves on old raised reefs. (Julius Behnke) Right: Two sea stars, a spineless sea-urchin like a football, and smaller, more prickly species are seen in a coral pool. (Alan Root)

once been submerged in shallow warm seas, and has later been slowly uplifted, reef limestones may occur over large areas, as in northeast Africa.

Typically the African fringing reefs consist of a rocky barrier about a hundred yards broad and exposed at low tide. Inland of this, and perhaps half a mile across, is the lagoon, with a few deep channels draining through the reef to the open sea. From the air one may see a continuous succession of ridges and pools through the clear waters, marking the growing coral or dead reefs. The outer surface of the reef, where the sea crashes and pounds, is difficult to explore, but the lagoons are one of the most fascinating of all natural habitats and can be studied with little difficulty.

LIFE IN CORAL LAGOONS

A marvelous variety of animals live in coral lagoons. Here they are not exposed to violent currents, and the water itself is mildly warm and lit by strong sunlight. The reef is an extremely colorful world. The corals themselves are bright-colored, as are reef fish and other animals, and the tropical sun shines down through clear waters onto patches of white coral sand alternating with rocky bars. The bottom is frequently covered with a dense growth of seaweed. Such seaweeds are often not brown algae, which are the common seaweeds of temperate coasts, but flowering plants related to the freshwater genus, *Potamogeton;* a species that is common off the East African coast is *Cymadocea ciliata.* These tropical seaweeds are not so luxuriant as the algae of temperate climates, but they nevertheless produce an abundance of plant food and shelter for small animals, and may be the food of sea cows.

Among the most conspicuous animals on coral reefs are sea urchins and starfish, more properly called sea-stars since they are not fish. Of sea urchins among the commonest are hatpin urchins *(Diadema)* with bright, jewel-like structures resembling eyes at the base of their spines. These urchins have long, brittle, black spines that break off easily and are sometimes filled with poison. They are partly a defense mechanism, but are also used in locomotion and they force an observer to watch his step.

Sea-stars can move about more rapidly than sea urchins, and some are formidable carnivores despite their inoffensive appearance. They eat mollusks or sometimes sea urchins. Bivalve mollusks, which close up too firmly to be opened by man, are defenseless against sea-stars. These are said to apply their sucker-like tube-feet to the shell of the mollusk and pull its two halves apart. The stomach of the sea-star is then extruded to engulf the fleshy parts of the mollusk, and eventually only the empty shell is left. Some bivalves, notably scallops, swim by expelling jets of water under pressure to escape the approach of a sea-star.

The largest bivalves of East African reefs are the giant clams, *Tridacna,* but here they do not usually grow to such a size as in the East Indies. They have thick, heavy, strongly-fluted shells that meet in a sinuous curve. In shallow water and when feeding, the clam opens the valves of its shell and extrudes a colorful mantle of flesh. On the mantle may be seen bright eyelike spots that are actually skylights admitting light into the mantle. Green algae live in the mantle and there they carry on photosynthesis converting, through the sun's energy, carbon dioxide into carbohydrates.

Just as interesting are the varied univalve mollusks of the reef such as the cowries, which vary from small, banded cowries *(Palmadusta clandestina)* to the large tortoiseshell and tiger cowries *(Callistocypraea testudinaria* and *Cypraea tigris).* One cowrie shell *(Monetaria minuta)* was formerly the standard form of East African currency. Cameo shells *(Cypraecassis rubra)* are quite common and there is an infinite variety of others from spiny *Murex* to huge conchs like *Tonna* or the long-horned *Lambis.* There are also many beautiful shell-less mollusks of the sea-slug family, while octopuses, which lie in shallow pools and dart off when disturbed, jet-propelled and screened by a cloud of ejected ink, are also mollusks.

Ornamental fish, some small, some large, abound among the coral. Noticeable are butterfly fish *(Chaetodon),* angel fish *(Platax pinnatus* and others), and surgeon fish, so called because of the sharp, lancet-like spine at the base of the tail. Also, found here are the moorish idol *(Zanclus cornutus)* and the coachman *(Hemiochus acuminatus),* both striking ornamental fish. In the caves and holes of the reef live moray eels and various rock cod; the largest rock cod, attaining five hundred pounds or more is *Promicrops lanceolatus.* Parrot fish *(Obliganthus, Callyodon* and *Bolbometopon)* actually eat corals and excrete the ground-up limy skeleton as coral sand. Spiny lobsters *(Panilurus* spp.) are common on the reef, and in the channels barracuda *(Sphyraena jello* and others) are understandably feared by swimmers. Outside the reef, sailfish *(Istiophorus gladius)* and marlin *(Makaira herscheli)* occur. There are also sharks and rays, not usually dangerous to men within the environs of the reef.

A MIGRATION ROUTE FOR BIRDS

The surface of the reef, and the inland lagoons and creeks, are very favorable feeding grounds for a variety of wading birds that migrate down the east coast of Africa in winter. They appear in numbers about September, stay for a time, and move on. Commonest of these are sanderlings *(Crocethia alba)* and curlew sandpipers *(Calidris testacea),* but there are many others, such as gray plovers *(Charadrius squatarola).* These all feed and rest chiefly along the open shore and less often out on the reef. Crab plovers *(Dromas ardeola)* breed in burrows along the Somali coast and also migrate down the east coast in the nonbreeding season.

Among the true sea birds the commonest are Hemprich's gull *(Larus hemprichi),* swift terns *(Sterna bergii),* crested terns *(Sterna bengalensis)* and white-cheeked terns *(Sterna repressa).* These may be seen out on the reef, or a little way offshore in a boat. They breed in large numbers on the Kiunga Islands in northern Kenya, and at other places along the coast. They may be found with migrant terns from temperate climates such as the common and black terns *(S. hirundo* and *(Chlidonias nigra).* But sea birds are never so common along tropical coasts as in temperate climates.

The coastal strip, usually only a few miles wide, which has better rainfall than much of the country inland, is also a favorite migration route for several land birds. Kites, various falcons, and eagles travel south down the coast. The most remarkable of these journeys is made by two small falcons: Eleanora's falcon *(Falco eleanorae)* and the sooty falcon *(F. concolor).* Both of these breed on islands—Eleanora's falcon in the Mediterranean and the sooty falcon in the Red Sea.

And both breed in late summer so as to take advantage of the first influx of palearctic migrant birds to Africa. After breeding, which is completed by mid-October, they migrate down the east coast to Madagascar, where they spend the winter—the rainy season—hawking insects. This migration is extraordinary in that they cling to the coast and do not travel overland, even though some of the Eleanora's falcons come from the North Atlantic shores of Morocco, and must first travel northeast, then east, then southeast and finally south to reach Madagascar.

The East African coast has several typical birds that do not occur elsewhere in Africa. The Indian house crow *(Corvus splendens)* and the house sparrow *(Passer domesticus)* are introduced species; both thrive in coastal towns but do not go far inland. Pied crows are common all along the beaches, scavenging scraps. A very different type of bird that is seen everywhere is the palm swift *(Cypsiurus parvus)*, a tiny creature that breeds under the swaying fronds of coconut palms. It is not confined to the coast but also breeds under palms inland. The underside of a palm leaf in a high wind is a very unstable breeding place, but the palm swift overcomes this hazard by gluing its eggs into its nest.

THE LUSH COASTAL STRIP

Just inland of the coast itself and stretching from Somali in the north to Zululand in the south, is a strip of land of varying width, made up of sedimentary formations overlying the continental foundation. At one time or another all this coastal strip has been submerged under the sea. The coastline of Africa was roughly blocked out in the Jurassic and Cretaceous periods 70,000,000 to 180,000,000 years ago, but has only been stable for about the past 25,000 years. Hence some of the sedimentary formations are ancient, while others have been laid down in more recent times.

The coastal strip has a hotter and often much wetter climate than much of the land on the plateau. Consequently the vegetation is generally very different from that of inland areas, and includes patches of forest and savanna forming a forest-savanna mosaic.

Many areas in the coastal strip are the remains of old lagoons, and are swampy and infertile. They often support only grass and doum palms *(Hyphaene thebaica)*. Forest is likely to be found on more elevated areas, and especially on the more fertile soils derived from old coral reefs. It is probable that in past wetter periods forest was more or less continuous from the west to the east coast. This is shown by the distribution of some animals and birds in East Africa. A common antelope of east coast forests is the suni *(Nesotragus moschatus)*, which is also found in the foothill forests of Mount Kenya and Kilimanjaro. Here the coastal animal and bird fauna mingle with West African elements. Abbott's duiker *(Cephalophus spadix)*, found in the forests of Kilimanjaro, is a close relative of the West African yellow-backed duiker that has become isolated here through the retreat of western forests.

Glossy starlings of the genus *Lamprocolius* are characteristic birds in savannas all over Africa. They are birds of strong flight, often locally migratory. Yet one species, *Lamprocolius corruscus*, is not found outside the coastal strip from Cape Province to Kenya. And very rarely does the southern banded snake eagle *(Circaetus fasciolatus)*, a large raptor, leave this coastal strip. Such curious facts emphasize the distinct ecological nature of this region.

WHITE RHINOS AND NYALA

The tropical coastal strip extends about as far south as St. Lucia Bay in Zululand. South of this inlet the proportion of tropical elements in the fauna drops off rapidly. Almost every family of animals and birds, the vegetation, and even viruses, are affected. St. Lucia Bay, which is scarcely large enough to be an impassable barrier, is probably not the real reason for this sudden change. The 18° C. isotherm (the line connecting all points on the earth's surface with mean temperatures of 18° C.) crosses the coast about this point. Only certain of the tropical plants and animals have been able to overcome this physiological barrier and penetrate farther south. Beyond St. Lucia the coastal strip also becomes much narrower and is an underwater continental shelf. South of St. Lucia the continent is still slowly emerging from the sea.

St. Lucia and its neighborhood used to swarm with large animals. It is now the southern limit of the hippopotamus; about four hundred of them live in the inlet. It is also one of the few known places in Africa where the great white pelican breeds, another being Lake Rukwa. Their breeding here is dependent on the food supply of fish, and this in turn is

Square-lipped or "white" rhinos have made a good recovery from near-extinction in the coastal bush of Zululand. (C. A. W. Guggisberg)

Overleaf: Lions have no particular habitat but occur wherever there is game in open country. A pride at a kill in the shade of a doum palm (Hyphaene thebaica), which is a common tree of coastal savannas. (Clem Haagner)

The Zululand nyala (Tragelaphus angasii) is the nearest relative of the Ethiopian mountain nyala, but is smaller and lives in an entirely different habitat. (Clem Haagner)

controlled by the influx of salt sea water at certain times of the year.

The once abundant large wild animals of this region have been grievously reduced and are now confined to two or three small reserves in thornbush and scrub forest country around the Umfolozi and Hluhluwe rivers. Ranches, sugar estates and cultivated areas surround these little reserves, yet they are places of outstanding interest. They contain the whole of the southern population of white rhinos, some black rhinos, and a large variety of other game such as buffalos, wildebeest, zebras, eland, greater kudus, giraffes, impala, and the southern or Zululand nyala.

The white rhinos of this area were once reduced to a few dozen, but with careful protection have increased to about seven hundred. They are now so numerous as to be an embarrassment, for the reserves are too small to hold all the stock. Some of the rhinos are being transferred to such other areas as the Kruger National Park, and to zoos. The white rhinos of these parts are not the rather shy, hunted beasts of the Sudan and western Uganda. With protection their placid nature has become evident and one can walk right up to the great beasts on foot. White rhinos are grazers, and black rhinos are browsers; Hluhluwe Reserve is the only place on the continent where both live naturally together.

The Zululand nyala *(Tragelaphus angasii)* is found in these reserves, in various other parts of the coastal plain and in the Kruger National Park. Superficially, especially in the shape of the male's horns, it resembles the Ethiopian mountain nyala, but its habitat is very different—coastal thornbush as opposed to giant heath on mountaintops. A close look at this animal shows that it is much smaller and shaggier than the mountain nyala. The females are bright red with many white side stripes, and in habits the beast is more like the lesser kudu of dry thornbush in northeast Africa than the Ethiopian mountain nyala.

The wildlife in these reserves demonstrates once again that

even heavy usage by wild animals damages the habitat less than ranchers. Hluhluwe is positively alive with animals. On most hillsides one may see impala, wildebeest and zebras, while in the bush there are an extraordinary number of kudus and nyala. It is fascinating to sit, as in a grandstand, and watch the different feeding habits of five or six species—for instance, the splendid kudus hidden in the thornbush, until, the sun glinting on their great spiral horns, they can be seen delicately nibbling leaves six or eight feet above ground.

These reserves are so small that they have to be carefully managed. They contain no lions, since neighboring ranchers would not tolerate them, and as a result the herbivores increase unchecked. Fortunately, nowadays surplus animals do not have to be destroyed. They are sold to farmers who wish to restock their lands with wild animals that can make better use of deteriorated areas of pasture than can domestic stock.

OFFSHORE ISLANDS

Islands are fascinating places, and there are many off Africa, each group different. In the Gulf of Guinea there is a string of small islands that are the tops of submerged volcanos. Fernando Po is the largest, and the nearest to the coast, followed by Principe, Sao Thome, and Annobon. Fernando Po, only twenty-three miles offshore and nine thousand feet high, is, like Mount Cameroon, covered by dense tropical forest, with giant lobelias at high altitudes. The fauna and flora of these islands indicate generally that they are the broken remnants of a peninsula that once extended outward from the African coast. But they have been isolated long enough for many endemic forms to develop.

In complete contrast to these tropical West African volcanos is Socotra, a barren island off Cape Guardafui—the most eastern point of Africa. Although it is not very far from the coast, it is difficult to visit, and it has developed an extraordinary number of endemic species, especially among reptiles. A recent ornithological expedition to the island discovered a new swift, not yet named, and there is an endemic breeding race of the European buzzard *(Buteo buteo)*. Among such groups as reptiles specialization is not surprising. But when one finds it in strong-flying birds like swifts that could easily move to the mainland were they so inclined, it is noteworthy. Some of the creatures that inhabit the island are more akin to Asian than to African species.

The Comoros are a group of four large islands—Grand Comoro, Moheli, Anjouan and Mayotte—lying to the north of Madagascar and nearest to the mainland of Africa. Of volcanic origin, they arose in the Miocene era, fifteen million years ago or more, and consequently have never been connected to the African continent. One of the volcanos, Mount Karthala, is still active. Their natural vegetation is a mixture of forest and grasslands, but has been greatly altered by man. Their fauna is an amalgam of African, Madagascan and Asian species. Each group is represented by rather few species, for each creature has had to cross the sea to reach the islands. From Madagascar, mongoose lemurs *(Lemur m. mungoz)* have colonized Moheli and Anjouan, and black lemurs *(L. macaco mayottensis)*, Mayotte. Birds, like the lemurs, have come chiefly from Madagascar, but some of the island animals have Asiatic affinities. Among four known species of bats, one is a flying fox of the Asiatic genus *Pteropus*. Insects are rather poorly represented and one can explore the Comoro forests without fear of being attacked by driver ants *(Dorylus)*. In recent times man has introduced several species of birds and mammals, such as guineafowl, Indian mynas *(Acridotheres tristis)*, bushpigs, rats, a wild cat, and, more useful, the insectivorous Madagascan tenrec *(Tenrec ecaudatus)*.

By far the most important and remarkable of all the islands near the African coast is Madagascar. Over one thousand miles long, and covering more than a quarter of a million square miles, it is a continent in miniature. It has three main geographic divisions consisting of a narrow eastern coastal plain rising in one or two sharp steps to the central highlands. These reach 8,655 feet at Mount Ankaratra, and then descend to the wider western coastal plain, which is much drier than the east. The varied topography results in a great variety of habitats. There are mangroves, coral reefs, tropical forests, savannas, semi-arid bushlands, lakes and even a small area of dune desert in the southwest. Many of the habitats found on the African mainland are repeated here, and much of the vegetation, especially savanna grasses, has come from the mainland. Yet Madagascar is in some ways utterly different from Africa and forms a zoogeographic region of its own.

MADAGASCAR'S STRANGE ANIMALS

Madagascar was probably cut off from the African mainland at least twenty million years ago. Most of the world's mammals have evolved since the Eocene period, and if Madagascar was isolated at that remote period, it would not be surprising if there were little else but very primitive mammals there.

We should therefore expect to find that those types of mammals evolving rather late in the great scheme of nature, such as carnivores, rodents, monkeys and antelopes, would be absent or poorly represented on Madagascar. And this is just what we do find. There are none of the abundant herbivores that characterize African grasslands, no powerful predators like lions or leopards, and no modern rats other than introduced species. In such conditions the ancient forms of life that existed in Madagascar when it was first separated from the mainland have been able to persist and to take advantage of many different habitats. Such ancient forms of life, persisting in isolation, are a common feature of life on islands, and they usually suffer as soon as man appears.

The absence of competition from more highly evolved primates has enabled the primitive lemurs to flourish on Madagascar. The nearest present-day relatives of lemurs are the galagos or bushbabies of Africa, the pottos of West African forests, and the loris of Ceylon. These are all rather closely related to the dwarf lemurs (Cheirogaleinae). But whereas dwarf lemurs are only one of a large variety of lemurs found in Madagascar, which includes nocturnal and diurnal species, the galagos, pottos and loris have only survived as nocturnal animals that do not compete with the diurnal, old-world monkeys.

The insectivores of Madagascar all belong to a family of primitive hedgehogs, the Centetidae, or tenrecs. All known members of this family are found in Madagascar, with the single exception of the West African otter-shrew, *Potamogale*, whose nearest relative is the aquatic tenrec, *Limnogale*. Most of the tenrecs are small creatures, some with long, some with

Aerial roots of this giant spreading fig tree have formed a mass of new columnar trunks, enabling the tree to spread out over a greater area. (Georges Bourdelon)

short tails, and some with a more or less spiny coat like a hedgehog's. The tenrecs may originally have been truly African, but they also have near relatives in the Antilles. Probably this indicates only that they are, like lemurs, survivors of a very old group, once far more widespread in the world.

The only carnivores on Madagascar are six endemic genera of the Viverridae, intermediate between the civet cats and mongooses of continental Africa. Again, they represent an old type which has been able to persist unchanged in Madagascar though undergoing further evolution on the continent. Madagascar rats all belong to a family of their own, the Nesomyidae, most nearly related to the continental Spalacidae.

In some instances the isolation of Madagascar has resulted in the persistence of animals that have totally disappeared from the African continent. There are no Agamid or Varanid lizards in Madagascar, though these are the common families of lizards on the continent. But on Madagascar there are two members of the American lizard family Iguanidae. There are no poisonous snakes or pythons there, but there are two species of *Boa,* again an American genus of constricting snakes. Most African genera of reptiles do not seem to have reached the island.

Madagascar birds, bats, and, curiously enough, amphibians, indicate some affinities with Asian fauna. Among these are Asian robins, *Copsychus,* certain owls *(Ninox),* and pigeons *(Alectroenas).* But a greater proportion of the bird fauna has African affinities, and many strong fliers such as fish eagles *(Haliaetus)* or harrier hawks *(Polyboroides)* may be recent immigrants. Among bats, the flying fox *(Pteropus)* occurs from the East Indies to Madagascar, the Comoros, and Pemba Island just off the mainland. There are no tree frogs (Hylidae) there, nor spade-footed toads (Pelobatidae), nor are there representatives of several other families common on the African continent. Among the family Microhylidae the Madagascar frogs are more like those of Malaysia than Africa.

There have been certain very recent introductions from Africa, some through the instigation of man. A bushpig, *Potamochoerus larvatus,* is quite common. It may have swum the Mozambique channel when the waterway was narrower than it is today, but this would be a considerable feat even for a wild pig. Guineafowl have been introduced in recent times, but crocodiles, to which sea water is no obstacle, probably crossed the channel of their own accord.

Man, as usual, has had far more destructive effect on the fauna than otherwise. Several very large species of subfossil lemurs that existed in later prehistoric times are thought to have been wiped out by early human settlers. In the Pliocene and Pleistocene eras there was a pigmy hippo, and the giant bird *Aepyornis,* possibly the fabled roc, also became extinct fairly recently. In modern times man has degraded seventy per cent of this island's vegetation and threatened the habitat of several species of lemurs.

THE REMARKABLE LEMURS

Lemurs are primitive primates; that is, they belong to the same group of mammals as monkeys or apes. Surviving in Madagascar after it became extinct in other parts of the world, the original stock has been able to evolve into a variety of forms that carry out many of the functions of monkeys, and indeed of several other animals. Lemurs range in size from that of a mouse to that of a large dog, and some extinct subfossil lemurs were as big as donkeys. Superficially some of them resemble monkeys, with a large brain case and a short muzzle, and one, the indris, has become tailless like an ape. Many lemurs are brightly or strikingly colored, with long woolly fur, and the majority are vegetarian and nocturnal.

Lemurs are divided into a number of subfamilies with very different characters. The Cheirogaleinae or mouse lemurs are all small animals chiefly arboreal and nocturnal, resembling bushbabies in their habits. They can run swiftly but cannot perform the huge elastic leaps of bushbabies. They make nests in hollow trees, and some of them become torpid in the dry season when food is short.

Except for the ring-tailed lemur *(L. catta),* which prefers rocky situations, the typical lemurs, Lemurinae, are all moderate-sized, arboreal animals. They are agile and active when awake, do not become seasonally torpid, and travel hand over hand along tree branches. The so-called gentle lemurs *(Hapalemur)* are chiefly nocturnal and live in bamboo thickets or reedbeds. *H. simus,* which lives in the reedbeds of Lake Alaotra, can be very easily caught on the ground and is partly diurnal. Its bamboo-loving relative, known as the gray gentle lemur *(H. griseus),* goes to sleep during the day and it too can be easily caught.

The true lemurs *(Lemur)* are larger animals and are often very beautiful. They have foxlike heads and long tails that they carry in a S-shaped curve. They are chiefly arboreal and often diurnal. They walk on all-fours, alternately running or leaping, and sit or squat. They groom their fur, either alone or for each other. One or another member of this genus eat almost anything from fruit to insects: the best-known is the ring-tailed lemur; the largest is the ruffed lemur *(L. variegatus);* and the handsomest, the black lemur *(L. macaco).* These lemurs are often docile and affectionate in captivity and are favorites in zoos.

The long tail possessed by most lemurs is apparently something of a nuisance. The sifakas *(Propithecus)* carry their tails coiled like a watch-spring between their legs. Sifakas are chiefly arboreal and diurnal, though they hide during the heat of the day. They move in fantastic leaps of up to thirty feet from tree to tree, and on the ground leap in an upright posture. They are gentle, not very intelligent, cannot be kept in captivity, and have the endearing habit of sunning themselves in the early morning with arms outstretched to catch the full warmth. This has given them the reputation of being sun-worshippers, and has helped to protect them from native hunters who might otherwise have killed them.

The largest of all living lemurs, the indris *(Indri),* is black, gray, and white, with a stumpy tail. It is diurnal and mainly arboreal but comes to the ground occasionally. In trees it progresses in remarkable sideways leaps from one vertical treetrunk to another. It is a forest animal, and is said to be partly carnivorous, eating birds' brains. The indris makes its presence known by extraordinary loud wailing or doglike howls, usually in the early morning or sometimes at night. This may be a form of territorial behavior, akin to the howling of some monkeys. It is regarded as sacred by the local people, but they have nevertheless destroyed its habitat and so endangered its survival.

The same has happened to perhaps the most remarkable of all lemurs, the aye-aye *(Daubentonia).* This highly specialized animal lives only in forests and bamboo thickets on the eastern border of the central plateau. It is nocturnal and arboreal, feeding on insects, birds' eggs and vegetable matter. Its most remarkable feature is a very much elongated and slender middle finger. With this it taps on dead logs to locate the larvae of wood-boring beetles. Having located its prey, it inserts its long middle finger, impales the grub on the claw and eats it. When the hole is too deep it chews the timber

A Madagascar succulent, a Pachypodium, typical of the strange vegetation of the semi-arid southwest part of the island. (Georges Bourdelon)

A tree hyrax (Dendrohyrax dorsalis) of Fernando Po, displaying its white back patch. More often heard than seen, the tree hyrax sometimes basks high up in great forest trees. (Horst Dischner)

till its claw can reach the victim. Fears have already been expressed that the aye-aye may be practically extinct.

Few of the species of lemurs have much chance of survival unless their habitat is protected. Those that live in savannas or reedbeds are better placed, but most lemurs, protected by isolation from competition with monkeys, may not long survive the demand for living space by the most dangerous of all primates, man.

LIVING FOSSILS

The Madagascar lemurs may be described as living fossils that have survived from much earlier ages. Such survival is easier on islands than on the continent, but even here there are some incredibly ancient survivals. The lungfish *(Polipterus* and *Calamoichthys)* are survivors of fishes, the Cnoanichthyes, whose ancestry dates back 400 million years and which are believed to be the ancestors of all forms of land vertebrates. The lungfish themselves never became very numerous, and they are an example of evolution apparently arrested and miraculously preserved to this day. Another branch of these fishes, the Rhipidistians, emerged from the water and became the ancestors of amphibia, reptiles, birds and mammals. The third group of these fishes, the Coelacanths, remained in the sea and, after flourishing for a time, apparently died out. The last living members were believed to have disappeared about seventy million years ago. But in 1938, a coelacanth, *Latimeria chalumnae,* made its dramatic reappearance after seventy million years of oblivion. The satisfaction of scientists must have been great when they found that the real coelacanth was almost identical with their reconstructions.

Since then, other coelacanths have been found. The first of these was caught by a native fisherman of Anjouan in the Comoros, on a hand line in sixty feet of water. It was recognized as a result of the descriptions and offers of rewards that had been sent out following the finding of the first coelacanth, and was described as a new species, *Malania anjouani.*

Africa has long retained its secrets, yet in the last decade or so a flush of extraordinary new knowledge has come to light. It is only since 1950 that the true value of the great African mammals, as the best possible users of the savannas, bush, and grasslands, has been appreciated. The story of the coelacanth is only one example among a flood of new discoveries that in some respects will date this book within a few years.

But the basic facts of life in Africa will not change so quickly. The earth will continue to oscillate on its vertical axis, and the rains will go on falling in the southern hemisphere at one season, and in the north at another. Birds, beasts, and plants, whose evolution over millennia has enabled them to take advantage of these varying conditions, will go on doing so provided that man does not interfere too drastically with the habitats concerned. On the continent of Africa man is having and will have the most severe influence on all the original vegetation and wildlife. His influence is likely to be intensified by population increases and by the political strife that is at present troubling the whole continent.

Man would do well to recognize in Africa as elsewhere that he himself is a species of animal wholly dependent upon natural conditions for his own survival. If he is to thrive, he must pay stricter attention to the details of his habitat than he does at present.

Index

Asterisks indicate pages containing illustrations

THE AUTHOR

Leslie Brown was educated as a zoologist and ecologist at St. Andrews University, Scotland, and at Cambridge. In 1940 he went to Nigeria and then in 1946 to Kenya as an Agricultural Officer. Rising to the position of Chief Agriculturist, Mr. Brown exercised a great influence in the development of African agriculture in Kenya. He has traveled widely in Africa and in the United States, India and Europe. He now lives on a farm near Nairobi.

Mr. Brown is also a well-known ornithologist and has written books on eagles and on flamingos and, with Dr. Dean Amadon of the American Museum of Natural History, recently completed a standard work on birds of prey of the world.

ENGRAVED AND PRINTED BY CONZETT AND HUBER OF ZURICH – DESIGNED BY ULRICH RUCHTI

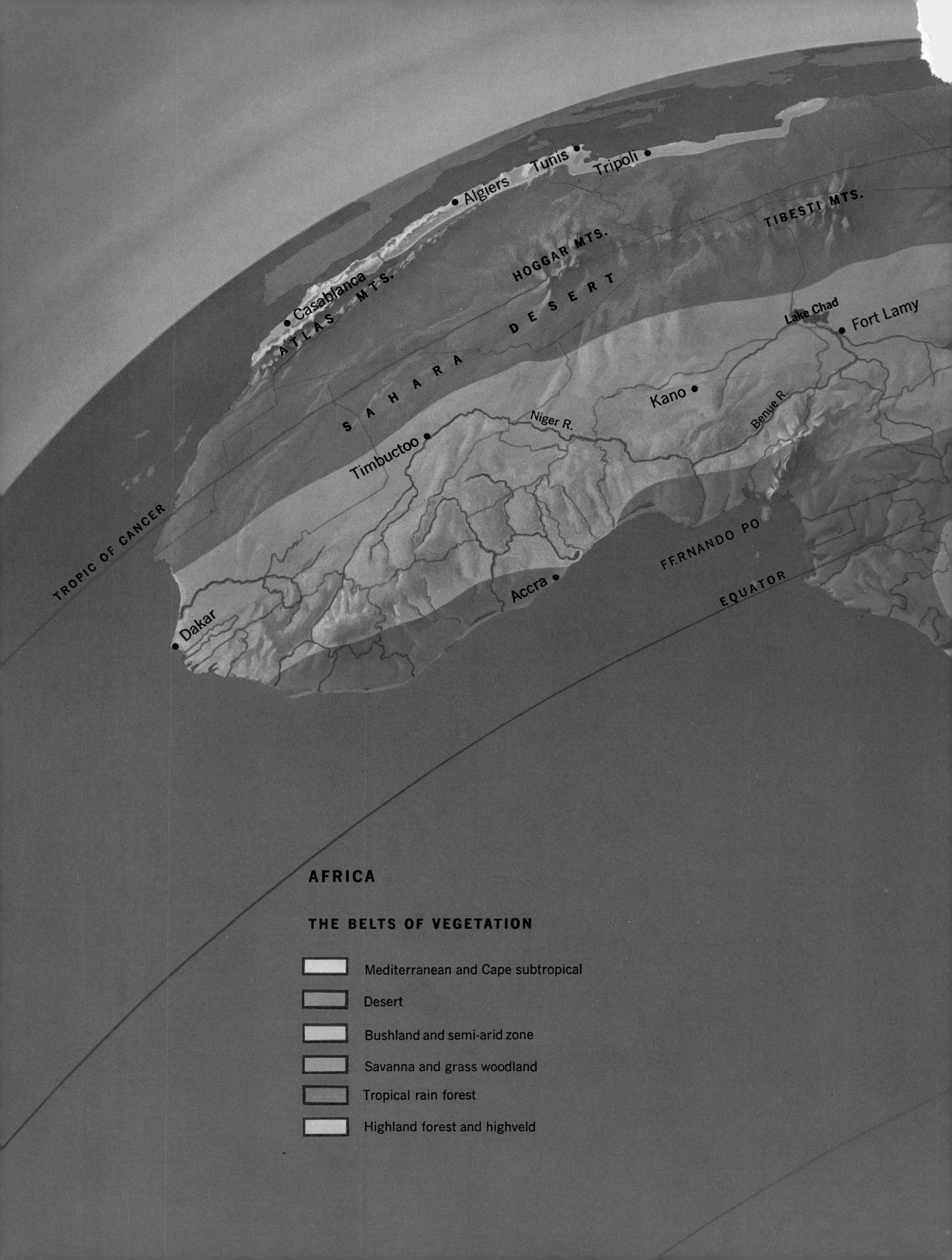

AFRICA

THE BELTS OF VEGETATION

- Mediterranean and Cape subtropical
- Desert
- Bushland and semi-arid zone
- Savanna and grass woodland
- Tropical rain forest
- Highland forest and highveld

Tunis
Tripoli
Algiers
TIBESTI MTS.
HOGGAR MTS.
Casablanca
ATLAS MTS.
SAHARA DESERT
Lake Chad
Fort Lamy
Kano
Niger R.
Benue R.
Timbuctoo
TROPIC OF CANCER
FERNANDO PO
Accra
EQUATOR
Dakar